Sounding Together

Sounding Together

Collaborative Perspectives on U.S. Music in the 21st Century

Charles Hiroshi Garrett
and Carol J. Oja, Editors

University of Michigan Press • Ann Arbor

Published in the United States of America by the
University of Michigan Press
Manufactured in the United States of America
Printed on acid-free paper
First published August 2021

A CIP catalog record for this book is available from the British Library.

Library of Congress Cataloging-in-Publication data has been applied for.

DOI: https://doi.org/10.3998/mpub.11374592

ISBN: 978-0-472-05433-6 (Paper : alk paper)
ISBN: 978-0-472-90130-2 (OA ebook)

This Open Access edition is made available through financial support from the Harvard University FAS Tenured Faculty Subvention Fund, the Harvard University Department of Music, and the University of Michigan Office of Research Faculty Grants and Awards Program.

Contents

The Politics of Historiography

Reaching Outward as Teachers and Scholars

Digital materials related to this title can be found on the Fulcrum platform via the following citable URL: https://doi.org/10.3998/mpub.11374592

Acknowledgments

With collaboration as its central mission, this book—not surprisingly—grew out of a collective effort, beginning with a two-day workshop sponsored by the Radcliffe Institute for Advanced Studies in 2017. For that opportunity, we are grateful to Julie Buchler, former Director of the Humanities Program at Radcliffe, and Rebecca E. F. Wassarman, its Executive Director of Academic Ventures and Engagement. The spirit of this project was kindled by the workshop's participants, including Marié Abe, Will Cheng, Louis Chude-Sokei, Daniel Goldmark, Glenda Goodman, Benjamin Harbert, Monica A. Hershberger, Ellie M. Hisama, Loren Kajikawa, Vijay Iyer, Tammy L. Kernodle, Alejandro L. Madrid, Ingrid Monson, Samuel Parler, Kay Kaufman Shelemay, Braxton D. Shelley, Michael Sy Uy, and Sherrie Tucker.

Throughout the process—from workshop to publication—we have been generously supported by the University of Michigan and Harvard University, our home institutions. Harvard's Department of Music provided a publication subvention, and we are grateful to Karen Rynne, the department's former Manager of Administration and Finance, for making those funds available. Open Access for the book was jointly underwritten by the Office of Research Faculty Grants and Awards Program at the University of Michigan and the FAS Tenured Faculty Publication Fund at Harvard. Meanwhile, the University of Michigan Press has consistently supported the book, starting with former editorial director Mary Francis, who championed the early stages of this project, and continuing with our exemplary editor Sara Cohen, assisted by Mary Hashman, Anna Pohlod, and Flannery Wise. Katie Callam and Joelle Tapas provided welcome editorial assistance, Grace Edgar prepared the index, and our anonymous reviewers helped us firm up the text during final revisions.

Monica Hershberger and Sarah Suhadolnik, who contributed a chapter, came up with the book's title.

Our families keep us on track, and we want to acknowledge their support in many dimensions. For Charles, to Saleema Waraich. For Carol, to her adult children Zoe and Wynn Oja Tucker.

Finally, we are grateful to our authors, a nimble and generous group of innovative scholars and musicians who were willing to take the leap and join a project that required creative risks and shared responsibility. It has been a great pleasure to work with and learn from them.

Introduction

CHARLES HIROSHI GARRETT AND CAROL J. OJA

Sounding Together: Collaborative Perspectives on U.S. Music in the 21st Century is a multiauthored, collaboratively conceived book featuring a diverse and cross-generational group of scholars, performers, and practitioners. It explores a wide range of musics, geographic locations, and moments in time, all as representatives of the vast network of musical cultures practiced both currently and historically in the United States. This collective project does not aim for comprehensive coverage; rather, our goal is to counter long-accepted norms in studying a subject with shifting parameters. Driving our venture is an appreciation for how working together gives rise to fresh ideas and propels innovative outcomes. We assert here, through collective example, that the study of US music is particularly fertile for collaborative interventions. Not only does it inherently cross dozens of disciplines, but it also traverses media, regions, geographies, nations, genres, economies, cultures, identities, and much more. It is literally all over the place, especially with the intensifying of globalization and migration and the ubiquitousness of media. As a result, both *inter*disciplinarity and *intra*disciplinarity are increasingly called for in the study of US music, and working together offers a means to attain those goals. To our knowledge, this is the first multiauthored collection of essays in the field of music that highlights collaboration, and we hope it is the first of many.

With this book, our authors join us in challenging traditional disciplinary boundaries, methodological approaches, conceptual frameworks, and scholarly insularity. We not only question foundational historiographic models—such as those related to notions of whiteness or the nature of mobility—but also imagine new ways to engage with traditional resources such as scholarly interviews and music reference works. At the same time, we emphasize cross-cultural inquiry, from ethnographies of immigrant musicians in a globalized United States to a bicultural perspective on US music in Japan during the postwar occupation. We seek varied vantage points to reappraise encounters of race, power, and social justice, from the ethics of politically conservative whites performing Black gospel, to a community engagement project designed to meet the diverse needs of students of color, to an assessment of the transhistorical impact of colonial conquest on Indigenous peoples.

This book tackles some of the ethical—the existential—challenges facing scholars studying music of the United States as we enter the third decade of the twenty-first century. In our current public discourse, hurled forward by twenty-four-hour news feeds, we hear a great deal about the humanities under threat, a nation at odds, a world in turmoil, and these complex challenges call out for a fresh approach to understanding the United States in multiple dimensions and from diverse perspectives. Music is a powerful form of human expression, and it proves especially resonant in a volatile world as sounds and the people who create and perform them traverse porous geographic and social borders. Even the term "American music," which has traditionally been used to label our field of study, has become politically charged, as it marginalizes—even ignores—traditions practiced within the Western hemisphere but outside the United States. For that reason, we intentionally embrace "US music" to demarcate the boundaries of our subject. All in all, our authors raise tough questions: How can we rethink the study of music-making in the United States? How can we envision a fusion of activism, scholarship, and teaching that addresses the growing challenges of the contemporary world, sometimes as a tool to advocate for change? How can we prepare our students for the evolving challenges of the twenty-first century? And how can we achieve these goals through collegial, mutually supportive means?

Our central response to these questions has been to embrace collaboration, resulting in a collectively conceived book that took shape in multiple stages, aiming to break out of long-established paradigms of solitude in humanities scholarship. The project began in 2011 when the two of us convened a colloquy for the *Journal of the American Musicological Society* in which five authors joined us to grapple with ways to reconceptualize the study of US music.[1] We wrote then of "a sense of destabilization—of living in a fundamentally different world, the dimensions and implications of which have yet to be discerned." University campuses were reeling from the 2008 financial crisis, with draconian budget cuts, especially to public institutions. At the same time, the election of Barack Obama as the nation's first Black president had opened a conversation about whether a "post-racial" apotheosis was underway, with hope that historic civil rights issues might finally be approaching resolution. With the election of Donald J. Trump in November 2016, those hopes were dashed, replaced by a white nationalist agenda that reignited debates over race, citizenship, and immigration. As this project developed, a sense of "destabilization" only deepened. The Trump administration radically unsettled many at home and around the globe, provoking a sharp escalation in political, economic, and social upheaval. Activism toward social justice pushed back aggressively, with Black Lives Matter and the Me Too movement as prime examples, asserting powerful rebukes to entrenched racism and sexism. At the same time, Covid-19 imperiled global health, with the United States struggling to implement basic preventative protocol and save lives.

Back in the spring of 2017, we took the next step in this project by convening a workshop at the Radcliffe Institute, designed as a brainstorming session focused on repositioning the study of music in the United States during the twenty-first century. That gathering was infused with a sense of social and political crisis, as the Trump agenda, then four months into activation, was being implemented radically and rapidly; at that point, the administration was already targeting immigrants, Muslims, and people of color with particular ferocity. We raised bedrock questions about our role as scholars, and our conversations ultimately inspired a number of authors to grapple head-on with the challenges and traumas of the Trump years. The location enabled us to bring together colleagues from around the country while including a strong contingent affiliated with Harvard and other Boston-area institutions. We were grateful to Radcliffe for diversifying the group further through the inclusion of four advanced graduate students (now alumni) as equal partners with junior and senior faculty.[2] Over the course of two days, we discussed research topics that felt urgent, and we considered the potential benefits of collaboration. We wondered about the value of continuing to identify as Americanists in an era increasingly marked by xenophobia, isolationism, and white nationalism. We considered how the increasing impact of migration and displacement challenges notions of nationhood and how, in turn, the idea of "nation" has been central to the identities and research agendas of US music scholars. We contemplated how musical production can be construed as the enactment of rights, and we shared ideas about research with potential to make a difference in the world. How, we wondered, can academics harness our scholarly training to address pressing needs on our campuses and in our communities?

Our workshop discussion formed an important phase in the genesis of this book, and we soon were embracing the collaborative impulse as a corrective strategy. That is, we increasingly viewed collaboration as a mode of innovation within arts and humanities scholarship. At the same time, it simply felt right to work with friends and colleagues as a way of addressing a shared yet somewhat inchoate sense of crisis. As we moved forward with publication plans, our circle expanded outward, with workshop contributors identifying collaborative projects and teaming with partners.[3] Each set of collaborators in this book formed on its own and pursued its chosen topic as a student pair, student-faculty pair, or faculty pair. As the book took shape, its disciplinary sweep expanded substantially to incorporate African and African American studies, American studies, communications, creative practice and critical inquiry, cultural studies, ethnomusicology, Indigenous studies, Latinx and Latin American studies, musicology, music theory, popular music studies, religious studies, and sociology. Broadening perspectives while optimizing resources, collaboration became a means for us to experiment with new research models, implement interdisciplinarity, and design projects built to maximize our collective strengths. Drawing on different spheres—whether chronological, methodological, disciplinary, technological, geographical, pedagogical, cultural, or linguistic—our collaborative teams pushed their thinking in unexpected directions.

This book demonstrates how collaboration can productively harness complementary skills and nourish comparative boundary-crossing research. Mixing genres, moving across time, exploring racial and cultural difference, synthesizing diverse perspectives, thinking intergenerationally, traversing geographical borders, combining disciplinary perspectives: these types of collaborative strategies are distinguishing features of *Sounding Together*. The process of working collaboratively emerges as a productive vehicle for collective action, whether expressed through the act of scholarly camaraderie or through responding directly—often pointedly—to the contemporary political climate.

Advocating for Collaboration in the Humanities

Collaboration is everywhere in the humanities, even if its prominence is not always recognized. As teachers, we collaborate with and learn from students, and we work with campus colleagues on governance and initiatives. As researchers, we share manuscripts with peers, exchange feedback and suggestions, and present our papers at conferences. We participate in writing groups, attend seminars and workshops, and lend our service to scholarly societies. We serve on editorial boards, coedit books, cofound journals, and stage conferences. All these activities present important opportunities for scholarly collaboration. Yet, despite such experiences, only a handful of the contributors to this book possessed prior experience with collaborative writing, and that is the norm for scholars in the humanities. Working and publishing in teams is common in other academic fields: indeed, it is everyday practice throughout the sciences. Yet in the humanities, long-held biases against collaborative work remain widespread, especially when it comes to evaluations for hiring, promotion, and tenure: the process of establishing individual credentials by producing single-authored work has long shaped training and scholarship for humanists. We seek to challenge these entrenched habits, and we hope this book will help energize a growing tide of interest in collaboration. Too many valuable projects simply cannot be accomplished by one person.

While in Canada and Europe collaborative research in the humanities has flourished for several decades, in the United States such research has only recently begun to blossom, with increased encouragement and support from funding agencies, scholarly societies, and academic institutions. In our case, the workshop sponsored by the Radcliffe Institute provided such an opportunity. The National Endowment for the Humanities and the American Council of Learned Societies recently have implemented fellowship programs for collaborative research, and many colleges and universities have established humanities "collaboratories"—dedicated programs that provide resources and training to support collective projects by humanities faculty, librarians, postdocs, students, and technical staff. Agreements between large consortia now fund multi-institutional collaborative ventures in pedagogy and collaborative research. Such collaborative impulses have been fueled, in part, by the enormous wave of interest over the past few decades in the digital humanities, a multidisciplinary set of initiatives that brings together digital technologies and computing resources with humanities scholarship and teaching. Although this collection is not designed as a digital humanities project, we look to the ways in which such interdisciplinary teamwork has shed new light on key questions in the humanities. Furthermore, the ubiquity of digital tools—especially real-time document creation tools such as Google Docs, cloud-based file-sharing utilities such as Dropbox, and digital conferencing tools such as Skype and Zoom—has removed logistical hurdles to the fluid sharing of texts and ideas that is necessary for successful collaboration.

The challenges of today's political and academic environment present an opportune moment for advancing collaborative work in US music studies, with the potential to build on activity taking place across the humanities. We are inspired by the pioneering work of Lisa Ede and Andrea Lunsford, two professors of English who have tirelessly sounded the call for collaborative research and writing in the humanities, and by interdisciplinary teams such as Judith W. Page and Elise L. Smith, who joined forces to combine their perspectives from literature and art history.[4] In the realm of music studies, collaborative work has found most traction in music education research, following the example of coauthored texts that populate the wider field of education. A number of significant collaborative books also have appeared in recent years throughout ethno/musicology, from *Danzón* by Alejandro L. Madrid and Robin Moore to *American Popular Music* by Larry Starr and Christopher Waterman.[5] It has become increasingly common in recent years for music scholars to form interdisciplinary teams and publish collaborative essays on focused topics.[6] A more extensive project took shape when Lisa Barg, Tammy Kernodle, Dianthe Spencer, and Sherrie Tucker formed the Melba Liston Research Collective and published their findings in *Black Music Research Journal* 34, no. 1 (2014).[7]

Despite an increase in collaborative initiatives in the humanities, such projects often receive far less recognition than solo-authored work. Many departments do not allow applicants for teaching positions to submit collaboratively written essays, and promotion and tenure committees often give far less weight to collaborative work. Consequently, many humanities scholars view collaborative research as a luxury and choose to postpone such projects until after tenure. We acknowledge there can be risks in collaboration, especially in terms of unexpected delays or obstacles, and graduate students and junior scholars need to be careful to focus on independent research alongside collaboration. Yet, overall, the process of collaboration holds enormous potential for all the reasons outlined here. We hope this volume will contribute to a change in perspective, supporting a more limber attitude on the part of faculty, administrators, and committees responsible for hiring, tenure, and promotion.

The Collaborative Process

Recognizing that collaborative research will be unfamiliar to some readers, we believe it may be useful to step back and reflect on our experiences working together. We hope that discussing the nuts and bolts of our collaborations will encourage others to explore such possibilities on their own. In addition to sharing advice for setting up a successful collaboration, we will also offer suggestions for navigating the inevitable challenges and bottlenecks that may appear along the way.

Scholarly collaboration is an experiment in process, requiring negotiation by individuals who learn to work together, seeking common ground while navigating difference. There is no single formula for assembling the right set of collaborators, since different projects have different needs and call for different types of expertise. But it is often the case—and this book represents a perfect example—that people who share common perspectives and research agendas are more inclined to collaborate. Collaborative projects that develop through friendships, mentoring relationships, and/or mutual admiration are often better prepared to navigate rough spots and bring a project to completion.[8] In other cases, such as campus-wide interdisciplinary initiatives, gathering a team that possesses the right combination of complementary strengths may take precedence. The essay by Rachel Wheeler (religious studies) and Sarah Eyerly (musicology), for example, blossomed through an exceptionally broad collaborative network also involving a scholar in linguistics, recording professionals, students, musicians, composers, and members of a Mohican descendant community.

Discussing issues surrounding intellectual property, attribution, and equity at the start of a collaborative project is wise, even if revisiting these issues over the course of a project may become necessary.[9] Who may present, adapt, reprint, or publish this work? How will each participant's contribution be acknowledged? For projects of extended duration, it may be helpful to plan in advance for tasks involving budgeting, grant preparation, and other administrative labor. Most such issues were resolved for this book as a result of two collective decisions. First, most teams of collaborators chose to work in equal partnership on their essays. Second, we decided to extend the reach of the book to a broader audience by publishing this collection as a printed book and also with Open Access (OA), which allows readers to view the collection in HTML format on the web under a Creative Commons (CC) license. Following the same rationale, we selected a type of CC license that allows the essays to be shared freely, as long as they are credited and remain unchanged, and also offers each set of collaborators the right to reprint their material.[10]

When a new project takes shape, collaborators often find it helpful to define its basic framework: shared objectives, key questions, a list of tasks, a timeline, an approximate word count. As one example from this volume, Glenda Goodman and Samuel Parler established a shared intellectual foundation by agreeing on a reading list before getting started. Specific roles and assignments may be spelled out at the beginning, or they may be assigned or exchanged as work progresses. No matter what size the collaboration, it is helpful to talk in advance about working styles, writing routines, time constraints, expectations, and deadlines. However the partnership forms, it will only succeed with plenty of communication and flexibility from everyone involved. Working together turns into a constant learning experience. Not only do collaborators discover how other scholars think, work, write, and solve problems, but the experience also fosters self-discovery about one's intellectual motivations, priorities, and blind spots. Constant intellectual exchange means there is no time for complacency, no lounging in a comfort zone, no succumbing to writer's block. The path toward completing a team project is not always predictable, and the process may lead to debates, conflicts, or other types of challenges requiring compromise or resolution. Our contributors found no better way to rejuvenate a project than by checking in with one another on a regular basis in person, on the phone, or online. Note that working collaboratively does not mean neglecting practices that fuel independent work. Sharing writing drafts with other colleagues, arranging for conversations with outside experts, presenting ongoing research at a conference, workshopping papers—all these sorts of activities also prove valuable for collaborative projects.

Just as there are many ways in which to shepherd the collaborative process, so too exist a wide variety of productive approaches to crafting and presenting collaborative writing. Some of our contributors divided their responsibilities precisely, as in the case of Braxton D. Shelley writing on race and gospel music, paired with a reflection from Cheryl Townsend Gilkes. Alejandro L. Madrid and Josh Kun chose to take a sequential approach, writing successive passages to build a lively dialogue. Several pairs of authors—among them Panayotis League and Kay Kaufman Shelemay—developed their ideas collectively, wrote their own case studies independently, and reconvened to complete their conclusions together. Others—including Naomi André and Michael Sy Uy, Monica Hershberger and Sarah Suhadolnik, Ellie M. Hisama and Lucie Vágnerová, Loren Kajikawa and Daniel Martinez HoSang—sought to present a single, synthesized voice, consistent in perspective, tone, style, and argument.

Collectively shaping a unified writing voice requires a substantial amount of planning, communication, and editing by coauthors.

Sometimes, however, it is more desirable to underscore different opinions by presenting individual experiences, signaling alternative perspectives, or advancing competing narratives. The essay by Charles Hiroshi Garrett and Daniel Goldmark, for example, alternates between a synthesized collaborative voice alongside individual passages (demarcated as such) that reflect distinctive perspectives on a *Grove Dictionary* project.[11] The dialogue between Kun and Madrid likewise employs a multivocal writing strategy that presents individual streams of thought and brings them together in conversation. Whether configured as a roundtable or through a more experimental format, it is not uncommon for collaborative projects to feature a handful of voices or an even more diverse array of participants. Multivocal writing can be especially powerful for its ability to resist scholarly conventions by rejecting a single narrative in favor of acknowledging difference, diversity, and debate.

Those new to collaboration often exchange successive drafts through e-mail, which seeks to ensure an orderly, sequential process, since only one person can work on the document at a time. Many contributors to this book, however, came to appreciate the benefits of writing together in Google Docs or some other mechanism for document sharing. These tools put partners in continual dialogue and generate a steady flow of feedback, suggestions, and ideas. It is a pleasure to take a break, then return to the screen and find that new prose has appeared or a rough passage has been smoothed over. Many essays in this book, including this introduction, would not have taken their final shape without its authors editing the same online document. Yet even with the capabilities of shared documents, many of our collaborators worked together—literally in one geographic location—for a designated period of time, whether to define their topic (Ohta and Oja), write vigorously side by side (Hershberger and Suhadolnik), or flesh out the ramifications of their findings (Uy and André). Among all these writers, Vijay Iyer's case is distinctive, for his contribution is based on an interview with Muhal Richard Abrams, who has since passed away, and Iyer poses their interactive conversation as a mode of collaboration, a dialogue between partners. In fact, an interview is the form of collaboration with the longest history.

Students today grow up in a climate in which collaborative work, team projects, and editing shared documents are commonplace educational activities. But for many of our contributors, writing has always been a solitary task undertaken in a private space. At first, collaborative writing may feel peculiar and improvisatory. It can be unsettling to share unbaked prose, and it takes time to feel comfortable about knowing when to propose edits without overstepping. Like any relationship, writing collaboratively requires practice, and rewards patience, respect, encouragement, fair critique, and communication. The more you work together, the more you build trust and accountability. And with a supportive writing partner, writers are free to take more chances, exploring ideas that would not have popped up if working alone. Working together also supplies a convenient remedy for writer's block, since collaborators can jump in to unstick tricky passages and find a path forward. The process of submerging one's writing identity in a collective text asks for individual flexibility, yet many find that this holistic process, leading to a fused piece of writing, accurately represents the collective nature of the endeavor.

Sounding Together: Innovative Approaches, Public Advocacy

All in all, then, we offer this volume to help shake up long-standing practices, both in challenging bedrock assumptions embedded in scholarship about music-making in the United States and in implementing collaborative authorship as a fruitful mode of innovation. Because collaborative work sparks dialogue and kindles comparative examination, it is particularly well equipped for raising fresh questions and breaking away from former constraints. Subjects we thought we understood are approached from new perspectives and held up to a different light. Older models relying on a Black/white racial dichotomy give way to more fluid, multidimensional, and intersectional understandings of identity. Combining forces by working in teams opens up new research vistas, enabling scholars to learn and grow together and to move more flexibly across time, place, region, and genre. Perhaps most importantly, collaboration brings together voices from otherwise separate sides of campus, builds fresh ties with the wider research world, and sets in motion rewarding connections between campus and community. It is a welcome antidote to an academic life that can at times feel balkanized and hyperspecialized.

Collaboration also governed an editorial decision that we made together with our authors in the final stages of preparing the book manuscript for publication in early July 2020. A month earlier, the murder of George Floyd Jr. in Minneapolis set off racial protests across the country, and as anger intensified over systemic racism, leading news networks and literary style guides began calling for change in a symbolic but powerful editorial detail, advocating for the capitalization of "Black."[12] Since this editorial change is still in transition, we gave our authors the choice to select the option that felt most comfortable.

Issues of race, nationalism, mobility, and identity permeate this book, starting with its first part, "Cross-Cultural Encounters across Time," which illustrates how collaboration holds special promise for cross-cultural inquiry. Researchers with shared interests may team up to better understand together a distant subject or draw upon distinctive disciplinary traditions to arrive at new questions. In "Music in Unexpected Places: Hearing New Histories of Early American Music," Sarah Eyerly and Rachel Wheeler launch the book by drawing on a rich set of interdisciplinary tools to shed new light on musical connections between Indigenous peoples and colonists. The arc of their research spans several centuries, beginning with the joint composition of a Mohican hymnal in 1756 by a German missionary and a Mohican leader, which reveals a complex interplay between European Christian values and Native American insights. Intertwining scholarship and social engagement, it then leaps to the authors' work with present-day Mohican descendant communities in recording new versions of the hymns. In the process, their essay highlights the importance of collaboration both in musical practice and in connecting Indigenous communities with their heritages. "US Concert Music and Cultural Reorientation during the Occupation of Japan: A Bicultural Perspective," by Misako Ohta and Carol J. Oja, moves in a different geographical and musical direction. Yet it too places US power and heavy-handed colonial actions under the microscope. Writing as citizens of Japan and the United States, the authors probe an out-of-balance cross-cultural exchange in which US concert music was introduced to Japanese audiences after World War II through public record concerts—literally, concerts in which phonograph recordings were played for audiences—as part of a massive effort to westernize Japanese culture. Decades later, the esteemed Japanese composer Torū Takemitsu, who was fifteen in 1945, shared fond memories of attending those concerts, exposing a complex cultural tangle: while the US concerts were one component of an imperialistic reorientation of Japanese society, they also became a vehicle for encouraging cross-cultural education and postwar understanding. Finally, in "Listening to and Learning from Music of the Global United States" Panayotis League and Kay Kaufman Shelemay advocate for the growing potential to study global musical traditions as practiced in the United States. Focusing on migration, they explore the performance, creativity, and circulation networks that emanate from migrant communities, and they demonstrate the power of comparative ethnography, drawing on case studies that consider the hybrid experiences of two musicians—one Ethiopian American and the other Greek

American. These musicians represent immigrant populations with different political histories, racial identities, and musical traditions. The essay also issues a call for greater scholarly attention to the extraordinarily diverse music of diasporic American communities within (and crossing beyond) the borders of the United States.

Essays under the title "Performance and Social Justice" comprise the second part of the book. Braxton D. Shelley's "Sounding Black, Acting White: Hearing Race and Racism in Gospel Performance" places two scholars in dialogue. Shelley ponders the politics of white gospel performers who are deeply intertwined with traditions of Black gospel even as they advocate for Donald Trump via online forums. While rethinking race, this essay also engages with social media to reimagine musicology's relationship to the virtual, pursuing an analytic that is both digital and humanistic, venturing toward a public musicology. What political and social responsibilities accompany sounding Black? Cheryl Townsend Gilkes—like Shelley both an academic and a practicing minster—offers a response: "Lift Every Voice? White Domination Still Matters, Even in Sacred Space: A Sociologist's Reflection on 'Sounding Black, Acting White.'" Gilkes meditates on the "predatory" history of white Americans in relation to Black culture, musing on the ongoing implications of cultural appropriation in sacred space, and wondering how Christian values can coexist with a politics of hate. In "*For the Daughters of Harlem*: Bridging Campus and Community through Sound," Ellie M. Hisama and Lucie Vágnerová call for institutions of higher education to make a commitment to public engagement. Together, they chronicle a music and technology workshop held at Columbia University for young women of color from New York City public schools. Serving as a site of collaborative learning and creative sound production, their ongoing program encourages students to reflect upon connections between music and identities—both individual and collective—such as gender, generation, race, ethnicity, and nationality. How can sound and music become an active force in the lives of these young women? What is its role in cementing friendships, building community, and mitigating the challenges of urban life? Established in the state of New York, which requires only two credits in the arts for high school students, the initiative "For the Daughters of Harlem" provides a new model of humanities-based sound-oriented work that promises to refresh debates in higher education about curriculum, teaching approaches, cultural diversity, and student demographics. In "The Law of Returns: Muhal Richard Abrams and Vijay Iyer in Conversation," Iyer engages in an intergenerational dialogue with composer-pianist Muhal Richard Abrams (1930–2017). One of the cofounders of the Association for the Advancement of Creative Musicians, Abrams raises philosophical and ethical concerns around community, empathy, difference, creative practice, and the category of the human. What unfolds is a conversation between two musicians exploring the nature of individuality in musical expression, including a rumination on why the AACM, as a core organization for musicians of color in Chicago, perceives itself as an "association" rather than a "collective."

The chapters in the next part, "The Politics of Historiography," interrogate the act of writing history in relation to unexamined political assumptions, even volatility. In "White Noise: Historiographical Exceptionalism and the Construction of a White American Music History," Glenda Goodman and Samuel Parler set out a series of provocative questions as they challenge the monolithic whiteness in US music scholarship. They do not claim that all such work focuses on music by white people—far from it—but rather that the historiography generated by Americanists needs to be critiqued alongside the foundational white supremacy so resoundingly present in the study of music overall. In the process they explore and contest the construction of whiteness and white masculinity in the United States with two iconic figures at distinct historical moments: first the late eighteenth-century psalmodist William Billings, then the mid-twentieth-century cowboy-singer Gene Autry. In "Exceptional Matters, Exceptional Times: A Conversation about the Challenges of US Music Scholarship in the Age of Black Lives Matter and Trump," Josh Kun and Alejandro L. Madrid launch a critique of scholarly writing from a different perspective, contemplating the divide in studying US music that has traditionally existed between musicology and American studies, with musicologists often asserting a certain entitlement over the subject. Acknowledging the daily chaos generated by the Trump administration, they propose the resulting disruption of norms as an opportunity to explore a new intellectual value system for discussing US music—one that is fundamentally pluralistic, inclusive, socially relevant, and critically engaged. Whether by confronting the impact of (de)colonization and critical globalization on contemporary musical life, by reconciling why immigrants are held in cells even as the sounds they produce float across borders, by asking why US music studies consistently relegate Latin@ and Latin American music to the margins of a fixed national imaginary, they argue that by listening differently we teach ourselves and our students new ways of documenting and understanding the evolution of music and musical politics in the United States. Yet another set of foundational questions underpins "Music, Travel, and Circuitous Reflections of Community," where Monica A. Hershberger and Sarah Suhadolnik probe how mobility—literally traveling and moving around—upends common structural categories in the study of US music. How does the "spatial turn" in humanities research—and its slippage of time, place, and space—push musical understandings in new directions? In what ways does music *move* musical communities, literally and metaphorically? How might such shifts productively push back against notions involving the musical "margins" and the "center"? Conceptions of genre tend to be fixed, they argue, and radical feminists such as bell hooks provide a means of exploring fluid personal and musical identities.

"Reaching Outward as Teachers and Scholars," the final part of the book, shifts to the pragmatic realms of teaching, publishing, and academic employment. Scholars connect with the public through all these avenues, and they—*we*—feel a deep obligation to disseminate information and ideas while touching individual lives, especially during the current unsettling era. In "Pedagogies of Music, Politics, and Race in US Music Studies," Loren Kajikawa and Daniel Martinez HoSang reflect on a three-year team-teaching venture at the University of Oregon, which focused on the intersection of music, politics, and race in the United States. Their project issues a challenge to reach not only beyond departments but across divisions in large universities (the arts, humanities, and social sciences), and they confront arguments against team teaching, which tend to focus on budgetary constraints and teaching loads. Such interdisciplinary pedagogy invites new perspectives in US music studies, offering a model in which diverse disciplines enjoy equal status. In "Finding Success inside and outside the Academy," Michael Sy Uy and Naomi André discuss the changing academic job market, with a special emphasis on young scholars of color. Acknowledging the waning number of tenure-track jobs in the humanities, as documented by the Mellon Foundation's Graduate Education Initiative, they consider how scholars increasingly need to develop new marketable skills, in addition to teaching. Doing so, they argue, is not only essential in a practical sense of obtaining employment but also carries the added benefit of opening humanistic research to wider audiences. In a fervent call to action, they draw upon their own experiences—one entering the musicology job market in the 1990s, the other in the 2010s. In "Collaborative Voices: Reimagining US Music Scholarship after *AmeriGrove II*," Charles

Hiroshi Garrett and Daniel Goldmark conclude the book by revisiting their shared experiences with editing *The Grove Dictionary of American Music*, second edition, in order to explore how various strategies, many involving collaboration, can guide future reference works in alternative, productive directions. Much has changed in a short time, including technological advances and methodological paradigms, so that new options have emerged to address challenges and predicaments faced during the Grove project. How might scholarly reference works reposition "US music" in a globalized world? What role do they play in the age of Wikipedia? The authors explore a range of possibilities, including open-source approaches, virtual reality platforms, and collaboratively written reference works.

The broad aim of this book, then, is to encourage scholars—in music circles and beyond—to explore the intersections between social responsibility, community engagement, and academic practices through the simple act of working together. These goals became increasingly urgent through each step of this project, which we have come to understand as a reflection of responses to the impact of the Trump presidency. We believe collective action resonates most powerfully in an age when the speed of communication dazzles yet the capacity to hear and empathize with one another feels compromised. Generating conversation and dialogue, of course, is what animates collaborative work. In the process, disciplinary constraints are jostled and new horizons open up, revealing unexpected vistas and proposing how we might move forward. We hope this volume will inspire others to find their own ways of sounding together.

A Note about Our Collaboration

We asked each of our pairs of authors to reflect on their collaboration, and we should do so too. Our friendship dates back to the 1990s, when Charles was an undergraduate student at Columbia University and worked with Carol's late husband Mark Tucker. Over the years our professional lives and interests have increasingly intertwined, although it was not until the 2011 colloquy in the *Journal of the American Musicological Society*, described earlier in this introduction, that we came to embrace scholarly collaboration. We kept searching for an opportunity to work together once again, ultimately convening the Radcliffe workshop and eventually producing this book. None of this would have been possible without today's technology, which held us in close contact while enabling our ideas to develop from a distance. Occasional phone calls and meetings kept us grounded, but virtually all of our collaborative work took place as part of steady e-mail conversations and within the set of Google Docs that guided virtually all elements of this project, from designing the workshop to editing the final essays. When life intervened to disrupt work rhythms for one of us, the other was usually available to step in. As a result, the project's momentum remained steady. We have always approached *Sounding Together* as a mutual endeavor, and that is also how we designed and crafted this introduction. Over the past decade we have come to cherish the act of writing collaboratively—inventing, tinkering, challenging, reimagining—and it is how we sought to assert our collective voice.

Notes

1. Charles Hiroshi Garrett and Carol J. Oja, "Studying U.S. Music in the Twenty-First Century," *Journal of the American Musicological Society* 64, no. 3 (Fall 2011): 689–719. Colloquy participants included Robert Fink, George Lewis, Gayle Sherwood Magee, Alejandro L. Madrid, and Sherrie Tucker. Other important calls for reappraisal include "Symposium: Disciplining American Music," introduced by Mary Wallace Davidson and featuring essays by Dale Cockrell, Guthrie P. Ramsey Jr., Anne K. Rasmussen, and Kay Kaufman Shelemay, in *American Music* 22, no. 2 (Summer 2004): 270–316, and *Rethinking American Music*, ed. Tara Browner and Thomas Riis (Urbana: University of Illinois Press, 2019).

2. Most, though not all, of our authors were involved in the Radcliffe workshop. Colleagues who participated there but were not ultimately part of the book include Marié Abe, Will Cheng, Louis Chude-Sokei, Benjamin Harbert, Tammy Kernodle, Ingrid Monson, and Sherrie Tucker. They contributed mightily to our overall discussions.

3. We also invited Sarah Eyerly and Rachel Wheeler to contribute an essay that would illustrate the dividends of their longer-term joint project.

4. Coauthored books by Lisa Ede and Andrea Lunsford include *Singular Texts / Plural Authors: Perspectives on Collaborative Writing* (Carbondale: Southern Illinois University Press, 1990) and *Writing Together: Collaboration in Theory and Practice* (Boston: Bedford / St. Martin's, 2011). Judith W. Page and Elise L. Smith reflect on coauthoring their book *Women, Literature, and the Domesticated Landscape: England's Disciplines of Flora, 1780–1870* (Cambridge: Cambridge University Press, 2011) in "Writing a Book Together," *Chronicle of Higher Education* (November 1, 2010), https://www.chronicle.com/article/Writing-a-Book-Together/125430

5. Alejandro L. Madrid and Robin D. Moore, *Danzón: Circum-Caribbean Dialogues in Music and Dance* (New York Oxford University Press, 2013), and Larry Starr and Christopher Waterman, *American Popular Music: From Minstrelsy to MP3*, fifth ed. (New York: Oxford, 2018).

6. Noteworthy examples include Daniel Goldmark and Utz McKnight, "Locating America: Revisiting Disney's Lady and the Tramp," *Social Identities* 14, no. 1 (2008): 101–20; Jason Stanyek and Benjamin Piekut, "Deadness: Technologies of the Intermundane," *TDR / The Drama Review* 54, no. 1 (Spring 2010): 14–38; and John Tresch and Emily I. Dolan, "Toward a New Organology: Instruments of Music and Science," *Osiris* 28 (2013): 278–98.

7. Other publications of note include Olivia Bloechl, Katherine Butler Schofield, and Gabriel Solis, "The Value of Collaboration," *Musicology Now* (March 20, 2017), http://www.musicologynow.org/the-value-of-collaboration/; Cathy N. Davidson, "What If Scholars in the Humanities Worked Together, in a Lab?," *Chronicle of Higher Education* (May 28, 1999), B4; and Jennie M. Burroughs, "No Uniform Culture: Patterns of Collaborative Research in the Humanities," *Portal: Libraries and the Academy* 17, no. 3 (July 2017): 507–27.

8. It is also possible to construct collaborative projects, such as dialogues or roundtables, meant to place in relief the perspectives of participants with sharply opposing views.

9. Delineating responsibilities, and including such commentary as part of the final publication, also helps to acknowledge the significance of each contributor's collaborative work and can provide valuable information to promotion, tenure, and hiring committees.

10. Creative Commons provides comprehensive information about the licensing process and the types of available licenses, addressing issues involving attribution, sharing, commercial purposes, and derivative works.

11. Charles Hiroshi Garrett, ed., *The Grove Dictionary of American Music*, 2nd ed., 8 vols. (New York: Oxford University Press, 2013).

12. In late June and early July 2020, the *New York Times*, *Washington Post*, and Associated Press, among other news outlets in the United States, decided to "capitaliz[e] Black when describing people and cultures of African origin" (Nancy Coleman, "Why We're Capitalizing Black," *New York Times*, July 5, 2020).

Cross-Cultural Encounters across Time

ONE | Music in Unexpected Places

Hearing New Histories of Early American Music

SARAH EYERLY AND RACHEL WHEELER

For over half a century, scholars from across the humanities have been wrestling with the complex legacy of colonialism in the United States. A range of new methodologies from various fields of study have sought to address the silences and biases of earlier histories. As scholars studying Native hymnody in mission contexts, we have been particularly drawn to methodologies emerging from Native American and Indigenous studies (NAIS) because of the emphasis on active collaboration with Native communities and interdisciplinary collaboration across academic disciplines. NAIS methods are particularly generative in calling for the centering of Indigenous viewpoints and research processes as integral to historical scholarship. In this chapter, we present our work to re-sound eighteenth-century Mohican-Moravian hymn texts in collaboration with two musicians and members of a church congregation, all from a descendant Mohican community, as a case study in the application of collaborative research methodologies and their potential application more broadly in US music studies.[1]

Our project began as an attempt to gain a fuller understanding of historic traditions of Mohican-language hymnody at Moravian mission sites and within the Moravian Church more broadly by combining insights from both of our disciplines—religious studies and musicology—in service of singing this repertory again. It has since evolved to include a number of different collaborators who also have a stake in this history: members of the Stockbridge-Munsee Band of Mohican Indians, a

Mohican descendant community; professional Mohican musicians and composers; a scholar in linguistics; recording professionals; and students at Florida State University and the University of Wisconsin-Whitewater. Together, we have traced the history of the creation of Mohican-language hymns at a number of different communities affiliated with the Moravian Church in New York and Pennsylvania in the mid-eighteenth century. In the process, we created a hymnal of Mohican-language hymns for use by the Church of the Wilderness on the Stockbridge-Munsee reservation in Bowler, Wisconsin, as a contribution to their ongoing efforts to incorporate more Mohican language into their regular services. The process of singing these hymns together for the first time in centuries and recording them in three different versions proved both deeply moving and instructive.[2]

From the outset, uncovering the story of these hymns was a puzzle that none of us could solve alone. Each one of us possessed important knowledge and skills, but it was only by putting the pieces together that we were able to see a fuller picture. Along the way, in constructing that picture, in singing these hymns, we have come to appreciate the benefits of collaborative research, particularly when put toward the task of resounding historic music. Our desire to hear the music and to sing the hymns again has been motivated by the conviction that the *process* itself of collaboratively investigating the Mohican hymns generates important new research questions, which, in turn, have shaped our interpretations of eighteenth-century Mohican-Moravian hymnody and its contemporary significance.

Decolonizing US Music Studies

Recent scholarship in Native American and Indigenous studies, settler colonialism, and critical race theory has called attention to the need for a further decolonization of historical scholarship by acknowledging alternate forms of knowledge and history-keeping that reflect Indigenous or non-European values and cultural practices. Such a process offers ways to engage more fully with the ethical and practical consequences of academic scholarship for modern Indigenous communities.[3] Many of the current themes and practices that have emerged in the fields of Native American and Indigenous studies can prove beneficial to musicologists looking to further these goals in the historiography of US music.[4] In a recent forum published in the *William and Mary Quarterly*, "Materials and Methods in Native American and Indigenous Studies," by

Alyssa Mt. Pleasant, Caroline Wigginton, and Kelly Wisecup, the authors outline four key practices that are necessary for the continued decolonization of the field of early American history. They include centering the active agency of Native peoples past and present, deploying a broader understanding of texts and archives to include the varied media through which Native peoples have communicated, including learning Native languages, recognizing the expertise of Native communities and knowledge bearers past and present, and understanding the "tribally specific genres, languages, chronologies, and geographic boundaries, which often contrast with European phenomena."[5] The authors further advocate for the value of local knowledge and conducting community-engaged and community-driven scholarship, as well as the recognition that Native perspectives and contexts are foundational to accurate and conscientious scholarship in early American history.[6]

We see these new directions as essential to creating richer narratives of the history of music in the United States, broadly speaking. Inspired by Philip Deloria's reframing of both Native and American studies—*Indians in Unexpected Places*—we advocate for new perspectives on musical contexts and places, especially as they pertain to the contributions of Indigenous musicians and communities, as important steps toward the decolonization of US music history.[7] What contexts and musical traditions remain undervalued and little explored? What have we relegated to the margins of US music history by prioritizing certain agendas and concerns over others? What *unexpected* places, questions, and materials might now be included? How might we reach beyond traditional narratives and histories to enrich our understanding of the musical past and of our country's diversity? What stands to be gained by inviting the contributions of scholars from a variety of disciplinary backgrounds, as well as descendant communities, to investigate the complex histories and continued resonances of historic musical traditions in the United States?

Tribal nations maintain deeply researched understandings of their pasts, often through the creation of historical centers and archives. Archival collections like the Arvid E. Miller Library on the Stockbridge-Munsee reservation contain significant holdings for historical research that complicate and sometimes contradict colonial histories.[8] Engaging with these materials and archives requires us as scholars of US music history to consider our ethical relationship to Native communities. How can musicologists create research that relies on materials held in colonial archives without implicitly or unconsciously replicating their biases? How can we be attentive to the stakes of our work for living Native peoples and their legal and cultural statuses? And how can we move beyond the cycle of simply acknowledging the importance of decolonization and take the concrete step of putting best practices into action?[9]

The task of creating richer historical narratives of US music also requires that we remain open to the multiplicity of Native experiences in the past and the present. Ironically, efforts to decolonize scholarship on Native communities has sometimes resulted in the valuing of certain categories of Native cultural and religious expression. Indeed, at first glance, it may seem that Mohican hymnody, a musical form with European musical roots, should not have been the first place we turned to study Mohican musical or religious traditions and practices. But the legacy and history of Mohican Moravian hymnody is also the legacy of a musical tradition that represented Native culture in critical engagement with non-Native cultural forms. This process can be seen in other modern-day Native-language hymn traditions, such as the Catholic and Protestant hymns of the Anishinaabe and Kiowa, and the adapted Christian repertory of Inuit Moravians. Although these musical forms were originally introduced by missionaries as a strategy to extinguish Native music and worship, they also became meaningful to Native populations. For many Anishinaabe, Kiowa, and Inuit people today, singing these pieces in Native languages, in forms adapted to their use and context, has become a way to maintain traditions and a sense of communal integrity in the face of rapid globalization and cultural instability.[10] As Native scholar Lisa Brooks has observed:

> The practice of Christianity in Native New England was syncretic, combining Indigenous and European spiritual practices, taking on its own character in relation to particular brands and movements of Christianity, and becoming a staple of life for many families, thus part of the fabric of communal identity and history. Now, we might not *like* that so many of our ancestors sought refuge in Christianity, and we may be able to see clearly in retrospect the damaging impact of such choices, but we should not deny our own histories and what we might learn from them or fall into the illusion that those choices made them somehow less Indian.[11]

Both Brooks and Native literary scholar Craig Womack argue that all religious expressions by Native peoples are deserving of attention, whether Christian, tribal, or any other variety, and contribute meaningfully to our understanding of Native individuals and communities.[12]

Similarly, Philip Deloria calls for moving beyond the often limiting cultural stereotypes of "Indian music" to explore the broader contexts of Native music, including engagement with non-Native musical traditions. Some excellent work has been done in this realm. John Troutman, in his book *Indian Blues: American Indians and the Politics of Music, 1879–1934*, examines the relationship between Native musical practices and federal Indian policy in the decades surrounding the turn of the twentieth century. Troutman argues that Native musicians engaged with non-Native musical forms as a method of resistance, survivance, and navigation of changing circumstances, even when confined by governmental and societal structures that threatened the erasure of traditional musics.[13] Similarly, David Samuels, in his provocative study of Apache country music, asks what the particular choice of country music makes possible for Apache musicians. Samuels suggests that country music, with its rootedness in place and longing for a more Edenic past, speaks powerfully to the experience of many Native peoples today.[14]

Our project engages similar questions: what were Native people able to express through engaging with the Moravian hymn tradition? In the eighteenth century this emergent Native hymnody showed signs of functioning as a means to preserve a distinct Native identity within a context of continuing colonialism. Michael McNally, Chad Hamill, Luke Lassiter, Clyde Ellis, and Ralph Kotay have all made similar arguments about Native engagement with Christian traditions of hymnody in a variety of different tribal and religious contexts.[15] Certainly, Christianity and the practice of Christian music traditions by Native people was intertwined with colonization. But the story does not end there. Structures of colonialism and distinctive traditions brought by both Mohicans and Europeans necessarily shaped their participation in and understanding of their collaborative hymn creation and use. But historical repertories like the Mohican-Moravian hymns also reveal the fluidity of musical practices across centuries. And they reveal the often hidden labor of Native musicians and hymn writers, as well as the necessity of collaboration in re-sounding historic musical repertories and in appreciating a fuller range of their meanings today.

We offer this chapter as an example of collaborative and community-driven research. While our project can't and shouldn't suggest a "one size fits all" approach, we hope that our work points to new methodologies and new narratives of US music that serve as an invitation to scholars who hail from a wide array of disciplinary homes.

Naaxkohmãak Osowheekuneenootuy 331 (Singing Box 331)

As with much research in historical musicology, our project began with a collection of manuscripts. On the shelves of the Moravian Church Archives in Bethlehem, Pennsylvania, in Box 331 of the Indian Missions collection, sit several small booklets of hymns dating to the 1740s (figure 1.1). Their titles announce that the language is Mohican. Most verses have a line in German above the Native-language stanza. At first glance, these documents would seem to be simply translations of popular German-Moravian hymns of the time. But a more careful look reveals them to be far more complex. A number of the Mohican stanzas are attributed to Native residents of the community, and an analysis of their content demonstrates that the stanzas are not translations, but new creations. The German heading indicates the chorale tune to be used rather than a source text, as might be assumed.

As material objects, the hymnbooks in Box 331 are an important, but sparse, representation of what was once a living, sounded tradition of hymn singing that brought together hundreds of Moravians, Native and European, in the mid-eighteenth century. These hymns were a significant element of community life in Mohican Moravian communities such as Shekomeko, New York, and Gnadenhütten, Pennsylvania. They were sung to and by the sick and the dying. They were sung at gravesides. They were sung by men while hunting. They were sung at communal feasts. They were sung for visitors, or when visiting other communities. They were sung to bring comfort, to call spiritual power, and to create and fortify community.[16] And, as written documents, the hymnbooks have become important cultural and linguistic records, silently preserving the tradition of Mohican-Moravian hymnody for over 250 years.

Long before we knew one other, both of us had visited the Moravian Archives and carefully paged through the hymns of Box 331. As a scholar of American religious history, Rachel's previous work on missions and Native adaptations of Christianity sparked her interest in the hymns as a way to explore how Mohicans engaged with Christian ideas.[17] But to proceed with unlocking the meaning of the hymns, she also needed to understand Moravian musical practices and the Mohican language. As a musicologist studying eighteenth-century Moravian music and performance practices, Sarah, too, had encountered the Mohican hymns of Box 331. She recognized many of the hymn tunes, prompting her to wonder how they might have sounded. But she lacked detailed knowledge of the history of the Moravian missions or the Mohican language, so she

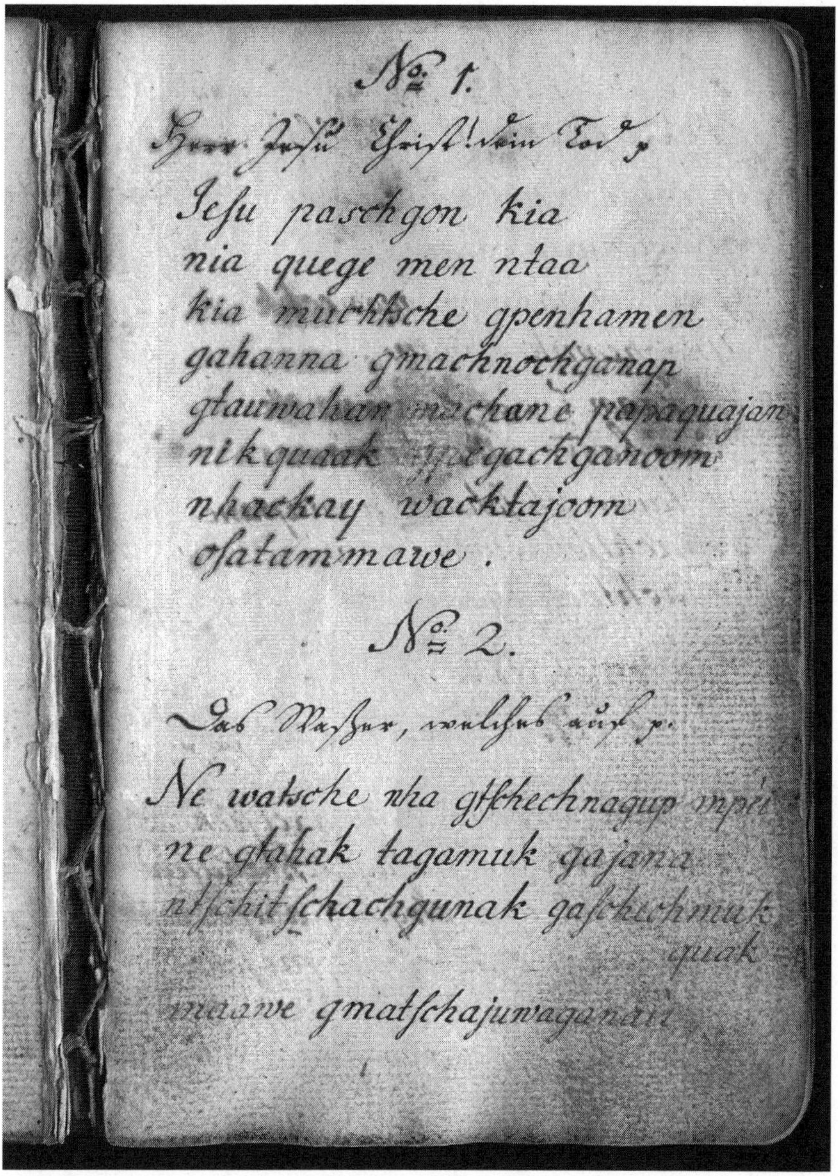

No. 1.

Herr Jesu Christ! dein Tod p

Jesu paschgon kia
nia quege men ntaa
kia muchksche gpenhamen
gahanna gmachnockganap
gtauwahan mechane papaquajan
nikquaak gpegachganoom
nhackay wacktajoom
ofatammawe.

No. 2.

Das Wasser, welches aus p.

Ne watsche wha gtschechnagup inpii
ne gtahak tagamuk gajana
ntschitschachgunak gaschechmuk
quak
maawe gmatschajuwaganan

Figure 1.1. First page of the hymnal "Verse zum Gebrauch bey den Indianern in Scattigok" (Verses for the use of the Indians in Pisgachtigok [Connecticut]), MissInd 331.2, Moravian Archives, Bethlehem, Pennsylvania. Reproduction courtesy of the Moravian Archives.

filed the idea away for a future project. We had both held these same texts in our hands, wondering how these hymns might have sounded and what they meant to the people who created them. Yet no matter how many years of expertise we had accumulated in our respective corners of Moravian studies, the texts remained stubbornly mute until we began conversations with each other and the many others—scholars and members of the Stockbridge-Munsee community—who we came to learn were also interested in studying and singing the Mohican hymns in that same archival collection.

The Stockbridge Mohican community descends from Housatonic and Mahican peoples who lived in the traditional Mahican homelands of the Hudson River Valley and the Housatonic Valley of western Massachusetts and Connecticut.[18] In 1735, the residents of two villages accepted the presence of a Congregational minister in their midst, hoping for the protections a New England-style town might offer. In 1740, the first German Moravian missionaries made contact with residents of another Mahican village, Shekomeko, roughly forty miles southwest of Stockbridge in Dutchess County, New York. The German Moravians kept the extensive records on which this project is based, but the conditions of colonialism led to a quick dissolution of a distinctively Mohican Moravian community, and thus no descendant community survives. The Stockbridges, however, have long remembered the significant ties of kinship that have bound Stockbridge and Shekomeko for centuries, and these ties prompted tribal historians Bernice Miller and Dorothy "Dot" Davids to seek out resources from the Moravian Archives.

Beginning in the late 1960s, these sisters undertook a series of trips to libraries, historical societies, and archives in ancestral locations in order to build a collection for the newly founded Arvid E. Miller Memorial Library on the reservation near Bowler, Wisconsin.[19] During a visit to the Moravian Archives sometime in the 1970s, the Stockbridge visitors were guided to the Indian Missions collection generally and Box 331 specifically for its wealth of Mohican-language material. Unfortunately, Bernice Miller's and Dorothy Davids's hopes that the Moravian sources would provide an accessible source for recovering Mohican history and language were quickly dashed. Archival assistant Lothar Madeheim later related how the Stockbridge visitors had left dismayed at how inaccessible the Mohican records were because of the difficult German handwriting.[20]

In recent years, language-revival efforts in the Stockbridge community have gathered momentum, although the task of language revival is fraught with challenges that are significant enough to have led some

Mohican community members to focus their efforts on learning Munsee rather than Mohican. First, the last native speakers of Mohican died in the 1930s, and those individuals were recalling language they remembered their parents and elders speaking decades earlier. Second, the body of archival and printed source material in Mohican is limited. So the Stockbridge Mohican community has sought the help of linguists in their project, including, most recently, Chris Harvey, a doctoral student at the University of Toronto, writing his dissertation on Mohican.[21] Chris is also collaborating on a grant with the Arvid Miller Library to produce a series of online classes to help community members to study Mohican. At the heart of these language revival efforts is Box 331 and its considerable collection of language materials.

In the end, our efforts to re-sound what we thought were obscure hymns led us to realize that many others had also visited Box 331 and contemplated the significance of these Mohican-language texts. The historical, musical, and linguistic reconstruction of the hymns was like putting together a puzzle: each person contributed their expertise, in the end making it possible to sing the hymns again. As a historian, Rachel conducted research in the larger Moravian mission collection with the aim of understanding how the Mohican-language hymns were created through the collaborative work of German missionaries and Native Christians. Through her musicological research, Sarah was able to identify the chorale tunes indicated by the single line of German that accompanied each Mohican hymn. She also considered the significance of polyglot hymnody to the Moravians' spiritual project.[22] Yet treating these sources as silent texts to be studied, rather than as shorthand representations of embodied, communally produced sound, felt insufficient. And so we set out to hear these texts once more.

Through the process of attempting to sing these hymns with our collaborators, we have gained deeper insight into the web of relationships that facilitated the creation and singing of the Mohican hymns in the eighteenth century. The rich sources in the Moravian records revealed that the hymns were not simply translations. They reveal instead that Mohicans called on the missionaries to devote themselves to the study of Mohican with Native teachers, and these teachers oversaw the composition of Mohican-language hymns. Many of the hymns were created by the Mohican leader, Tassawachamen (baptized as Joshua), and his second wife, Bathsheba, in collaboration with the German missionary Johann Christoph Pyrlaeus and his wife, Susanna Benezet. This was very much a community-based practice, and the hymns were not written or sung alone. They depended on the collaborative work of individuals such as Joshua and Johann Christoph, Bathsheba, and Susanna.[23] They depended on relationships between Native and European Moravians, and between communities who were bound up in structural forces of colonialism and imperialism, yet whose experience of those forces were mediated through personal, familial, spiritual, and communal relationships. The resulting Mohican-language hymns were then put to use in Native communities to carry on various types of ritual work in domestic and communal settings. Hymns were often sung when visitors arrived in town, or when delegations traveled to other communities. Thus, it became clear to us that the hymns could not be understood as simply a mechanism of colonization. Rather, they represented Mohican efforts at sustaining community through ceremonial practice.

Likewise, our twenty-first-century project to re-sound these hymns was necessarily deeply collaborative and relational, bringing together scholars, musicians, and community members who had all found their way to the Mohican hymns for quite different reasons. It was our desire to hear the hymns of Box 331 that led us to record three different versions of eight of those hymns, two done in collaboration with members of the Stockbridge community.[24] The stark differences in these three sets of recordings represent a sort of aural shorthand for the varied ways in which we might approach eighteenth-century musical texts, particularly those that originate in Native communities. Hearing these hymns in three modes has helped us to appreciate more fully the silences that loom over the voluminous Moravian records. Moravian missionaries wrote far more about Native people than did their Anglo-Protestant counterparts, yet volume alone cannot make up for the paucity of Native voices. Reconstructing the performance practices of Native Christians is virtually impossible using these records. By contrast, the available documentary record regarding European-Moravian musical practices is both broad and deep. The extensive mission records include only a scant few references to how Mohican singers sounded, leaving us to wonder whether they adapted Moravian musical aesthetics or how their singing of the hymns reflected Native musical traditions.

Our first set of recordings, therefore, re-sounds the Mohican-Moravian hymns using information on performance practices gleaned from Moravian sources. These recordings hew closely to eighteenth-century Moravian ideals of musical worship and were produced by the early music choir at Florida State University. They reflect our best understanding of how the hymns would have sounded *if we assume* adherence to the ideals of eighteenth-century European-Moravian music for worship.

Before we could proceed with efforts to sing and record the hymns, we had to confront the challenge of language. It quickly became clear that we could not simply rely on the German phonetic representation of the Mohican language from the eighteenth-century hymnals. How proficient were the missionaries in German? Could Mohican sounds even be adequately represented with German phonetics? Were the missionaries attuned to the subtleties of the Mohican language? Because Mohican has long been a "sleeping" language, we turned to linguist Chris Harvey for assistance. Working with historical archival sources and his study of related Algonquian languages, Chris was able to provide us with spoken word recordings of our selected hymns and transcriptions using IPA (international phonetic alphabet). He also corrected the grammar and orthography of the Moravian versions of the hymn texts.

The absence of information on the hymn tunes mentioned in the hymnals posed an additional challenge in reconstructing the hymns as sounded pieces of music. There were no chorale books on this side of the Atlantic containing the tune repertory that would have been in use in Moravian communities in Pennsylvania, New York, or Connecticut in the mid-eighteenth century. Fortunately, during a research trip in 2004 to the Moravian Archives in Herrnhut, the original church settlement in southeastern Germany, Sarah located several small manuscript chorale books from that time period. They were undated, but Moravian archivists Paul Peucker and Rüdiger Kröger used contextual clues to date them to the 1740s and 1750s.[25] Consulting the Herrnhut chorale books allowed Sarah to reunite the Mohican texts with contemporary versions of the chorale tunes. Before the hymns could be sung, however, the chorale manuscript needed to be decoded from the original figured bass, which included only the bass and soprano parts and numerical figures that represented the harmonic structure. To accomplish this, Sarah enlisted the help of Joshua Tanis, a doctoral student in music theory. Josh wrote alto and tenor parts for the singers, and ensured the hymns were singable and harmonically correct, according to Moravian musical principles and standard harmonic and voice-leading rules for eighteenth-century counterpoint. Using Josh's editions, Sarah and her students worked collaboratively to sing and rebalance the text settings and musical underlay for the Mohican words using Chris's spoken recordings and IPA transcriptions to produce a final edition of the music. Weeks of choir rehearsals followed, conducted by ethnomusicology student Drew Griffin and accompanied by organ student Teodora Mitze-Cîrciumaru on a continuo organ, which could imitate the quiet sound of eighteenth-century Moravian organs. Sarah also coached the singers on the aesthetic practices of Moravian singing. Finally, in February 2018, the singers and organist held a recording session with engineer John Hadden, a specialist in early music recording, on the FSU campus (Florida State University, "Jesu paschgon kia," recording 1; https://doi.org/10.3998/mpub.11374592.cmp.6).[26]

In this first set of recordings, we consciously privileged Moravian musical practices when filling in the gaps created by the enigmatic hymn texts; in doing so, we adhered to today's practices of historically informed performances of eighteenth-century music, which typically rely on written documents. Our FSU recording strove to recreate the Moravian aesthetic that encouraged singers to sing "as if there were only *one* voice, so that the focus of the singing was upon the group and not on individual voices."[27] We knew Mohican singers incorporated these musical and aesthetic practices when singing Moravian hymns in multiethnic gatherings of Moravians, but because archival records preserving information on the performance practices of the Mohican hymns are particularly sparse, we could not determine if Native singers might also have chosen to incorporate Mohican musical practices into their hymn singing. We also knew that several Mohican Moravians received extensive training in European musical practices, but the archives remained silent on how their previous knowledge of Indigenous musical practices influenced their performance of Native hymnody.[28] In the end, we realized that if we only relied on our knowledge of Moravian musical styles to fill in the gaps of the historical record, we might effectively be replicating the silencing of Mohican voices. Therefore, we felt it was important to create additional recordings that would restore Mohican voices to the reconstruction process.

Building cautiously from what we knew of northeastern Native musical practices and contextual evidence from the Moravian mission records, we began to construct a picture of how Mohican Moravians participated in hymnody during the eighteenth century, and especially how they did so in ways that carried on the function of Native communal and ceremonial music. Contextual clues about the use of hymnody among the eighteenth-century Mohican Moravian community suggested that communal hymn singing served as a means of preserving community among and between various Native communities and of forging new ties with European settlers in the face of the pressures of colonialism, while also being an occasion of giving thanks to the spirit beings who provided for the well-being of the community. Just as traditional practices, such as the Big House Ceremony, forged and reinforced communal ties at the time between the community and their neighbors, hymns seemed to have served a very similar function. Hymns brought communities together in common purpose.[29]

Our second set of recordings made at the Church of the Wilderness on the Stockbridge reservation, like our first set, was therefore more about the insights gained through the collaborative process of singing the hymns than producing a specific musical or aesthetic product. In this case, the recordings were intended to assist with the community's ongoing efforts of language revitalization and engagement with Mohican history.[30] They were also intended to serve as a resource for ongoing study of Mohican-language hymns for use by the congregation. These recordings present reharmonized versions of the original chorale tunes by Brent Michael Davids, a composer living on the reservation.[31] Brent undertook the work of cultural translation to render the distant eighteenth-century German chorale tunes accessible to a contemporary congregation affiliated with the Evangelical Lutheran Church of America. It is worth noting that Brent's involvement in this project reflects the long-standing Mohican tradition of valuing community over orthodoxy: while he is an avowed atheist and not a member of the congregation, he views his work on this project as supporting his community in their varied religious expressions while connecting to Mohican history and language.

In August 2017, during our trip to the reservation, Paul Johnson (pastor of the Lutheran Church of the Wilderness) and church council president and tribal council member Greg Miller expressed considerable interest in learning Mohican hymns as a way to connect with their heritage and reinforce bonds of community among those who identify as both Christian and Mohican. In response, Brent updated the arrangements and harmonizations of the chorale tunes, from which we created a hymnal including eight hymns.[32] Brent's editions transformed the original eighteenth-century chordal harmonies into harmonies that would be more appealing to a modern church congregation. He also shortened the English translation of the Mohican text so it could be inserted above each musical phrase, and he added chord indications that could be read more easily by guitarists and other musicians familiar with tablature notation, rather than standard Western staff notation. The results were flexible, modern versions of the hymns that could be used in a number of different musical contexts (figure 1.2).

Jesus, To You Alone

Moravian Archives, Bethlehem, Pennsylvania, MissInd 331.2 and MissInd 331.3
"Verses for the use of the Indians in Pisgachtigok (Connecticut)"
Mel. *Herr Jesu Christ! Dein Tod/In dulci jubilo,* Arr. Brent Michael Davids
Text and Music Research: Sarah Eyerly, Chris Harvey, and Rachel Wheeler

Figure 1.2 a and b (facing page). "Jesu paschgon kia" in a modern edition prepared from the Moravian chorale tune "Herr Jesu Christ, dein Tod / In dulci jubilo." Arrangement by Brent Michael Davids (used by permission).

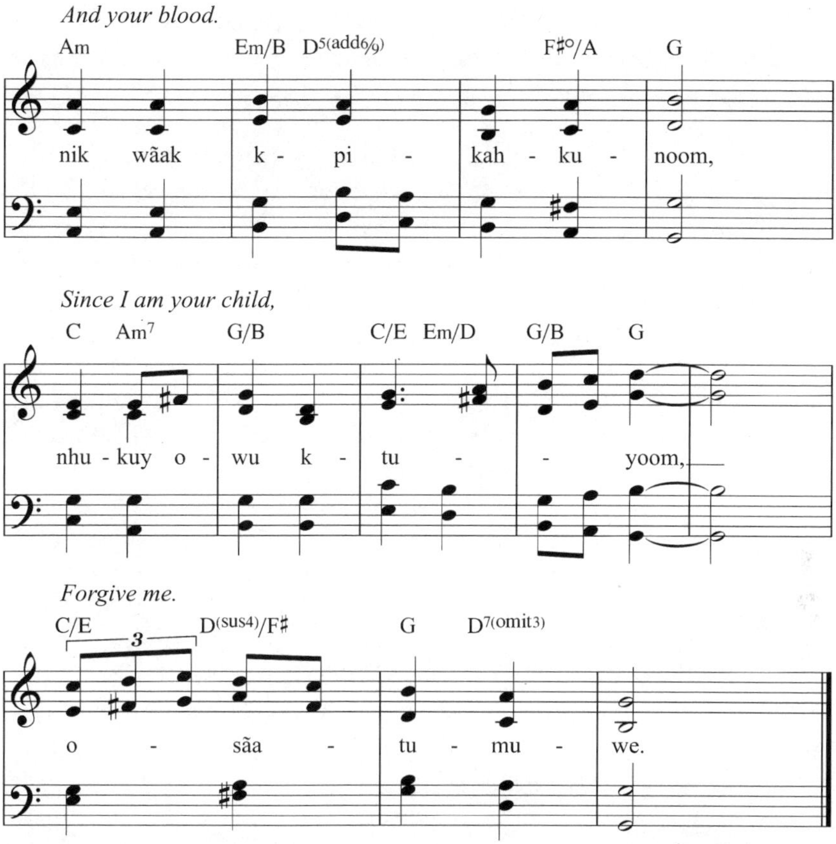

In the summer of 2018, we gathered at the Church of the Wilderness to rehearse the hymns with the congregation, thereby creating a permanent record of Brent's musical settings for future study and use by the congregation. At Brent's suggestion, we timed our visit to coincide with a Mohican history seminar held at the North Star Casino on June 22.[33] The next day, we gathered at the Church of the Wilderness on Moh He Con Nuck Road, whose name recalls the tribe's homelands along the Mahicanituck (Hudson) River.[34] Pastor Paul and Greg Miller had invited the community to the church for a potluck and a day of learning and recording the hymns. After setting up the recording equipment, members of the congregation and broader community began to arrive, ranging from small children to the elderly. Choral students from the University of Wisconsin-Whitewater recruited by Brent's colleague, choral faculty member Robert Gehrenbeck, also arrived to assist in learning the hymns for the recording session.[35]

Once everyone had settled in, Greg welcomed the singers, and introduced the project. Then, we began to learn the hymn "Jesu paschgon kia" ("Jesus to You Alone"). Sarah spoke the Mohican words line by line, and the participants repeated them. Then, Amanda O'Donnell, one of the choral students, rehearsed each of the four parts (soprano, alto, tenor, bass) with the singers. We practiced each hymn several times, and then recorded them, with Brent serving as recording engineer. Over the course of the day, we were able to record all eight hymn verses, with a break for a shared lunch (figure 1.3) (Church of the Wilderness, "Jesu paschgon kia," recording 2; https://doi.org/10.3998/mpub.11374592.cmp.7).

During our visits to the Stockbridge reservation, several themes became clear from our conversations with members of the community and congregation that suggested a remarkable survivance of Mohican community and lifeways from the eighteenth century to the present. Maintaining relationships with spirits, with ancestors, with other Native communities, and with broader communities across the United States was clearly an ethical and spiritual priority. The community saw their Christian identity not as a break from a Mohican past, but a continuation. In his welcoming remarks, Greg spoke of the tribe's history, stressing that affiliation with Congregational, Moravian, and Lutheran mission projects was not an abandonment of Mohican traditions: "Speaking from my heart, I can tell you the Mohican people . . . always embraced the teaching of their elders . . . that each one of us is born with all that we need to know." Regardless of denominational affiliation, Greg affirmed that Mohicans had always relied on broader spiritual understandings of personal and communal morality: "We don't need the Bible. We don't need to argue over all kinds of different things, over what's right, what's wrong. It's in our hearts. And that's what our people always taught us." Community has always been more important than doctrine: "I just think that our ancestors throughout the years worked towards keeping community together. And what people think they gave up to do that we didn't necessarily do, because with a wink our parents have always taught us . . . about what it took to keep us as a community strong. . . . And we blended those together and we kept that strong and we do that yet today." This idea continues to find expression in the church's liturgical use of the Mohican term *Pachtamawas* (the one to whom we pray) to represent the concept of God. For Greg and other church members, speaking and singing Mohican provided a sense of connection to "the old folks . . . and what they went through," as well as

Figure 1.3. Recording session at the Church of the Wilderness, Bowler, Wisconsin (June 2018). Photograph by authors.

the opportunity "to learn from [our] ancestors."[36] As Greg expressed, "Singing these songs that our ancestors probably never heard for over two hundred years made my heart grow fond."[37]

The collaborative recordings made at the Church of the Wilderness in June 2018 served several intersecting but not identical aims. For the community, the recordings were an opportunity to support and strengthen their community by incorporating the language and music of their ancestors. As scholars, we hoped that our work could serve community aims. We also recognized that our scholarship was transformed by engagement with community members who generously shared their perspectives on the contemporary legacy of the eighteenth-century mission projects.

Finally, our third set of recordings was done in collaboration with contemporary Stockbridge Mohican musician Bill Miller.[38] Bill is a singer-songwriter and Grammy-winning musician whose music spans multiple genres, from traditional Native American flute to classic rock, blues, gospel, and sacred music. Like eighteenth-century Mohicans involved in the development of a Native Moravian hymn tradition, Bill views his work as a musician and artist as spiritual work done in service of community, broadly conceived. The constant of Bill's long career has been a melding of musical genres and an exploration of the complex racial and religious history of the United States through the lens of his own experiences as a Stockbridge Mohican of Native American and German American ancestry. Bill's music resonates powerfully with a wide audience because he calls attention to the sometimes painful, sometimes creatively inspired cultural conflicts that are foundational to our country's history. In Bill's words, participating in this collaborative project became a means of building "a connection between me and my past and America."[39]

In Bill's recordings, he set several of the eighteenth-century Mohican hymn texts to new music that reflected his adaptations of traditional Native musical forms. Bill began to work on the hymns in April 2018, when he gathered with Rachel, Sarah, and Chris in preparation for a public presentation and performance at the Eiteljorg Museum of American Indians and Western Art in Indianapolis. Over the course of a few days, we worked together in a basement classroom on the campus of Indiana University-Purdue University Indianapolis (IUPUI) to pool our separate but overlapping stores of knowledge. Chris coached Bill on pronunciation of the Mohican words, and Bill recalled phrases he had learned from his elders as a child. Sarah talked about the Moravians' ideas on the spiritual purposes of communal singing. Rachel shared bits of research from Moravian archival records about how and when the hymns had been created and sung by Mohicans in the eighteenth century. Bill's memories of learning to hunt with the older men of his community and their practice of singing to the deer were remarkably parallel to archival accounts of Mohican elder, Joshua, and other Mohican men speaking of the spiritual inspiration behind their singing, and their practice of singing while hunting. Again and again, in the course of our rehearsals, Bill stressed the importance of listening: to his elders who encouraged him to listen in the woods as he learned to hunt, to his musical teachers who taught him to listen to the sounds of nature in order to learn to play the traditional Native American flute, and to Chris while shutting his eyes to better hear the sounds without the distraction of the written word. Bill made the connection to listening explicit, linking these various acts of listening to finding the inspiration to put new music to the words of the Mohican verses: "It's very sacred to me, and I know what I heard in the woods with the other hunters. I know what I heard at powwows with these old men, how they sing. . . . And that's what I did [in the recording session]."[40]

When he started the process of learning the Mohican hymns, Bill preferred not to listen to the German chorale tunes that had originally been used to sing the Mohican texts. The result was a very different musical take on the pieces that helped us to appreciate the extent to which the original chorale tunes had exerted a distinct sonic presence that almost overshadowed the Mohican voices of "Jesu paschgon kia" and other hymns. Bill's versions of the hymns provide a new way to experience and hear the texts themselves. Since Bill's versions were created through improvisation, there was no need to transform them into notated pieces of music. The oral nature of Bill's versions also allows the possibility to transform future iterations of the hymns into different combinations of texts and tunes that reflect new ideas about the meaning of the Mohican words (Bill Miller, "Jesu paschgon kia," recording 3; https://doi.org/10.3998/mpub.11374592.cmp.8).[41]

In the end, Bill's recordings of "Jesu paschgon kia" and other hymns were one culmination of years of collaboration, and ultimately, inspiration: "It's bringing the past up to now, and it is powerful to hold this thing, this song, hundreds and hundreds of years old and then put it in my breath and put it in my soul and then bring it out in the present tense."[42] Bill's versions of the hymns should not be heard as replicating the sounds of eighteenth-century Mohicans. Rather, Bill's recordings privilege his voice as a contemporary Mohican musician re-sounding sacred ancestral texts.[43] For Bill, as for his Mohican ancestors, music has long translated experiences of spirit into sound, offering a means to call down spiritual power and build community.

Hearing New Histories of US Music

We have sought throughout this project to reprise historic music in ways that recognize Native agency past and present. Archives produce silences as well as reveal particular worldviews, but we believe a broadly collaborative process and approach to historical research functions to reveal and reinstate Native agency that has often been overlooked in the documentary records that have been used to construct narratives of early American history. The various methods of musical reconstruction we have deployed help us to "hear" more clearly the presences and absences of the eighteenth-century textual sources. Using the standards of European-based historical performance in Moravian communities for the first recordings, we were able to make use of the rich Moravian records to create what might mistakenly be seen as highly authoritative musical reconstructions. But, in the end, the German-ness of the musical sounds completely overshadows the Mohican-ness of the words and the Mohican contribution to the creation of the hymns. We caution that this first set of recordings should remind listeners of the silences of the archives rather than persuade us that we are stepping back in time to hear history. Had we stopped with this recording, we would have encouraged this misunderstanding. Our second set of recordings produced in collaboration with the congregation of the Church of the Wilderness speaks to the ways that Native communities past and present navigate the mixing and melding of inherited tradition with new resources and how they do so with the aim of reinforcing community ties. The recordings produced with the congregation of the Church of the Wilderness, like the other recordings, were not created as musical products, but rather document the active engagement of the community in the process of constructing historical memory, strengthening communal ties, and revitalizing the Mohican language. Finally, our third set of recordings represents the experiences of one Mohican man and musician whose process of setting centuries-old Mohican words to his own music was itself a powerful spiritual experience fueled by his lifelong efforts to create community through music.

While these collaborative methods have significant potential, they also pose a set of challenges that were quite new to us as historians. This includes acknowledging that there are multiple viewpoints and perspectives on archival sources like the Mohican-Moravian hymns within the Stockbridge community. For many, the legacy of Christian missions among Mohican communities is one of tremendous loss and pain, and so there is an understandable desire not to revisit the personal and cultural trauma of Mohican experiences with missionaries.[44] The different resonances of these sources for different members of the Stockbridge community highlight the fraught nature of Native adaptations of Christianity and the ongoing impact of colonialism for modern descendant communities. The commitment to work collaboratively also pressed us to reflect on the utility of academic scholarship beyond the academy and the extent to which it serves contemporary communities. As scholars, we have been accustomed to writing for those who share common disciplinary commitments. Our work with Native communities and individuals who have an altogether different investment in the sources has pushed our work in new directions. As non-Native academics, and as cultural descendants of European American settlers, this project had a different resonance for us than for our Mohican partners.

The result for us was a move toward prioritizing relationships in our scholarship: with texts, with other scholars, with communities who have a stake in the production of scholarship. This approach only became more valuable as we committed to a different set of priorities and methodologies, and it was far more generative than approaching these manuscripts from a singular disciplinary perspective. The resulting hymn recordings inexorably shifted our understanding of our historic subject, helping us to appreciate in new ways both the losses inflicted by colonialism and represented in archival silences, and also the survivances, which we likely would not have seen—or heard—if we had remained in our disciplinary academic silos.

This prioritizing of relationships called for by the methods of Native American and Indigenous studies also offered a welcome way to reframe our thinking about what it means to be a scholar, particularly on a topic not often discussed in academic publications: the balancing of family life and academic production. We are both mothers of young children and have often wrestled with the disparity of our lived experience and the academic ideals of the intrepid scholar off for months working in distant archives, followed by monastic hours in front of the computer, resulting in book dedications thanking the family for tolerating these extended absences. When we had independently come across the Mohican-Moravian hymns, we were both excited but also discouraged, each wondering how we could possibly devote the necessary time to mastering a new discipline that could help interpret these documents. Over the years as our collaboration grew, we both came to a deep appreciation of this different mode of scholarly endeavor. Modern academic life, with its whir of teaching responsibilities and ever-expanding service obligations, often means that we have few occasions with colleagues at our home institutions for sustained conversations about our scholarly work. Conferences offer opportunities to connect with other specialists in our fields who are familiar with our research, but the snatches of conversation during coffee breaks and the few minutes at the end of paper presentations do not provide an opportunity for sustained intellectual engagement and development of our thinking. In contrast, we have found this type of collaborative project to be a welcome chance to engage in a shared endeavor rooted in our core academic commitment that led to a further expansion that grew to include other academics, our students, our colleagues, and our local communities. In other words, new communities developed around the collaboration itself, which in turn has fostered friendships that carry beyond our shared project (figure 1.4). As Chris Harvey expressed when we met to work on the recordings in Indianapolis: "The reason I was *invited* here was because I have a background in the language and I can understand the words. But the reason why I *came* here is because I've met comrades, colleagues. I've met friends who I'm gonna hopefully work with for a good long time."[45]

Our experience working on this narrowly focused collaborative project has also given us pause to reflect on its larger implications for US music studies. The very process of creating these recordings points to the unique potential of musical performance to further decolonize scholarship on early American music. Musical performance is an inherently social and collaborative activity, and it is particularly inviting of the contributions of nonacademic collaborators. Especially in the realm of historical performance practices, to truly create nuanced interpretations of past musical traditions, we must necessarily draw upon a complex blend of diachronic and synchronic evidence that includes the voices, languages, and musical traditions of Indigenous communities.

Throughout this project, we have been reminded of the words of Abenaki basketmaker Judy Dow, quoted by Lisa Brooks: "We all have pieces of the puzzle, and it is only by coming together that we can hope to reconstruct the full picture."[46] This metaphor can apply to the historical creation of a body of Mohican hymns by German and Mohican Moravians, as well as our work in the present. In the eighteenth century, various reeds—Mohican tradition, Moravian music, and the larger context of colonialism—were woven together to create the basket of Mohican-Moravian hymnody. That particular basket served different purposes for the Mohicans and the Moravians who contributed to its construction, but it was nonetheless a shared creation. Quite different patterns emerged depending on the admixture of various strands. And, to mix metaphors, the distinctive pattern that emerged with the weaving together of the various strands created a new and *unexpected* site of early American music.

As scholars in the twenty-first century studying this historic "basket" of Mohican hymnody, none of us alone possesses the range of knowledge needed to understand all of the different reeds used in the basket's construction, nor the interpretive skills needed to appreciate the range of meanings attributed to that basket by those who used it to carry what was precious to them. The same can be said of the study of US music more broadly. Our work does not lead us to a new "grand narrative" of the history of music in the United States, nor does it convince us that we ought to study US music as an abundance of distinct and separate

Figure 1.4. Bill Miller, Chris Harvey, Sarah Eyerly, and Rachel Wheeler, Richmond, Virginia. Photograph by authors.

strands. Rather, we believe the study of music in this country is the study of the infinitely varied baskets produced out of the encounters of different cultures and musical traditions within the varied geographical contexts of Native nations, colonialism, and empire. The music found in these unexpected places is testimony to the rich and combinative musical heritage of the United States.[47]

When he speaks to student groups, Bill Miller often tosses out a question: "What is Mohican music?" After watching students struggle to come up with an answer, he'll play a riff on Johnny Cash's "Folsom Prison Blues" or Eric Clapton's "After Midnight" and say, often with a mischievous grin, "Now, that's Mohican music!"

Notes

This project would not have been possible without a wide circle of collaborators. The authors would like to offer special thanks to members of the Stockbridge Mohican community, including Nathalee Kristiansen and Yvette Malone of the Arvid E. Miller Historical Library/Museum; the congregation of the Church of the Wilderness, especially Pastor Paul Andrew Johnson and council president Greg Miller; Brent Michael Davids; Bill Miller; and too many others to name! The authors have benefited from the encouragement and support of many scholars, including Jon Butler; Philip Deloria; Michael McNally; Paul Peucker, Thomas McCullough, and the staff at the Moravian Archives; Martha Hill, Scott Shoemaker, and the staff of the Eiteljorg Museum; and their colleagues and students in the Religious Studies and Native American and Indigenous Studies programs at Indiana University–Purdue University Indianapolis (IUPUI), and the Musicology area at Florida State University (FSU), and Douglas Winiarski and Andy McGraw at the University of Richmond. This project would not have been possible without financial support from the American Council of Learned Societies, the IUPUI Arts and Humanities Initiative, and the New Frontiers in the Arts and Humanities initiative at Indiana University, as well as sabbatical and research support from IUPUI and FSU.

1. Where possible, we avoid using "American" to describe the United States, since that term also encompasses other countries within North America, Central America, and South America, consistent with editorial practice in this volume. In referencing musical practices in the eighteenth-century missions of the Moravian Church, we employ the terms "early North American" or "early American" as geographical, not geopolitical constructs, since our historical subject predates the founding of the United States.

2. For a brief overview of the whole project, see the short documentary film *Singing Box 331*, https://www.youtube.com/watch?v=96JxDaDYgss&feature=emb_logo. This film accompanies our article "Singing Box 331: Re-sounding Eighteenth-Century Mohican Hymns from the Moravian Archives," *William and Mary Quarterly* 76, no. 4 (October 2019): 649–96. A digital companion version of the article, containing additional videos, recordings, and other multimedia elements, can be accessed at https://oieahc.wm.edu/digital-projects/oi-reader/singing-box-331-rachel-wheeler-sarah-eyerly/

3. As Linda Tuhiwai Smith has argued, the act of decolonizing history is intertwined with the act of valuing Indigenous knowledge and knowledge production: "To hold alternative histories is to hold alternative knowledges. The pedagogical implication of this access to alternative knowledges is that they can form the basis of alternative ways of doing things. Transforming our colonized views of our own history (as written by the West), however, requires us to revisit, site by site, our history under Western eyes. This in turn requires a theory or approach which helps us to engage with, understand and then act upon history." Tuhiwai Smith, *Decolonizing Methodologies: Research and Indigenous Peoples* (London: Zed Books, 1999), 34. For recent sources on decolonizing American history, see Susan Sleeper-Smith et al., *Why You Can't Teach United States History without American Indians* (Chapel Hill: University of North Carolina Press, 2015); James H. Merrell, "Second Thoughts on Colonial Historians and American Indians," *William and Mary Quarterly* 69, no. 3 (July 2012): 451–512; David Treuer, *The Heartbeat of Wounded Knee: Native America from 1890 to the Present* (New York: Riverhead Books, 2019); Robert Warrior, ed., *The World of Indigenous North America* (New York: Routledge, 2015); Chris Andersen and Jean M. O'Brien, eds., *Sources and Methods in Indigenous Studies* (London: Routledge, 2017);

Lisa Brooks, *Our Beloved Kin: A New History of King Philip's War* (New Haven: Yale University Press, 2018); Brooks, "Awikhigawôgan ta Pildowi Ôjmowôgan: Mapping a New History," *William and Mary Quarterly* 75, no. 2 (April 2018): 259–94; Christine M. DeLucia, "Locating Kickemuit: Springs, Stone Memorials, and Contested Placemaking in the Northeastern Borderlands," *Early American Studies* 13, no. 2 (Spring 2015): 467–502; DeLucia, *Memory Lands: King Philip's War and the Place of Violence in the Northeast* (New Haven: Yale University Press, 2018); Jeffrey Glover and Paul Chaat Smith, eds., *Colonial Mediascapes: Sensory Worlds of the Early Americas* (Lincoln: University of Nebraska Press, 2014); Jean M. O'Brien, *Firsting and Lasting: Writing Indians Out of Existence in New England* (Minneapolis: University of Minnesota Press, 2010); Craig N. Cipolla, *Becoming Brothertown: Native American Ethnogenesis and Endurance in the Modern World* (Tucson: University of Arizona Press, 2013); David J. Silverman, *Red Brethren: The Brothertown and Stockbridge Indians and the Problem of Race in Early America* (Ithaca, NY: Cornell University Press, 2010); Jace Weaver, *The Red Atlantic: American Indigenes and the Making of the Modern World, 1000–1927* (Chapel Hill: University of North Carolina Press, 2014); Claire Smith and H. Martin Wobst, eds., *Indigenous Archaeologies: Decolonizing Theory and Practice* (New York: Routledge, 2005). For foundational works on settler colonialism, see Patrick Wolfe, "Settler Colonialism and the Elimination of the Native," *Journal of Genocide Research* 8, no. 4 (December, 2006): 387–409; Wolfe, "The Settler Complex: An Introduction," *American Indian Culture and Research Journal* 37, no. 2 (2013): 1–22; J. Kēhaulani Kauanui, "'A Structure, Not an Event': Settler Colonialism and Enduring Indigeneity," *Lateral* 5, no. 1 (Spring 2016). We have also found the work of Native literary critics particularly helpful. See especially the essays by Craig Womack and Lisa Brooks in Craig S. Womack, Daniel Heath Justice, and Christopher B. Teuton, eds., *Reasoning Together: The Native Critics Collective* (Norman: University of Oklahoma Press, 2008).

4. Some recent examples of decolonial work in music history and ethnomusicology that take up these themes include Victoria Lindsay Levine and Dylan Robinson, eds., *Music and Modernity among First Peoples of North America* (Middletown, CT: Wesleyan University Press, 2019); Olivia Ashley Bloechl, Melanie Diane Lowe, and Jeffrey Kallberg, eds., *Rethinking Difference in Music Scholarship* (New York: Cambridge University Press, 2015); and the *Journal of the Society for American Music*'s special issue "Music, Indigeneity, and Colonialism in the Americas," 13, no. 4 (November 2019), including articles by Jessica Bissett Perea and Gabriel Solis ("Asking the Indigeneity Question of American Music Studies," 401–10) and Glenda Goodman ("Joseph Johnson's Lost Gamuts: Native Hymnody, Materials of Exchange, and the Colonialist Archive," 482–507).

5. Alyssa Mt. Pleasant, Caroline Wigginton, and Kelly Wisecup, "Materials and Methods in Native American and Indigenous Studies: Completing the Turn," *William and Mary Quarterly* 75, no. 2 (2018): 210. A further extension of this conversation can be found in a forum devoted to a critical review of recent NAIS scholarship by historian David Silverman: "Historians and Native American and Indigenous Studies," *American Historical Review* 125, no. 2 (April 2020): 517–51. Respondents to Silverman's review include leading figures in the field of NAIS, Christine M. DeLucia, Alyssa Mt. Pleasant, Philip J. Deloria, and Jean M. O'Brien.

6. Mt. Pleasant, Wigginton, and Wisecup, "Materials and Methods," 208.

7. Philip Joseph Deloria, *Indians in Unexpected Places* (Lawrence: University Press of Kansas, 2004).

8. For an excellent discussion of the creation of the Arvid Miller Library as an expression of sovereignty, see Rose K. Miron, "Mohican Archival Activism: Narrating Indigenous Nationalism," PhD dissertation, University of Minnesota, 2018.

9. This echoes the call made by Mt. Pleasant, Wigginton, and Wisecup to "complete the turn" to integrate Native American history: "Materials and Methods," 209.

10. See Luke E. Lassiter, Clyde Ellis, and Ralph Kotay, *The Jesus Road: Kiowas, Christianity, and Indian Hymns* (Lincoln: University of Nebraska Press, 2002); Michael David McNally, *Ojibwe Singers: Hymns, Grief, and a Native Culture in Motion* (New York: Oxford University Press, 2000); Tom Gordon, "Found in Translation: The Inuit Voice in Moravian Music," *Newfoundland and Labrador Studies* 22, no. 1 (2007): 287–314; Tom Artiss, "Music and Change in Nain, Nunatsiavut: More White Does Not Always Mean Less Inuit," *Études/Inuit/Studies* 38, nos. 1–2 (2014): 33–52; and Sarah Eyerly, "Mozart and the Moravians," *Early Music* 47, no. 2 (May 2019): 161–182. Although Moravian hymn singing and the soundscapes of mission communities were a form of colonialism, on an individual and community level people were modifying hymns and adapting them. Native Moravians were not passive actors enmeshed in colonial processes. In studying the Moravian missions, we might take some inspiration from Sarah Rivett's reexamination of missionary transcriptions of Native American languages. Rather than emphasizing a process of language erasure, Rivett has sought to highlight the adaptive power and survivance of Native languages. Even as missionaries sought to convey Christian theology through new linguistic mediums, Native languages often resisted simple acts of translation, instead preserving and encoding different theologies and religious worldviews in their very structures and grammars. While many Native American languages ceased to be spoken languages during several centuries of colonial contact, Rivett argues that the essential grammatical elements of those languages survived in missionary transcriptions to encode the cultures and religions they represented. See Sarah Rivett, *Unscripted America: Indigenous Languages and the Origins of a Literary Nation* (New York: Oxford University Press, 2017).

11. Lisa Brooks, "Locating an Ethical Native Criticism," in Womack, Justice, and Teuton, *Reasoning Together*, 262 n. 30.

12. Craig S. Womack, "Theorizing American Indian Experience," in Womack, Justice, and Teuton, *Reasoning Together*, 353–410.

13. Gerald Vizenor defines survivance as "an active sense of presence, the continuance of native stories, not a mere reaction, or a survivable name." Gerald Vizenor, *Manifest Manners: Narratives on Postindian Survivance* (Lincoln: University of Nebraska Press, 1999), vii. This theme of renunciation of narratives of dominance and tragedy, and Native agency and presence in shaping contemporary Native culture, in conversation with modernity and Native traditions, is central to much of NAIS scholarship following Vizenor. See also Vizenor, "The Ruins of Representation: Shadow Survivance and the Literature of Dominance," *American*

Indian Quarterly 17, no. 1 (1993): 7–30; Vizenor, *Survivance: Narratives of Native Presence* (Lincoln: University of Nebraska Press, 2008); John Troutman, *Indian Blues: American Indians and the Politics of Music, 1879–1934* (Norman: University of Oklahoma Press, 2012).

14. David W. Samuels, "Singing Indian Country," in *Music of the First Nations: Tradition and Innovation in Native North America*, ed. Tara Browner (Urbana: University of Illinois Press, 2009), 141–59.

15. Lassiter, Ellis, and Kotay, *Jesus Road*; and Luke E. Lassiter, "'From Here On, I Will Be Praying to You': Indian Churches, Kiowa Hymns, and Native American Christianity in Southwestern Oklahoma," *Ethnomusicology* 45, no. 2 (2001): 338–52; McNally, *Ojibwe Singers*; and Chad Hamill, *Songs of Power and Prayer in the Columbia Plateau: The Jesuit, the Medicine Man, and the Indian Hymn Singer* (Corvallis: Oregon State University Press, 2012). See also David W. Samuels, *Putting a Song on Top of It: Expression and Identity on the San Carlos Apache Reservation* (Tucson: University of Arizona Press, 2004). For recent scholarship on music in the context of missionaries active in the Northeast, see Robin Leaver, "More Than Simple Psalm-Singing in English: Sacred Music in Early Colonial America," *Yale Journal of Music and Religion* 1, no. 1 (February 2015): 63-80; Olivia Ashley Bloechl, *Native American Song at the Frontiers of Early Modern Music* (New York: Cambridge University Press, 2008); Glenda Goodman, "'But They Differ from Us in Sound': Indian Psalmody and the Soundscape of Colonialism, 1651–75," *William and Mary Quarterly* 69, no. 4 (2012): 793–822; Beverley Diamond, *Native American Music in Eastern North America: Experiencing Music, Expressing Culture* (New York: Oxford University Press, 2008); and Patrick Erben, *Harmony of the Spirits: Translation and the Language of Community in Early Pennsylvania* (Chapel Hill: University of North Carolina Press, 2012). Christine DeLucia has argued persuasively for greater attention to the aural encounters of colonialism in "The Sound of Violence: Music of King Philip's War and Memories of Settler Colonialism in the American Northeast," *Common-Place*, special issue on early American music, 13, no. 2 (Winter 2013), http://commonplace.online/article/sound-violence-music-king-philips-war-memories-settler-colonialism-american-northeast/. Literary scholars have looked at Samson Occom's hymnody for what it tells us about Native authorship. See Joanna Brooks, "Six Hymns by Samson Occom," *Early American Literature* 38, no. 1 (January 1, 2003): 67–87.

16. We have written more broadly elsewhere about the history of the Moravian missions in relation to the Mohicans and the place of hymnody within the mission: Wheeler and Eyerly, "Songs of the Spirit: Hymnody in the Moravian Mohican Missions," *Journal of Moravian History* 17 (Spring 2017): 1–26. A more detailed analysis of the modern recordings and the history of the Mohican-Moravian hymns, especially the hymn "Jesu paschgon kia," can be found in Wheeler and Eyerly, "Singing Box 331."

17. Rachel Wheeler, *To Live upon Hope: Mohicans and Missionaries in the Eighteenth-Century Northeast* (Ithaca, NY: Cornell University Press, 2008).

18. The Stockbridge Munsee Band of Mohicans has federally recognized tribal status. For a history of the tribe, see Dorothy Davids, *A Brief History of the Mohican Nation: Stockbridge Munsee Band* (2001; Bowler, WI, revised 2004); and James W. Oberly, *A Nation of Statesmen: The Political Culture of the Stockbridge-Munsee Mohicans, 1815–1972* (Norman: University of Oklahoma Press, 2005).

19. According to Dorothy Davids, at least twenty research trips were undertaken by groups of tribal youth and elders beginning in 1969. Davids, *A Brief History*, 8. See also Miron, "Mohican Archival Activism."

20. Carl Masthay, *Mahican-Language Hymns, Biblical Prose, and Vocabularies from Moravian Sources, with 11 Mohawk Hymns (Transcription and Translation)* (St. Louis, MO: C. Masthay, 1980), 1. This visit may have been part of the 1972 trip made by a delegation of women from the Stockbridge reservation documented in the travel journal by Kristy Miller, housed in the Arvid Miller Library.

21. Chris Harvey, "The Diachronic Phonology of Mahican" (PhD diss. in linguistics, University of Toronto, in progress).

22. For more information on Moravian singing practices, see Sarah Eyerly, *Moravian Soundscapes: A Sonic History of the Moravian Missions in Early Pennsylvania* (Bloomington: Indiana University Press, 2020), https://doi.org/10.33009/moraviansoundscapes_music_fsu; Eyerly, "Mozart and the Moravians"; Eyerly, "The Sensual Theology of the Eighteenth-Century Moravian Church," in *Christian Congregational Music: Performance, Identity, and Experience*, ed. Monique Ingalls, Carolyn Landau, and Tom Wagner (Ashgate, 2013); and Eyerly, "*Der Wille Gottes:* Musical Improvisation in Eighteenth-Century Moravian Communities," in *Self, Community, World: Colonial Education in a Transatlantic World*, ed. Heikki Lempa and Paul Peucker (Bethlehem: Lehigh University Press, 2010), 201–27.

23. For a fuller discussion of this collaborative process of composing the texts and setting them to chorale tunes in the eighteenth century see Wheeler and Eyerly, "Singing Box 331," and Wheeler and Eyerly, "Songs of the Spirit."

24. For more information on the recording process, see Wheeler and Eyerly, "Singing Box 331," and the digital companion edition with accompanying audiovisual materials.

25. The Moravian Archives in Herrnhut hold two copies of a chorale book likely prepared by the Moravian composer Christian Gregor, H.4 and H.4a, and also an older chorale book of tunes in use before Gregor's standardization of Moravian hymn tunes in 1784 (H.3, H.2).

26. The recordings of the Mohican hymns produced at Florida State University involved the collaborative work and contributions of a number of students and faculty. We would like to express our thanks to singers Vivianne Asturizaga, Rachel Bani, Laura Clapper, Drew Griffin (singer and conductor), Teodora Mitze-Cîrciumaru, Kevin Speer, Ryan Whittington, and Kaitlin Zardetto-Smith. We would also like to thank music theorist Joshua Tanis, who created the alto and tenor parts; recording engineer John Hadden; and the Florida State University College of Music for the use of facilities and recording equipment.

27. "Verlass der vier Synoden der evangelischen Brüder-Unität, von den Jahren 1764, 1769, 1775, und 1782," Paragraph 917, Moravian Archives, Bethlehem, Pennsylvania.

28. Lawrence W. Hartzell, "Joshua, Jr., Moravian Indian Musician," *Transactions of the Moravian Historical Society* 26 (1990): 1–19; Laurence Libin, "What Instrument Did Joshua Make?," *Proceedings of the 6th Bethlehem Conference of Moravian Music* (n.p., n.d.), 46–50.

29. Dennis Kelley offers a particularly useful theoretical framework for understanding contemporary Native political activism, language revival efforts, and

practice of Christianity, including Christian music, as being forms of ceremony that carry on traditional Native ideals of maintaining relationships with human and other than human beings. Kelley, *Tradition, Performance, and Religion in Native America: Ancestral Ways, Modern Selves* (New York: Routledge, 2015).

30. The congregation at the Church of the Wilderness already recites the doxology in Mohican, and sings hymns from many different Christian traditions. According to former pastor Melinda (Shriner) VanderSys, the congregation began using the Mohican doxology around 1996 in a translation by Marlene Molly Miller. Email communication from Paul Andrew Johnson to Rachel Wheeler, November 22, 2018.

31. Brent is a prolific and accomplished composer of concert music, film scores, and music for dance and theater. He is also a recording engineer, and recently became a codirector of the Lenape Center in New York. His website can be found at http://filmcomposer.us/. Brent is committed to promoting musical education among Native youth locally, regionally, and nationally, including collaborative projects with Robert Gehrenbeck, the director of choral programming at the University of Wisconsin-Whitewater.

32. Our current recordings, and musical editions shared with the Church of the Wilderness, represent a selection of eight hymns. The choice of these particular hymns was driven by Sarah's ability to identify the referenced hymn tunes from the eighteenth-century Mohican hymn booklets. It is our hope to add additional hymns, and their musical settings, to the repertory of Native language hymns available for use. We are currently producing a hymnal featuring the eight hymns in both eighteenth-century and modern arrangements, along with an accompanying CD, in conjunction with the Moravian Music Foundation, based in Winston-Salem, North Carolina.

33. The one-day seminar included sessions by Native and non-Native scholars and community members. Presenters included, among others, Jeremy Mohawk, representing the tribe's Language Committee, the Trustees of Reservations, who manage the Mission House in Stockbridge, Massachusetts, and community youth, who read aloud the words of their ancestors dating back to the eighteenth century.

34. "Stockbridge-Munsee Mohican History," *Tribal Histories*, accessed November 17, 2018, https://www.pbs.org/video/wpt-documentaries-stockbridge-munsee-mohican-history/; Davids, *A Brief History*, 1.

35. In addition to Pastor Paul, Greg Miller and Brent Michael Davids, community members participating included Yvette Malone, Kane Granquist (minor), Kora Burr (minor), Linda Miller, Miles Miller (minor), Patrick Bailey, Douglas Miller, Katie Lewis, Barbara Stephenson, Starlyn Tourillott, Meryl Miller (minor), Caroline Lepscier, Clarissa Vele, and Elsie Utke. Students from the University of Wisconsin-Whitewater included Amanda O'Donnell, Hana Worsham, Dan Szelogowski, David Baker, and Dan Worsham.

36. Katie Lewis, interview, June 23, 2018, Bowler, Wisconsin.

37. Greg Miller, interview, June 23, 2018, Bowler, Wisconsin.

38. Bill's full discography can be found at https://billmiller.co. To learn more about Bill's involvement in this project, please see the video from the digitally published version of our article "Singing Box 331" at https://youtu.be/O02kQ-lYLis

39. Bill Miller, interview, April 5, 2018, Eiteljorg Museum, Indianapolis, Indiana.

40. Bill Miller, interview.

41. Scott Deal, professor of music technology, and Harry Chaubey, doctoral student, served as recording engineers. Postproduction work on the recording was completed by Andy Nathan.

42. Bill Miller, interview.

43. On the notion of reprise, see chap. 1 of Kelley, *Tradition, Performance, and Religion in Native America.*

44. Marlene Molly Miller (Mohican Nation, Stockbridge-Munsee Historical Committee), writes candidly about the negative influence of Christian ideas in her community and the need for a rebirth of Mohican traditions in Robert Steven Grumet, ed., *Voices from the Delaware Big House Ceremony* (Norman: University of Oklahoma Press, 2001), xxii–xxiii. On the legacy of Christian missions, see Rose Miron, "Fighting for the Tribal Bible: Mohican Politics of Self-Representation in Public History," *Journal of the Native American and Indigenous Studies Association (NAIS)* 5, no. 2 (September 22, 2018): 91–123.

45. Chris Harvey, interview, April 5, 2018, Eiteljorg Museum, Indianapolis, Indiana.

46. Lisa Brooks, *The Common Pot: The Recovery of Native Space in the Northeast* (Minneapolis: University of Minnesota Press, 2008), xxxiv.

47. Catherine Albanese highlights the "combinative nature" of American religion as its defining feature. Albanese, *America: Religion and Religions*, 5th ed. (Boston: Wadsworth, 2013). David Stowe has made a similar point about American sacred music: "The story of sacred music, like many others that have been told about America, is one of cross-pollination and syncretism taking place amid encounters marked by conquest and exploitation. Out of these social collisions, cultural boundaries have been challenged, redefined, reinforced, and sometimes dissolved." David Stowe, *How Sweet the Sound: Music in the Spiritual Lives of Americans* (Cambridge, MA: Harvard University Press, 2004), 7. See also Stephen A. Marini, *Sacred Song in America: Religion, Music, and Public Culture* (Urbana: University of Illinois Press, 2003).

TWO | US Concert Music and Cultural Reorientation during the Occupation of Japan

A Bicultural Perspective

MISAKO OHTA AND CAROL J. OJA

Since World War II, Japan and the United States have enjoyed a close political and cultural alliance, and musicians have played an important role in that relationship. A famous case of such an interchange involved the composers John Cage and Tōru Takemitsu, and it exemplified how notions of "place" were fluid in cultural transmission. In the early 1950s, Cage studied the Japanese tradition of Zen Buddhism in New York City; he did so with D. T. Suzuki, the renowned philosopher who had recently arrived from Japan, and Cage's music was deeply impacted by that experience. Then in 1961 Takemitsu heard the first Japanese performance of Cage's Concert for Piano and Orchestra at the Sogetsu Art Center in Tokyo, a hotbed of avant-garde experimentation. This encounter brought Takemitsu in contact with Cage's conceptual realms of "chance" and "indeterminacy," which in turn had been shaped by his study of Zen Buddhism, and it also prodded Takemitsu to confront his postwar ambivalence about Japanese culture.[1]

Here we place our focus on an earlier aspect of cultural exchange between Japan and the United States that has gone largely unexamined: the introduction of contemporary American concert music into Japan during the US occupation that followed World War II. Doing so opens a new perspective on the intense westernization of Japan after the war—a cultural exchange built on radically unequal power structures. We begin with the Japanese surrender on August 14, 1945, and end with the Treaty of San Francisco at the end of April 1952. General Douglas MacArthur was appointed as Supreme Commander for the Allied Powers (SCAP), wielding enormous authority from General Headquarters (GHQ) in Tokyo. Thus a symbiotic cultural relationship resulted, and it was managed and implemented by the US government, experienced by Japanese audiences and American occupying personnel, and chronicled by Japanese music critics in both English- and Japanese-language newspapers. For the Japanese of this era, the occupation yielded six years of strict censorship and ideological control. At the same time, they steadily built new relationships with the occupiers and their culture, and the Japanese media vigorously introduced American films and popular music. The war had been devastating for Japan, destroying major cities and infrastructure. Many civilians lost everything—family members, homes, livelihood, basic dignity—and the atomic bombs dropped on Hiroshima and Nagasaki produced staggering destruction. Many Japanese were starving, and there was a crisis with refugees and orphans. After the Japanese surrender, some 6.5 million Japanese were stranded in Asia, Siberia, and the greater Pacific area, and in 1948, the number of orphaned and homeless Japanese children was estimated at 123,510.[2] These numbers were staggering, reflecting the abject comprehensiveness of the defeat. Thus during the postwar period, the Japanese needed to make a fresh start—to rebuild their lives completely—and the US occupation offered the resources to do so. The turnaround from being dire enemies to collaborating as allies happened with astonishing speed. In the process, the Japanese experienced an unprecedented encounter with US culture and music. At the same time, however, this aid came at a huge cost, for Japan was forcibly colonized. The United States wielded "naked power," writes historian E. Taylor Atkins, "over its vanquished former foe."[3]

As citizens of Japan and the United States—who teach at universities in our respective countries—we challenged ourselves with finding a topic for this book on collaboration that would benefit from our different cultural perspectives, and we settled on a case study in global US music, a cross-cultural archival research project that was sufficiently targeted to accommodate the brief length of the assignment. As a result, we place our focus on the introduction of US concert music into Japan during the occupation through two interrelated areas of cultural exchange.[4] First, we explore a series of "record concerts"—literally concerts in which audiences gathered together to listen to recordings being played on a turntable—that were held at libraries and public centers established by the United States through its Civil Information and Education Division, which was part of SCAP and known as CIE.[5] These events featured the music of US composers, most often alongside staples from the European canon, and the choice of repertory, as well as the adjustments in programming that occurred over time, are fascinating. Second, as a direct outgrowth of the record concerts, we turn briefly to postwar productions in Japan of the operas of Gian Carlo Menotti, which were also initially sponsored by CIE and became an important force in reviving Japan's infrastructure for the performance of Western opera.

Remarkably, Tōru Takemitsu (1930–1996) was among those who attended the record concerts. In a lecture given decades later at the Japan Society of New York City, he reflected on the occupation era—he was fifteen in 1945—and recalled going "very, very frequently" to the CIE library in Hibiya (part of Tokyo). "There I also sought out American music," Takemitsu remembered. "Through hearing the music of Roy Harris, Aaron Copland, Walter Piston, Roger Sessions, and such great American composers, I was introduced to an unknown world. . . . For me, after having tasted the bitter, miserable experiences of the war years, this music seemed full of hope."[6]

Reconstructing a history of these concerts has been challenging. The events took place in an extreme environment where the very existence of a shared listening experience, void of human performers, bore witness to a stripped-down yet resourceful era. We bring to this project distinct cultural perspectives as well as different pools of knowledge and access to information, and we recognize the voluminous existing literature about the occupation.[7] One of our goals has been to draw on that scholarship—on research published in both Japan and the United States—as a way of bridging the language barrier that often inhibits Americans from accessing Japanese scholarship in American studies.[8] The introduction of US music to Japan during the occupation has been most studied in Japan, especially through the important foundational research of Masaaki Ueno and Akihiro Taniguichi.[9] Building on their work, we draw upon primary sources that have been largely unexplored: coverage of US concert music in two of the main Tokyo newspapers of the day, both of which are digitized. For our purposes, the core such publication is the *Nippon Times*, an English-language paper known from 1956 as the *Japan Times*, and the second is *Yomiuri shinbun*, one of the most prominent and widely circulated Japanese-language newspapers.[10] Both were subject to censorship by GHQ.

The readership of the *Nippon Times*, founded in 1897, included both foreigners and Japanese who knew English. During the occupation, it functioned as an important source of information and opinion for the sizable American presence in Tokyo, yielding a complicated scenario. "Cultural exchange," reported an internally produced history of the newspaper, "is an activity in which *The Japan Times* has been engaged since it began."[11] A contemporaneous assessment called the *Nippon Times* "the organ if not the creature of the Japanese government's foreign office," and GHQ controlled that office during the occupation.[12] At the same time, the *Yomiuri shinbun* dates to 1874, and from the outset it established a reputation as a major literary arts publication. By 1941, *Yomiuri shinbun* had the largest circulation of any daily newspaper in the Tokyo area, and today it continues a commitment to broad-ranging cultural affairs in theater, arts, music and sports. In 1945, *Yomiuri shinbun* also came under the control of GHQ.[13] In probing censorship during this period, media historian Teruo Ariyama writes that the Japanese were "obedient" to GHQ's interventions.[14] In relation to CIE's record concerts, the *Nippon Times* announced the events regularly; it did not, however, offer reviews or critiques. Similarly *Yomiuri shinbun* gave listings only, although less consistently than the *Nippon Times*.[15] Thus our main sources for this essay reported on the dissemination of US music through the medium of announcements, with little critical appraisal. At the same time, these newspapers were subjected to American censorship.

In short, we interrogate a shared history as publicly documented and digitally accessible, aiming to draw on our respective cultural perspectives.

US Music in Japan before the Occupation

When the occupation's strategists began introducing American compositions to the Japanese after World War II, they reinvigorated cultural interchanges that dated back to Commodore Perry's famous arrival in 1853. In other words, some US music already had a notable presence in Japan. Perry brought both a brass band and a blackface minstrel performance to Japan, and subsequent visitors, especially missionaries, introduced American hymns together with the songs of Stephen Foster, which became especially popular.[16] In the late nineteenth and early twentieth centuries, the Japanese were developing a deep reverence for European high art, especially that of Austria and Germany (Mozart, Beethoven, Wagner), and German music teachers in Japan had a strong

Figure 2.1. In this photograph from the early 1950s, Misako Ohta's mother Sakiko Ohta (on the right), born in 1935, plays with Japanese friends pretending to enact an American-style wedding in Tokyo. From Misako Ohta's personal archives.

impact, including Raphael von Koebel (1848–1923) and August Junker (1868–1944).[17] As a result, US compositions that had roots in the Austro-German tradition had some degree of familiarity to Japanese audiences. To provide a context for CIE's record concerts of music by American composers, we offer a synoptic history of selected musical encounters between the two cultures.

Notable interactions often resulted from travel by Japanese musicians, dancers, and other performers to the United States during the early twentieth century. Takagi Tokuko (1891–1919), for example, studied dance in New York City in the 1910s, and after returning to Japan, she played a major role in the development of "Asakusa opera" in Tokyo.[18] Asakusa fused operetta, musical theater, and theatrical revues into a distinctive idiom that was wildly popular in Japan. Another early cultural mediator was the conductor and composer Kosaku Yamada (1886–1965), who visited the United States from 1917 to 1919 and reported to his fellow citizens about the American music he heard, pushing back against the Japanese tendency at the time to be dismissive of American culture and music. While in the United States, Yamada worked with the Japanese dancer Michio Itō and the American composer Charles Tomlinson Griffes, and in 1918 he conducted an orchestral concert of his own compositions in Carnegie Hall.[19] It was an extraordinary event, and the *New York Times* credited Yamada as "the first conductor and composer who ever led such forces here in any music original with Japan."[20] Yamada, in turn, reported to readers in Japan that the "power of Americanism" opened a space for intercultural artistic expression.[21]

Another notable interchange occurred on July 4, 1937, when concerts of Japanese and US music were transmitted over the radio and across the Pacific—between Tokyo and the United States—to celebrate Independence Day.[22] From Tokyo on July 5 (a date that accommodated the time difference), the famed composer and koto player Michio Miyagi performed his *The Sea in Spring* (*Haru No Umi*) and *Rokudan* with the New Symphony Orchestra (now the NHK Symphony Orchestra) conducted by Naotada Yamamoto. From the United States on July 4, the program included *The Invincible Eagle* by John Philip Sousa, *Woodland Sketches* by Edward MacDowell, *The Serenade* by Victor Herbert, and an orchestral work by Henry Hadley, conducted by Ernest Gill.[23]

In 1939, Masao Koga (1904–1978), a leading Japanese composer of popular music, visited New York City and reported back to Japan: "Stephen Foster's typically American folk songs enjoy a tremendous vogue in Japan, and one hears 'Swanee River' and 'Old Folks at Home' more often in Tokyo than in New York."[24] Newspaper articles and advertisements before the occupation show that Foster was the most famous American composer among the Japanese, with his music disseminated vigorously through songbooks, recordings, and radio.

During World War II, these cultural alliances fractured as political antagonisms infiltrated the arts. As part of the Axis Alliance, the Japanese intensified their commitment to Austro-German traditions while banning music with English lyrics, which included most American music. Jazz was forbidden, as were the beloved tunes of Stephen Foster—all in an environment of strict censorship and governmental control of journalism and the media. An intriguing example of critical attitudes toward music of the United States appeared in March 1945, during the final phase of the war, when the music critic Naoe Monma (1897–1961) wrote articles for both the *Nippon Times* and *Asahi shinbun* that focused on minstrelsy, jazz, and Foster. While the tone was propagandistic, the critique embedded an inconvenient truth:

> American prejudice against the colored people not only manifested itself in the untold cruelty lashed [*sic*] against the Negroes, but the American stage took up the subject of their misery and tragic distress and made Negro minstrels appear in public performances. . . . And to see that the misery of the colored people was made a theme for show[s], entertainment, and livelihood is astounding to say the least. . . . In the musical industry too America made . . . inroads into Japan, with the Christian hymns and songs for school children. But now all such music has been banished from our homes, school rooms and concerts.[25]

Attitudes toward US music changed radically during the occupation, persuaded by US propaganda. In 1946, Yoichi Hiraoka (1907–1981), a Japanese xylophone player who had worked as a professional musician in the United States before the war, wrote a book, *Reader for American Music,* which drew on firsthand observations.[26] After Pearl Harbor, he lost his job at NBC radio in New York and returned to Japan, where he performed professionally with a focus on European classical music. During wartime censorship, instrumental music from the European classical tradition, which carried a universalist cachet, offered the appearance of neutrality.[27] In the foreword to his 1946 book, Hiraoka wrote:

> With this defeat Japan is being changed, and I feel that Japanese people start to search for true information about America in every aspect. I have many memories from my twelve years living in America. . . . I should say that the superficial image about American music culture by the Japanese is a terrible mistake: "By power of money they buy expensive world-class artists and display them as their own." From my own experience, this sort of prejudice is a gross injustice. I saw that American musicians work hard and have a serious desire to learn, and they live in an intensely competitive society. Japanese musicians can and should also learn a lot from them.[28]

As a result, the Japanese were compelled to make a rapid turnaround, from censoring American music during the war to embracing it heartily in the immediate aftermath. The military structure set in place by the occupying US forces turned to soft power—that is, cultural and economic persuasion—to compel the Japanese to embrace American ideology and values.

Hearing US Music at CIE Record Concerts

Against this history of Japanese-American musical interactions in classical music, the CIE Library and Information Center in Hibiya, an area in Tokyo that houses the city's major cultural institutions, announced that the "first of a series of recorded American music concerts" was scheduled for July 27, 1948 at 5:30 p.m. The series would be devoted exclusively to classical music composed in the United States—no American jazz or Top 40 hits.[29] The initial program included Samuel Barber's *Second Essay for Orchestra,* Deems Taylor's *Through the Looking Glass* (also for orchestra), and "Negro spirituals" performed by Marian Anderson. The anticipated audience was relatively small: "Tickets for 150 Japanese patrons of the library may be obtained from the librarian."[30] Subsequent concerts in this inaugural cluster featured the following composers, works, and performers:

- August 6, 1948: Barber, Cello Sonata; John Alden Carpenter, Symphony no. 2; and "Negro spirituals" (sung by the Wings Over Jordan Choir).
- August 27, 1948: Louis Gruenberg, Violin Concerto (Jascha Heifetz and the San Francisco Symphony), and "The Wayfaring Stranger" (sung by Burl Ives).
- September 3, 1948: Virgil Thomson, *The Plow That Broke the Plains* (Hollywood Symphony, conducted by Leopold Stokowski), and Charles Martin Loeffler, *A Pagan Poem* (Eastman-Rochester Symphony).[31]

Viewed in relation to the performance norms of Western classical music, the concept of a "free record concert" is striking to contemplate, giving a stark sense of how Japan had been ravaged by the war. By featuring recordings, these concerts provided an opportunity to hear new releases at a moment when few Japanese could afford to purchase them. They also resourcefully capitalized on the easy transportability of 78 rpms in an era before the international stars of classical music could travel to Japan. Change was taking place rapidly. In 1951 the violinist Yehudi Menuhin was among the earliest virtuoso guests to Japan, and others followed, notably the African American singer Marian Anderson in 1953.[32] Her recordings of spirituals, in turn, had been featured in the initial CIE concert.

GHQ opened its first CIE Library and Information Center in the

Figure 2.2. CIE library in Hibiya in 1947. From Madoko Kon, *Library Concepts in Modern Japan: Reformation after World War II* (Tokyo: Bensei Publishing, 2013), 100.

Hibiya area of Tokyo in November 1945, initially doing so at a temporary site that was replaced within a few years by a "two-story, modernistic library next to the U.S. Army's big Ernie Pyle Theater," reported the *Nippon Times*. "The libraries have proven one of the most popular innovations of the Occupation."[33] Subsequent branches soon appeared in Kyoto and Nagoya, and fourteen others were added in 1948, eventu-

Figure 2.3. Donald Beckman Brown (1905–1980), chief of the Information Division of GHQ, gazing at a turntable with Japanese high school students. This photo was taken on June 10, 1948, and the recording in his hand was *Oklahoma!* From: 日本の高校生とCIE音楽担当官 [Japanese high school students and CIE music officers] 横浜開港資料館所蔵 [held in Yokohama Archives of History], which houses a Don Brown Collection of foreign books and magazines about Japan.

ally totaling twenty-three such facilities. The CIE libraries aimed to reach Japanese citizens as part of GHQ's broad-ranging propaganda campaign, at the same time as they provided an intellectual refuge at a time when access to resources was extremely limited. They stocked American publications, such as *Reader's Digest,* which went on sale in a Japanese translation in June 1946.[34] The libraries essentially functioned as community centers, showing films and offering a variety of services. English conversation classes were reportedly among "the most popular" programs: "In addition to availing themselves of at least 5,000 American and British books and 400 current periodicals all in English, at each Center, [the] Japanese have shown an enthusiastic response for the educational activities of the Centers."[35] Thus CIE's libraries hosted both grassroots and specialized activities, and they helped construct a dynamic web through which transnational propaganda locked arms with friendship.

In tracking record concerts of American classical music, we focused on events at CIE libraries in Hibiya (with the first concert in July 1948); the city of Yokohama, which is thirty-five kilometers to the south of Tokyo (beginning in October 1948); and Shinjuku, a ward of Tokyo (September 1949). We selected those CIE locations simply because they listed events in the *Nippon Times*.[36] We use the terms "classical music" and "concert music" interchangeably here, signaling works by US composers that were based, if even partly, on high-prestige European traditions of symphonic, vocal, chamber, and solo composition. In studying the overall philosophy behind CIE's music programs, Masaaki Ueno observed that the number of professional Japanese musicians interested in performing new American compositions was limited, which was another reason for CIE to rely on recordings. He too emphasized the strong link between the American compositions featured at these events and European models, which meant the new American music was written within an aesthetic framework familiar to Japanese audiences.[37] At this point in time, the CIE concerts largely displayed American traditionalism in composition rather than avant-garde experimentation.

The record concerts of US classical music also pushed back against the immense postwar popularity of jazz, which "came to represent the cultural power of the victor," observes E. Taylor Atkins in his history of Japanese jazz.[38] Jazz clubs sprang up soon after peace was declared, ending the wartime prohibition, and radio was a powerful medium for jazz during the occupation, with active programming through NHK and Armed Forces Radio. Classical music, mostly European but also some by Americans, also appeared on the radio, but the sounds of the United States were most often associated with jazz. NHK (Nippon Hōsō Kyōkai, or Japan Broadcasting Corporation) was essentially the BBC of Japan, and it was controlled by CIE during the occupation.[39]

Thus the American music heard in CIE's record concerts fell into a special category between jazz and European classical music, even as it competed with both. It was separate yet related, offering a highbrow vision of American creative expression. As a result, CIE's record concerts introduced new repertory to the Japanese—doing so within the spirit of advancing Americanization—at the same time as they featured works that were fundamentally comprehensible. Notably, the composers involved were overwhelmingly white and thoroughly male.[40] Also notable was the integration of a few recordings that didn't fall strictly—or at all—into the art-music tradition. The first wave of record concerts in 1948 illustrated this tendency. The spirituals recorded by the African American contralto Marian Anderson, for example, represented a hybrid drawing upon the texts and tunes of so-called slave songs, which Anderson performed in piano-vocal concert arrangements.[41] An entirely different performance tradition for spirituals was represented by the Wings Over Jordan Choir from Cleveland, which gained a following in the United States through radio broadcasts. Finally, CIE included the folk singer Burl Ives, who, like Wings Over Jordan, had national exposure through a radio show.[42]

The commercial recordings featured at CIE's concerts were largely issued by Columbia or Victor. The same year as the concerts began, SCAP signed a royalty arrangement with those two companies, authorizing the sale of records by US artists through Japanese subsidiaries. Additionally, the major labels were supplemented by releases from small companies and noncommercial sources; the latter mostly included material from American radio broadcasts and releases by the US government.[43] The Columbia recordings in the initial concerts from 1948 included a mixture of folk, classical, and gospel: Burl Ives (released in 1941/1944), Deems Taylor (1938), and Wings Over Jordan Choir (1941). Those from Victor were all classical, plus spirituals: Marian Anderson (multiple recordings of spirituals), Gruenberg (released in 1945), Loeffler (1942), and Thomson (1947). As for small labels, Barber's Cello Sonata was issued in 1947 on Concert Hall Society, a subscription label founded the previous year.[44] With both Barber's *Second Essay* and Carpenter's Second Symphony, commercial recordings do not appear to have been released by 1948. A noncommercial disc of the Barber was "duplicated" from an NBC radio broadcast on February 15, 1947, and perhaps it was played by CIE.[45] With the Carpenter, no recording, whether commercial or governmental, has yet been located.[46]

In fact, some of these recordings—as well as the aesthetic choices they embodied—appear to have been modeled on the Office of War Information (OWI), a cultural propaganda agency that existed from June 1942 to September 1945 and provided a crucial predecessor to CIE. The works in CIE's initial set of concerts featured most of the same composers as in OWI's radio programs and libraries. One OWI memo titled "Examples of Records for Information Centers" lists Copland, Gershwin, Griffes, Hanson, Loeffler, MacDowell, Schuman, and Taylor among the American composers to be featured; significantly, these names were included alongside—and were greatly outnumbered by—staples from the European repertory.[47] The American concert music programmed by OWI, writes Annegret Fauser, had been used "to open channels of communications so as to win over the hearts and minds of the citizens of Allied and neutral countries." At the same time, "It contributed to creating a positive view throughout the world of the United States as a cultured and peace-loving nation."[48] These goals remained central in the American occupation of Japan as CIE continued to endorse the aesthetic tendencies of OWI: both agencies favored music that was thoroughly tonal, composed in well-established forms such as symphonies, sonatas, concertos, and operas. In addition, much of this music fit into the category of "Americanist composition," a well-established if wide-ranging rubric that encompassed works with a recognizable and nationally inflected sound.[49]

In postwar Germany, a mission of cultural reorientation continued with the US occupation forces, running concurrently with initiatives in Japan. In Germany, information centers were set up, as Amy Beal puts it, as "fundamental tools of reeducation."[50] They were most often called "America House," and they too offered concerts of recorded music. The parallels between the Japanese and German immediate postwar programs are striking, with initial programming in Germany focused on "institutionally bound American composers," which is Beal's term for figures such as Howard Hanson, Walter Piston, and Roger Sessions, whose music was also solidly present at the CIE events in Japan.[51] In 1947, an article in the *Nippon Times* illustrated how US cultural propaganda efforts were directed simultaneously across both the Atlantic and the Pacific. Titled "American Music Hailed: Europeans Appreciate Serious Works Even More than Jazz," it quoted Carlos Moseley, "a former concert pianist who is a music specialist for the United States State Department's Office of International Information and Cultural Affairs." Mosely highlighted an "Americanist" aesthetic vision and acknowledged shifting trends:

> He says that the past generation of American music composers had produced works that were derivable [*sic*] of European music. New music, he says, is unadulterated American and has been described by leading musicians abroad as "fresh, dynamic and vigorous."[52]

Another notable publication demonstrating ties between propaganda efforts in Europe and Japan appeared in 1948 in *Arts Today*, a cultural affairs section of *Yomiuri shinbun*. The article was written by Harrison Kerr, then chief of the Music and Art Unit of the War Department's Reorientation Branch, and it was published in Japanese. Kerr acknowledged knowing little about Japanese music, and he argued that American jazz and classical music were inherently different, advocating for music to "cross national boundaries" with greater success if it is "played repeatedly."[53]

CIE's concerts in Japan, then, had parallels in the postwar reconstruction of Europe, and they ultimately served as a bridge, both chronologically and ideologically, between OWI's initiatives with allies during the war and the better-known (and much-studied) Cold War propaganda programs. The latter included the US Information Agency (USIA) established in 1953 and initiatives that resulted from the International Cultural Exchange and Trade Fair Participation Act of 1956.[54]

While American repertory dominated the initial set of record concerts at the Hibiya CIE library, its reign was short-lived, replaced in April 1949 by programs that either integrated US works with European classical repertory or focused solely on European works. That is, the concerts were rebooted on April 8, 1949, when "the first of a series of recorded concerts" (that is, the "first" in a *new* series) included Beethoven's Symphony no. 7 alongside Ferde Grofé's *Grand Canyon Suite*; a week later Beethoven's Piano Concerto no. 3 was paired with Copland's *Rodeo*.[55] The concerts at CIE's Hibiya center then continued on a weekly basis, with a related set of concerts also taking place at the CIE center in Shinjuku. On the whole, works by Beethoven were prominent, often paired with an American composition and yielding curious combinations. They included Beethoven's Ninth Symphony with David Diamond's incidental music to *Romeo and Juliet* (at Hibiya on September 8, 1949, and Shinjuku on October 19, 1950); Beethoven's Fifth with David Guion's orchestral arrangements of *Chester* by William Billings and "Arkansas Traveler" (Shinjuku, November 10, 1951); Beethoven's Ninth with Harl MacDonald's *San Juan Capistrano* (Shinjuku, December 8, 1951); Beethoven's Kreutzer Sonata Op. 47 with Elie Siegmeister's *Ozark Set* (Shinjuku, April 26, 1952).[56] Occasional high-low juxtapositions were fascinating—also startling—as when Beethoven's Ninth immediately preceded a square dance class (Shinjuku, December 14, 1950).[57] Just as often, the concerts were thoroughly European, and this tendency became more pronounced as the 1950s progressed. Here, too, there were direct parallels with reconstruction efforts in Germany, where the infrastructure for performance of the European canon was being rebuilt at the same time as new US compositions were introduced.[58]

From the outset, moderators officiated at CIE's record concerts, which added a human dimension to events that were otherwise mechanized. Initially Clarence Davies served that function, doing so as "head of the music unit of the Motion Picture and Drama Division" of CIE, a position he assumed in April 1946. Davies represented a typical figure employed by the occupying Americans. He had deep experience with Japanese culture, having lived there since 1920. Before the war, Davies worked for the *Japan Advertiser*, an English-language newspaper; Davies was identified at various times as its business manager and as music and drama critic.[59] He also exemplified another core trait for GHQ affiliates: US service during the war. In Davies's case, he had moved to Honolulu in 1941, working for the Office of War Information in its First Radio Broadcasting and Leaflet Group, Psychological Warfare Section. He returned to Tokyo when the war ended.

Beginning in early 1949, a new moderator stepped in at the CIE Library in Hibiya, identified by *Nippon Times* as Ernest Satow and as being "in charge of the weekly series of free record concerts."[60] His full name was Yoshiro Ernest Satow (1927–1990), and he made quite an impact at the concerts. Satow was then in his early twenties, with a law degree already completed in Japan, and he continued as moderator until leaving in September 1951 to study music history at the University of Oklahoma, then art history at Columbia University. Born and raised in Japan, Satow's heritage was biracial, with a Japanese father and an American mother who was a missionary.[61] Before the war, Satow's father, Tai'ichirō, worked for NHK, so there was a family tie to the media and culture industry. Yoshiro obtained the job of CIE moderator because of compiling a postwar discography of Western classical music that had been released in Japan.[62]

In retrospect, Yoshiro Satow represented an important transitional phase for the CIE record concerts, serving as moderator between the Anglo-American Davies and a series of Japanese academics, music critics, and representatives of global record companies. Like Davies, Satow had a prewar tie to the upper echelons of the English-speaking community in Tokyo. In a way, this transition can be viewed as a microcosm of the American occupation overall, with initial dominance from Americans and eventual transference of leadership to the Japanese.

Japanese music critics and record-company representatives increasingly took over as moderators at CIE's record concerts, solidifying the tie between the global media industry and the US government. This new phase was possible in part because of SCAP's agreement in 1948 with Columbia and Victor. Hiroshi Terajima, an affiliate of Columbia Records, served as moderator of a concert in 1950, and Koichi Nishiyama, identified in *Nippon Times* as being "of Keio University," took over from Satow at Hibiya in September 1951.[63] Meanwhile, Mamoru Watanabe (1915–2007) moderated a substantial number of concerts at Shinjuku and Yokohama

Figure 2.4. The photos in this cluster feature Yoshiro Ernest Satow. In the group image (upper left), he is in the center, surrounded by family members (from the left): Tai'ichirō (Yoshiro's father), Emiko Dorothy (his sister), and (on the right) Grace (his mother); and an unidentified American (possibly Donald Brown). Published in *Geijutsu Shinchō* 50, no. 6 (Tokyo: Shinchō-sha, June 1999), 60. Courtesy of Morihiro Satow.

beginning in June 1951, then also at Hibiya the following year; he was a noted music critic and affiliate of Nippon Victor.[64] Finally, Masami Warashina (1915–1993) was another moderator from within the record industry, first listed for a concert at the Shinjuku CIE library in 1951.[65]

There were notable moments and trends in the concerts. Leonard Bernstein, who subsequently built a strong relationship with Japan, had recordings of two of his symphonies played on the CIE programs.[66] His Symphony no. 1 (*Jeremiah*) was heard in September 1949 at the opening of the CIE library in Shinjuku, and his Symphony no. 2 ("The Age of Anxiety") was on the program at the Hibiya library in June 1951.[67] Programming the *Jeremiah* Symphony on September 25 (1949) meant that it was heard during Rosh Hashanah, one of the most important Jewish holidays, and that work gestured audibly to Bernstein's Jewish heritage. Overall, the CIE libraries paid respects to the Jewish holidays, especially with recordings of music by the composer Ernest Bloch. A recording of his *Schelemo* (*Hebrew Rhapsody*) was heard at Yokohama (October 18, 1951) and Shinjuku (two days later) in concerts that took place a week after Yom Kippur.[68] His Concerto Grosso appeared on a record concert at Hibiya on September 26, 1952, a few days before Yom Kippur.[69]

The music of Aaron Copland marked another notable trend in the record concerts, with more appearances than by any other American composer. The works heard included his *Rodeo* (Hibiya, April 1949); *Quiet City* (Hibiya, May 1951, October 1951, December 1952), Sonata for Violin and Piano and Two Pieces for Violin and Piano (at Hibiya on different dates in 1951); *Piano Blues* (Hibiya, November 1952); and *Lincoln Portrait* and *Billy the Kid* (at Shinjuku on different dates in 1952).[70] Broadway musicals also turned up at the record concerts: Jerome Kern and Oscar Hammerstein II's *Show Boat* (Hibiya, 1949), Kurt Weill and Arnold Sundgaard's *Down in the Valley* (Hibiya, 1951), and Richard Rodgers and Hammerstein's *Carousel* and *The King and I* (Yokohama, 1952).[71]

Also striking was the relatively late introduction of the music of George Gershwin, whose compositional fusions of jazz and concert music turned up at CIE around the same time as Broadway musicals. The CIE center in Hibiya kicked off with a recording of Gershwin's *Porgy and Bess*, introduced by Satow in April 1951.[72] *Rhapsody in Blue* followed that October (Yokohama), and *An American in Paris* appeared in March (Hibiya).[73] Gershwin's music was played as CIE's programming grew more hybrid. Significantly, his work was already well known in Japan through the international distribution of his recordings and films, articles in the popular press, radio broadcasts, and concert performances.

Menotti's Operas in Postwar Japan

The operas of Gian Carlo Menotti marked a special case in CIE's record concerts, ultimately gaining a strong position in Japanese performance over a long period of time. In the record concerts, Menotti's *Amelia Goes to the Ball* (overture), *The Telephone* (complete opera), and *Sebastian* (ballet suite) were featured at CIE's Hibiya center in May 1951; a year later, *The Medium* was played twice at the Shinjuku library.[74] A multilayered backdrop preceded these events, merging a Japanese passion for opera with the occupation's political mandate, also intermingling record concerts with live performances. CIE, together with related branches of the occupying forces, played a central role at every turn.

Before the war, "opera" in Japan meant major European works. Between 1938 and 1945, for example, the operas most often produced there were *La Bohème, La Traviata, Cavalleria Rusticana, Tosca, Faust, Fidelio,* and *Lohengrin*.[75] After the war, opera was revived in Japan as part of the overall reconstruction effort, and doing so involved raising considerable cash. A major step in a new direction occurred early in the process—in August 1946—when an "ambitious and lavish" production of Gilbert and Sullivan's *The Mikado* took place in English at the Ernie Pyle Theater in Tokyo, a venue under the management of GHQ that sponsored performances for occupation personnel. The production was supported by the Special Services Detachment Production Unit, and it boasted a transnational cast "including 30 Japanese in the chorus, 30 Japanese dancers, 30 American soldiers, and three American civilian actresses, and an orchestra of 18 Americans and 34 Japanese."[76] GHQ's production was an audacious—even outrageous—move, rebooting postwar opera in Japan by ending a sixty-one-year prohibition of *The Mikado,* a work that had been banned because of offensively stereotyping both the Japanese and their emperor. Yet Japanese performers participated in the work's postwar production, apparently viewing it pragmatically as an opportunity to regain careers suspended during the war, and drama historian Tara Rodman argues that *The Mikado* also became a means for the Japanese to project "cosmopolitan identities."[77]

Another noteworthy production of *The Mikado*—and an immediate predecessor to the introduction of Menotti's operas in Japan—occurred in January 1948 when a Japanese-language staging was mounted by the Japanese soprano Miho Nagato, founder of the Nagato Opera Company in Tokyo. CIE was once again involved, with a special performance for Allied personnel in February.[78] The operetta took place in Hibiya

Public Hall, this time with an all-Japanese cast and orchestra, and representatives of the imperial family attended, sitting prominently in the front row, where they "smiled throughout the performance but did not applaud."[79] Their presence projected an unsettling image of subjugation to the occupiers, at the same time as it was complex, sanctioning *The Mikado* for a modern Japan. Miho Nagato actively cultivated the support of CIE for the production, and she paid tribute to its westernizing agenda, emphasizing the importance of staging operas from abroad in order to contribute to a new democratic era.[80]

Both these productions of *The Mikado* laid the groundwork for the next major initiative of the Nagato Opera Company: Menotti's *The Old Maid and the Thief*, which opened in February 1949 at the Shinbashi Enbujō Theater in Tokyo.[81] The Tokyo Philharmonic Orchestra performed, and the lyrics were in Japanese.[82] Like so much of the American classical music being heard around the same time at CIE's record concerts, *The Old Maid and the Thief* had strong roots in European traditions. Furthermore, it had been singled out for official endorsement when in 1948 CIE released a list of eleven modern American dramas "for local [Japanese] presentation"—that is, productions endorsed under the watchful gaze of censorship. *The Old Maid and the Thief* was cited there, together with Thornton Wilder's *The Skin of Our Teeth*.[83] At the end of March 1949, the production of *The Old Maid and the Thief* moved to Hibiya Hall, where Nagato's company performed for Allied personnel, doing so under the sponsorship of the Eighth Army Educational Center. In a gesture of cross-cultural exchange, the performance was combined with "Kabuki dances."[84] CIE's record concerts of Menotti began in 1951, hence subsequent to these productions.

Menotti's operas continued to be popular after the occupation, with productions all over Japan, and ultimately, they have garnered a special place in Japanese culture. In 1955 Menotti's *The Consul* was produced by the Fujiwara Opera Company; in 1957 *The Telephone* was broadcast in Japanese over the radio; in 1960 *The Saint of Bleecker Street* had its Japanese debut; and in 1973 Menotti visited Japan for the first time.[85] Overall, the Japanese had a predilection for the fusion of opera, operetta, and musical theater represented by Menotti's work, with a warm reception in Japan for European operettas produced in the Japanese language and staged within Japanese cultural contexts.[86] Three years after the war, Toyokichi Hata, stage director for the famed Takarazuka Revue, advocated that the Japanese should not imitate "grand opera" but rather create their own opera buffa, aiming for broad-based entertainment—that is, the kind of middlebrow niche where Menotti thrived.[87] And there were important historical precedents: musical theater works like *The Threepenny Opera* by Bertolt Brecht and Kurt Weill had been already popular in Japan during the 1930s.[88]

As of 2016, Menotti's operas had been staged in Japan 278 times, and in 2017 Menotti was ranked among the top ten opera composers from abroad whose works were staged in Japan that year. Notably, he was the only American, enshrined among opera's European titans, and Menotti's popularity marked one of the most long-lasting outcomes of the record concerts sponsored by CIE. To provide some context: Mascagni's *Cavalleria Rusticana* is a particular favorite in Japan, with 237 stagings in Japan since 1923, but not as many as the operas of Menotti.[89] In 2017 alone, works by Menotti were produced eighteen times in Japan, and that year, the top ten opera composers from abroad were, from top to bottom, Puccini, Mozart, Verdi, Bizet, J. Strauss II, Donizetti, Offenbach, Menotti, and Wagner and Mascagni (tied for last).[90]

Impact of CIE's Record Concerts

So what did CIE's record concerts add up to? The lasting popularity of Menotti's operas in Japan offers one perspective on their impact, giving a sense of how CIE's cultural politics resulted in choosing "institutionally bound" Americanist composers. Yet another perspective on the resonance of the concerts circles back to the Japanese composer Tōru Takemitsu, whose interactions with John Cage opened this essay. While visiting the CIE library in Hibiya during the occupation, Takemitsu experienced new music by American composers for the first time. He also met kindred spirits—emerging Japanese composers and creative artists of his generation—and he became aligned with a group that called itself Jikken Kobo, or Experimental Workshop, which was active in Tokyo from 1951 to 1958. Jikken Kobo was made up of young Japanese visual artists, performing musicians, composers, poets, and lighting engineers who hungered for access to the newest Western art in an era when few Japanese had the resources to purchase musical scores or recordings, let alone travel. Several in the group were friends with Yoshiro Ernest Satow, one of the early and influential moderators of CIE's concerts. During a 2013 roundtable in Tokyo, then-elderly members of Jikken Kobo shared memories of attending the record concerts at CIE's library in Hibiya.[91] Composer Joji Yuasa (b. 1929) recalled that he and fellow composer Kuniharu Akiyama (1929–96) often visited Satow's CIE office, which "was located just in the middle of the central Ginza (4th floor of the Wako Department Store Building) and [they] went together to the 'German Bakery' to have a cup of coffee."[92] Yuasa continued:

> In the postwar period, the CIE library was the only place where we could see American contemporary arts and listen to American contemporary music. If we didn't go to the CIE library, we could not listen to American contemporary music. There were LPs from the United States played at the recorded concerts, and they had some scores at the CIE library. I copied Copland's pieces by hand before becoming a member of Jikken Kobo.

Composer Kazuo Fukushima (b. 1930) also remembered visiting CIE's Hibiya library frequently, where he met other members of Jikken Kobo, including Akiyama and visual artist Katsuhiro Yamaguchi (1928–2018). He recalled Satow's commentary at Thursday evening record concerts: "Their recorded materials had scores as supplements, and regular attendees listened to music while reading scores." Yamaguchi saw Takemitsu there, and artists on the 2013 panel concurred that the CIE library was a place where young Japanese artists, writers, and musicians could network with one another, even if their aesthetic inclinations and artistic mediums differed.

Viewed in the round, then, CIE's project of introducing American concert music into Japan opened much-needed opportunities for Japanese creative figures and the general public, who were collectively emerging from the traumas of World War II and its aftermath. At the same time, CIE's initiatives yielded a heavy-handed imposition of American political ideologies and artistic practices that aimed to flip Japanese tastes toward the West. The result was a complex cultural negotiation—partly well-intended outreach but mostly strategic indoctrination. The *Nippon Times* and *Yomiuri shinbun* offer an on-the-ground view of what took place, documenting a time when libraries, in terms of both their physical structures and their contents, provided refuge in a shattered landscape, offering the Japanese access to ideas and information from the outer world, albeit that access was defined by American censorship and cultural advocacy. The overall process marked an important stage in the globalization of concert-music composition, performance, consumption, and reception, even as CIE's record concerts and cultural interventions yield a stark image of cultural supremacy in action.

Reflections on Our Collaboration: A Postscript

This essay grew out of steady transnational research and communication, with Misako in Kobe, Japan, and Carol in Cambridge, Massachusetts. Once we defined a topic and commenced the work, the challenges became increasingly pragmatic: that is, each of us accessed the materials available in our country and for which we had language comprehension. We opted to fuse our voices in the text, rather than presenting separate narratives, and that choice responded to logistical limitations, including the relatively short length of this chapter. Predictably, our individual interpretative contributions reflected our national orientations. Misako raised questions to clarify the concerts' many-layered Japanese contexts, especially emphasizing Japan's long-standing tie to Austro-German music; she also prodded us to explore the continuing prominence of Menotti's music in Japan. Carol, meanwhile, recognized the American composers programmed by CIE as representing aesthetics that were mostly, but not completely, conservative. Together—via conversations over Skype and e-mail—we assembled the puzzle pieces.

Even though the topic of this article is highly focused, it opens a window onto the kinds of historical research and transcultural methodologies that are germane to studying globalized classical music cultures. For one thing, our research fused secondary literature from Japan and the United States. Perhaps most fundamentally, we emerged with an interpretation of the materials that differs substantially from the perspective either of us would have shaped on our own. We also found ourselves gravitating to bicultural figures. Yoshiro Ernest Satow represented the main such case—a young intellectual of Japanese and American parentage who was raised in Japan, interpreted to Japanese audiences the new American music heard at CIE's concerts, became involved in the early stages of Jikken Kobo, and then went on to study in the United States, eventually returning home to Japan. In many ways, Satow stands as an intriguing example of postwar mobility. He listened and learned transculturally, becoming the kind of cosmopolitan figure who was highly prized in an increasingly westernized Japan.

Notes

All translations from Japanese to English are by Misako Ohta. We are grateful to the following: Professor Annegret Fauser, University of North Carolina; Peter Laurence, Librarian for Recorded Sound and Media, Loeb Music Library,

Harvard University; Professor Morihiro Satow, Doshisha University; Yukako Tatsumi, Curator, Gordon W. Prange Collection and East Asian Studies Librarian, University of Maryland; Makiko Tada, Librarian, Kobe University Library for Human Development Sciences; Joelle Tapas, copy editor with an expertise in Japanese.

1. Tōru Takemitsu, "Contemporary Music in Japan," interpreted by Peter Grilli, *Perspectives of New Music* 27, no. 2 (Summer 1989): 199. Takemitsu's ambivalence about Japanese music was common in the postwar period, and it was exemplified in a pamphlet published by the occupation forces that addressed the question of what music to teach in Japanese schools: "Considerable discussion was held about a very basic problem: what of the conflict between western and traditional [Japanese] music? The difficulty lies in the fact that Japanese music uses the quarter tone system. . . . From the view point of the musician the argument is to eliminate Japanese music from the schools and teach only western music. However, this is tantamount to deciding that a whole segment of Japanese culture, which is very much still alive, will not be considered part of the heritage that schools should pass on." "GHQ/SCAP Civil Information and Education Section 13 September 1946 / Mombusho Curriculum Committee Regular Triweekly Conference," in *Ongaku kiso kenkyū bunkenshū* 音楽基礎研究文献集 [Foundational research texts on music], ed. Ezaki Kimiko 江崎公子 (Tokyo: Ōzora-sha, 1991), 14:27.

2. John W. Dower, *Embracing Defeat: Japan in the Wake of World War II* (New York: Norton, 1999), 48, 61.

3. E. Taylor Atkins, *Blue Nippon: Authenticating Jazz in Japan* (Durham, NC: Duke University Press, 2001), 171.

4. Our first collaboration led to the article: Katherine Callam, Makiko Kimoto, Misako Ohta, and Carol J. Oja, "Marian Anderson's 1953 Concert Tour of Japan: A Transnational History," in "Transpacific Currents," ed. Gayle Magee, special issue, *American Music* 37, no. 3 (Fall 2019): 266–329. Through that research, we recognized the largely untapped resource of newspaper criticism in chronicling Anderson's tour, which in turn revealed unexplored aspects of musical interchanges during the occupation.

5. The organization was sometimes abbreviated as CI&E, but we have opted for the more prevalent and shorter CIE.

6. Takemitsu, "Contemporary Music," 200.

7. Aoki Shin 青木深, *Meguriau monotachi no gunzō: Sengo Nihon no Beigun kichi to ongaku 1945–1958* めぐりあうものたちの群像: 戦後日本の米軍基地と音楽 1945–1958 [Portraits of encounters: American military bases and music in postwar Japan, 1945–1958] (Tokyo: Ōtsuki Shoten, 2013); and Tōya Mamoru 東谷護, *Shinchūgun kurabu kara kayōkyoku e: Sengo Nihon popyurā ongaku no reimeiki* 進駐軍クラブから歌謡曲へ: 戦後日本ポピュラー音楽の黎明期 [From occupation forces clubs to popular songs: The dawning of popular music in postwar Japan] (Tokyo: Misuzu Shobō, 2005). Dower's book *Embracing Defeat* is a central history of the occupation in English. Overall, there is less scholarship about the reception of American concert music in postwar Japan than about jazz and popular music. Meanwhile, classical music in the occupation era has largely been chronicled in relation to European repertory. See Tonoshita Tatsuya 戸ノ下達

也, *Ongaku wo dōin seyo: Tōsei to goraku no jūgonen sensō* 音楽を動員せよ: 統制と娯楽の十五年戦争 [Mobilize music: The fifteen-year war between regulation and entertainment] (Tokyo: Seikyūsha, 2008).

8. In the early twenty-first century, the vast majority of Japanese academics are fluent in English, while the study of Japanese is rare in the United States.

9. Ueno Masaaki 上野正章, "Shakai kyōiku toshite no Amerika ongaku: Senryōki no Nihon ni okeru CIE no ongaku seisaku ni tsuite" 社会教育としてのアメリカ音楽: 占領期の日本におけるCIEの音楽政策について [American music as social education: The CIE's music policy during the occupation period in Japan], *Ongakugaku* 音楽学 [Journal of the Musicological Society of Japan] 45, no. 2 (1999): 99–109; Taniguchi Akihiro 谷口昭弘, "Senryōki ni okeru Amerika kurashikku ongaku no juyō: Genjō hōkoku" 占領期におけるアメリカ・クラシック音楽の受容: 現状報告 [Reception of American classical music during the occupation: Status report], *Kunitachi Ongaku Daigaku ongaku kenkyūjo nenpō* 国立音楽大学音楽研究所年報 [Annual report of the Music Research Institute at Kunitachi College of Music] 29 (2016): 57–73.

10. Throughout this essay, we use the transliteration (and spelling) *shinbun*, which means "newspaper" in Japanese. Subsequent research on our topic could investigate archival traces of CIE's work in Japan. Doing so was beyond our scope.

11. Don Brown, "Japan Times in Vanguard: Pioneer of Cultural Exchange," *Japan Times*, March 22, 1962. Reprinted in Hasegawa Shin'ichi 長谷川進一, ed., *Japan Taimuzu monogatari* ジャパンタイムズものがたり [History of the *Japan Times*] (Tokyo: Kabushiki-gaisha Japan Taimuzu, 1966), 191. Note that Brown is pictured here in figure 2.3.

12. Robert H. Berkov, "Press in Postwar Japan," *Far Eastern Survey* 16, no. 14 (July 23, 1947): 162.

13. *Yomiuri shinbun 120-nen shi* 読売新聞120年史 [120-year history of the *Yomiuri shinbun*] (Tokyo: Yomiuri Shinbunsha, 1994), 187.

14. Ariyama Teruo 有山輝雄, "Senryōki no media tōsei 1: Shinbun" 占領期のメディア統制1: 新聞 [Media regulation during the occupation period 1: Newspapers], *Kan* 環 [Circle] 22 (July 2005): 263–66.

15. The *Nippon Times* listed dates and program information for the record concerts, while *Yomiuri shinbun* published sporadic listings for the events with no information about the repertory performed.

16. Regarding Perry and minstrelsy: Victor Fell Yellin, "Mrs. Belmont, Matthew Perry, and the 'Japanese Minstrels,'" *American Music* 14, no. 3 (Autumn 1996): 257–75. Japanese artists documented Perry's minstrel show: *Kaiga shiryō ni miru Edo no yōgaku kotohajime* 絵画資料にみる江戸の洋楽事始め [The beginning of Western music studies in the Edo period as seen in visual records] (Okayama: Tsūyama Yōgaku Shiryōkan, 2017), 18–19. Regarding Foster in Japan: Sugimoto Minako 杉本皆子, *Fosutā no ongaku: Amerika bunka to Nihon bunka* フォスターの音楽: アメリカ文化と日本文化 [The music of Foster: American culture and Japanese culture] (Tokyo: Kindai Bungeisha, 1995), especially chap. 4 (pp. 48–92); and Kazuko Miyashita, "Foster's Songs in Japan," *American Music* 30, no. 3 (Fall 2012): 308–25.

17. Nishihara Minoru 西原稔, *"Gakusei" Bētōben no tanjō: Kindai kokka ga motometa ongaku* 「楽聖」ベートーヴェンの誕生: 近代国家が求めた音楽 [The birth of

the great musician Beethoven: Music that the modern nation sought] (Tokyo: Heibonsha, 2000), 18.

18. *Routledge Encyclopedia of Modernism*, s.v. "Asakusa Opera," by Yoshiko Fukushima, accessed March 28, 2020, https://www.rem.routledge.com/articles/asakusa-opera. See also Aaron M. Cohen, "Tokuko Nagai Takagi (1891–1919): Japan's First Actress," *Bright Lights Film Journal*, June 27, 2014, https://brightlightsfilm.com/tokuko-nagai-takagi-1891-1919-japans-first-actress/#.Xn-VWC3MxTY.

19. Kosaku Yamada also used the first name "Kósçak." A chronology of his US visit appears in David Pacun, "'Thus We Cultivate Our Own World, and Thus We Share It with Others': Kósaçk Yamada's Visit to the United States in 1918–1919," *American Music* 24, no. 1 (Spring 2006): 68.

20. "Japanese Conducts Own Native Works," *New York Times*, October 17, 1918.

21. Yamada Kōsaku 山田耕作, "Amerika no ongaku I" アメリカの音楽 (上) [American music I], *Yomiuri shinbun*, June 17, 1919; Yamada Kōsaku 山田耕作, "Amerika no ongaku II" アメリカの音楽 (下) [American music II], *Yomiuri shinbun*, June 18, 1919.

22. "US-Japan Exchange Broadcast on July 5," *Nippon Times*, July 3, 1937; "Koten, kindaika sōkyoku to Amerika ongaku to no kōryū" 古典, 近代化箏曲とアメリカ音楽との交流 [Interchange between traditional and modernized koto music and American music], *Yomiuri shinbun*, July 5, 1937.

23. *Yomiuri shinbun* and American newspapers include different details about this event. "Amerika ongaku to no kōryū" lists the NBC Orchestra broadcasting from New York. The *Boston Globe* states: "Ernest Gill's Orchestra from San Francisco." "Radio listings," *Boston Globe*, July 4, 1937.

24. "Japan's Ace Composer in New York to Do a Song of the United States," *Nippon Times*, October 2, 1939.

25. Naoe Monma, "Anglo-American Anthems: Negro Music Forms Basis of American Jazz," *Nippon Times*, March 23, 1945. Also: Monma Naoe 門馬直衛, "Akunaki yajūsei: Ongaku ni miru Amerikajin katagi" 飽くなき野獣性: 音楽に見るアメリカ人気質 [Insatiable savagery: American character as seen in music], *Asahi shinbun*, August 30, 1944.

26. Hiraoka Yōichi 平岡養一, *Amerika ongaku tokuhon* アメリカ音楽読本 [American music reader], 1946, E-0018, Gordon W. Prange Collection, University of Maryland. This forty-six-page book was censored by GHQ. Two more histories of American music appeared in rapid succession: Hattori Ryūtarō 服部龍太郎, *Ongaku suru Amerika* 音楽するアメリカ [America makes music] (Tokyo: Gakufu Shuppansha, 1947); Miura Atsushi 三浦淳史, *Gendai Amerika ongaku* 現代アメリカ音楽 [Contemporary American music] (Tokyo: Shinkō Ongaku Shuppansha, 1948).

27. Tsūzaki Mutsumi 通崎睦美, *Mokkin deizu: Hiraoka Yōichi ten'i muhō no ongaku jinsei* 木琴デイズ: 平岡養一 天衣無縫の音楽人生 [Xylophone days: Hiraoka Yōichi and a musical life of artlessness] (Tokyo: Kodansha, 2013), 171. Tsūzaki pointed out that Hiraoka continued to program Western classical music during the war, even if other Japanese musicians played nationalistic pieces. Because of that, he has not garnered much attention from Japanese scholars studying music

during World War II. See also Akiko Goto, "Yoichi Hiraoka: His Artistic Life and His Influence on the Art of Xylophone Performance" (DMA diss., University of North Texas, 2013).

28. Hiraoka, preface to *Amerika ongaku tokuhon*, 2.

29. "Recorded Concert Set," *Nippon Times*, July 25, 1948.

30. "Recorded Concert Set." Overall, it is hard to gauge the size of audiences. An article from 1950 suggests that a significant following had emerged over two years: "Many thousands of Japanese attend record concerts organized and conducted by CIE's Music Department, and other thousands flock to record concerts at the CIE Information Centers." "Western Music in Japan," *Music Educators Journal* 36, no. 3 (January 1950): 33.

31. Listings appeared in *Nippon Times* with some version of the heading "Social & General: CIE Record Concert": August 6, 1948; August 27, 1948; September 3, 1948. Some listings included information about performers, while others did not.

32. "Japanese Concert Fans Buy Up 13,000 Tickets for Menuhin in 4 Hours," *Nippon Times*, August 2, 1951. Regarding Marian Anderson's concert tour: Callam et al., "Marian Anderson's 1953 Concert Tour." Regarding foreign musicians in Japan in the 1950s: Yamazaki Kōtarō 山崎浩太郎, *Ensō shitan 1954/55: Kurashikku ongaku no ōgon no hibi* 演奏史譚 1954/55: クラシック音楽の黄金の日日 [Tales of performance history 1954/55: Golden days of classical music] (Tokyo: Arufa Bēta Bukkusu, 2017); Minagawa Hiroshi 皆川 弘至, "Kurashikku ongaku bunka juyō no hensen: Gairai ensōka ni yoru konsāto-shi e no ichi kōsatsu" クラシック音楽文化受容の変遷: 外来演奏家によるコンサート史への一考察 [Aspects in the reception of "Classical Music" culture: A survey concerning the history of concerts by visiting performers], in "Ongaku hyōgen gakka tokushūgō" 音楽表現学科特集号 [Special issue on studies of musical expression], special issue, *Shōbi Gakuen Daigaku Geijutsu Jōhō Gakubu kiyō* 尚美学園大学芸術情報学部紀要 [Bulletin of the Faculty of Informatics for Arts, Shobi University] 4 (2004): 71–164.

33. "Japanese Flock to CIE Libraries," *Nippon Times*, October 10, 1949. Additional information: "Visitors Flock to CIE Libraries," *Nippon Times*, May 24, 1949.

34. Barak Kushner and Sato Masaharu, "Digesting Postwar Japanese Media," *Diplomatic History* 29, no. 1 (January 2005): 27.

35. "Japanese Flock to CIE Libraries."

36. Announcements of inaugural record concerts: [Hibiya] "Recorded Concert Set," *Nippon Times*, July 25, 1948; [Yokohama] "Data Furnished on School Board," *Nippon Times*, September 29, 1948; [Shinjuku] "Music Notes and Calendar," *Nippon Times*, September 25, 1949.

37. Ueno, "Shakai kyōiku," 107–8.

38. Atkins, *Blue Nippon*, 171.

39. The broadcasting of American concert music on NHK and Armed Forces Radio is outside the purview of this study.

40. An exception within the recorded repertory listed by *Nippon Times* was William Grant Still's *Afro-American Symphony* (Scherzo), heard at a record concert in Hibiya in April 1951. Social and General, *Nippon Times*, April 13, 1951. We have located no listings for compositions by American women.

41. The noted American journalist Earnest Hoberecht (1918–1999) included a biography of Anderson in a book published in a Japanese translation in 1947: Earnest Hoberecht, *Gendai Amerika jinbutsuden* 現代アメリカ人物伝 [Biographies in contemporary America], trans. Ōkubo Yasuo 大久保康雄 (Tokyo: Masu Shobō, 1947), 15–19.

42. Robert Marovich, "Wings Over Jordan," in *Encyclopedia of American Gospel Music*, ed. W. K. McNeil (New York: Taylor & Francis, 2005), 429–30; "Burl Ives," by Cheryl A. Brauner, revised by Paul F. Wells, *Grove Music Online*, July 25, 2013, https://doi-org.ezp-prod1.hul.harvard.edu/10.1093/gmo/9781561592630.article.A2241775

43. Atkins, *Blue Nippon*, 173.

44. All recording dates come from the online international library catalog WorldCat, accessed April 12, 2020, https://www.worldcat.org/; or Carol J. Oja, ed., *American Music Recordings: A Discography of 20th-Century U.S. Composers* (Brooklyn: Institute for Studies in American Music, 1982).

45. This recording is listed in SONIC: Sound Online Inventory Catalog of the Library of Congress, s.v. Samuel Barber, *Second Essay*, accessed April 27, 2020, https://star1.loc.gov/cgi-bin/starfinder/15433/sonic.txt

46. Recordings pressed through OWI and by US government agencies after the war are difficult to find and often uncataloged, yet emerging steadily.

47. Memorandum, "Examples of Records for Information Centers. Types of Music for all Centers: Chosen to Illustrate America's Catholic Tastes," n.d., RG 208, Box 13, Archives of the Office of War Information, National Archives, College Park, Maryland. Thanks to Annegret Fauser for generously sharing a pdf.

48. Annegret Fauser, *Sounds of War: Music in the United States during World War II* (New York: Oxford University Press, 2013), 76. The OWI memo states the following in its introduction: "A note on Jazz: Our primary purpose is to use these record[ing]s to develop cultural relations, not to sell American music—serious or popular—as such. Therefore, if it is easier to answer German-made charges that America is culturally backward by showing our appreciation and development of serious music than to sell them Am Jazz, *the thing to do is to sell our Haydn and Mozart*, leaving other things for other times" (the emphasis is ours). "Examples of Records," n.d., Archives of the Office of War Information.

49. Emily Abrams Ansari, *The Sound of a Superpower: Musical Americanism and the Cold War* (New York: Oxford University Press, 2018). Ansari's introduction (pp. 1–27) defines the shifting stylistic and political parameters that shaped the designation of "Americanist."

50. Amy C. Beal, *New Music, New Allies: American Experimental Music in West Germany from the Zero Hour to Reunification* (Berkeley: University of California Press, 2006), 33.

51. Beal (p. 3) focuses largely on the extraordinary support in Germany after the war for American "experimentalist" composers, such as Henry Cowell, Ruth Crawford, Charles Ives, Carl Ruggles, and Edgard Varèse, which is a different aesthetic realm from the CIE record concerts in Japan.

52. "American Music Hailed: Europeans Appreciate Serious Works Even More than Jazz," *Nippon Times*, February 19, 1947. Moseley later had multiple leader-

ship roles with the New York Philharmonic, overseeing its move from Carnegie Hall to Lincoln Center in 1962.

53. Harrison Kerr, "Beikoku ongaku to Nihon" 米国音楽と日本 [American music and Japan], *Gendai no geijutsu* 現代の芸術 [Contemporary arts] (Tokyo: Yomiuri Shinbunsha Bunka-bu, 1948). Kerr appears in Beal's book at various points (e.g., pp. 19–20).

54. In addition to Ansari, see Danielle Fosler-Lussier, *Music in America's Cold War Diplomacy* (Oakland: University of California Press, 2015).

55. Social and General, *Nippon Times*, April 8, 1949; Social and General, *Nippon Times*, April 13, 1949.

56. Beethoven 9: "Music Notes and Calendar," *Nippon Times*, September 4, 1949; Social and General, *Nippon Times*, October 17, 1950; and Announcements, *Nippon Times*, December 6, 1951. Beethoven 5: Announcements, *Nippon Times*, November 8, 1951. Kreuzer Sonata: Announcements, *Nippon Times*, April 25, 1952.

57. Social and General, *Nippon Times*, December 13, 1950.

58. Beal chronicles postwar efforts to help the Berlin Philharmonic and other major institutions of classical music in Germany (p. 12), and she also discusses Leonard Bernstein's tour of Germany in 1948, funded by OMGUS (US Office of Military Government in Germany, which was the German corollary to GHQ and SCAP) (p. 22).

59. "Davies Joins CI&E," *Nippon Times*, April 21, 1946; and "'Old Japan Hand' Dies Unexpectedly," *Nippon Times*, October 23, 1953.

60. Social and General, *Nippon Times*, August 2, 1951. One source describes Satow as Davies's "assistant"—see "Western Music in Japan," 33.

61. Satow later became a noted photographer, with photos published in the *New York Times*. For example: Yoshiro Satow, "Cityscape: Autumn," *New York Times*, November 29, 1959. In 1962, Satow returned to Japan as a correspondent for *Life*; then in 1973 he was appointed professor at Kyoto City University of Arts. The information in this paragraph about Yoshiro and Tai'ichirō Satow comes from Morihiro Satow, ed., *Y. Ernest Satow: Selected Photographs* (Tokyo: Kodansha, 1998), 123; "Y. Ernest Satow" Y・アーネスト・サトウ, Morihiro Satow, accessed April 27, 2020, http://web.kyoto-inet.or.jp/people/b-monkey/YES.html; and Morihiro Satow, e-mail to Carol J. Oja, January 18, 2019.

62. Satow, e-mail. As of this writing, the discography has not been located.

63. Terajima moderated a concert at the Shinjuku CIE library: Social and General, *Nippon Times*, October 17, 1950. Nishiyama's first concert is listed in Social and General, *Nippon Times*, August 2, 1951. In both cases, we have not been able to locate biographical information.

64. Selected listings of Watanabe as moderator in Social and General, *Nippon Times*, June 30, 1951; and Announcements, *Nippon Times*, May 14, 1952. Watanabe became a professor at Musashino College of Music and Tokyo University.

65. Announcements, *Nippon Times*, December 12, 1951. Warashina taught at Keio University, and he worked as the music director of Mainichi Broadcasting Company.

66. Bernstein's relationship with Japan culminated in 1990 when he was among the founders of the Pacific Music Festival in Sapporo. For more about

Bernstein and Japan, see Mari Yoshihara, *Dearest Lenny: Letters from Japan and the Making of the World Maestro* (New York: Oxford University Press, 2019), which was in press as we wrote this chapter.

67. Symphony no. 1: "Music Notes and Calendar," *Nippon Times*, September 25, 1949. While the listing vaguely states, "Symphony by Leonard Bernstein," the work must have been no. 1 (*Jeremiah*), which Bernstein composed and recorded in 1942. Symphony no. 2: Social and General, *Nippon Times*, June 28, 1951.

68. Announcements, *Nippon Times*, October 16, 1951; October 19, 1951.

69. Announcements, *Nippon Times*, September 24, 1952.

70. The following concert listings appeared in *Nippon Times* under the headings "Recorded Concerts Today," Social and General, or Announcements: [*Rodeo*] April 13, 1949; [*Quiet City*] May 24, 1951, October 18, 1951, and December 3, 1952; [Sonata for Violin and Piano] May 18, 1951; [Two Pieces for Violin and Piano] June 14, 1951; [*Piano Blues*] November 13, 1952; [*Lincoln Portrait*] April 18, 1952; [*Billy the Kid*] May 22, 1952.

71. Listings in *Nippon Times*, under the same headings as above: [*Show Boat*] May 20, 1949; [*Down in the Valley*] June 19, 1951; [*Carousel*] February 6, 1952; [*The King and I*] February 20, 1952.

72. Social and General, *Nippon Times*, April 27, 1951.

73. *Rhapsody in Blue:* Social and General, *Nippon Times*, October 2, 1951; *An American in Paris:* Announcements, *Nippon Times*, March 5, 1952.

74. *Amelia Goes to the Ball* and *The Telephone:* Social and General, *Nippon Times*, May 10, 1951. *The Medium:* Two pairs of record concerts at Shinjuku featured *The Medium*, with one act per event. All listed under Announcements in *Nippon Times:* [Act 1] April 3, 1952; [Act 2] April 8, 1952; [Act 1] May 14, 1952; and [Act 2] May 30, 1952.

75. Masui Keiji 増井敬二, *Nihon opera-shi: 1952* 日本オペラ史: 1952 [History of opera in Japan to 1952] (Tokyo: Suiyōsha, 2003), 293–324.

76. "U.S. Army to Stage Opera 'The Mikado,'" *Nippon Times*, August 7, 1946.

77. Tara Rodman, "A More Humane Mikado: Re-envisioning the Nation through Occupation-Era Productions of *The Mikado* in Japan," *Theatre Research International* 40, no. 3 (2015): 289. Rodman discusses the various productions; while she included one reference to *Yomiuri shinbun*, she did not appear to consult the *Nippon Times*.

78. "'Mikado' Play Extends Run," *Nippon Times*, February 1, 1948.

79. Peter Kalischer, "Imperial Family Members Enjoy 'The Mikado' Staged by Japanese," *Nippon Times*, January 31, 1948. This production was directed by Michio Itō, who had returned to Japan from the United States, and Miho Nagato played the role of Yum-Yum.

80. Nagato Miho 長門美保, "Gaikoku sakuhin no jōen" 外国作品の上演 [Performing foreign pieces], *Gendai no geijutsu* 現代の芸術 [Contemporary arts] (Tokyo: Yomiuri Shinbunsha Bunka-bu, 1948), 230–31.

81. An advertisement for *The Old Maid and the Thief* identifies Nagato's troupe as "the same opera company [that] played MIKADO in Dec." *The Old Maid and the Thief*, advertisement, *Nippon Times*, February 3, 1949. The Shinbashi Enbujō Theater was demolished by Allied bombs during the war; it was subsequently rebuilt and opened in 1948, not long before this production.

82. "Amerika gendai opera jōen" アメリカ現代オペラ上演 [Performance of contemporary American opera], *Yomiuri shinbun,* January 8, 1949. The production was reportedly "well received by the Japanese." "Western Music in Japan," 33.

83. The other plays listed are little known today: "On the Stage: 'Our Town,'" *Nippon Times,* June 10, 1948. Regarding CIE's authorization of the Menotti opera: "Amerika gendai opera jōen."

84. "Music Notes and Calendar," *Nippon Times,* March 27, 1949. An earlier two-part article in *Nippon Times* compared the similarities in dramatic spectacle between opera and Kabuki: Keizo Horiuchi, "Points of Similarity Exist between Kabuki and Opera," pts. 1 and 2, *Nippon Times,* May 28, 1948; May 29, 1948.

85. "Fujiwara Kagekidan no myūjikaru purei 6-gatsu *Ryōji* jōen e" 藤原歌劇団 のミュージカルプレイ6月『領事』上演へ [June performance of *The Consul* by the Fujiwara Opera Company], *Yomiuri shinbun,* February 3, 1955; "Futari dake no kikageki Menotti no sakuhin *Denwa*" 二人だけの喜歌劇 メノッティの作品『電話』[Menotti's *Telephone* a comic opera just for two], *Yomiuri shinbun,* November 11, 1956; "*Burikkā-gai no Seija* Nihon de shoen"『ブリッカー街の聖者』日本で初演 [First performance of *The Saint of Bleecker Street* in Japan], *Yomiuri shinbun,* June 1, 1960; "Hatsu rai-Nichi no opera sakkyokuka Menotti ni kiku: Sosaetī ha kirai" 初来日のオペラ作曲家メノッティに聞く: ソサエティーは嫌い [Asking opera composer Menotti on his first visit to Japan: Disliking society], *Yomiuri shinbun,* October 16, 1973.

86. Masui, *Nihon opera-shi,* 372; "Shin operetta keishiki: Bōdobirian mo chōshū" 新オペレッタ形式: ボードビリアンも徴収 [New operetta form: Vaudevillian also included], *Yomiuri shinbun,* February 4, 1949; Kikuta Kazuo 菊田一夫, "Komikku opera" コミックオペラ [Comic opera], *Yomiuri shinbun,* February 7, 1951.

87. Hata Toyokichi 秦豊吉, "Nihon opera no michi" 日本オペラの道 [The way of Japanese opera], in *Gendai no geijutsu* 現代の芸術 [Contemporary arts] (Tokyo: Yomiuri Shinbunsha Bunka-bu, 1948), 229; Matsuda Naoyuki 松田直行, "Hata Toyokichi no *Shō:* Teigeki myūjikarusu ni itaru rinen to jissen" 秦豊吉の『ショウ』: 帝劇ミュージカルスに至る理念と実践 [Hata Toyokichi's *Show:* Theory and practice in musicals at the Imperial Theatre], in *Komazawa tandai kokubun* 駒沢短大国文 [National literature at Komazawa Junior College] (Tokyo: Komazawa University, 2001), 62–76.

88. In the 1930s, *The Threepenny Opera* became popular in Japan through recordings, film, and stage. The work's first performance there in 1932 brought together singers and actors from operetta, theater, and cabaret: "Mondai no Senda Koreya-kun shingekidan no hataage: Fūgawari na varaeti gekijō" 問題の千田是也君 新劇団の旗揚げ: 風変わりなヴァラエティ劇場 [Senda Koreya launches new theater company: Eccentric variety playhouse], *Asahi shinbun,* January 28, 1932. According to advertisements in the *Yomiuri shinbun,* the 1931 film *Die 3 Groschen-Oper* was shown in Japan until at least 1943. Presumably it was banned under wartime censorship. In 1953, advertisements for the film resumed. See Misako Ohta, *Kurt Weill: A Sociocultural History of Musical Theater* (Tokyo: Iwanami Shoten, forthcoming); and Misako Ohta and Sachiko Hiyama, "Kurt Weill: The *Threepenny Opera* in Japan / The *Threepenny* Fever in Its Early Days," *Bulletin of Graduate School of Human Development and Environment, Kobe University* 14, no. 1 (September 2020), 37–54.

89. Opera Information Center of Opera Research Center, Showa University of Music, accessed April 17, 2020, https://opera.tosei-showa-music.ac.jp/search/Search/Results?filter%5B%5D=composers%3A%22ジャン・カルロ・メノッティ%22&lookfor=メノッティ&type=AllFields&informationType[]=Find_PerformanceInformation

90. Ishida Asako 石田麻子, "Nihon opera kōen 2017" 日本のオペラ公演2017 [Opera on stage in Japan 2017], in *Nihon opera nenkan 2017* 日本のオペラ年鑑 2017 [Opera in Japan yearbook 2017] (Tokyo: Agency for Cultural Affairs; Opera Research Center at Showa Academia Musicae, 2018), 81.

91. "Jikken Kōbō membā ni yoru zadankai" 実験工房メンバーによる座談会 [Roundtable with members of Jikken Kōbō], in *Jikken Kōbō-ten: Sengo geijutsu wo kirihiraku* 実験工房展: 戦後芸術を切り拓く [Jikken Kobo exhibition: Cutting through postwar art] (Tokyo: Yomiuri Shinbunsha; Japan Association of Art Museums, 2013), 256–59. We are grateful to Morihiro Satow for telling us about this catalog.

92. The Wako Building was one of the few that survived the Allied bombings, and it served as the PX store for the US military during the occupation. In 1998, it was selected as a landmark of the City of Tokyo by the Japan Federation of Architects. Sanko Estate, *Wakō biru* 和光ビル [Wako Building], accessed April 17, 2020, https://www.sanko-e.co.jp/download_file/view/772/281

THREE | Listening to and Learning from Music of the Global United States

PANAYOTIS LEAGUE AND KAY KAUFMAN SHELEMAY

American ethnomusicologists and historical musicologists have tended to work more often than not outside the boundaries of the United States. Indeed, American ethnomusicology, as it developed under the influence of American anthropology, privileged research—until well into the third quarter of the twentieth century—in small, remote communities abroad, whether the rain forest or the isolated village. At the same time, historical musicology focused on European music histories and styles, with scholarly attention to musics of North America emerging only well into the twentieth century.

This foreign focus was in contrast to a number of other national research traditions, such as those from Eastern Europe and Latin America, where researchers have tended from the inception of ethnomusicological scholarship to privilege studies at home.[1] Meanwhile, scholars who did undertake research in North America often specialized mainly in Indigenous American traditions such as Native American musics or in traditions, like African American musics, that originated in the United States as an outcome of early forced migrations.

In addition, the large and continuing waves of transnational migration from the mid-twentieth century forward, both voluntary and forced, stemming from a variety of locales beyond Europe, have rendered the United States a site of extraordinary musical diversity. While the rising heterogeneity of American musical resources has paralleled the maturation of US music scholarship, only recently has the music of global North

America attracted scholarly attention. This living and expanding archive of US music is the subject of our essay, where we envision a future in which scholars of American musics prioritize working at home amid a global array of traditions.

Americanists today have a rich array of subjects that promise to enliven and diversify US music studies and reshape the broader field of musical scholarship. First, multiple waves of migration to the United States can be tracked through their impact in establishing a new, transnational musical scene. Second, research in the United States promises a remapping of networks of musical performance, creativity, and circulation, especially as traditions from different regions of the world interact in global America. Third, as migrant populations put down ever-deeper roots and consolidate their economic, cultural, and political capital in the US context, they play an increasingly pivotal role in national conversations about race, ethnicity, and cultural politics. Musical practices are part and parcel of all of these processes, and often take on surprising new meanings when they are repurposed to address the needs of migrant musicians and audiences.

For our case studies, we profile musicians from the Greek American and Ethiopian American diasporas who are deeply involved in global jazz, among other hybrid styles, and provide an opportunity to contrast the experiences of individuals from two lively immigrant populations with different political histories, racial identities, and musical traditions.[2] They have in common a number of important sociopolitical and artistic features that, we argue, move them into productive dialogue despite their superficial differences. These features include departure from their respective homelands in the wake of armed conflict and sudden political changes; sustained engagement with musical and cultural formations that developed in their new home in the United States; and the development of novel strategies to meld the modal, rhythmic, and poetic character of their respective homelands' traditions with various aspects of global popular music.

Hundreds of thousands of Anatolian Greeks fled their ancestral homeland of present-day Turkey following the Greco-Turkish War of 1919–22 and the destruction of Greek communities in Asia Minor; the ongoing violence and subsequent expulsion of Orthodox Christians from Anatolia forced many to depart for points abroad, including Greece and the United States. At a later date, Ethiopian migration began primarily as a response to the Ethiopian revolution in 1974, and continued through periods of ongoing instability and violence well into the twenty-first century, forcing Ethiopians of diverse ethnic and regional backgrounds to flee the Horn of Africa. Many settled in the United States, where by the turn of the twenty-first century they numbered the largest Ethiopian community living outside its historical homeland.

We present these case studies by focusing on two individual artists from the Greek American and Ethiopian American communities, with Panayotis contributing the Greek American section and Kay focusing on Ethiopian Americans. Then, together we conclude by contrasting and comparing these materials in relation to insights they offer for the study of musics of the global United States in the twenty-first century.

Expanding the Zone of Musical Pilgrimage: Lefteris Kordis's Mediterranean Jazz

Though systematic Greek migration to North America stretches back at least to the late eighteenth century with the ill-fated colony of New Smyrna on Florida's Atlantic Coast, the largest waves of immigrants came in the century after the majority of the Greek mainland declared independence from the Ottomans in 1822. The period between roughly 1880 and 1920, in particular, saw as many as five-hundred-thousand Greeks, mostly men, enter the United States. They were predominantly economic migrants abandoning a flailing economy and the social upheavals of the Balkan Wars (1912–13) and Greco-Turkish Wars of 1897 and 1919–21.[3] They were joined in the 1920s by Anatolian Greek refugees fleeing the destruction of their ancestral homes in Asia Minor by the victorious Young Turk army and an associated program of genocide against Ottoman minorities that resulted in the murder of one and a half million Armenians and perhaps as many as half a million Greeks from all over Asia Minor; this series of tragedies became known collectively to Greeks as the "Great Catastrophe."[4] The greater Boston area, including the Somerville and Watertown neighborhoods and the North Shore industrial hub of Lynn, received a particularly large number of Anatolian refugees. Some, like the former inhabitants of worldly and European-oriented places like the port city of Smyrna and the island of Lesbos, maintained some of their Asia Minor traditions while participating fully in the economic, cultural, social, and political life of their new homes.[5] Others, such as the Pontian Greeks from the southern shores of the Black Sea, led more insular lives as a community, preserving their distinct (and, to other Greeks, confounding) linguistic and musical idioms into the twenty-first century. For the most part, today's approximately two million American and 275,000 Canadian residents of Greek descent—many of them belonging to the third, fourth, or even fifth generation in North America—are able to participate simultaneously in several different fields of cultural expression in terms of Greek identity: regional cultural associations organized according to an ancestral village or province; a generalized sense of Greek ethnicity that sets them apart from other Mediterranean and Balkan communities; observation of Orthodox Christianity; and, increasingly, representation in popular culture based on stereotypes of garrulous, impulsive revelers ready to dance and feast at the drop of a hat (or the breaking of a plate).

After a fallow period that stretched over the 1990s and early 2000s, the recently reinvigorated field of Greek American studies has begun to engage critically with both the multiple histories of this diaspora and its increasingly complex connections to other migrant communities in terms of artistic expression. Inspired in large part by Yiorgos Anagnostou's pioneering work on the development of white ethnicity among Greeks in America over the course of the twentieth century,[6] researchers are beginning to complement work in folklore and comparative literature with studies of music in the Greek American experience. A notable example is the recent volume *Greek Music in America*, edited by Tina Bucuvalas, which covers a wide range of popular, folk, and liturgical genres and features contributions from ethnomusicologists, folklorists, archivists, and, notably, practitioners of traditional Greek music and dance—many of whom are themselves members of the Greek American diaspora.[7] Perhaps because of the relative dearth of scholarship on the musical facets of the Greek American experience over the last 150 years, most of this necessary work has focused more on artifacts and archives than on ethnography, attempting to piece together the community's histories rather than navigate the shifting currents of what it means to be a Greek musician in the United States at the end of the twenty-first century's second decade. In a similar vein, most researchers working on Greek music in America—one of the present authors included—have concentrated on the traditional musics brought to the United States by migrant communities, such as regional folk dance music, oral poetry, and Byzantine chant.

Here we take a different approach, profiling pianist Lefteris Kordis, a performer and composer with deep roots in the musical and cultural traditions of Anatolia and minority communities of mainland Greece, who has developed his artistic identity and philosophical orientation over two decades of living in the United States, studying and practicing genres grounded in the African American experience: jazz, blues, gospel, and contemporary tonal approaches to improvisation. Though Lefteris was born a few miles from Athens and began playing music there as a small child, his entire adult life and nearly all of his performing career have been spent in the Boston area, first as an undergraduate and then doctoral student in jazz performance at the New England Conservatory and now as a professor at Berklee College of Music and its affiliated Global Jazz Institute. Today, aside from teaching improvisation, theory, composition, and ear training at these institutions and his private studio, Lefteris is at the creative forefront of the burgeoning global jazz movement, combining elements of the folk, popular, and liturgical music of Greece and the Balkans with the harmonic vocabulary and improvisational audacity of contemporary jazz. But, unlike some of his colleagues, Lefteris resists categorizing his compositions as a simple fusion of disparate influences. Instead, he insists on a holistic conceptualization of his music and its philosophical and practical underpinnings; all of it, he argues, emerges out of necessarily hybrid experiences and memories that are simultaneously personal and ancestral, an imbrication of Anatolian heritage and daily life as a transnational artist in New England. As we shall see, this is borne out in the musical details of his work, particularly on his 2016 album release, *Mediterrana*.[8]

Lefteris's lifelong engagement with musical traditions that were developed, nurtured, and constantly reinvented predominantly by Black artists immediately calls to mind two other Greek American pianists whose lifelong involvement with the world of American jazz stretches back to the immediate aftermath of the Great Catastrophe. The first is composer, producer, bandleader, and Rock and Roll Hall of Fame inductee Johnny Otis, who was born Ioannis Alexandros Valiotis in 1921 to Greek immigrant parents in Northern California and made a decision at a young age to live, musically and socially, as a member of the African American community; he did so in a conscious rejection of selective racism and white supremacy.[9] The second is legendary jazz pedagogue Charlie Banacos, who was born in 1941 in the Greek immigrant enclave of Lowell, Massachusetts, and whose groundbreaking ear-training methods had a profound impact on thousands of students, including luminaries such as Michael Brecker, Mike Stern, Wayne Krantz, Danilo Pérez, and, at the end of Banacos's life, Lefteris. Lefteris's studies with Banacos had a deep and lasting impact; aside from the technical and conceptual tools that he gained, revolutionizing his approach to composition and improvisation, he was impressed by Banacos's single-minded, spiritual devotion to music, exemplified in this quotation from Banacos:

Figure 3.1. Lefteris Kordis. Photo by Jarvis Chen.

> Music for me is like religion. In every religion there are the preachers who are touring all over the world to preach about religion, and the monks, who sit in a basement, practice for themselves, and teach others. I am the monk.[10]

This ascetic orientation takes on simultaneously mystical and practical dimensions in Lefteris's life and work. Stepping into his home studio or being in his presence during a performance—whether sharing the stage or observing from the audience—one is immediately aware of an environment swirling with consciously focused creative energy, what Lefteris simply calls "the zone." Talking to Lefteris about this zone and the relationship between his formative musical experiences and his current work reveals a trajectory that immediately calls to mind Banacos's analogy to spiritual discipline: a lifetime of exhaustive analytical and technical practice infused with a series of almost mystical encounters with the physical vibrations of musical sound and the bodies that produce them, encounters that have served as way stations of initiation and lasting inspiration on his own journey as an artistic pilgrim.[11]

Lefteris was born in 1977 in Elefsina, a medium-sized town on the northwestern outskirts of Athens that in antiquity was the site of the Eleusinian Mysteries, annual initiations into the cult of the goddess Demeter and her daughter Persephone. Lefteris's neighborhood, Sinoikismos, was built in the 1920s in the wake of the Great Catastrophe to house refugees arriving from Asia Minor, including his paternal grandfather, who survived the burning of Smyrna as a toddler, and his maternal grandmother, a Turkish-speaking Greek from a village in Cappadocia. His mother's father was an Arvanitis, a descendant of Albanian-speaking migrants to the southern Balkans in the late Middle Ages, and his father's mother was born in the mountainous Roumeli region of central Greece. Aside from these communities, the neighborhood was home to a sizable population of Turkish-speaking Muslims from Serres in Greek Macedonia and a number of settled Roma. The music of these diverse migrant communities permeated young Lefteris's childhood in the 1980s; celebrated Greek clarinetists played for dancing every weekend at an outdoor stage in front of his grandmother's house, and the streets behind echoed with the sounds of three-day-long Turkish weddings, which the entire neighborhood attended. At home, he absorbed the Asia Minor repertoire sung at family gatherings, and sat for hours by the radio with his grandfather listening to the great voices of *dimotika*, the folk music of central Greece. His Smyrna-born grandfather was a chanter of Orthodox liturgical music, and his great-uncle ran a Byzantine music school where Lefteris learned the basics of that modal singing tradition.

As a child, Lefteris was particularly fascinated by the various drums he saw and heard around him, and at the age of four convinced his mother to sign him up for lessons at a local *odeion*, or music school. When they entered the building, he was immediately drawn to a drum set in the corner of the room, and he went into something of an ecstatic trance: "I have such a vibrant memory of seeing those drums for the first time. . . . I don't know where my mother went, but I sat there at the drums and I lost myself." He was awakened from his reverie by the director informing him that he was too young to take drum lessons. But if he started on piano for a year he could then take them up. He agreed, and though he became so absorbed by the piano that he never formally studied the drums, he believes that his approach to playing the keyboard bears a significant percussive influence.

Another quasi-mystical childhood experience that left a profound mark on Lefteris connects this early fascination with drums with a lifelong affinity for Romani music and musicians. One of his second-grade classmates in Elefsina was a much older Roma boy who had been repeatedly ignored by school staff and made to repeat the same grade time and again. Lefteris heard him play the *tuberleki* goblet drum and followed him around the schoolyard at recess one day begging him to demonstrate the Romani *tsiftetelli*, or belly dance rhythm. While his other friends ran off to play soccer, Lefteris overturned a cylindrical metal trash can and handed it to his classmate. "This guy, who everyone mocked and looked down on because of his race and his accent, played an incredible *tsiftetelli* that took hold of my body and transported me. . . . I remember it now and my hair still stands on end." This was the first of many encounters with Roma musicians over the course of Lefteris's life; as he explains, "I have a special connection with them that goes back very far. I never looked at them in the racist way that the majority of Greek society does—to me, they're my brothers, the same with the Turkish speakers and other kids from my neighborhood."

Throughout his adolescence, Lefteris focused on classical piano and music theory at the National Odeion in Athens, studying with German school pianist Eva Stange. Simultaneously, he attended classes in traditional music at the Music Gymnasium and Lyceum of Pallini with some luminaries of the thriving *paradosiaka*, or urban Greek folk music scene,[12] and he spent his free time at his home piano, picking out John Lennon's solos on Beatles records, experimenting with free improvisation, and fulfilling requests for folk and popular songs. "I became the household jukebox," Lefteris remembers. "My family and their friends would grill me on everything from the ballads of his childhood to postwar *rebetika*, the bouzouki music of films and nightclubs."

At eighteen, Lefteris left home to study classical piano at Ionian University on the island of Kerkyra (Corfu). There he had another significant experience. Hearing that he was interested in learning more about jazz, a friend sent him a copy of Keith Jarrett's massively influential album *The Köln Concert*, a live recording of solo piano improvisations performed at the Cologne Opera House in January 1975. Lefteris describes his reaction to putting on the cassette tape in his dorm room one rainy winter afternoon:

> It sent a shock through my body. I thought, "Oh, this is jazz? This is what I've been doing all along!" Not on the profound level that he

> was, of course, but improvising and telling stories at the piano. It was a transcendental experience. I went into a state that I can't describe in words—but I couldn't control my tears or my consciousness. It was something primordial. I just lost myself, I disappeared. And I knew that's how I should play classical music—Beethoven, Brahms, all of that. I suddenly understood all those things about interpretation that hadn't clicked yet, through the world of jazz.

Lefteris formed a group with other students and began playing jazz standards at a local bar, going progressively deeper into his explorations of the repertoire and idiom. In the summer of 2000 he and his partner, singer Panayota Haloulakou, traveled to Boston for a summer program at Berklee College of Music. Though the classes were helpful, most significant was being in such an international, culturally pluralistic US environment for the first time. Hanging out at the legendary Wally's Café, watching the avant-garde jazz group The Fringe, and being around young improvising musicians from all over the world changed everything for the two young artists and opened their ears and minds to new worlds of musical possibility. After finishing their degrees in Greece, Lefteris and Panayota moved to Boston on Fulbright fellowships to study at the New England Conservatory, where Lefteris completed an MA and DMA in jazz performance, working with saxophonist Steve Lacy, trombonist Bob Brookmeyer, pianists George Russell and Danilo Pérez—now his colleague at the Global Jazz Institute—and, of course, Charlie Banacos.

Most importantly, Lefteris says, he met and got to know African American musicians for the first time and experienced, up close, specifically Black ways of making and understanding music. "It was something far beyond what I could hear on records. It was that groove, that vibration that you get from being in the physical presence of another person who brings their lifetime of experiences and their inheritance, to bear on what they're communicating in that moment." At some point, a friend asked him to sub on a gig playing organ at an African Methodist Episcopal church, which led to a regular engagement for weekly services and a profound musical and spiritual apprenticeship. When he began playing at the church, Lefteris had already completed years of intensive study, was a seasoned professional performer, and had listened to hundreds of hours of gospel and blues. But, accompanying the preacher, a septuagenarian native of New Orleans, he felt new physical vibrations that helped him make connections that had eluded him previously.

> I had listened to Blind Willie Johnson, for example, and thought, OK, that's the blues, I get it, but I hadn't understood anything until feeling it in my body, hearing and feeling those vibrations. And then I said, ahh, *that's* jazz!—one of the many things that is jazz, anyway. But that's the *folk* element of the music, that's where it comes from—I felt that with my body, that *this* blues was the prime source of the music that captivated me. The choir sang in French Creole, something else I didn't even know existed. And the preacher helped me a lot. I know how to improvise, my ears work very well, but he helped me understand how to improvise together with him, to find his note and to follow, to harmonize, but not just with chords, through rhythmic structures too, and how to improvise together in the context of preaching—the deeper context, not "Hmm, I'll put an E diminished chord over his A flat because it'll sound cool," but communication on a deeper level, not even looking at or thinking about my hands, just feeling and reacting.

For the first time Lefteris was taking all the work he had done in the practice room—all the technique, all the transcribing, all the ear training with Charlie Banacos and his other mentors—and letting it flow out of him in truly spontaneous, inherently communicative creation.

Parallel with his immersion into the various worlds of African American popular and sacred music, Lefteris continued performing the music of his childhood in the new context of New England's Greek diaspora, playing keyboard at weddings, baptisms, parish socials, and nightclubs. This, too, was a mind- and repertoire-expanding experience; he would routinely receive calls to play for communities from parts of Greece whose local repertoire was completely unfamiliar to him.

> So I needed to learn, for example, dozens of songs from Agrinio in western Greece, heavy clarinet music; I had to do a ton of research for those gigs, and it opened my mind hugely, influenced me deeply. I'm preparing a project now of seven tonal "watercolors" that are inspired by the way Giannis Vasilopoulos plays the clarinet. And it all started because of a wedding for some people from Agrinio and having to learn their repertoire.

While immersing himself in American jazz, Lefteris also established a reputation as one of the few non-Pontian Greek keyboardists capable of playing the Black Sea migrant community's complex, angular dance music, which accompanied the *kementzes* (a three-string upright fiddle) and *daouli* (a double-headed bass drum) over rapid five- and seven-beat rhythmic cycles. In these situations, he says, propelling circles of shoulder-shaking dancers around the floor, he came to a realization analogous to his epiphanies about the zone of intensely focused collaboration that surrounded the Creole preacher in the African Methodist Episcopal church as Lefteris accompanied him.

> Suddenly I understood the huge responsibility that I have, rhythmically speaking. I understood that when I'm playing in that context, I'm not making art or fooling around; I have to be 100 percent present to move that united body of stomping feet. . . . I understood the relationship with the dancers, the lead dancer, that back and forth—and that helped me to understand, by extension, how I can open a channel with the audience at a concert, with the musicians around me. It doesn't always work, but I've understood that it's possible through those experiences with Pontian dancers.

Over nearly two decades of living, studying, and working in Boston, all of these cumulative experiences have allowed Lefteris to, as he puts it, find some distance from the four "trees" of his genealogy, rooted in the Cappadocian hinterland, the Aegean coast of Asia Minor, the Greek-Albanian community of Attica province, and the mountains of central Greece. From this new distance, he explains, he can see "leaves and branches and even roots that I never perceived before, and I can water them differently. And I can experience the traditions that we have in Greece in a different context, see the connective tissue that unites us with Turks and Bulgarians and Israelis and Egyptians and Italians and others."

This distance, and the awareness of these connections—gained through all those years of intensive study and immersion in the world of contemporary improvisation and compositional techniques—have led Lefteris to explore new ways of nourishing that ancestral bower, drawing simultaneously on the modal traditions of Greek, Turkish, and Balkan music and the tonal prerogatives of modern jazz to cultivate entirely new growth. One recent approach that has borne exceptional fruit in the form of his 2016 recording *Mediterrana* is his practice of taking various *makams*—the modal melodic pathways of Near and Middle Eastern folk, classical, and liturgical music—adjusting their intervals to the even-tempered piano, and then building chords and working out harmonic functions and progressions based on the modified *makam*'s melodic identity in a diatonic environment. For example, instead of the seventh chords of the diatonic major mode from C—C major 7, D minor 7, E minor 7, F major 7, G dominant 7, A minor 7, and B diminished 7—the *makam neveser*, which is characterized in its modified even-tempered form by a major second, minor third, raised fourth, minor sixth, and major seventh (from C, the pitches C–D–E♭–F#–G–A♭–B), produces the following chords: C minor major 7 (i maj7), D dominant flat 5 (II7 ♭5), E♭ augmented major 7 (III+ maj7), the first inversion of an A♭ dominant 7 (functioning here as a #IV7), G major 7 (V maj7), A♭ major 7 (♭VImaj7), and B minor 6 (vii-6). Applying this process to the repertoire of commonly-played *makams* in the Greek and Turkish modal system produces dozens of new tonal environments to choose from in addition to the standard Western major and minor modes.[13]

Lefteris, like his mentor Charlie Banacos, speaks about these tonalities and chord qualities in terms of colors, each of which has a unique, unmistakable character. Many of the central melodic and harmonic ideas on *Mediterrana* are based on what Lefteris calls a major sharp 2 color, where the seventh degree of the scale is major (in the context of *makam*, "natural" in the Pythagorean sense) when the melody is ascending and flattened on the descent. These are prominent features of the fourth plagal mode in Byzantine music, for example, and the *makam rast* in Greek, Turkish, and Arabic music.[14] For his part, Lefteris interprets this color in terms of the bright, nourishing light of the Mediterranean sun: a sun that he misses terribly, feels deprived of in his daily life in gloomy New England, but whose memory, and the knowledge that it exists, gives him hope. And the figure of the stylized goddess of light portrayed on the cover of the album is an apt metaphor for what Lefteris strives to be through his music: a channel for the connections between heritage, personal experiences, ancestral memories, and the ever-opening moment of the now that leads into the future.

Two of the pieces on *Mediterrana* are particularly resonant examples of this spirit-saturated and memorial approach to composition and improvisation—in Lefteris's words, music as "imagination, fairy tale, and emotion"—inspired by quasi-mystical experiences analogous to the others discussed earlier. The result is deeply transcultural. The opening track, "In the Land of Phrygians," was born out of Lefteris's visit several years ago to his grandmother's native village of Sinaso (now Mustafapaşa in Turkish), in the Nevşehir area of Cappadocia in central Turkey. As he tells it, the composition—which begins with an improvisation on the *ney*, or end-blown cane flute, by his old schoolmate Haris Lambrakis before the entrance of the core jazz ensemble of piano, bass, and drums, augmented by a microtonal pitch-shifting keyboard reminiscent of Romani wedding ensembles—came out of his experience of being physically present on that ancestral soil while recalling his grandmother's vivid tales of her youth there, of friendships and harmonious relations with her Turkish neighbors. As he walked through the streets of the village, looking at abandoned houses and empty flowerpots, he began to weep.

> I don't believe that we only carry around our own experiences, but also those of previous generations, and things that haven't been solved, so to speak; we have to solve them so that they're not passed on. I think the refugee element is very strong in this way, in other peoples too. It's something that is passed on, it doesn't leave easily. That pain of being a refugee, of being uprooted—my body tells me that it's lived it, even though in my own life it never happened to me. That pain, and those memories, give me a direction.

Another composition from *Mediterrana*, "Journey with Pilgrims," engages even more explicitly with a metanarrative of forced migration, loss, imaginative return, and spiritual inheritance. Through instrumental role-playing between the piano, chromatic harmonica (played by Israeli Roni Eytan), and *laouto*, or steel-string lute (played by fellow Greek Vasilis Kostas), the three musicians featured on the track interpret characters, scenes, and emotional memories from a trip Lefteris took with his grandparents as a small child to a shrine on the island of Evia near Athens. The shrine houses the remains and relics of the eighteenth-century Saint John the Russian of Cappadocia, the patron of Lefteris's maternal grandmother's native region; everyone on this particular trip, he recalls, was an Asia Minor refugee or descendant thereof, and their chartered tour bus was full of singing, clapping, and dancing for the entirety of the journey. When they arrived and paid their respects, they took young Lefteris into the room where the saint's relics were housed; the priest dressed him in John's belt, hat, and tunic, for him to take his blessing:

> It was a completely metaphysical experience. I saw his desiccated remains, but I wasn't afraid . . . I felt that energy. Everyone was so focused, so together, one body, one community on a pilgrimage. Afterwards we all went to a tavern. They brought out wonderful

> Anatolian food. They produced a guitar, an accordion, and a drum, and we sat singing and eating under the grape arbor, the sun's rays falling through the leaves. . . . All of that stayed with me all these years as a magical experience. So that piece, "Journey with Pilgrims," is as if you're standing on a hill watching them being bathed in the sacred light of that sun of my childhood.

Facing the ever-increasing difficulties of making a living performing this kind of art—"The deeper I go into my relationship with music, my fellow musicians, with God, if you like, the more challenging things get professionally"—Lefteris views his role as a music educator as the most direct and powerful way he can make a real difference in the lives of young people from all over the world who have come, as he did two decades ago, to study jazz in Boston. He sees himself not simply as an instructor who comes to campus to teach harmony, theory, composition, rhythm, and improvisation, but as someone with a responsibility to remind students of their common humanity and boundless potential. Reflecting on this responsibility in the specific context of twenty-first-century America, in a social and political environment rife with hateful rhetoric, alienation, and casual cruelty, Lefteris offers a concrete example of how the jazz vocabulary that he has internalized can change the way we listen to the world around us:

> Here's something very basic but very profound, going back to the core qualities that I learned from Charlie Banacos. If we take the major seventh chord and add extensions—if we proceed through all of them until we get to a flat 15 (in the context of a C major 7, a D♭ two octaves above the root C), some students say, "Hey, that flat 15 is forbidden. Flat 2 on top of a major seventh is an avoid note!" But if we take it arpeggiated, it's just a step. Same with the fourth, it's an avoid note in major seventh. And it grows from there. When we make this relationship between consonance and dissonance liquid, things start to shift. The conception of consonance begins to expand; before the student couldn't hear the sharp 11 or the flat 15, and then they can. It sticks! It's not an avoid note anymore, it doesn't cause dissonance. And then it becomes beautiful. And if you accept dissonances in music, if you contextualize them in a philosophical sense in society, you start accepting people and ideas that don't conform to your preconceived notions. Until one day you hear all twelve notes of the chromatic scale in the context of a major seventh chord and

> everything sounds consonant, like a symphony. That's what it is! Our earth, all the people, colors, nationalities, animals, nature . . . that's an example. I tell them: you're studying *music*! You have a tool in your hands, one of the most powerful tools there is. It's not just to play concerts and get applause and likes on Facebook. It can work magic, and it can heal.

In its melding of Anatolian and Black Atlantic elements through spiritually charged bodily experience, Lefteris Kordis's music is complex and expansive, with ample room for the engaged listener to find a diversity of provocative propositions. In the spirit of fellow pilgrims Johnny Otis and Charlie Banacos, it is one of the latest iterations of a century-old zone of contact between Greek migrants and African American popular music; but in its explicit mining of ancestral vibrations from the Greek Aegean, it may prove to be a template for more sustained and consonant dialogue between the inherited past and the ever-emergent present.

Hearing the Multiple "Sonic Homelands" of the Ethiopian American Diaspora[15]

The violence of the Ethiopian revolution (1974–1991) along with the Eritrean civil war marked the beginning of a mass migration from the Horn of Africa to destinations worldwide.[16] Of the estimated five million refugees who have departed from Ethiopia, Eritrea, and Somalia from 1974 until the present, musicians constituted only a small, and on the surface, seemingly inconsequential number. However, the United States quickly became the site of the largest community of Ethiopians outside of their historical homeland, with a notably large number of musicians settled in the Washington, DC, metropolitan area.[17]

The Ethiopian diaspora is in the early twenty-first century an intensely heterogeneous musical scene. One finds repertories associated with traditional Ethiopian ethnic musics widely performed, especially at Ethiopian restaurants, community events, and domestic celebrations such as weddings. Many Ethiopian Orthodox churches have been founded across the United States, with more than a dozen Orthodox institutions as well as additional Ethiopian churches of both evangelical and other denominations in Washington, DC, alone; most Ethiopian Orthodox congregations seek to perform as much of the esoteric Ethiopian chant tradition as available clergy can muster. Finally, there is an active Ethiopian popular music scene that runs the stylistic gamut of musical repertories drawn from Ethiopian and African American genres, especially jazz, hip-hop, and blues, as well as some styles in world music, such as reggae.[18]

Since the end of the Ethiopian revolution in 1991, musical life in the Ethiopian American community has reestablished ties to musical developments in Ethiopia, with considerable movement of musicians and repertories back and forth between homeland and diaspora. Ethiopian singers come for tours of varying length across the United States and Canada, visiting clubs and mounting concerts in major Ethiopian centers such as the Washington, DC, metropolitan area, Los Angeles, the San Francisco Bay Area, Seattle, Atlanta, Dallas, Houston, Chicago, Las Vegas, Minneapolis, New York, Boston, and Toronto. Since 1991, too, Ethiopian musicians have traveled back to Ethiopia to perform concerts, with a number returning since the early 2000s for extended visits, and a few to reestablish residency in Ethiopia.

The Ethiopian American diaspora thus provides an example of a rapidly changing musical scene that has sustained dialogue with its historical homeland. Additionally, there are sizable Ethiopian diaspora communities located across Africa, Europe, Australia, and Canada that are also in constant, close touch with their counterparts in the United States through active concert circuits, travel, ubiquitous internet connections, and a variety of digital sound media. This case study seeks to shed light on the complex interaction of the Ethiopian American musical community with other Ethiopians in their homeland and in diaspora locales abroad to demonstrate that the Ethiopian diaspora in the United States is in fact a lively musical contact zone,[19] not a bounded Ethiopian American diasporic musical scene. A representative case study can clarify the creative processes through which Ethiopian diasporic musical styles have become transnational hybrids, combining elements of a variety of Ethiopian traditional and popular musics with a range of American popular traditions, as well as influences from a panoply of other styles that float in and out of musicians' experience from multiple sources.

For insight into the musical processes at work here, I focus on the career and music of Ethiopian American singer-songwriter Meklit Hadero. Meklit was born in the Ethiopian capital, Addis Ababa, although her father was from the Kambata ethnic group in the southwestern Ethiopian region today known as the Southern Nations, Nationalities, and Peoples Regional State.[20] Her mother was from the Amhara community dominant in Ethiopian political life until the beginning of the revolution. Meklit spent her first year in the care of family members in Ethiopia after her parents departed shortly after her birth in 1980 for

Figure 3.2. Meklit Hadero. Photo by Camille.

medical fellowships in East Germany. They were reunited in Europe during 1981, and a year later, the Hadero family received asylum in the United States. They lived in a number of American locales, including Iowa, New York, and Florida, a peripatetic existence during which Meklit was exposed to Ethiopian music primarily by auditing her parents' collection of cassettes. But Meklit was also early on "a student of the greats like Joni Mitchell and Bob Dylan" and had a "special affection for Leonard Cohen," whose music she encountered through hearing Nina Simone's version of his song "Suzanne."[21] Meklit identifies herself as an Ethiopian American who lives "on both sides of the hyphen," an apt description as well of her musical identity.[22]

A graduate of Yale in 2002 with a degree in political science, Meklit has resided since 2004 in the San Francisco Bay Area. Her musical career was launched when she composed her first song in 2005 and subsequently released her first album in 2007. With six albums now in circulation, the last two published by Six Degrees Records, Meklit's music has climbed the iTunes World Music and North American Community and College Radio World Music charts. She has also performed at major venues and festivals nationally and internationally, was named both a TED Global Fellow and TED Senior Fellow, and has undertaken residencies at various academic institutions.[23]

Known for her thoughtful lyrics, Meklit has come over time to embrace a number of styles. Her first commercial CD, *On a Day Like This*,[24] moves through the course of a day, narrating different moods and experiences in its ten songs. But the tight temporal focus belies its stylistic diversity as Meklit experiments with multiple styles from jazz to blues, accompanying many songs with her acoustic guitar and an ever-changing, unconventional band constituted of electric guitar, bass, drumkit, bass, cello, viola, piano, a variety of woodwinds and brass, and even a Middle Eastern *ney*. Meklit credits her inspiration to multiple sources, and her musical styles shift rapidly within and among the songs, for instance, incorporating New Orleans-like instrumental choruses (Track 2, "Float and Fall"); blues ballads (Track 4, "You and the Rain"); and innovative covers of classics such as "Feeling Good" (Track 5) from the 1964 musical *The Roar of the Greasepaint—The Smell of the Crowd*.[25] Meklit's treatment of this well-known song is unconventional and borders on the cross-cultural, as it begins with a solo *ney* introduction followed by a long, unaccompanied vocal passage. On this first album, Meklit's Ethiopian homeland influences are clearly apparent: included is a well-known traditional song in the Amharic language, "Abbay Mado" ("Beyond the Nile"), popularized by renowned Ethiopian singer Mahmoud Ahmed on his breakthrough album *Ere Mela Mela*.[26] The only song not in English on the album, "Abbay Mado," features a syncopated rhythm underscored by the call-and-response between Meklit's voice and the solo trumpet part. Subsequent songs on *A Day Like This* have an Afro-Latin/Caribbean twist with occasional blue notes, appearance of the clave, and big-band sound. Throughout, Meklit reshapes her vocals in classic blues style, inflecting different timbres and bending the pitch. In sum, Meklit's first album moves across multiple repertories of different cultural origins, embracing styles from folk to jazz to blues, and incorporating influences of African American, Latin, and Ethiopian origin.

Meklit's 2014 CD *Meklit: We Are Alive* exhibits a similar heterogeneity of repertory and styles. One listener summed it up with the observation that Meklit is "constantly bringing together the tattered corners of a disparate and fragmented world."[27] Once again, Meklit embraces multiple styles and repertories: The title song, "We Are Alive," incorporates elements of samba and a variety of sonic effects, "including a Casio that sounds like an electric kalimba."[28] Most songs on this CD are composed by Meklit, with the exception of a traditional Ethiopian tune "Kemekem" ("I Like Your Afro"), along with a soul-influenced cover of Sting's "Bring on the Night." Meklit's "A Train" riffs on Billy Strayhorn's classic song for the Ellington Orchestra, "Take the A Train."

Other tracks provide a glimpse of Meklit's deep engagement with Afrofuturism, an African American philosophy and aesthetic usually attributed to the creativity of jazz musician Sun Ra (1914–1993) and described as an "intersection of imagination, technology, the future, and liberation."[29] The term *Afrofuturism* was coined by cultural critic Mark Dery in 1994, describing philosophical and artistic exploration that seeks "to unearth the missing history of people of African descent and their roles in science, technology, and science fiction."[30] Meklit's songs such as "Stuck on the Moon" reflect this aesthetic, which emerged full blown on the CD *Copperwire Earthbound* in collaboration with fellow Ethiopian diaspora musicians Gabriel Teodros and Burntface (Elias Fullmore).[31] *Copperwire Earthbound* traces the path of a "crew of rogues" in a missing space craft (named *Copperwire*) stolen to an unknown location at an unknown time, with destinations of Addis Ababa and places beyond the solar system and Milky Way. Afrofuturism is also closely wedded to diaspora consciousness in Meklit's 2017 CD *When the People Move the Music Moves Too,* especially the stunning track "Supernova," also released as a music video.[32] Meklit notes that "when someone asks you where you are from, you name a country and it means something. . . . But beyond place, there are older stories, of hydrogen, helium, and the stars."[33]

If each of Meklit's songs rarely remains within a single style, blending jazz, modern pop, soul, folk, and influences from outside the United States, her listening public is equally diverse. Her performances take place at varied sites such as the Berklee College of Music in Boston (March 22, 2014) and San Francisco's Yerba Buena Center for the Arts (May 21, 2016). In concert, Meklit often acknowledges and credits influences, for instance, paying homage to The Roots, the Philadelphia hip-hop band whose 1999 album *Things Fall Apart* reinforced Meklit's Ethiopian heritage, invisible to her at a time "when Ethiopia was not mentioned."[34]

Meklit summarizes her style as follows:

> I was born in Ethiopia, grew up in Brooklyn, and have lived for the past 14 years in the San Francisco Bay Area. These places are my sonic homelands and I make music that touches all of them. I am inspired by the unique melodies, rhythms and scales of Ethiopia. I am moved

> by the improvisation of Jazz. . . . The way it lets you make the music new every time you play it, and the connection it gives me to the heart and history of the US. I am a singer-songwriter at the core, deeply influenced by that American folk ethos that anyone can sing their truth if they can strum a chord or two.[35]

Meklit first traveled back to Ethiopia in 2001 after the revolution ended, visiting her homeland with her mother; her first duo performance there was in 2009.[36] Meklit's experience as an Ethiopian American musician raised in the United States in the 1980s and 1990s, incorporating ample contact with Ethiopia through recordings and the emerging internet and culminating with travel to the homeland, reflects a process of musical learning common to many young Ethiopian American musicians of her generation. This process also lays bare a deeper understanding of the manner in which Ethiopian diaspora musicians are global in their musical styles and artistic agendas, and the nature of the influences on them.

Here we must take into account an Ethiopian musician whose musical influence Meklit acknowledges and who is responsible for her turn in recent years to the style known as "Ethio-jazz." From early on, Meklit was familiar with the music of Mulatu Astatke, a revered and ubiquitous artistic presence both at home in Ethiopia and in the global diaspora through his widely circulated recordings and frequent concert tours. During her first whole-band concert in Addis Ababa in 2011, Meklit looked out into her audience and was thrilled to see Mulatu Astatke sitting in the front row; the two subsequently spent several afternoons together talking about music, and Meklit took to heart Mulatu's advice to "just keep innovating," making a commitment to innovate through the inspiration of Ethio-jazz.[37]

Mulatu's career also provided a model for Meklit in its global scope and hybrid musical style. A brief discussion of his pathway enables us to appreciate how the study of one diaspora musician has immediate implications for exploring the pathway of others. As the first prominent Ethiopian musician to live in the United States well before the 1974 revolution, Mulatu provided not just a highly successful musical model for Meklit, but also a kindred spirit. After a year in Boston during 1959–60, when he enrolled at the forerunner of the Berklee College of Music and then lived in New York City, Mulatu combined his knowledge of a full range of styles of Ethiopian secular and sacred musics with his exposure to African American and Latin jazz, innovating the Ethio-jazz style.

Although he returned to Ethiopia in the late 1960s after years composing, performing, and recording in New York City and subsequently maintained his primary residence in Ethiopia, Mulatu continued to spend long periods outside of Ethiopia performing internationally, sojourning for lengthy periods in the United States, where his daughter eventually settled and where he maintains deep musical ties.[38]

Meklit has observed that "Ethio-jazz comes from a hybrid soul."[39] But the style itself is so heterogeneous and flexible that it was possible for her to embrace Ethio-jazz and not just reproduce the past. In many ways, Meklit's jazz explorations constitute a series of new musical innovations that draw on the innovations of another. A brief look at Mulatu's experience can permit a better grasp of yet another dimension of Meklit's complex musical world.

Building on a musical foundation acquired in England, Boston, and New York, steeped in modal jazz, bebop, and Latin jazz, Mulatu joined traditional melodies and modes from his Ethiopian homeland with these global styles. Thus Mulatu's instrumental jazz is constructed of sonic content from his Ethiopian past, fused with the musical styles and even specific melodies he heard over time and in different places.[40] For instance, Mulatu's best-known composition, "Yekermo Sew," quotes and transforms as its refrain a melody borrowed from "Song for My Father," an instrumental piece composed in 1964 by Cape Verdean American jazz musician Horace Silver.[41] Melodic quotations and stylistic borrowings thus tie Mulatu's music simultaneously to the sonic world of his Ethiopian past as well as to the American jazz scenes of Boston and New York in the late 1950s and 1960s. Mulatu's compositions also implicitly acknowledge the sources of their own borrowings. For instance, "Yekermo Sew" (translated colloquially as "A man of experience and wisdom"), which dates to the late 1960s, foregrounds instruments that came into prominence during that period, including the Fender Rhodes electric piano as well as other new technologies of the day such as the "fuzz box" pedal that creates distortion in electric guitar sounds.[42] The sound of Mulatu's music thus locates itself both temporally and spatially in different times and places. One prominent devotee of Mulatu's music, the American film director Jim Jarmusch, so clearly perceived the imaginative geography of Mulatu's music that he referred to "Yekermo Sew" as "traveling music" and used this composition to accompany scenes of travel for the soundtrack of his 2005 film, *Broken Flowers*.[43] Mulatu's music does not map place in a cartographic or visual sense, but rather, through processes of musicking, recreating a sonic record of times and locales that inspired and continue to compel its composer/performer's creativity and style. Similarly, Meklit's compositions, most particularly her 2017 album, *When the People Move the Music Moves Too,* follow their own original path, uniting musical and human movement, drawing on familiar Ethiopian brass riffs and rhythms, Indigenous instruments, modes, and, occasionally, languages. At the same time, Meklit's style partakes fully of the twenty-first-century singer-songwriter's palette, tempered by the worlds of African American and Afro-Latin musics along with the aesthetics and racial politics that have shaped them.

Conclusions

There are clear and compelling parallels between the artistic and personal paths taken by Lefteris Kordis and Meklit Hadero over the course of their careers. Both were born in nations with millennia-old histories as cultural crossroads and the site of incessant mixing of peoples and ideas, whose respective musical heritages share a great deal of connective tissue through the modal liturgical music of Eastern Orthodox Christianity and a rich stew of influences from regional folk and classical musics, particularly genres associated with Muslim populations. Both are members of transnational diasporas that defy any simple notion of bounded communities, diasporas whose constant movement to and from the homeland have turned the entire globe into a fluid zone of cultural contact. Migration to the United States and immersion in genres innovated and developed primarily by Black musicians—jazz, blues, funk, and a diversity of Afro-Latin musics—led both Lefteris and Meklit to find deeply personal voices as performers and composers, pushing their art in new directions while consciously building on the analogous work done by previous generations of migrant musicians from their respective communities. And while one of them focuses primarily on instrumental improvised music and the other on songwriting, both pay conscious homage to collective pasts by articulating a profound connection that fuses spiritual and material heritage.

This examination of the two artists' work and respective philosophies also reminds us that, even in the absence of lyrical content or overt partisan posturing, musical creation in the migrant context is explicitly political. Each composition, each performance, each trip to the recording studio tracks the musician's perception of their place in society and their aspirations for the future. This political dimension is even more apparent through Lefteris's and Meklit's shared commitment to spreading the transformative power of music through education and community engagement projects. As artists who benefited from life-changing apprenticeships with community elders, both have committed themselves to passing on this aspect of the American migrant experience while blazing their own personal paths.

The catalytic influence of African American culture, music, and philosophy on the artistic and personal evolution of both Lefteris and Meklit points to an obvious but nonetheless important distinction between the two musicians and the scenes in which they operate. As an African-born American, Meklit presents and identifies as a person (and woman) of color, and views her music as uniting Ethiopian inspired rhythms, melodies, and instruments with African American repertories. But beyond fusing Ethiopian and African American musical styles, she considers her most recent album, *When the People Move the Music Moves Too*, as explicitly setting forth "the way that cultural shifts follow migration."[44] For Meklit, this builds on her own intimate relationship to African American identity:

> Growing up, man, hip-hop was one of those few places where I felt seen as an African woman. . . . I'm really interested in linking Ethiopian music and African American music and telling that story of inter-relationship, on these shores. I always think about how I'm here as an African woman because of the Civil Rights Act—that's when the immigration codes were opened up and African people were no longer restricted from coming to the States. Everything that I am stands on the shoulders of the Civil Rights Movement and the struggles of Black people in this country for justice and equality.[45]

On the other hand, Lefteris belongs to an ethnonational group that, despite enduring race-based discrimination in the early twentieth century in many places in the United States, completed its transition to ethnic whiteness and associated white privilege a full generation before his birth. His European citizenship, migration to America as a young adult, and residence in one of the nation's most progressive cities only increase his experiential distance from the racial tensions endemic to the musical culture in which he has lived and worked for the last two decades. Regardless, his deeply felt awareness of his refugee heritage, and status as an immigrant in an increasingly xenophobic political climate, have undoubtedly contributed to his affective and philosophical affinity for the power and beauty of African American musical culture.

Here we have taken a look at two immigrant musicians in the United States, both of whom innovate in incorporating and wedding multiple musical styles from their natal homelands, their adopted American home, and the wider world all around. Multiple streams of influence flow into their musics, which in turn contribute to a new stream of global American musical expression. What may have once been characterized as "American ethnic musical subcultures" today attracts new and diverse listening publics. As Meklit has eloquently observed, we must acknowledge that US music has carved out meaningful cultural space for new hybrid identities and provides a framework within which people can gather, connect, reflect, and grow collectively. Here we experience a new world of sonic expression "under the umbrella of American music," in the words of Joanna Ladd reviewing a CD by Meklit. "[It] wouldn't have been made anywhere else in the world, so doesn't that make it of this place?"[46]

Notes

1. See, for example, Oskár Elschek, "Ideas, Principles, Motivations, and Results in Eastern European Folk-Music Research," in *Comparative Musicology and Anthropology of Music: Essays on the History of Ethnomusicology*, ed. Bruno Nettl and Philip V. Bohlman (Chicago: University of Chicago Press, 1991), 91–109; and Gerard Béhague, "Reflections on the Ideological History of Latin American Ethnomusicology," in Nettl and Bohlman, *Comparative Musicology and Anthropology*, 56–68.

2. Our collaborative process emerged from our many discussions of the role of music in migratory processes in general as well as in the lives of individual musicians. Shelemay participated in the 2017 Radcliffe seminar hosted by Garrett and Oja, and in light of the resonance between the two case studies presented here—which we had been talking about for years—invited League to collaborate with her on this article.

3. Alexander Kitroeff, "Greek-American History and Unauthorized Immigration," *National Herald*, October 15, 2015, 13.

4. See Renée Hirschon, *Heirs of the Great Catastrophe: The Social Life of Asia Minor Refugees in Piraeus* (New York: Berghahn Books, 1998) and Richard G. Hovanissian, ed., *Looking Back, Moving Forward: Confronting the Armenian Genocide* (New Brunswick, NJ: Transaction Publishers, 2003).

5. See Panayotis League, "Echoes of the Great Catastrophe: Re-sounding Anatolian Greekness in Diaspora" (PhD diss., Harvard University, 2017).

6. See Yiorgos Anagnostou, *Contours of White Ethnicity: Popular History and the Making of Usable Pasts in Greek America* (Athens, Ohio: Ohio University Press, 2009).

7. Tina Bucuvalas, ed., *Greek Music in America* (Jackson: University Press of Mississippi, 2018).

8. Lefteris Kordis, *Mediterrana*, Inner Circle Music, 2016.

9. George Lipsitz, *Midnight at the Barrelhouse: The Johnny Otis Story* (Minneapolis: University of Minnesota Press, 2010).

10. Lefteris Kordis, "'Top Speed and in All Keys': Charlie Banacos's Pedagogy of Jazz Improvisation" (DMA diss., New England Conservatory, 2012), 6.

11. All quotations and biographical information in this section are taken from a series of personal interviews by Panayotis League with Lefteris Kordis in Brookline and Boston, Massachusetts, conducted from January 2016 to December 2018, and translated from Greek by League.

12. See Eleni Kallimopoulou, *Paradosiaká: Music, Meaning, and Identity in Modern Greece* (Burlington, VT: Ashgate, 2009).

13. For an exhaustive analytical study of a roughly analogous process of harmonization of *makam* music in the context of mid-twentieth-century Greece, see Risto Pekksa Pennanen, "The Development of Chordal Harmony in Greek Rebetika and Laika Music, 1930s to 1960s," *British Forum for Ethnomusicology* 6 (1997): 65–116.

14. See Walter Feldman, *Music of the Ottoman Court: Makam, Composition, and the Early Ottoman Instrumental Repertoire* (Berlin: Verlag für Wissenschaft und Bildung, 1996).

15. Kay Kaufman Shelemay thanks Meklit Hadero and Mulatu Astatke for multiple interviews, performances, and assistance in preparing this case study, carried out between 2007 and 2020 in Cambridge, MA, Stanford and San Francisco, CA, and Addis Ababa. Note that Ethiopians are traditionally called by their first names.

16. A small number of privileged Ethiopians traveled abroad to study in the years following the end of World War II. Mulatu Astatke, whose influence will be discussed below, was the first Ethiopian musician to study abroad in the mid-1950s, spending more than a decade living in Wales, Boston, and New York City. See Kay Kaufman Shelemay, "Ethiopian Musical Invention in Diaspora: A Tale of Three Musicians," *Diaspora* 15, no. 2–3 (2006): 303–20.

17. The exact numbers of migrants from the Horn of Africa to the United States is unclear for a variety of reasons enumerated in Steven Kaplan, "Ethiopian Immigrants in the United States and Israel: A Preliminary Comparison," *International Journal of Ethiopian Studies* 5, no. 1 (2010): 71–92. A reasonable estimate is approximately one million Ethiopians, Eritreans, and Somalis nationwide, with a concentration of perhaps 250,000 in the Washington, DC, metropolitan area. Musicians in the Washington, DC, area estimate that there are at least 150 musicians from the African Horn performing secular styles, along with numerous church musicians performing the liturgy at local Ethiopian and Eritrean churches. The second largest Ethiopian diaspora community, located in Israel, numbers nearly 120,000 (Kaplan, "Ethiopian Immigrants," 74).

18. Kay Kaufman Shelemay, "Music in the Ethiopian American Diaspora: A Preliminary Overview," in *Proceedings of the 16th International Conference of*

Ethiopian Studies, vol. 4, Svein Ege, Harald Aspen, Birhanu Teferra and Shiferaw Bekele, eds. (Trondheim: Norwegian University of Science and Technology, 2009), 1153–64.

19. James Clifford, "Museums as Contact Zones," chap. 7 in *Routes: Travel and Translation in the Late Twentieth Century* (Cambridge, MA: Harvard University Press, 1997).

20. This is one of the nine regional states into which Ethiopia was divided in 1991 at the end of the revolution. Donald Crummey, "Ethiopia," in *Encyclopaedia Aethiopica*, vol. 2, ed. Siegbert Uhlig (Wiesbaden: Harrassowitz Verlag, 2005), 396.

21. Siddharta Mitter. "For Meklit Hadero, Keeping It Real and Varied," *Boston Globe*, July 10, 2011.

22. Meklit Hadero, interview by Shelemay, Stanford, CA, December 11, 2015.

23. See Meklit's website at https://www.meklitmusic.com/ and the Yerba Buena Center for the Arts announcement of Meklit's appointment as the organization's chief of program at https://ybca.org/wp-content/uploads/2019/10/YBCA_2019-20_Season_Brochure_v7.1_LI-web.pdf, accessed November 14, 2020.

24. Meklit, *On a Day Like This*, Porto Franco Records, 2010.

25. This song, composed by Newley and Bricusse, entered Meklit's repertory through her engagement with the work of singer Nina Simone, who included a rendition of the song as the first track of her studio album *I Put a Spell on You*, Philips, 1965.

26. "Ere Mela Mela" (both the album and its title song) have a long history. First recorded in 1975 by Mahmoud Ahmed on Kaifa Records, the album was reissued in 1986 by producer Francis Falceto on the Crammed Discs label in Belgium and widely circulated. When Falceto initiated the *éthiopiques* series in 1999, he issued *Erè Mèla Mèla* as the seventh CD in that series. The song "Abbay Mado" is on both the original vinyl recording and the 1999 CD. See Francis Falceto, liner notes, *Erè Mèla Mèla*, Buda Musique, 1999.

27. Walter Mosley, "Seeking a Unified Field," liner notes, Meklit, *We Are Alive*, Six Degrees Records, 2013.

28. Thom Jurek, review of Meklit, *We Are Alive*, AllMusic, n.d., https://www.allmusic.com/album/we-are-alive-mw0002613363, accessed November 14, 2020.

29. Ytasha Womack, *Afrofuturism: The World of Black Sci-Fi and Fantasy Culture* (Chicago: Chicago Review Press, 2013), 9.

30. Womack, *Afrofuturism*, 17. Also see Mark Dery, "Black to the Future: Interviews with Samuel R. Delany, Greg Tate, and Tricia Rose," in *Flame Wars: The Discourse of Cyberculture*, ed. Mark Dery (Durham, NC: Duke University Press, 1994), 180.

31. Gabriel Teodros, Meklit Hadero, and Burntface, *Copperwire Earthbound*, Porto Franco Records, 2012. Gabriel Teodros (b. 1981) is an Ethiopian American rapper who lives in Seattle and a cousin of Meklit Hadero. Burntface is an African / Black Power collective with two dozen musicians, singers, rappers, web designers, activists, teachers, and visual artists. Originally an Ethiopian rap group, begun by Elias Fullmore (aka "The Profit") while he was in college in Atlanta, that released an underground classic recording, "U Abesha?" (Are

You Ethiopian?"), the collective grew to incorporate both Ethiopian and African American rappers. Today Elias lives in Los Angeles, and there are Burntface communities in Los Angeles, Seattle, Houston, New York, New Orleans, San Diego, Tanzania, and Addis Ababa. For more details on Burntface and its "revolutionary marketing," see Elias (Fullmore), *Tadias Online*, 2003, http://www.tadias.com/v1n5/AE_2_2003-3.html, accessed November 14, 2020.

32. Meklit, *When the People Move the Music Moves Too*, Six Degrees Records, 2017. For "Supernova" see https://www.youtube.com/watch?v=MvHnrEh63SE

33. Shelemay field notes, Stanford, CA, May 21, 2016.

34. Shelemay field notes, Stanford, CA, May 21, 2016.

35. Meklit Music, http://www.meklitmusic.com/faq, accessed November 21, 2020.

36. Mitter, "Meklit Hadero"; Meklit, interview by Shelemay, Cambridge, MA, March 26, 2019.

37. Mitter, "Meklit Hadero."

38. See Kay Kaufman Shelemay, "Traveling Music: Mulatu Astatke and the Genesis of Ethiopian Jazz," in *Jazz Worlds / World Jazz*, ed. Philip V. Bohlman and Goffredo Plastino, eds. (Chicago: University of Chicago Press, 2016), 239–57.

39. Shelemay field notes, Meklit Hadero in concert ("This Was Made Here: A Diasporic Odyssey"), Yerba Buena Center for the Arts, San Francisco, May 21, 2016.

40. Instrumental jazz was performed in Ethiopia as a result of the close alliance between Ethiopia, the United States, and Europe during and after World War II. Brass instruments of Western manufacture were introduced into Ethiopia much earlier, just before the turn of the twentieth century, and a distinctive style of Ethiopian big-band music was already quite popular in Ethiopian urban settings by the 1950s. Although Mulatu surely created a new, hybrid jazz style in the form of Ethio-jazz, he was not the first to perform jazz in his native land.

41. "Yekermo Sew" uses the common jazz form that begins with a distinctive "head," in this case a transformation of both the melodic phrasing and rhythm of Silver's melody along with expansion of its accompanying ostinato figure to reiterate the interval of an octave. The head is followed by a contrasting bridge, after which the head is repeated. This refrain is followed by a series of solo improvisations, after which the refrain returns. See Shelemay, "Traveling Music," 2016, for a lengthier discussion of "Yekermo Sew." See David H. Rosenthal, *Hard Bop: Jazz and Black Music* (New York: Oxford University Press, 1992), 48, for a history of the Horace Silver's "Song for My Father," from which Mulatu quoted, as well as Horace Silver, *Let's Get to the Nitty Gritty: The Autobiography of Horace Silver*, ed. Phil Pastras (Berkeley: University of California Press, 1966). Horace Silver died in New York on June 18, 2014.

42. Tony Bacon and Lynn Wheelwright, "Electric Guitar," *Grove Music Online*, January 31, 2014.

43. Jim Jarmusch, *Broken Flowers*, Focus Features, 2005. "Yekermo Sew" can be heard on Francis Falceto, ed., *Ethiopiques 4: Ethio-jazz & Musique Instrumentale 1969–1974* (Paris: Buda Records, 1998). Most of the music mentioned here can be accessed through commercial recordings or on YouTube.

44. Joanna Ladd, "Bursting into Color: Meklit's New Album 'When the People Move, the Music Moves Too' Blossoms with Ethio-jazz and Big-Name Guests," *48hills*, May 2, 2017, https://48hills.org/2017/05/meklit/

45. Ladd, "Bursting into Color."

46. Ladd, "Bursting into Color."

Performance and Social Justice

FOUR | Sounding Black, Acting White

Hearing Race and Racism in Gospel Performance

BRAXTON D. SHELLEY

WITH A REFLECTION BY CHERYL TOWNSEND GILKES

In the tense days that followed Donald J. Trump's inauguration as the forty-fifth president of the United States, an expression of support for the new president landed a gospel singer in a controversy from which she has yet to recover. Rather than simply stating her political preference, gospel artist Vicki Yohe shared on Instagram a sepia-colored meme, which shows a white man with long hair carrying luggage across a frontier-like landscape. According to the meme's caption, this man's inner thoughts were predictably fixated on travel: "ON MY WAY BACK TO THE WHITE HOUSE." Beneath the meme, posted January 22, 2017, Yohe wrote, "March all you want, protest all you want, President DONALD J. TRUMP is our President for at least 4 years, no weapon formed against him will prosper! You know you are doing something right when there is so much opposition !!! #exciting-times." As she weaponized scripture against the many marches that took place that January, Yohe used this Instagram post to assert that Trump's inauguration marked the return of Jesus, and a kind of righteousness, to the seat of executive power. Jesus was the baggage carrier—Trump, the reason for his return. While there is much in this post with which many have taken issue, Yohe was absolutely right about at least one thing: excitement was on the way, but it was not the kind for which she hoped.[1] As the aforementioned statement traveled across the digital landscape, multitudes of social media users reacted against the striking dissonance they experienced between Yohe's political utterance and the sonic politics that she, a white woman and self-described "black gospel singer," had practiced throughout her career.

This essay ponders the politics of black gospel performance, which, while often implicit, came into clear relief around the election of Donald J. Trump. The controversies surrounding Vicki Yohe's, Paula White's, and Tina Campbell's vocal support for the United States' forty-fifth chief executive highlight the understudied relationship between black gospel and the racialized character of American Christianities.[2] I will argue that these disputes disclose what is generally unspoken: gospel's function to many black religious communities is not simply liturgical, but it is also political. As the aesthetic form that binds together the diffuse network of churches, denominations, and practices often referred to as simply "the black church," the black gospel tradition carries a political burden—a necessary concern for black life.[3] To many, this sonic responsibility seemed to rule out supporting Trump's presidential candidacy.

The chapter begins with the storm surrounding African American gospel singer Tina Campbell's vote for Trump, using it to outline the politics of gospel, a mode of hearing that understands musical sound as an indication of political solidarity. I then proceed to Vicki Yohe's contradictory performances of an idealized musical blackness and a materialized political whiteness, examining interview data and social media posts alongside performances of "Because of Who You Are" and "I'm at Peace." The essay's third section takes a similar look at Paula White's preaching, another problematic venture toward a fetishized sonic blackness. Throughout, I will use the controversy surrounding Yohe's and White's dissonant sonic and political choices to grapple with the multiple, contradictory notions of race that pervade gospel performance. Although both Yohe and White have used gospel sound to cultivate long-standing relationships with African American religious communities, their political preferences suggest that their "ministry" is animated by a mishearing of this tradition. Their claims to hear and perform race, when compared to their incapacity to see or hear racism—in a meme or in a presidential candidate's discourse—expose the contradictions that animate their musical practice. Yohe's and White's simultaneous pursuit of a sonic blackness—the ultimate symbolic capital in Pentecostal worship contexts—and refusal of liberative politics represents an attempt to have it both ways: as they try to live on both sides of what Jennifer Lynn Stoever has called "the sonic color line"[4] they also demonstrate what I, following George Lipsitz, define as a possessive interest in blackness.[5] To conclude, the discussion turns away from these controversies to focus on their virtual venues, to what these cases suggest about how music scholars might make use of the veritable profusion of data—memes, tweets, and posts—that is produced and disseminated on social media platforms every day. I will suggest that these controversies highlight the roles music plays in "the technosocial production of race."[6]

"Whose Side Are You On?": The Politics of Gospel

According to exit poll data, 96 percent of African American women voted against Donald J. Trump in the 2016 general election. While 2 percent voted for a third party or failed to respond to the survey, a full 94 percent of black women voted for Hillary Clinton.[7] Both a continuation of long-standing voting patterns and a tangible reaction against the racist and sexist words and deeds that saturated the Trump presidential campaign, this collective exercise of the franchise gave vent to what the philosopher Tommie Shelby has called "a political mode of blackness." According to Shelby, this politics constitutes "a set of antiracist principles and goals [demonstrated by] commitment to those principles and goals and by identifying with, showing special concern for, being loyal to, and trusting other blacks."[8] Against this collective were the 4 percent of black women voters who supported Trump's candidacy, among whom gospel singer Tina Campbell is a particularly noteworthy case. As one-half of the Grammy Award–winning duo Mary Mary, a gospel fixture since 1999, Campbell spent two decades establishing herself as a skilled vocalist. From 2012 to 2017, as a costar on the VH1 reality television show named for her musical duo, Campbell added texture to her larger-than-life persona. By repeatedly inviting concert and television audiences into the musical, confessional, and personal dimensions of her life, she placed her musical persona in conversation with the ordinary duties and anxieties she managed each day. As she emphasized her capacity to relate to the fullness of her fan's experiences, Campbell unwittingly set the stage for the tremendous backlash that erupted when news of her vote for Trump spread in early 2017. As knowledge of her political preferences rent the cords of identification and understanding that had been woven between the singer and her audiences, Campbell faced significant commercial consequences: during this months-long controversy, the *Christian Post* reporter Christine Thomasos noted that "Tina Campbell . . . had to postpone her tour due to low ticket sales weeks after receiving backlash for revealing that she voted for President Donald Trump."[9] While Campbell explained her vote with reference to "some of the candidate's views on Christianity," she offered no list of specific statements or positions, leaving her audiences to imagine that her vote and its justification revealed an unexpected affiliation: Campbell suddenly seemed to have more in common with the roughly 81 percent of white evangelical Christians who supported Trump than with the black women who had been her strongest supporters.

The manifold negative reactions to Campbell's political choice were poignantly summarized in writer and theologian Candice Benbow's article, "Oh, How I love White Jesus: On Travis Greene, Tina Campbell, Vicki Yohe and Paula White."[10] Benbow, writing about Campbell's vote for Trump and gospel singer Travis Greene's decision to perform at an inaugural event, argued that the artists' largely black audiences "deserved their accountability to us. We deserved that they took stock in how their words and behaviors would impact us. Because more than Trump, more than the White evangelicals who now will invite them to their churches as tokens, we have been here for them."[11] What is at issue in Benbow's plea for accountability—and in the viral outrage that she channeled—is not a question of essentialism, but of expectation, sonic promises seemingly broken by contradictory actions. How does sound suggest solidarity? Campbell's paradigmatic gospel singing—robustly embodied growls, melismatic lines, and ecstatic movements—produces what Fred Moten calls a "phonic materiality,"[12] an affective surplus that doubles Roland Barthes's "vocal grain."[13] As Campbell's body and voice emphatically indwell each other, they materialize race and belief, yielding performances of what Ashon Crawley calls "Blackpentecostal breath."[14] Sonic blackness makes Campbell's performance of a political mode of whiteness all the more contestable. The dismay that took form in Benbow's demand for "accountability," then, vents an expectation for consonance between the sonic and political dimensions of Campbell's aesthetic. Moving beyond Campbell and Trump, what does this moment of rupture reveal about the politics that animate the black gospel tradition?

Campbell's controversy, and those of Yohe and White, to which we will soon turn, locate gospel's politics in the tangled threads of race and religion that pervade American religious history. In the aforementioned essay, Benbow contends that both Campbell's vote and explanation "ignor[e] the tradition of resistance upon which Christianity stands." But Benbow's contention is decidedly partisan, reflecting a liberationist strand of American Christianity's messy fabric. Taken together, Campbell's justification and Benbow's jeremiad illustrate American

Christianity's enduring function as a site and source of racial and political contradiction, such that the term "American Christianities" becomes a more fitting referent. As the sociologist Cheryl Townsend Gilkes has written, the fact that "American society's most segregated moments were also its most sacred moments . . . both reflected and generated the braided realities of religion, race and community."[15] Throughout its history, Gilkes asserts, American Christianity has been populated by opposing forces: "At the same time . . . dominant groups sharing ideologies of dominance and supremacy 'congregate' to segregate others, the segregated and excluded congregate to resist subordination and to assert their humanity."[16] From chattel slavery through the civil rights movements, from those who opposed women's suffrage to those who battle what Michelle Alexander terms "the New Jim Crow," American Christianities have been marked by persistent antagonism between "two civil religions."[17] In view of this, a phrase from a popular praise chant, "Whose side are you on?" functions as a synecdoche for the politics of gospel.

As one of the chief aesthetic products of the black church, gospel has been variously defined as a "crystallization of the African American aesthetic," "a symbol of ethnicity," and an exemplar of "ethnocentric energy."[18] The genre's political burden reflects the site of its emergence, the black church, a primary arena of the black public sphere, a collective function that, as Evelyn Brooks Higginbotham recounts, crystallized during Jim Crow, when, "by law, blacks were denied access to public space, such as parks, libraries, restaurants, meeting halls, and other public accommodations. In time the black church—open to both secular and religious groups in the community—came to signify public space."[19] Not a monolithic zone, "The church also functioned as a discursive critical arena—a public sphere in which values and issues were aired, debated, and disseminated throughout the larger black community." As it emerged from sites of ecclesial oppression and in clandestine assemblies,[20] the black church began as an oppositional space, in which, to return to Gilkes, to "construct ideas and strategies that contest and resist domination."[21] Many of the ideas and strategies that emerged from these religious collectives were materialized in sound. Both the "hidden transcripts" of the antebellum spiritual and the musical backdrop for many civil rights protests confirm the primacy of musical sound to liberative pursuits.[22] Thus, the politics of gospel reflects an intense focus on electoral choice in the community theater of the black church, from the earliest decades of the independent black church movement through the present moment. For, as Mark Anthony Neal writes, "Unlike mainstream concepts of representational voting, African-Americans [have] often viewed the franchise as something that was communally derived."[23] While its implications extend into brick-and-mortar edifices, the debates that are at issue in this essay began in digital forums of "the black church." These technosocial venues organize individuals and groups who, as articulated by Raphael G. Warnock, "consciously and unconsciously, live within the conflicting intersectionality of being black and Christian in America."[24] Like previous iterations of black religious assembly, what we might call *the virtual black church* continues to be animated by tensions between its priestly and prophetic functions, and by questions of the relative emphasis that should be placed on piety and protest, personal salvation and social justice. In fact, these online platforms paint an unusually vivid sense of the complexity and variety of black Christian thought. Notwithstanding these disputes, the collective derivation and exercise of the franchise—the fact that roughly 90 percent of African Americans vote in opposition to an equal percentage of white evangelicals—reveals the endurance of a political mode of blackness. If, as Tommie Shelby proposes, "[Blackness] should be understood in terms of one's vulnerability to antiblack racism,"[25] we can then understand how support for a candidate like Trump would be taken to transgress something fundamental, particularly when performed by those whose public life has been so bound up with the sonic substance of black Christian belief.

In the aftermath of the 2016 presidential election, the politics of gospel became a topic of viral attention through the controversies of Yohe and White, two white women who nevertheless have pursued identities as black gospel vocalists and exhorters. Yohe, a singer, and White, a preacher, have both built careers on sounding "black." Before turning to these matters, I want to emphasize that the black/white binary employed in the title and throughout this essay does not suggest that I subscribe to a reductionist understanding of racial (or other categories of) identity; rather it highlights the dyadic racial ideologies at work in these two cases. As Jennifer Lynn Stoever contends, "The black/white binary has never been about descriptive accuracy, but rather it is a deliberately reductionist racial project constructing white power and privilege against the alterity and abjection of the imagined polarity of 'blackness.'"[26] Hovering outside each enactment of this interracial exchange, this "sounding black," is an invisible and unmarked white musicality that, even if not the aesthetic preference, is still given the high ground of normativity.

Vicki Yohe

While she had been singing professionally since 1992, Vicki Yohe's fame ascended rapidly after her 2003 release *I Just Want You*, the album that formalized her connection to the Pure Springs Gospel label, led by CeCe Winans, a member of gospel's storied Winans family.[27] Yohe's description of this new business arrangement is cast in emphatically spiritual terms. In a 2006 interview, Yohe repeatedly expressed a desire to be "anointed," a supplication reiterated in one of that CD's tracks, a song Yohe composed when she was just sixteen years old, "Anoint Me, Lord." Yohe's tangled conceptions of musical style, race, and "the anointing" came to the fore when she discussed the marked career shift that followed the aforementioned CD's release:

> My father was a pastor of a mostly black congregation . . . [M]y father and mother both sang with a lot of soul. We always had Edwin Hawkins and Andrae Crouch playing in our house. That was the kind of music I grew up around. I'd record songs and felt like I was anointed but [creatively] I didn't feel like "this is really me." I struggled with that until I signed with CeCe Winans. I told the people at Winans' label, "Listen, I know the music I need to be singing and I know the style and I just haven't had anybody who really hit it, you know?"[28]

These comments clarify that Yohe's search for her musical self was also a quest for a new way to monetize her decades-long investment in black gospel music.

On January 22, 2017, two days after President Trump's inauguration, one of Yohe's social media posts revealed a different kind of investment. The much-discussed meme's essentially recombinant shape—the depiction of Jesus as a luggage-bearing pioneer, heading back to the White House—was amplified by Yohe's comments about the futility of protest. The red-hot controversy that followed this post prompted Yohe to issue apologies on radio and various social media platforms. The moment was kinetic, "the resistance" was mounting, but the intensity of the conversation that surrounded this social media post is, in some ways, surprising, mostly because of how unsurprising—demographically speaking—was her support for candidate Trump. I want to fasten onto the image and its reception for its insights into a broader set of questions: Why is it that this white evangelical support for Trump would come as a surprise, capable of eliciting the aforementioned outrage? How might this scene elucidate gospel's sonic politics? In what follows, I will contend that her many performances in black churches, in which she sang the repertoire mostly closely associated with them, both produced and relied on beliefs about the relationship between the sound of her voice and her relationship to black people. These expectations were breached by Yohe's practice of two contradictory politics of identity.

The meme in question communicates three interconnected messages. The first that Donald Trump's impending inauguration would be the cause for Jesus to return to the seat of executive power, a suggestion that runs counter to many perceptions of the forty-fifth president as an unsavory and immoral actor, one whose actions and character seem completely contradictory to Christianity. The second implication, which flows from the first, is that the Obama administration marked a moment when divine grace, signified here by the physical presence of Jesus, was absent from the White House. This constitutes a spiritual kind of birtherism: even as President Obama's birthright is no longer up for intelligent debate, Yohe and many others were certain that he could not also have been "born again." Third, this critique of the Obama presidency, which, according to the political commentator Roland Martin, "insults the faith of President Obama," doubles as a broadside against "the black church" as an invalidation of the institutions, individuals, and practices that have been so central to this singer's career.[29] This question of Yohe's relationship to black Christianity is intensified by the image, by the depiction of Jesus as a white man with long hair walking across a frontier-like landscape. While the retrospective illustration of a white pioneer Jesus is dissonant with the race and phenotype of the historical Jesus, it is highly consonant with the Jesus that has been the idol of white supremacists for centuries.[30] The resistance to such characterizations of Jesus's identity is materialized in memes that embed sociotheological critique in unlikely visual references. One paradigmatic digital artifact, posted by Facebook user Mar Mar Penn, repurposes an image of a bowl of cereal, which contains one regular cheerio in a sea of chocolate cheerios, to contest the fictive whiteness many project onto the historical Jesus. The meme humorously recalls the theologian James Cone's contention that "Jesus is black," which is an assertion that Jesus takes the side of the oppressed in their pursuit for liberation.[31] Interpreted in this context, Yohe's meme seems to suggest the opposite, that Jesus is aligned with white racism. If, as Lisa Nakamura proposes, "The internet allows 'common' users to represent their bodies and deploy their bodies in social, visual and aesthetic transactions," this deployment of a figurative body of Christ constitutes an aesthetic performance of whiteness, contrary to Yohe's aesthetic pursuit of sonic blackness.[32]

In stark contrast to the white identity politics that pervade the rhetoric of her chosen candidate, Vicki Yohe's musical personality has long been suffused by an interracial preoccupation. In a 2012 NPR interview Yohe, a white woman, discussed her approach to music-making in strikingly racial terms:

> White people want to come in and they want to sing the few songs, hear a sermon, and be out in 30, an hour, 90 minutes. Black people, we want to come in—look, we. See? *You see white but I'm really black.* OK. Black folks' songs, we're going to repeat a line about 40, 50 times. It's just kind of a cultural thing.[33]

Yohe's half-humorous deployment of "they" and "we" in this quotation illustrates her insistent efforts to position herself as a bearer of the black gospel tradition—a black gospel singer. While it might be tempting to think of this quotation as a jestful allusion to a much deeper fount of musical and cultural knowledge, the singer's much-maligned meme clarifies that her understanding of the tradition she claims really is that vacuous: that gospel music is thought to be a religious expression divorced from its creators' experiences of and resistance to white racism.

Yohe's gleeful appropriation of the reified traits she sees as central to a musical kind of blackness evidences what the sociologist George Lipsitz calls "the possessive investment in whiteness."[34] Lurking behind Yohe's desired blackness, "as the unmarked category against which difference is constructed, whiteness never has to speak its name, never has to acknowledge its role as an organizing principle in social and cultural relations."[35] Since, as Lipsitz notes, "Race is a cultural construct . . . with deadly social causes and consequences," Yohe's acquisitive zeal merits suspicion. The singer's metamusical commentary clarifies her investment, not in "an egalitarian mode of Spirit," but in the demarcation of "the sonic color line . . . a socially constructed boundary that racially codes sonic phenomena such as vocal timbre, accents, and musical tones."[36] Yohe's statement and practice "produces, codes, and polices racial difference through the ear, enabling us to hear race as well as see it."[37] When read against the much-discussed meme, Yohe's forceful answer to what Nina Eidsheim has called "the acousmatic question"[38] invites yet another interrogative: why "sound black" if Jesus is white? I suggest that, more than an attempt to distinguish herself from other singers, or to make space for herself with black audiences, Yohe's desire to sound black evidences a *possessive interest in blackness.* In Yohe's Pentecostal context, one where visible, audible, and palpable signs of divine presence—"the anointing"—are the most important qualities for musicians or ministers, a performance of musical blackness that, in Jennifer Lynn Stoever's words, can "trump notions of authenticity proffered via visible phenotype"[39] becomes the ultimate symbolic capital. Yohe's fetishization of "sounding black," that is, a kind of stereotyping that simultaneously idolizes and reviles, fuels the dissonance between her musical and political choices.[40] A possessive commitment to racial difference links Yohe's investment in whiteness and interest in blackness, which allows the former to extract value from the latter.

But how does Yohe pursue this musical blackness in her oeuvre? While the comment referenced above locates musical blackness in a kind of repetitive impulse, Yohe turns her performances toward ecstasy by aestheticizing musical meter. Consider Yohe's recording of Martha Munizzi's ballad "Because of Who You Are."[41] In her recording—and many enactments of this gospel ballad, Yohe begins with a heteroglossic declaration of adoration, "Hmmm! I worship you, Lord. Ooooooo, thank you. Hmmmmm! Thank you, Lord. I love you, Lord." These words adorn the keyboardists' iteration of the last two measures of the song's ten-bar A section, creating a compound introduction, which is elided into Yohe's initial statement of the song's verse:

> Because of who you are, I give you glory.
> Because of who you are, I give you praise.
> Because of who you are, I will lift my voice and say:
> Lord, I worship you because of who you are!
> Lord, I worship you because of who you are!

After Yohe's first iteration of this A section, the ensemble and the rhythm track enter to restate this material, making room for the soloist to adlib. Like the ensemble's entrance, the transition to the eight-bar chorus is announced by anacrustic instrumental accents. The motion into the chorus is especially significant because it highlights two concomitant inflections: (1) a shift from choral unison to harmony and (2) a rhythmic shift from an austere backbeat to percussive elements that sound on every sixteenth note of the B section. In this chorus, Yohe and the ensemble exclaim:

Jehovah Jireh, my provider!
Jehovah Nissi, Lord, you reign in victory!
Jehovah Shalom, my Prince of Peace!
And I worship you because of who you are!

After they cycle through one more iteration of the verse and two more presentations of the chorus, the second of which is intensified by a semitonal modulation, the ensemble and most of the instruments evacuate the texture, leaving Yohe and the keyboardist to finish the song with the freedom with which it began. This ending gesture reinterprets the fairly conventional "(ac)cumulative introduction,"[42] defining it as the first phase of a metrical experience that is bookended by the delayed entrance, gradual intensification, and eventual removal of the rhythmic track. While Yohe's performance of "Because of Who You Are" is an exemplar of "praise and worship," a genre "generally regarded as a subgenre of [contemporary] Christian and black gospel music,"[43] I contend that the iterative inflection of the song's form creates conditions for Yohe's performance of a musical blackness. The halting transitions created in the compound introduction, at the ensemble's entrance, at the beginning of the chorus, through the final chorus's semitonal modulation, and by the dramatic final reduction of the song's texture enact the kind of "irruptive gestures" that Moten finds "in the break"[44] of characteristically black expression. These affective articulations also enact the formal logic that I have elsewhere called "tuning up," a song-based incorporation of the black sermon's escalation from speech to song.[45]

Another of Yohe's standards, "I'm at Peace," has an even more dramatic relationship to rhythm and meter.[46] First, I want to note that this is the selection Yohe presented at the funeral of Alton Sterling, a black man killed by police in Baton Rouge, Louisiana, in July 2016. While her presence at this funeral, at the height of the Black Lives Matter movement and just months before Trump's election, points to the real ties she formed with various black religious communities—a reason for the intensity of the controversy surrounding her support for Trump—the sonic features of her performance are also quite remarkable. The song functions as a paradoxical source of assurance:

I'm at peace,
even though my heart is breaking.
I'm at peace.
I never thought I would be shaken.

But you came and laid your hands on me and now . . .
Oh oh Lord, you came and laid your hands on me and now . . .
I can see: my storm has moved away.

The song consists of one basic unit, which is never accompanied by any level of regular percussion. Her iteration of this verse, which gets repeated with slightly modified words, flows freely, standing apart from the groove-centricity of many gospel songs. Floating above the virtuosic rolling accompaniment on the keyboard, Yohe's repeated descent from the alto D♭ down to A♭ begins a tonal progression that does not reach resolution until the lyric "storm has moved away." Built into each stanza are moments where the singer breaks the flow of the lyrics to emphasize the Lord's arrival into the place of chaos. As the song unfolds, the disruptions are extended: the song's one section is fragmented, allowing for the reiteration of the key lyrics, "You came and laid your hands on me" and "You died for me on Calvary." Near the end of the performance, Yohe inserts lines from another gospel song, the Winans's "Ain't No Need to Worry," demonstrating both her mastery of the gospel repertory and her improvisational abilities. "I'm at Peace" aestheticizes a musical device that the religious studies scholar Ashon Crawley has written about, a "tendency in black gospel music to make any rhythmic song arrhythmic, to slow down standard so that the singer can play around and toy, tinker and trouble the structure. A mundane song gains new life by way of evacuating it of any such architectonics, yielding the song to a critique of normative modes of organization itself."[47] In "I'm at Peace," and throughout her catalog, Yohe treats a dialectical relationship to rhythm/meter as a device with which to access musical blackness.

Taken together, the aforementioned performances and the NPR interview illuminate the preoccupation with being a "black gospel singer" that made Yohe's support for Trump, as declared through the pioneer meme, grounds for consternation. A January 22, 2017, Facebook post from writer and activist Shaun King distills much of the reaction to Yohe's post.[48] King wrote an open letter to Yohe, citing his "need to strongly come against much of what [she,] a white 'Gospel' singer widely known for singing to Black audiences has done here." King makes three points: (1) a defense of President Obama's Christian faith, (2) an enumeration of Donald Trump's public and personal immorality, 3) a rewording of Yohe's post: "What I think you mean is that WHITE JESUS, and white supremacy are returning to White House. That is why you shared an image of a random white man with luggage. That's not Jesus and Donald

Trump is not ushering in the return of Jesus. Anyway, this is why fewer and fewer people want anything to do with American Christianity. It is simply a cover for your whiteness."[49] As King braided together questions of theology and race, he reanimated the many similar debates that have constituted American religious history.

Yohe's response to King, and many others who pushed back against her posts, proceeds from the familiar position of white evangelicalism. Although her post from January 23, 2017, begins with an apology for any hurt she may have caused, she immediately turned to a recapitulation of the basic belief behind the much-maligned meme, asserting, "It is true that I am excited by the thought of a government that will protect Christianity and not attack it."[50] This thinly veiled desire for "religious liberty," or, more accurately, "Christian supremacy," is buttressed by the claim that the policies of the Obama administration "went against what most Christians believe." Before outlining her post's negative reception—"continual attacks" and "vulgar messages"—and financial impact—canceled "ministry dates" and individual boycotts—she sought to soften the impact of her post by hiding behind the medium: "I posted this pic quickly after someone sent it to me."[51] In so doing, she blames both the unnamed sender, the unknown creator, and the sharing features of Instagram and Facebook for the decision to post. About this I make two observations: first, the fact that her virtual network was populated by those who would approvingly share such an image offers a richer sense of the contradictions between her purported sonic blackness and her resolutely white politics; second, that this image came to her attention did not require her to share it, with or without the aforementioned caption. At issue here is the question of technical mediation. While Yohe attempts to yoke causality to the sharing functions of Instagram and Facebook, the relationship between device and user, or the "actantial shape," is much more complex.[52] Facebook and other social media sites facilitate sharing; they afford and, indeed, encourage such dissemination, but they do not determine it. Sharing a post or meme, as Yohe did, is one of the central aesthetic acts through which race, belief, and other categories of human expression are materialized in the digital form. I want to suggest that sharing this meme/caption should be understood as an analogue to Yohe's singing, an affective performance that reverberated across the viral networks often referred to as Black Twitter.[53] Yohe's post constituted a digital performance of a distinctly political whiteness that invalidated her pursuit of sonic blackness, causing her to be disinvited from traditional musical venues—canceled.

Paula White

Like Yohe, Paula White, a Florida-based pastor, who has emerged as one of President Trump's most vocal evangelical allies, has come under scrutiny because of the dissonance between her radically conservative politics and her sonic investment in the black church. While at first glance, the support of a prominent evangelical minister for the candidate who won 81 percent of the evangelical vote would not seem to be remarkable, the racialized sonic politics White has practiced throughout her public career makes her alliance with the forty-fifth president the source of significant controversy. In a discussion of his mother's ministry with *Washington Post* writer Julia Duin, White's son, Bradley Knight, detailed relationships his mother developed while doing "inner-city" ministry work, associations that also became formative homiletic influences. As his mother "learned their vocabulary and cadence," Knight suggested, "the black community told her: you're a white girl who preaches black."[54] While one might take issue with the stereotypical sentiments expressed in Knight's comment, his words do point to a well-known aspect of Paula White's career.

Paula White's sermon "Can You Dig It?," delivered to a crowd of approximately fifty thousand (predominantly African American) women in 2000 at Bishop T. D. Jakes's "Woman Thou Art Loosed" conference, marked a critical moment in her path to fame. The sermon is drawn from 2 Kings, chapter 3, a text that depicts ancient monarchs struggling to feed their armies and animals in the midst of a drought-ravaged battle. These kings' path out of natural disaster hinged on their obedience to a prophetic command to dig ditches despite the scarcity of rain. White likened this prophetic utterance to the "illogical instructions" God gave to her "every time there was a dilemma." More than just obedience to an "illogical instruction," the act of digging would also create space for the ground to receive the promised downpour. According to White's sermonic scripture, when those caught in this precarious scene obeyed the prophet's instruction, the sky opened, yielding a torrent that enabled the kings, their armies, and their livestock to survive. In White's hands, this familiar story became a contemporary directive for the women who filled the storied Georgia Dome: they could experience transformation in their lives if they, like the ancient kings, would but dig.

In the climactic phase of her sermon, White made a marked shift in the sound and form of her delivery—she dug into the aesthetic resources of the black gospel tradition. Departing from her initial conversational style of delivery, a fairly unmarked mode of preaching, White turned toward incantation, hovering around A♭ as a tonal center. As she trained her utterances into a metrical flow, she also engaged the form of aestheticized breathing that scholars and practitioners of black preaching often refer to as "whooping." This musical shift, "tuning up," provided White a heightened musical space in which to oscillate between testimony and exhortation.[55] She proclaimed:

> I'm not a novice. This is not my first time. This is not my first dig.
> I know what it is to turn a corner and not know what utility is gonna be cut off.
> I know what it is to be on government cheese.
> I know what it is to have a baby look you in the eyes and not know how you're gonna put food on the table.
> I know what it is to have to pray for a raven to feed you.
> But God [said], "Paula . . . dig!"[56]

White recounted her own past difficulties, hoping that her words would resonate with her audience, inviting them to see themselves in her. As the ellipses in the preceding sentence illustrate, White interrupts her spoken discourse to dig out three shovelfuls of dirt. As she embodied the crux of her sermon, she emphasized this heightened sonic space's concomitance with a physical elevation: during this ecstatic phase of her message, White made the ancient scene come alive by preaching, not just from a lectern, but standing in a kind of sandbox. Preaching from this illustrative device, a box full of dirt, she held both a shovel and a microphone in her hands. She used these two tools to transmute the scripture's ancient desert into the host of contemporary sites that require believers to dig.

White's sermon displays an experiential focus that is a hallmark of black preaching traditions "where a moment is created in which the remembrance of a redemptive past and/or the condition of a liberated future transforms the events immediately experienced."[57] In both form and content, White recapitulates the pervasive belief that faithful actions can use spiritual power to transform one's material existence. In this case, the necessary action was digging, an ideal metaphor for the spiritual labors frequently referred to by such terms as "tarrying," "travailing," "pressing," and "tapping-in," each of which denotes the embodied pursuit of divine blessing. White exclaimed:

Dig
Dig your way into your blessing!
Dig your way into your breakthrough!
Dig your way out of depression!
Dig your way!
I came to "Woman Thou Art Loosed" to give you a shovel!
Dig!
Dig!

If you dig you're gonna hit something!
If you dig you're gonna hit something!
You dig. [With] every little scoop of dirt
You're getting closer to your breakthrough.
You're getting closer to water.
You're getting closer to your promise.
Get up and dig.

But I'm tired.
Dig anyway. Get up and dig.
But they're laughing at me.
Dig anyway. Get up and dig.
But they're making fun of me.
Dig![58]

Here White turned her thematic anchor into a rhetorical and musical motif, recalling the music theorist Elizabeth Margulis's claim that "when language is being repetitive, language is being musical," and demonstrating a practical mastery that is one of the controversy's conditions of possibility.[59] White, like Yohe, clearly understands how to articulate certain formal features of the black gospel tradition without expressing a commitment to its political entailments. Just a cursory glance at the text reveals a characteristically musical preoccupation: White's repetitive deployment of recursive rhetorical techniques like epistrophe and anaphora constructs what the musicologist Guthrie P. Ramsey Jr. calls a "troping cycle."[60]

While instrumental accompaniment to this kind of sermon is customary, vocal accompaniment is unusual. White's sermonic conclusion is not hers alone. In this climactic phase, White's proclamation is amplified by a largely African American band and by a tenor vocalist who echoes salient parts of her message. Although antiphonal exclamations are expected from congregations, what this tenor adds to White's performance is foregrounded. Like the preacher, the singer has a direct microphone. These musicians, which we might assume to be members of White's musical staff and, therefore, used to taking part in these emergent moments of proclamation, constitute an ensemble of vital importance to this sermon. At the center of this group is the keyboardist, who would probably be termed the "music director." His intense focus on White enables him to follow her utterances and gestures, leading the ensemble's creation of a "participatory musical framework against which highly idiosyncratic and innovative improvisation can take place."[61] As White abandons speech in favor of iterative digging, the band plays the following harmonic progression, A♭, G♭, E, G♭, A♭, or I–VII–VI–VII–I. In doing so, they create an autotelic musical cycle, a vamp, which I think of as "a musical technology of transcendence."[62] Every time the preacher lifts a shovel filled with dirt, the band moves to the next chord in the sequence, using tonal motion to assert the transformative power of digging.

These sonic transformations converted the thousands of women gathered by this sermon into one big congregation. At the same time, this musicality staked White's own claim to characteristically black modes of preaching. While I earlier referenced the shovel with which White preached, I also want to note the thousands of miniature shovels that had been prepared and distributed to the multitude of conference attendees. Armed with these icons of White's sermonic tool, many conference-goers dug into the air in response to the preacher's exhortation. Although the gift of tokens of a conference theme is not uncommon, their integration into White's sermonic presentation reveals the stagecraft that preceded this event, an intention and artful capacity to craft an experience that, while bringing audiences into "the presence of God" would also collapse the distance between White and her audience—fomenting such a sense of identification that she would be described as preaching like a black woman.[63] This very sentiment, detailed in an interview with White's son, also emerged in the anthropologist Marla Frederick's discussions with black religious women in Halifax County, North Carolina. While Frederick found that her informants frequently tuned out televangelists' statements that supported Republican candidates and policies, the reaction against White was not so nonchalant.[64] In White's case the ease with which she was received as "preaching like a black woman" reveals the relationships she cultivated with audiences. As Frederick observes, "White's ministry is based on her testimony [of] struggle."[65] But while the preacher's experiences with poverty, abuse, and illness were received as sincere links between her and largely black audiences, her support for Trump seemed to ignore the multiplicative force of race in the American context, an ignorance that retrospectively defines her attempts to "sound black" as exploitative appropriations of black aesthetics, not performances of solidarity. I want to suggest that this has to do with White's attempts to practice two contradictory politics of identity. The controversy surrounding her support for President Trump shows that the homiletic "vocabulary and cadence" mentioned in the aforementioned article and practiced in "Can You Dig It" is not so easily disentangled from the political concerns of African Americans.

In the spring of 2019, White handed over leadership of the predominantly African American, Tampa, Florida, church she founded and pastored to her son and daughter-in-law, Bradley and Rachel Knight. Despite White's explanation that she installed the new pastors to allow her to focus on other goals, the church's new pastor, White's son, references a frayed relationship with the black community and charges of betrayal in the article that announces the pastoral transition.[66] It seems that the form of White's preaching and the character of her politics produced a dissonance too great for many congregants' ears. In the fall of 2019, White accepted a position in the White House's Office of Public Liaison, serving as an adviser to the president's Faith and Opportunity Initiative.[67] As White's transition points to a larger trend of African Americans leaving white evangelical congregations, it recalls Cleophus LaRue's argument that the distinctiveness of black preaching lies in an expectation that God will act in the material world on behalf of the black downtrodden.[68] While LaRue de-emphasizes the role of sound in black preaching, his theopolitical insights find a witness in Ashon Crawley's notion of "Blackpentecostal breath." Writing about performances of Dorinda Clark-Cole and Juandolyn Stokes, two other prominent women preachers, Crawley makes an observation that illuminates the discordant relationship between White's preaching and political controversy, proposing that preaching

> produce[s] the sonic space as discontinuous and open, open to the other voices that both preceded her moment of being overcome with Spirit—such that other women gathered around, held and hugged her—and extended the preacherly moment by sociality, through opening up and diffusing the very grounds for the concept of preaching, for listening, for breathing.[69]

Crawley contends that such openness, enacts "violence against any form of marginalized oppression."[70] For White, as for Yohe and Campbell, vocal support for Trump represented a forceful turn away from the communities that had sustained her ministry—movement away from affirming sociality, itself, in favor of a white nationalist politics. By lending her voice to shroud President Trump's inauguration, White House events, and campaign rallies in Pentecostal language, White turned black aesthetics against black people.

Through its analysis of the controversies that arose in response to "black" gospel artists' support for Donald J. Trump's presidential campaign, this essay has illuminated the racial politics of the black gospel tradition. The artists' desire to practice contradictory politics of identity—to be black gospel singers and support a candidate whom one prominent commentator has called "the first white president"[71]—highlight both the status of race as a floating signifier and these musicians' preoccupation with racial difference. In point of fact, the musical devices Yohe and White use to pursue blackness clarify that understandings of sonic blackness are as slippery as other categories of race. Although both Yohe and White seem to understand specific deployments of musical meter as a technique of blackness, their aesthetic pursuit takes them in opposite directions. Yohe's singing is punctuated by a desire for freedom from fixed meter, but White's sermons seek to achieve ecstasy through an emergent sense of regular temporality. While this is related to the different realms of the gospel traditions that the two vocalists occupy, songs and sermons, both share a sense that musical blackness is materialized through emphatic assertions of difference.

Yohe's case, in particular, highlights a conflict between two aesthetic forms, the song and the meme. As such, it is a productive site from which to reflect on the methodological issues that are raised by these controversies. While it is clear that the most salient feature of Yohe's radioactive post was the kind of graphical digital artifact that is typically referred to as a meme, what does this category entail? Paula Harper's definition of the meme as "a constellation of material, comprised of recognizable iterations of a particular pattern or form, sometimes with no particular single referent or point of origin" elucidates this question.[72] Harper's definition clarifies the meme's plural ontology as a set of articles whose coherence activates a dialectic of repetition and difference. The memetic grammar of the image Yohe shared is best understood with reference to the many different captions that could have been applied to the image in question. While any number of absurd and humorous messages can be communicated with any such artifact, the form Yohe shared reflected a decision to use this image to make a political assertion about Jesus and Trump, race and belief.

I first came into contact with Yohe's Jesus meme, and the news stories it elicited, on my Facebook timeline. The application's aggregation of many friends who share interests and concerns in such an accessible place meant that my Facebook timeline quickly became an index of this meme's virality: in just a few seconds of scrolling, I came across more than a dozen iterations of this image. My active presence in what Zeynep Tufekci calls "the networked public sphere" made avoiding this image nearly impossible.[73] But this is a recent impossibility. As Tufekci writes: "The networked public sphere has emerged so forcefully and so rapidly that it is easy to forget how new it is. Facebook was started in 2004 and Twitter in 2006. The first iPhone, ushering in the era of the smart, networked phone, was introduced in 2007. The wide extent of digital connectivity might blind us to the power of this transformation. It should not. These dynamics are significant social mechanisms, especially for social movements, since they change the operation of a key resource: attention."[74] As virtual attention has fixated on the kinds of support exemplified by Yohe's meme, the expressions of outrage have taken their own memetic character. For example, Facebook user Arlen Harris's post inverts the lyrics from Mary Mary's first hit to critique Tina Campbell's support for President Trump: "Tina better hope someone take the shackles off her mind and Chrisette better hope 45 builds that bridge she talked about instead of his wall. Either way, they both continue to be CANCELLED."[75] One of gospel producer Kevin Bond's recent Facebook posts aestheticizes hashtags, declaring "#PaulaWhite #Duped #The #Church & now we're seeing the #Fruit! #Discernment."[76] Facebook user Anita Armstrong used one of Paula White's public pages to make this post:[77]

> It's Amazing how Paula White Got Rich OFF Black Churches 🙄
> And Now You A Spiritual Leader To TRUMP 🙄 Racists."

Armstrong and Bond's reiteration of hashtags, emojis, and other characteristic elements of social media syntax highlight the digital epistemology that shapes contemporary political debate—much of which explicitly concerns or engages music itself. As these online forums become increasingly primary venues of cultural production, they will require musicologists to expand the analytic tools used to mine these viral archives. If "viral" and "archive" (like "digital" and "material") seem like non sequiturs, these contradictions might prove productive, dramatically expanding the kinds of data available to scholars of expressive culture. For example, the online setting of the debates explored in these pages has made it possible to study reactions from a political commentator like Roland Martin, a revered gospel musician, Kevin Bond, and users with less status as social media influencers. As such, these digital platforms yield a clearer picture of both the pervasiveness of a given opinion and the richly textured variety that emerges when these ideas are iterated by numerous individuals.

What kind of musicological object is a Facebook post? What might a music scholar make of a meme? I contend that the creation and circulation of such artifacts—what Paula Harper terms "viral musicking"[78]—are digital performances that materialize the intercalation of aesthetic preference and social categories like race and belief, such that sharing a meme becomes an ideal way to act white or to undertake any other kind of affiliation. The kind of strategic essentialism often at work in the production of virtual socialities suggests that memes provide an instructive way to think about White and Yohe's investment in a reified kind of black musicality. The two vocalists' ironic juxtaposition of sonic modes of blackness and political modes of whiteness share the meme's tendency to conjoin the incongruous. While such satirical recombinations often have humor as their goal, the absurdist Jesus meme yielded more pain and anger than howls of laughter. That a swift social media post could powerfully interrupt a decades-long musical relationship reveals the convergent resonance of these virtual practices. Such enactments are saturated with intermedial reference, promiscuous connections that link each sharing event to precedents, while inciting memetic rearticulation. I call this digital antiphony. As the evidence of interaction, such posts also outline the paths through which more traditional subjects of musicological focus are disseminated. Therefore, tracing the digital circulation of these affects promises to yield analytical tools for rethinking thorny questions about music's imbrication with various aspects of identity.

Notes

This chapter and the "reflection" from Cheryl Townsend Gilkes grew out of our many conversations about the combination of race and politics in the black gospel tradition and in American Christianity, more broadly. This long-running dialogue was shaped by our shared interests in black preaching and black sacred music and by shared space in the pulpit of Union Baptist Church in Cambridge, Massachusetts.

1. See, for example, "Gospel singer Vicki Yohe apologizes for Trump posting," Associated Press, January 23, 2017, https://apnews.com/55338bbd270243 4083606681838d0f0f

2. Catherine A. Brekus and W. Clark Gilpin, *American Christianities: A History of Dominance and Diversity* (Chapel Hill: University of North Carolina Press, 2011), 1.

3. Though problematic, I use the term as a heuristic to describe black religious collectives.

4. Jennifer Lynn Stoever, *Sonic Color Line: Race and the Cultural Politics of Listening* (New York: New York University Press, 2016).

5. George Lipsitz, *The Possessive Investment in Whiteness: How White People Profit from Identity Politics* (Philadelphia: Temple University Press, 1998).

6. Sanjay Sharma, "Black Twitter? Racial Hashtags, Networks and Contagion," *New Formations* 78 (2013): 46–64.

7. "Exit Polls: Election 2016 Results," November 23, 2016, https://www.cnn .com/election/2016/results/exit-polls

8. Tommie Shelby, *We Who Are Dark: The Philosophical Foundations of Black Solidarity* (Cambridge, MA: Belknap Press of the Harvard University Press, 2007), 251.

9. Christine Thomasos, "Tina Campbell Postpones Tour Due to Low Sales Amid Backlash for Trump Support," *Christian Post*, October 26, 2017, https:// www.christianpost.com/news/tina-campbell-postpones-tour-low-sales-backlash -for-trump-support.html

10. Candice Benbow, "Oh How I Love White Jesus: On Travis Greene, Tina Campbell, Vicki Yohe and Paula White," *CandiceB*, January 29, 2017, https:// www.candicebenbow.com/post/oh-how-i-love-white-jesus-on-travis-greene-tina -campbell-vicki-yohe-and-paula-white

11. Benbow, "How I Love White Jesus."

12. Fred Moten, *In the Break: The Aesthetics of the Black Radical Tradition* (Minneapolis: University of Minnesota Press, 2003), 1.

13. Roland Barthes, "The Grain of the Voice," in *Image, Music, Text*, trans. Stephen Heath (New York: Farrar, Straus, and Giroux, 1977), 179–89.

14. Ashon T. Crawley, *Blackpentecostal Breath: The Aesthetics of Possibility* (New York: Fordham University Press, 2017).

15. Cheryl Townsend Gilkes, "Still the 'Most Segregated Hour': Religion, Race and the American Experience," in *The SAGE Handbook of Race and Ethnic Studies*, ed. Patricia Hill Collins and John Solomos (Los Angeles: SAGE, 2010), 417.

16. Gilkes, "Most Segregated Hour," 416.

17. Michelle Alexander, *The New Jim Crow: Mass Incarceration in the Age of Colorblindness* (New York: New Press, 2012); Andrew Michael Manis, *Southern Civil Religions in Conflict: Civil Rights and the Culture Wars* (Macon, GA: Mercer University Press, 2002).

18. Pearl Williams Jones, "Afro-American Gospel Music: A Crystallization

of the Black Aesthetic," *Ethnomusicology* 19, no. 3 (September 1975): 373–85; Mellonie Burnim, "The Black Gospel Tradition: Symbol of Ethnicity" (PhD diss., Indiana University, 1980); Guthrie P. Ramsey Jr., *Race Music: Black Music Cultures from Bebop to HipHop* (Berkeley: University of California Press, 2003).

19. Evelyn Brooks Higginbotham, *Righteous Discontent: The Women's Movement in the Black Baptist Church* (Cambridge, MA: Harvard University Press, 1993), 3.

20. See Albert Rabtoeau, *Slave Religion: the "Invisible Institution" in the Antebellum South* (Oxford: Oxford University Press, 1978).

21. Gilkes, "Most Segregated Hour," 416.

22. James C. Scott, *Domination and the Arts of Resistance: Hidden Transcripts* (New Haven: Yale University Press, 1990).

23. Mark Anthony Neal, *What the Music Said: Black Popular Music and Black Public Culture* (New York: Routledge, 1999), 5.

24. Raphael G. Warnock, *Divided Mind of the Black Church: Theology, Piety, and Public Witness* (New York: New York University Press, 2014), 9.

25. Shelby, *We Who Are Dark*, 251.

26. Stoever, *Sonic Color Line*, 21.

27. Tony Cummings, "Vicki Yohe: A Blue-eyed Gospel Diva Who Seeks 'the Anointing,'" *Cross Rhythms*, November 5, 2006, http://www.crossrhythms.co.uk/articles/music/Vicki_Yohe_A_blueeyed_gospel_diva_who_Seeks_the_anointing/24631/p1/

28. Cummings, "Vicki Yohe."

29. Roland S. Martin, Twitter post, January 22, 2017, 6:10 p.m., https://twitter.com/rolandsmartin/status/823352297384275972

30. Regarding racial imagination and Christian theology, see J. Kameron Carter, *Race: A Theological Account* (Oxford: Oxford University Press, 2008).

31. James Cone, *A Black Theology of Liberation* (Maryknoll, NY: Orbis Books, 1970), 116–36.

32. Lisa Nakamura, *Digitizing Race: Visual Cultures of the Internet* (Minneapolis: University of Minnesota Press, 2007), 208.

33. Vicki Yohe, "Gospel Diva Vicki Yohe On 'Sounding Black,'" interviewed by Michel Martin, *Tell Me More*, NPR Music, December 20, 2012, audio 28:31, https://www.npr.org/2012/12/20/167709027/gospel-diva-vicki-yohe-on-sounding-black. Emphasis added.

34. Lipsitz, *Possessive Investment in Whiteness.*

35. Lipsitz, *Possessive Investment in Whiteness*, 1.

36. Stoever, *Sonic Color Line*, 11.

37. Stoever, *Sonic Color Line*, 11.

38. Nina Sun Eidsheim, *The Race of Sound: Listening, Timbre, and Vocality in African American Music* (Durham, NC: Duke University Press, 2019), introduction.

39. Stoever, *Sonic Color Line*, 11.

40. I follow Homi Bhabha's notion of fetishization, which is outlined in "The Other Question," *Screen* 24, no. 6 (November–December 1983): 18–36.

41. Vicki Yohe, "Because of Who You Are," *I Just Want You*, Pure Springs Gospel, 2003, CD.

42. Mark Spicer, "(Ac)cumulative Form in Pop-Rock Music," *Twentieth-Century Music* 1, no. 1 (2004): 29–64.

43. Birgitta Johnson, "Back to the Heart of Worship: Praise and Worship Music in a Los Angeles African-American Megachurch," *Black Music Research Journal* 31, no. 1 (Spring 2011): 109.

44. Moten, *In the Break.*

45. Braxton Shelley, "Sounding Belief: 'Tuning Up' and 'the Gospel Imagination,'" in *Exploring Christian Song,* ed. M. Jennifer Bloxam and Andrew D. Shelton (Lanham, MD: Lexington Books, 2017), 173–94.

46. Vicki Yohe, "I'm at Peace," *I'm at Peace,* Shanachie Entertainment, 2011, CD.

47. Crawley, *Blackpentecostal Breath,* 259.

48. Shaun King, "Dear Vicki Yohe," Facebook, January 22, 2017, https://www.facebook.com/shaunking/posts/dear-vicki-yohethis-is-disgusting-you-are-disgusting-for-saying-it-i-was-a-pasto/1277179958987586/

49. King, "Dear Vicki Yohe."

50. Vicki Yohe, "I never want to hurt anyone," Facebook, January 23, 2017 (post has been deleted but there are many screenshot images and quotations).

51. Yohe, "I never want to hurt anyone."

52. Bruno Latour, "On Technical Mediation: Philosophy, Sociology, Genealogy," *Common Knowledge* 3, no.2 (1994): 33.

53. Sharma, "Black Twitter?"

54. Julia Duin, "She Led Trump to Christ: The Rise of the Televangelist Who Advises the White House," *Washington Post,* November 14, 2017, https://www.washingtonpost.com/lifestyle/magazine/she-led-trump-to-christ-the-rise-of-the-televangelist-who-advises-the-white-house/2017/11/13/1dc3a830-bb1a-11e7-be94-fabb0f1e9ffb_story.html

55. Shelley, "Sounding Belief."

56. Paula White, "Can You Dig It?" (sermon, Atlanta, GA, July 2000). An excerpt of the sermon is posted on YouTube: Georgia Wool, "Can You Dig It 4 Paula White," https://www.youtube.com/watch?v=GoH-RytnIEw, accessed December 14, 2020.

57. Frank Thomas, *They Like to Never Quit Praisin' God: The Role of Celebration in Preaching* (Cleveland: United Church Press, 1997), 31.

58. Paula White, "Can You Dig It?"

59. Elizabeth Hellmuth Margulis, *On Repeat: How Music Plays the Mind* (New York: Oxford University Press, 2014), 57.

60. Ramsey, *Race Music,* 60.

61. Ingrid Monson, *Saying Something: Jazz Improvisation and Interaction* (Chicago: University of Chicago Press, 1996), 89.

62. Braxton D. Shelley, "Analyzing Gospel," *Journal of the American Musicological Society* 72, no. 1 (Spring 2019): 181–243.

63. Duin, "She Led Trump to Christ."

64. Marla Frederick, "Rags to Riches: Religion, Media, and the Performance of Wealth in a Neoliberal Age," in *Ethnographies of Neoliberalism,* ed. Carol J. Greenhouse (Philadelphia: University of Pennsylvania Press, 2010), 235.

65. Frederick, "Rags to Riches," 228.

66. Duin, "She Led Trump to Christ."

67. Jeremy W. Peters and Maggie Haberman, "Paula White, Trump's Personal

Pastor, Joins White House," *New York Times*, October 31, 2019, https://www.nytimes.com/2019/10/31/us/politics/paula-white-trump.html

68. Campbell Robertson, "A Quiet Exodus: Why Black Worshipers Are Leaving White Evangelical Churches," *New York Times*, March 9, 2018, https://www.nytimes.com/2018/03/09/us/blacks-evangelical-churches.html; Cleophus J. LaRue, *The Heart of Black Preaching* (Louisville, KY: Westminster John Knox, 2000), 3.

69. Crawley, *Blackpentecostal Breath*, 45.

70. Crawley, *Blackpentecostal Breath*, 45.

71. Ta-Nehisi Coates, "The First White President," *The Atlantic*, October 2017, https://www.theatlantic.com/magazine/archive/2017/10/the-first-white-president-ta-nehisi-coates/537909/

72. Paula Harper, "Unmute This: Circulation, Sociality, and Sound in Viral Media" (PhD diss., Columbia University, 2019), 19.

73. Zeynep Tufekci, *Twitter and Tear Gas: The Power and Fragility of Networked Protest* (New Haven: Yale University Press, 2018), chap. 1.

74. Tufekci, *Twitter and Tear Gas*, 29–30.

75. Arlen Harris, Facebook post, October 27, 2017, https://www.facebook.com/arlen.herrell/posts/10104693686147345

76. Kevin Bond, Facebook post, June 22, 2019, https://www.facebook.com/MrKevinBond/posts/10155928163066601

77. Anita Armstrong, Facebook post, July 23, 2019, https://www.facebook.com/realpaulawhite/posts/10157662307397313

78. Harper, "Unmute This."

Lift Every Voice?

White Domination Still Matters, Even in Sacred Space: A Sociologist's Reflection on "Sounding Black, Acting White"

CHERYL TOWNSEND GILKES

The 2016 presidential election was a dramatic lightning flash that illuminated and revealed the persistent racial fissures of the American landscape. Perhaps the most vexing and troubling was the dramatic racial divide among American Christians. White evangelicals supported someone whose lifestyle and personal history seemed anathema to the values of a supposedly Christian nation. Three significant women in religious popular culture, two gospel singers (one white and one black) and a popular white megachurch preacher and pastor of a predominantly black church, discovered that their support for Donald Trump initiated a firestorm among their black followers. As Shelton and Emerson demonstrate in their 2012 study, *Blacks and Whites in Christian America*, "Controversial racial issues as well as past and present injustices and inequalities are ideologically meaningful to both black and white Protestants."[1] Braxton Shelley reveals a dimension of this ideological meaning by highlighting the importance of understanding racialized upheaval in America's sacred sphere. His illumination of the racial politics of sacred cultural production reminds us that white domination and the defense of it is a fact of American life, even in sacred space. My reflection reinforces the importance of Professor Shelley's musicological analysis by drawing upon classical and contemporary sociological and historical approaches to race and the history of African American Christianity, commonly called "the black church."

The racial politics of cultural production in the United States have always been generative, symbiotic, and persistently predatory. This has been especially evident in secular popular culture. Examples abound of starving African American blues and R & B songwriters selling their compositions for a pittance or of white performers popularizing black compositions for white audiences, especially during the era of Jim Crow segregation. Most recently Ken Burns's exploration of country music, a clearly white-identified genre of US music, points to the generative relationships between African American mentors and their white disciples who became the avatars of country music.[2] African instruments and styles were shared across racial boundaries, a sharing that began during slavery and continued across time, establishing a predatory and symbiotic relationship between black musical expression and white appropriation.

Such sharing has taken place in sacred space as well. Analyzing and criticizing predatory racial politics in sacred space is a complicated task, however, since it confronts the presumption that black and white Christians love and serve and worship and praise the same God. The requirement to "love one another" further complicates matters. While it has become easy to critique popular music as a cultural production developed in the context of racial oppression, focusing on the sacred is more of a problem.

As Professor Shelley's exploration of this particular political moment demonstrates, such a focus is a necessary task. When white people use black culture, sacred or secular, black people are required to scrutinize, criticize, and ask, "Which side are you on?" Professor Shelley points out that white people in a "racialized social system," to use Eduardo Bonilla-Silva's term, are able "to turn black aesthetics against black people."[3] The United States has been specifically and historically white supremacist and anti-Africanist, producing weaponized ideas and styles to argue for and maintain cultural dominance. This is at the heart of minstrelsy and other forms of stereotyping through entertainment. As the behavior of Vicki Yohe and Paula White indicates, this dynamic lives in sacred spaces too.

At a recent conference, sociologist Orlando Patterson pointed out that the United States is the only white majoritarian formerly slave society.[4] The cultural consequences of this reality have always been puzzling and distinctive. Scholars have explored and argued over the origins and ownership of expressive cultural artifacts associated with black

Americans. Use of black music by whites has too often been distorted into an assumption that black creativity derives from white expression. What sociologist Joe Feagin identifies as the "white racial frame" shapes responses to and interpretations of black cultural production.[5] This is even true in sacred space.

While black church "origins" are clearly "oppositional," there is more. The sacred is where African cultural capital was marshaled and coordinated for survival in the Americas and for the creation of African American culture. Anthropologists Sidney Mintz and Richard Price argue, and I agree, that the epicenter for the creation of African American culture can be located in what Mintz and Price identified as the "'exchanged' ritual assistance" that occurred among Africans of different ethnic origins in the slave communities of the Americas.[6] The religion of the US slave community, the fundamental source of African American sacred music, was a consequence of such ritual exchange. Within those communities, Africans and their descendants pursued the most consequential interfaith conversations, conversations that not only explored the nature of God/Spirit but also evaluated critically the Christianity that white people eventually offered, although reluctantly at first. The music is a map of the agency and oppositional stance that constitute the deep roots and grounding of the black church.

The current political lightning flash—this vexing relationship between the Trump administration and white evangelicals—clarified and illuminated the importance of exploring American religion and liturgical space as a problem in the power politics of race. One Sunday morning, around 1998 or 1999, I accidentally tuned in to a white conservative televised megachurch service. I was drawn by the music—the white singer was singing gospel style. I was listening and not watching until my goddaughter—a precocious five-year-old—started watching and indignantly demanded to know, "Why aren't there any black people there?" When I actually looked, I saw American flags and bunting draped throughout the sanctuary, and the pastor turned out to be a well-known antifeminist conservative and undercover racist who was part of Jerry Falwell's Moral Majority. The idolatries of wealth, whiteness, and Americanism were abundantly evident. And the white soloist was singing in an African American gospel style.

From their American beginnings, white evangelical Protestants have exploited and appropriated black voices for their own purposes. During the Great Awakening, a preacher known as Black Harry Hoosier (1750–1810) served as an "opening act" for Bishop Francis Asbury (1745–1816), one of the founders of Methodism.[7] White people sometimes preferred camp meetings where enslaved black people were present and singing.[8] And some written texts for spirituals were transcribed by white people, who learned the language of their enslaved nannies and enslaved playmates.

Like the origins of minstrelsy, cultural appropriation in sacred space is an assertion of power. White people are free to invade and borrow, and black people are powerless to prevent white people's invasion and borrowing. Furthermore, white intruders are allowed to resist learning about, changing, and sharing the burdens that black people routinely face. Paula White's emergence as Donald Trump's spiritual adviser is a case in point. When she came to Trump's attention, he took her under his wing and took her to dinner at a Michelin-rated restaurant in Trump Tower—an experience that prompted her to enroll in an etiquette school to learn proper table manners.[9] How she managed not to gain those basic skills while immersed in African American sacred space is indicative of her fundamental resistance to the authority and leadership of black people. Anyone raised in a black church knows that it is impossible to eat a meal and not be nudged and corrected by women of *all* social classes who model and advocate correct behavior. My own fieldwork at a national Pentecostal women's conference involved five thousand women sharing formal meals together, and if any of them did not arrive knowing correct table etiquette, they had learned it by the end of the week. As Alice Walker opined in *The Color Purple*, "I know white people never listen to colored, period. If they do, they only listen long enough to be able to tell what to do."[10]

Instead, Paula White chose to be the Elvis Presley of black preaching. It is well known that Presley was singled out by record producers to market black music to white audiences. While black people served as backup singers in the recording studio—Whitney Houston's mother, Cissy Houston, being a famous example—Presley's backup singers on the road were white. A famous short story by Alice Walker, "Nineteen-Fifty-Five," reimagines a Presley-type character seeking out the composer of his songs, figuratively seeming to be Big Mama Thornton, in order to learn the origins and meanings of his recordings and to enable him to sing with more authenticity.[11]

Black religious spaces are political spaces. And black religious spaces are cultural spaces. Religious spaces are what Evelyn Brooks Higginbotham identified as the black "public sphere."[12] Unlike white space, black spaces are not exclusionary, especially religious spaces.

The rule is "Whosoever will, let them come." Public spheres such as the National Baptist Convention are spaces where debates such as the one between "Booker T. and W. E. B." are observed and adjudicated as well as the space where controversial new musical compositions like Thomas A. Dorsey's gospel music are presented and disseminated. For black folks, the connections among the sacred, the political, and the cultural have been constant and dynamic.

According to Bernice Johnson Reagon, African American sacred music can be the tape measure of American history.[13] The traditions of sacred music are a mirror of American progress embedded in black voices. The intrusion of white evangelicals into the black sacred voice may be reflective of a new set of alignments generated by the rise of "prosperity gospel." In a 2019 presentation before the Society for the Scientific Study of Religion, Jason Shelton suggested that these new alignments could possibly signal what he tentatively called "the death of the Black Church."

Music and preaching are the discourses central to the black church. Along with ecstatic worship, something institutionalized and formalized in a variety of black Pentecostal and Holiness experiences, these three constitute the basic pillars identified by Du Bois as the core of "the Negro church."[14] However, authority is embedded in the preaching. The preacher is also, in Du Bois's formulation, a leader. Although white people appropriate, exploit, and commodify the entire black religious package—that is, the music, preaching style, and ecstatic worship—white America resists and rejects black leadership and authority. After Reconstruction, as has been widely studied, black leadership and authority were derided as "Negro domination." The presumptions of permanent and unquestioned white authority and domination are built into the white racial frame that shapes white approaches to black culture.

It is also possible that white people want to preach like black people and sing like black people because those activities pay well. Black congregations—from storefront to megachurch—highly value great preaching and singing. Those congregations pay far better than similarly situated white congregations.[15] The power that white people exercise, furthermore, provides opportunities to exploit style and cultural artifacts for their own benefit. Yohe and White, like many white people before them, exploit black people, their styles, their culture, and communities as step stools to reach the ladder of mobility leading to prosperity and the American Dream. This is what settlers, enslavers, and European immigrants have done in the past, and this strategy persists and has been rendered visible in contemporary sacred space.

In his classic work *The Souls of Black Folk,* Du Bois asked a question that still reverberates today: "Your country? How came it yours?"[16] It is a question that goes to the heart of race, culture, ownership, and the problem of white domination in a society where "the gifts" of black folk—material and expressive—remain exploited and unacknowledged. Written during the nadir of race relations when the backlash to black political participation generated the rise of Jim Crow and the era of lynchings and racial massacres, Du Bois recognized the importance of African American creativity and agency in the making of the America that white people insisted was theirs alone. Current issues evident in social media illuminate dramatically the deeper cultural history—sacred and secular—that has shaped the United States as a racialized social system. Tina, Vicki, and Paula remind us that the dynamics among African American cultural generativity and its confrontations with white predation and appropriation are still very much a powerful undercurrent in the political river of American cultural production. In this current moment of racial resentment and backlash, fostered by a politics of hate, white domination still matters, even in sacred space, and every voice lifted in that space must answer the question, "Which side are you on?"

Notes

1. Jason E. Shelton and Michael O. Emerson, *Blacks and Whites in Christian America: How Racial Discrimination Shapes Religious Convictions* (New York: New York University Press, 2012), 168.

2. Dayton Duncan and Ken Burns, *Country Music: An Illustrated History* (New York: Penguin Random House, 2019).

3. Eduardo Bonilla-Silva, "Rethinking Racism: Toward a Structural Interpretation," *American Sociological Review* 62, no. 3 (June 1997): 465–80. The resonance of the phrase "Which side are you on?" arrived at independently by Monica Hershberger and Sarah Suhadolnik, also informs chapter 9 of this volume.

4. Orlando Patterson, "The Continued Significance of Race, Class, and Culture," paper presented at "William Julius Wilson Retirement Symposium," Harvard University, September 12, 2019, https://hutchinscenter.fas.harvard.edu/WJW2019

5. Joe R. Feagin, *The White Racial Frame: Centuries of Racial Framing and Counter-Framing* (New York: Routledge, 2010).

6. Sidney W. Mintz and Richard Price, *The Birth of African American Culture: An Anthropological Perspective* (Boston: Beacon Press, 1992), 45–46.

7. Internet resources describing the origins of American Methodism include descriptions of the effectiveness of Hoosier's preaching as he traveled with Asbury. The Wallbuilders website includes helpful resources on eighteenth-century African American preachers including Hoosier: https://wallbuilders.com/black-history-issue-2005/

8. Minuette Floyd, *A Place to Worship: African American Camp Meetings in the Carolinas* (Columbia: University of South Carolina Press, 2018), 18. The following website provides a brief description of the musical and cultural exchanges that occurred in camp meetings during slavery: https://www.jeremyaaron.com/folk-music-timeline/slavery-and-the-african-american-spiritual

9. Elizabeth Dias, "Meet the Pastor Who Prays with Donald Trump," *Time*, September 14, 2016, https://time.com/4493530/donald-trump-prayer/

10. Alice Walker, *The Color Purple* (1982; repr. San Diego: Harcourt Brace Jovanovich 1992), 195.

11. Alice Walker, *You Can't Keep a Good Woman Down* (San Diego: Harcourt Brace Jovanovich, 1981).

12. Evelyn Brooks Higginbotham, *Righteous Discontent: The Women's Movement in the Black Baptist Church, 1880–1920* (Cambridge, MA: Harvard University Press, 1993), 7.

13. Bernice Johnson Reagon, "'Take Your Burden to the Lord, Leave It There': The New 20th Century Social Music and African American Survival in the City" (Special Topics forum, Annual Meeting of the American Academy of Religion, Washington, DC, November 22, 1993). See also Bernice Johnson Reagon, *We'll Understand It Better By and By: Pioneering African American Gospel Composers* (Washington, DC: Smithsonian Institution Scholarly Press, 1992).

14. W. E. B. Du Bois, "Of the Faith of the Fathers," in *The Souls of Black Folk* (1903; New York: Bantam Books, 1989), 133–45.

15. This reflection is based on personal experience and numerous conversations with other clergy.

16. Du Bois, "Of the Sorrow Songs," in *The Souls of Black Folk*, 186.

FIVE | *For the Daughters of Harlem*

Bridging Campus and Community through Sound

ELLIE M. HISAMA AND LUCIE VÁGNEROVÁ

This is an era where we have to encourage that sense of community particularly at a time when neoliberalism attempts to force people to think only in individual terms and not in collective terms. It is in collectivities that we find reservoirs of hope and optimism.

—Angela Davis

It's so important for these high schoolers to have an opportunity to come to Columbia and sit face to face with Ebonie, and be able to say, "If she's doing this, I can do this."

—Matthew D. Morrison, workshop leader

I think it's beyond important to have workshops and opportunities like this one where our talents and passions are acknowledged.

—Michelle Cabrera, workshop participant, age fifteen

Our workshop "For the Daughters of Harlem: Working in Sound" is a site of collaborative learning, critical reflection, and creative production.[1] Recognizing the documented and palpable underrepresentation of women—and particularly women of color—in music technology and audio production as well as in music criticism and scholarship, we conceived of a public outreach project held at Columbia University for young women of color from New York City public schools. In a free, daylong workshop, they discussed, made, recorded, and produced their own "sound work." Drawn from high schools and a middle school in the Bronx, Brooklyn, and Manhattan, the students worked in teams with faculty, alumnae/i, and students from Columbia University's Department of Music and its Computer Music Center. At the end of the workshop, they presented and discussed their collaborative pieces in an evening showcase. As of this writing, two iterations of the project have taken place, in April 2018 and October 2018, with twenty-five participants from nine different schools in all, and we anticipate expanding the program at Columbia and possibly assisting other institutions in developing their own, site-specific versions of the project.[2]

"For the Daughters of Harlem" takes up the mission of its seed funder, the Collaborative to Advance Equity through Research (CAETR), a nationwide collaborative of over fifty universities, colleges, and nonprofit groups "committed to taking meaningful action to support and improve research addressing the lives of women and girls of color"[3] and focused on "studying and addressing the educational, health and social services disparities faced by women and girls of color."[4] Ironically, the resources and decentralized funding of CAETR, an initiative of the Obama White House, bear out some of these very disparities when compared to Barack Obama's well-funded signature program for men and boys of color, "My Brother's Keeper."[5] We drew our project's name from the words of Kevin Young, director of the Schomburg Library Center for Research on Black Culture, a branch of the New York Public Library in Central Harlem. In discussing the return of Sonny Rollins's personal archive to Harlem and the Schomburg's recent acquisition of the archive of James Baldwin, a native of Harlem, Young observes: "That's one of our big desires: to bring the sons and daughters of Harlem back home."[6] Like the efforts of the Schomburg Center, the "Daughters" project is fundamentally site-specific. We reflect upon the demographics of New York City, the spaces and places of Columbia University's arts and music facilities in Harlem, and the power and significance of producing and archiving musical work.

The aims of this essay are threefold: First, we argue that "sound work," recording, and production are valuable platforms in which students can productively reflect upon connections between music and identifications such as gender, generation, race, ethnicity, and nationality. We introduce several key theoretical concepts in the opening seminar discussions and draw connections to the hands-on music-making workshops. Second, we chronicle the logistics and content of the "Daughters" workshops and show how the project bridges campus and community through sound. In so doing, we provide a template for other universities and colleges to conceive of and launch similar programs. Last, we reflect on an institution's responsibility to listen to and engage with its neighbors and the public, and we envision how a commitment to public outreach programs and service-learning can positively impact student demographics and curricula in college and university music programs.

We structured the workshop as follows:

1. Students, organizers, and workshop leaders met for breakfast and spent the morning in a humanities-oriented discussion session.
2. Students broke into small groups for several hours of hands-on performing, recording, and production, convening over snack breaks.
3. Students regrouped for another humanities-oriented workshop to reflect on their process, share their work with their peers, and prepare for the final showcase and reception.
4. Students presented their work at an evening showcase attended by families, the university community, and the public, followed by a dinner reception.

We opened the workshops with a humanities-based seminar in which we explained the impetus behind the "Daughters" project. Prompted by sociologist Tia DeNora's foundational text *Music in Everyday Life*, which we discuss in more depth below, a lively discussion with the students about everyday uses of music broke the ice, allowing participants to get to know the workshop organizers, leaders, and each other.[7] Students shared some of their experiences with music as listeners (e.g., admiring Kanye West's musical talent while acknowledging their distance from his politics) and performers (e.g., singing solo in a church).

After exploring DeNora's argument that we commonly use music to make sense of who we are, students worked collaboratively at Columbia's Computer Music Center (CMC) in recording studios with professional equipment. Formerly the Columbia-Princeton Electronic Music Center (CPEMC), the facility is the oldest center for electronic music research in the United States.[8] Groups of three or four students rotated throughout the day among the four workshop leaders, who were Columbia faculty, students in music and sound art, and music professionals, ensuring that every student worked with every workshop leader. The demographic, disciplinary, and artistic diversity of workshop leaders shaped the culture and outcomes of the sound work.[9]

By the end of the studio sessions, each group had produced at least one "sound work." In the October 2018 workshop, students reflected on what they had produced in a second humanities-oriented session led by musicologist Matthew D. Morrison and music producer, audio engineer, and singer-songwriter Ebonie Smith. Morrison exhorted the students to "find your inner musicologist!" in thinking about the role of sound in the students' lives, and detailed Smith's considerable professional accomplishments to the students. Morrison introduced vocabulary the students could use to describe their sound work, and they shared their experiences in collaborating and the ideas behind their recorded work. Smith listened intently to each student piece, and provided valuable feedback in a riveting master class on the work of music producers. A closing public showcase in which each piece was played and discussed provided a venue for participants to share their creations with peers, families, teachers, the Columbia and Barnard community, and the community in Harlem and Morningside Heights. A public discussion of the aims and outcomes of the workshop concluded the showcase.

Why "Sound Work"?

Students were invited to "work in sound" without further prompts, unrestrained by traditional rubrics of song, music, or sound art. In the words of workshop leader and Columbia School of General Studies[10] student Sondra E. Woodruff II, "The use of the term *sound* instead of music or piece relieves the participants of any rules that are relegated to either term. It also offered a universal platform for these participants to be unapologetically young girls of color. The mindset they created in was not hindered by expectations. The work they produced was intentionally theirs, and above all, like sound, it was heard."[11]

To illustrate the range of possibilities implicit in the term "sound work," we shared excerpts of the workshop leaders' highly distinctive work in the opening seminar-style discussion. Students listened to an excerpt from Courtney Bryan's Black Lives Matter oratorio *Yet Unheard* (2017) for classically trained singers and orchestra and David Adamcyk's percussion piece titled *Six Drawings by* [Julia] *Randall* (2012), a piece played on a rubber balloon by percussionist Diego Espinosa Cruz Gonzalez. Woodruff's song "All My Love" (2018) and Rachel Devorah Rome's electronic work using recordings and synthesis of birdsong (*Cybird Drone*, 2018) prompted a lively discussion by the students. In introducing the students to a catalog of sound work that may not be juxtaposed in a genre-based course on contemporary music, we wanted to demonstrate the rich diversity of approaches to composition today and to emphasize that there is no single type of composer, genre, or style of music that we were privileging. Composers can span a range of identifications across gender, race, ethnicity, age, and so forth. One may start with a riff, instrumental experimentation, a set of lyrics, a jam session, or the recording of an acousmatic sample.

Further, we thought it important to present work for electronic and/or acoustic instruments and noninstruments such as birds and balloons alongside songlike popular idioms. Women musicians often face the assumption that they are vocalists, and they are socially rewarded for vocal, rather than instrumental, work. Electronic composer and vocalist Pamela Z describes the voice as "the tool that women seem to be expected to excel in using."[12] The workshop made ample space for musical work that is *not* traditionally associated with girls' or women's music-making: sampling, beat-making, instrumentals, engineering, and production. The variety of genres, styles, and idioms drawn upon by the workshop leaders demonstrated that the space was available for creating and valuing difference rather than homogeneity, with significant aesthetic and social implications. While application forms filled out by the participants suggested that popular idioms were more familiar to some than the more experimental ones, the students spent the workshop learning and using a wide range of techniques demonstrated by their teachers, and they approached their sound work with enthusiasm and creative freedom.

NYC Public Schools: Underresourced and Segregated

Our insistence that the workshop serve students in the public school system and not from independent schools initially made it challenging to locate participants. We were approached by one music teacher from an independent school who expressed interest in having their students participate in the program, but we maintained that the workshop must be open only for students at public schools, given the significant disparity in resources between public and independent schools in the city. Inadequate funding within the New York public school system, perceptions of the arts as optional or extracurricular, and the city's drive to create smaller schools in the last two decades have all contributed to a scarcity of music programs in New York City high schools. A 2018 *New York Times* article about music in New York City public high schools charts how small schools, even if broadly beneficial to students, fail to support robust music programs, instead "prioritiz[ing] core academic subjects."[13] That music is not understood as a "core" curricular offering in New York City public schools was well established in the 1970s when thousands of arts teachers were laid off in the wake of an economic crisis that brought New York City to the brink of bankruptcy.[14] The objective of contemporary education to turn out successful workers and consumers and the system's attendant focus on standardized testing have also contributed to a long-standing lack of support for the arts. It is telling that even the very scarce coverage of vanishing music classes typically focuses on the documented correlation between music education and higher test scores in other "core" subjects such as math and science, and on the advantage of having a background in the performing arts that students can note in their college applications.[15]

The New York State Department of Education requires that students take only two credits in the arts—any art form—throughout their high school coursework.[16] Only 57 percent of high schools provide music classes, compared to 93 percent providing classes in the visual arts, and whereas about a quarter of students in ninth and tenth grades take a music class, only a sixth do so in eleventh and twelfth grades.[17] Yet "stronger arts programs" ranks sixth among "top family request[s] for school improvements" in New York and first in mentions of specific subject areas, while "stronger enrichment programs (e.g., afterschool programs, clubs, teams)" tops the list.[18] Additionally, the above figures do not reveal further disparities within the public school system, which is the most racially segregated in the United States:[19] viewed along the axis of race and ethnicity, Asian and white students in New York overwhelmingly benefit from better-rounded programs than Black and Hispanic students. In March 2019, only seven Black students were among the 895 admitted to the competitive public Stuyvesant High School,[20] whose student demographics in 2018 were 74 percent Asian, 18 percent white, 3 percent Hispanic, and 1 percent Black, with no English-language learners or students with special needs.[21] The school's music program, meanwhile, boasts a Music Appreciation course, five bands, four choruses, a yearlong Beginning Woodwind/Brass course, and AP Music Theory.[22]

It is in the context of this dearth of resources and programming for public school student populations distributed along sharp color lines that the "Daughters" workshops are taking root. The initiative responds to several of the aforementioned issues head-on. The workshops seek to (1) share the robust material and institutional resources of a private, Research 1 university with underresourced public schools; (2) prioritize and encourage teenagers' thinking about, discussing, and making sound work; and (3) broach in seminar-style discussions the topics of gendered and racialized inequities in musical, technological, and university spaces.

Resources and Collaboration

Perhaps the most powerful resource that the "Daughters" initiative brought to participants, however, was the very cohort of workshop leaders listed above—many of them faculty, students, and alumnae/i of the university—working intensively with the students in a free workshop. In terms of material resources, Columbia University's Computer Music Center is replete with recording technologies, though it has only one fully equipped recording studio. For the workshop, an additional studio-like room with a piano and a computer was set up, together with a classroom with a DAW (digital audio workstation). Neither had any significant soundproofing, and both were outfitted with additional recording setups, comprising a digital audio interface, a mixer, microphones, and monitor speakers. This made three recording spaces in all.

While state-of-the-art recording technologies were part of the program's draw, we also wanted the students to be able to continue the work on their own, developing the skill of learning how to establish recording setups in nonstudio spaces. In the planning stages, we considered using free, open-source audio software such as Audacity in place of expensive professional alternatives such as Logic Pro and Pro Tools. If we had chosen Audacity, students could have continued similar projects at home or on school computers. Our eventual decision to introduce students to professional DAWs was, in the end, swayed by workshop leader fluency and our desire to share resources that allow the broadest possible range of musical effects and procedures. We provided each student with a canvas bag (and fabric markers to decorate the bags) and a USB drive so that they could take home the sound work they created. We may conceivably use the open-source controller Arduino, the audio-editing platform Audacity, or other more accessible tools in future workshops.

The first workshop was supported by a seed grant from CAETR and funds from the Heyman Center for the Humanities / Society of Fellows, and the second workshop was funded by an Action Grant from Humanities New York and a Public Outreach Grant from the Center for Science and Society. A number of relatively modest contributions from other units at the university supplemented these funds. Three of the project organizers (Hisama, Vágnerová, and Zosha Di Castri) collaborated previously on the international symposium "Women, Music, Power: A Celebration of Suzanne G. Cusick's Work," which provided valuable experience in organizing, budgeting, and raising funds for a large-scale event with over forty participants.[23] We paid all graduate students working for the symposium at an hourly rate that was then more than double the minimum wage; at "Daughters," we also paid graduate students and budgeted in honoraria, travel, and lodging costs as necessary to all workshop leaders who were not full-time Columbia faculty.[24] Woodruff, a former Logic Pro instructor and recording artist, demonstrated her expertise as a student volunteer at the April 2018 workshop; recognizing her deep well of experience and her skills in mentoring high school students, we invited her to participate as a compensated workshop leader in the October 2018 iteration.

Our regular meetings, often over breakfast or coffee, quickly became the backbone of our collaborative workflow: we discussed to-do lists (and housed them in Google Docs), prioritized, and divided individual tasks. These activities included writing funding requests and grant applications; preparing the budget; hiring graduate students to assist with specific tasks; inviting workshop leaders; designing and writing content for our website; locating students by advertising the workshops; securing studio time and booking university spaces; communicating with students, teachers, parents, and guardians; obtaining parent/guardian consent for photo and video documentation of the event; designing and producing printed materials; purchasing workshop materials; securing catering for breakfast, lunch, and the dinner reception; and more. These larger tasks would often be divided into more detailed lists: for example, we compiled a list of individual schools, parent mailing lists, social workers, public school administrators, and not-for-profit organizations, divided the responsibilities of contacting them, and annotated the list with the date and nature of our contact, as well as any notes regarding responses and follow-up. We housed all documents—grant applications, the budget, event flyers, student applications and surveys, our to-do list, event photos, and so on—in a shared Google Drive. Thus, the most recent version of all files was always available to both of us, minimizing the need to check in over e-mail, and we could easily loop in other personnel (workshop leaders, graduate student workers) on relevant files and folders.

It is important to underscore that a project like ours need not be extremely costly to mount if full-time faculty are willing to plan, organize, and run the workshops, and if external grants, internal funding, or in-kind donations can be secured to cover honoraria for external workshop leaders, hourly wages of student workers, print materials, meals, and a reception, USB drives, tote bags, and fees for venues, facilities, and security services, if any. Organizers should consider asking for any monetized venues to be donated or discounted as a significant contribution to a community engagement project; we acknowledged the contributions of departments, institutes, and centers on the project website, departmental website, posters, other print materials, and in a video and article prepared by *Columbia News.*[25] In lieu of professional digital audio workstations, organizers may also consider using free audio-editing platforms such as Audacity or working with inexpensive open-source controllers such as Arduino. That is, the "Daughters" program should not be contingent on institutions owning costly equipment or allocating considerable internal funding. Using an accessible set of tools, after all, may open up exciting possibilities for students' future work at home or school.

DeNora and the Power of Representation

The "Daughters of Harlem" initiative is grounded in the writing of sociologist Tia DeNora, who argues in her book *Music in Everyday Life* for the importance of recognizing the role of music in constituting self-identity. DeNora's ethnographic interviews of fifty-two British and American women probe how music can be understood as an organizing force of the everyday, both personal and social: "Music works as an ordering material in social life . . . [a material that is] pressed into action," writes DeNora.[26] By considering how music is "pressed into action," "Daughters" extends DeNora's work while teasing out its implications for intersectional analysis along the axes of race, ethnicity, and class, which are not fully examined in her text.

DeNora valuably explores music as a medium of what she calls the "care of self,"[27] such as when music is used as a "resource" of mood management. However, the structural issues that cause particular populations to lack—and therefore *need*—"care" in the first place are not fully drawn into consideration in her text. Expanding upon her ideas, we thus asked: what forms of musical self-care mitigate the particular stresses of sexism, homophobia/transphobia, racism, anti-immigrant bias, and economic injustice? How can sound and music be "pressed into action" in the lives of young women of color in New York? What is the role of sound and music in cementing friendships and communities? Asking these questions decentered the emphasis on music's "practical," measurable value—its power to raise test scores in other subjects or to boost a college application, for example—and instead recognized the importance of music as a resource in the "ongoing constitution of [individuals] and their social psychological, physiological and emotional states . . . [their] self-regulatory strategies and socio-cultural practices for the construction and maintenance of mood, memory, and identity."[28]

In the discussion-oriented portions of the workshops, we explicitly addressed the gendered and racial barriers that motivate the "Daughters" initiative, palpable in STEM-adjacent fields, in the academic disciplines that study music, and at elite institutions such as Columbia. With the students, we shared personal experiences while addressing systemic issues through statistics and examples of initiatives designed to address gendered and racial barriers. For example, we introduced the students to an initiative of John Johnson, a professor of astronomy who has established a program that invites undergraduate students of color to explore astronomy research through social justice education at Harvard's Banneker Institute.[29] We also presented data reflecting the stagnating numbers of Black and Latinx faculty at Columbia,[30] and the effects of universities' efforts to recruit undergraduates from established high schools and not from those with a less recognized profile and track record.[31] At the end of the workshop, students received a resource list of local and national organizations providing music-oriented education as well as broadly academic opportunities for high school students.

That the participants' intellectual and creative work took place in majority women-of-color spaces was a central motivation for the project as well as a factor that shaped its outcomes. We shared words from workshop leader Courtney Bryan that spoke to the power of seeing herself represented in the late composer and pianist Geri Allen. In Bryan's words: "From both the innovative sound I heard and the image of someone who looked like me (never underestimate the power of representation), I realized a path in front of me."[32] Ebonie Smith similarly spoke to feeling liberated by online archives such as Women's Audio Mission, SoundGirls, Girls Make Beats, and Female Frequency, as well as her own project Gender Amplified, all of which spotlight the work of women producers. In turn, Matthew Morrison noted how important it was for the participants "to see themselves represented . . . it's really wonderful for students to have the opportunity to . . . sit face to face with one of the top-notch producers, engineers, and songwriters in the country, Ebonie Smith."[33] The cohort of workshop leaders we invited thus represented women and people of color among professional composers, musicians, recording artists, producers, and university faculty. As Smith added, non-creative roles in the music industry also have palpable effects on its creative dimension: "It enriches our industry . . . to have women in every facet of the business. Not just in production, engineering, but also in A&R, in marketing, in development, business development, in legal. . . . It's so important to ensure that the industry that I'm in reflects the world that I live in."[34]

Student participants also strongly responded to seeing themselves represented alongside other women of color. In the workshop application, a returning participant noted:

> I was a part of the workshop earlier this year and what interested me most then and now was the opportunity to be able to not only make music, but learn about music; with other women who not only have the same interest as me, but also look like me. Sometimes media lacks representation and women of color aren't given the same opportunities as others.[35]

Bryan commented on the participants' joy in working with each other and with the instructors[36] and her own deep satisfaction as a workshop leader: "I know these workshops for the Daughters of Harlem are very important work that will lead to realization of dreams for many young girls at such an important age."[37] She reflected on the success in transferring ideas from the "Daughters" initiative to young musicians in Florida, through her duties as the Mary Carr Patton Composer-in-Residence at the Jacksonville Symphony:

> [I'm] thinking about [our] workshops from earlier in the year, especially with the excitement on young people's faces when they actually hear what they can do with their own improvisations as a group. I'm visiting different schools (elementary, junior high, high school) and having them improvise on sounds of their neighborhoods and also answering questions about being a composer, etc. I borrowed some from the discussion you and Lucie led about why we listen to music and the role of music in our lives with one of the schools. It's so fun![38]

Part of the success of the "Daughters" initiative lay in the workshop leaders' ability to engage with high school students, translating their teaching of college-age students to a younger group. Doing so enabled them to emphasize the playful, fun aspects of music-making alongside the hard work put in over the course of the workshop. From the workshops the young women learned new software and technological skills, engaged in discussions of music as a technology of self, created sound work, collaborated with students from other schools, experienced a workday at a university campus, and made new friends.

Student Sound Work

Participants addressed issues of social difference and identity directly in the sound work they produced, often taking up the activist meanings of "having a voice." Voice-oriented pieces featured original sung lyrics, spoken-word poetry, choral singing, and rap and freestyle. The voice also took on accompanying roles through backing vocals, beatboxing, and processed vocals sampled in instrumental textures. Along with the voice, participants employed acoustic instruments (percussion, piano), electric instruments (guitar, bass), digital samples from popular music, sounds of the classic Roland TR-808 Rhythm Composer 808 drum machine, and synthesized samples and effects native to various DAWs.[39]

Conceptually, several of the sound works that emerged from the workshop thematize self-love as a political attitude, particularly for women of color. In one of the pieces, for example, a simple minor piano groove sparsely accented by bass guitar and percussion leads into spoken word poetry celebrating Black womanhood (a sixteen-note hi-hat sample kicks in with the voice): "I identify myself as a Black woman, I wouldn't change it for the world. My skin so pure with golden undertones that it is amplified with just the subtle kiss of sunlight."[40] A set of sung lyrics from another piece, accompanied by beatboxing, similarly present the theme of self-love and self-confidence: "I am my kind of hero / and though I may seem a little crazy / I don't care as long as I'm me."[41] This song returns to a belted chorus, every line punctuated by a descending vocal flourish: "I will scream on the top of every mountain I reach / I will sing when I reach the goals I wanted to achieve / I will be me / and no one can change me."[42] Beatboxing, historically derived from drum machine sounds but not reliant on electricity and expensive technology, allows the song to exist outside of the recording studio, perhaps "on the top of every mountain." The same group of students produced a fast-paced freestyle—an endless catalog of "[I] feel like . . ." statements—that flows urgently ahead of the beat supplied by table percussion. The rapper vacillates between addressing, and calling out, the second person (the listener?): "feel like I know I'm worth your time / feel like you don't value my time," and the third person: "feel like nobody really cares"; "feel like it's not that I don't think I'm enough / feel like it's that people 'round me don't care enough." In this freestyle, self-love is framed not as an indulgence but as a bulwark against carelessness: "feel like can nobody tell me otherwise / feel like I love myself / feel like I made myself whole again / feel like I don't care what you think."[43]

Several of the sound works also address themes of cultural lineage, genealogy, and family. The spoken word poem by Group C ends with a meditation on "the endless tradition of knots and tangles" (the insistent hi-hat dropping out for the rest): "It's unknown what reminds myself of myself. It's a sweet debt that you can't comprehend unless you were it."[44] One participant brought in poetry she wrote about her experience as a member of an immigrant family and prompted her working group to brainstorm ideas for musical settings. The resulting piece, titled "Heartbeat," accompanied by a guitar and bass ostinato in minor, takes on the third-generation immigrant experience through a spoken-word poem followed by verse rapped by another group member, both bilingual in English and Spanish: "Your broken English has been made out to be funny . . . I recognize how hard it must be for you to be . . . we stand on the stained concrete of your ancestors' blood." Gesturing to immigrant family histories in the United States, the rapped verse opens in Spanish, the voice cloaked in mild distortion evocative of a megaphone indicting current attitudes toward Hispanic immigrants:

> Perdón, mi presidente, no te quiero confundir / solamente es mi vida que quiero vivir / perdón Mami, tú sabes que toda mi vida he sabido que tú no has podido vivir / land of the free, home of the immigrants / freedom in the home but not in the streets.

At a time defined by anti-immigrant rhetoric and separations of families at the southern border of the United States, the very bilingualism of the song sends a powerful message. The politely worded diss ("I'm sorry, my president, I'd hate to confuse you") contrasts with the tawdry speech and tweets of its addressee.

The open-ended formulation *working in sound* thus yielded participants' creative work that directly addressed issues of social difference, social justice, personal family history, and national political climate. Participants' interaction with workshop leaders in the studios typically began with an explanation of the sonic and emotional effect they would like to convey in their piece, and then experimenting with and learning how to achieve it sonically and technically. In the end, participants called up the expressive and technical strategies—lyrical repetition, contrasting instrumental textures, a mix of vocal styles, rhythmic strategies, various recording techniques and digital effects—of a number of different sound-based genres to amplify the social message of their sound work.

Critical Making and Recording

In studying social inequities next to learning technological skills, and in harnessing critical thinking and hands-on creative experimentation, we recognized that participants in the "Daughters" workshops engaged in what design theorists refer to as "critical making." Broadly speaking, critical making is a practice that regards technology (and the process of "making") as fundamentally social. The framework reflects a belief that hands-on creative and technical exploration can be a form of critical thinking, and conversely that humanities- and activist-based forms of inquiry—not just engineering skills—should be the cornerstone of technological engagement. Anne Balsamo calls this "tinkering as a mode of knowledge production"[45]—a paradigm rooted in a kind of thoughtful experimentation. In centering the social dimension of technology, critical making invites addressing the gendered, racial, and class barriers that define technologized, musical, and institutional spaces. The practice foregrounds the process rather than the product of creation, and destabilizes the false binary between cognitive thought and "embodied, . . . community-oriented" work.[46]

Reflecting these principles, during the final seminar and evening showcase at Columbia's Maison Française, students not only presented their pieces but also shared insights about their group's workflow, methods of collaborating, and what they learned from one another and the workshop leaders. The emphasis was not on individual authorship of finalized and completely polished pieces, but instead on collaborative sound work oriented toward a particular community of listeners (family members, teachers and social workers, the community) at a particular time (evident in references to contemporary artists and the thematization of current political issues) in a particular place (Columbia University, Harlem). "Critical making" was by no means an absolutist guiding principle for the workshops, but the concept valuably captures the reciprocity of intellectual-theoretical and creative-technical work that took place, as well the project's valuing of collaboration and community over individual achievement.

Furthermore, the rubric of critical making invites thinking about the process of recording as a site of agency rather than a neutral stepping-stone to a finished product. The opportunity to record their own sound work thus momentarily restituted the right to *make a record of one's activity* to young women of color. At a time characterized by the proliferation of civic surveillance, data capitalism, and private policing of institutions including campuses, museums, public transit stations, and shopping malls—all of which disproportionately affect communities of color—the act of aiming a microphone, sliding a fader, or applying a digital effect to one's own sound work is a small claim to agency. We were reminded of this policing of youth of color just days after the first "Daughters" workshop took place, when teen brothers Thomas Kanewakeron Gray and Lloyd Skanahwati Gray, members of the Mohawk tribe who were wearing T-shirts of the death metal bands Cattle Decapitation and Archspire, were pulled from a Colorado State University college tour by university police based on the 911 call of a white mother who was also on the tour: officer body-camera video of the brothers, their names, and hometown circulated in the press, while the woman remained anonymous.[47] In a small way, "Daughters" participants thus took control of some of the very mechanisms of recording that frequently oppress communities of color.

"Gym Crow Must Go!": Institutions & Communities

A critical thread of our seminar discussions addressed our academic institution's responsibility to listen to and communicate with its neighbors. Our opening seminar discussion of racial inequities reflected on Columbia University's long and fraught relationship with the community of Harlem, a historically Latinx and Black neighborhood in upper Manhattan.[48] As Woodruff emphasized in a video interview for Columbia News, "Columbia is *in* Harlem."[49]

In 1968, community members and Columbia students protested Columbia's plan to build a fitness center in Morningside Park with a separate entrance for residents of the neighborhood, many of whom were Black, citing the institution's encroachment upon a community in buying up property in Harlem and evicting residents.[50] In her 2015 book *A Storm Foretold: Columbia University and Morningside Heights, 1968,* Christiane Crasemann Collins focuses on the community involvement in the protest; Collins, a historian of urban planning with master's degrees in art history and library science, and the wife of George Collins, a professor of art history at Columbia, was part of the community-based protests that led to the university's abandonment of the project in April 1968.[51] Other leaders in the protest included Bob McKay, Maria Miller, Justus Poole, Suki Ports, Rev. Kendall A. Smith of Beulah Baptist Church in Harlem, the Columbia chapter of Students for a Democratic Society (SDS), and Columbia C.O.R.E., the university chapter of the Congress on Racial Equality.[52] When Columbia University broke ground on a new campus in West Harlem in 2008, intending to build what Mayor Michael Bloomberg described as a "modern, academic mixed-use development with 6.8 million square feet of new state-of-the-art facilities," community organizers protested the legal designation of the neighborhood as "blighted" and the granting of "eminent domain" to the project.[53]

Several of the student participants shared their experiences moving out of West Harlem, Hamilton Heights, and Washington Heights to outer boroughs due to gentrification and rising rents, and one participant watched Columbia's Manhattanville campus take shape from her family's apartment in the Grant Houses public housing project located just across the intersection of Broadway and 125th Street. In a public speech made at an annual Martin Luther King Day march, eighth-grade students from an independent, sliding-scale Upper West Side K–8 school noted the controversy of Columbia's Manhattanville campus.[54] Inviting students from public schools to Columbia's campuses—both the Morningside campus at 116th Street as well as the spaces of the new School of the Arts on the Manhattanville campus in West Harlem on 127th Street—was thus central to our project, which was designed to increase equity and inclusion in the academy, welcoming community members to campus to use resources that are otherwise unavailable to those who are not students or faculty, and reflecting the justification of eminent domain as being *for public utility*.

Happily, academics in some currents of music studies, such as applied ethnomusicology, have long thought about their intellectual work within the vocabularies of public utility and social justice. Writes Jeff Todd Titon, one of the editors of *The Oxford Handbook of Applied Ethnomusicology*:

> Applied ethnomusicology is best regarded as a music-centered intervention in a particular community, whose purpose is to benefit that community—for example, a social improvement, a musical benefit, a cultural good, an economic advantage, or a combination of these and other benefits. It is music-centered, but above all the intervention is people-centered, for the understanding that drives it toward reciprocity is based in the collaborative partnerships that arise from

> ethnomusicological fieldwork. Applied ethnomusicology is guided by ethical principles of social responsibility, human rights, and cultural and musical equity.[55]

This approach to music-centric academic work is self-consciously interested in reciprocity—in addressing and redressing the "disparities often found between the university community, and the community within which it is located and *upon whose service labour it depends.*"[56] Public-outreach is charity: universities often rely on the natural, infrastructural, and human resources of a surrounding community, so it is equitable to share our resources in return.

Music departments can also benefit from applied programming: at a time when many faculty are rethinking their music curricula and confronting the cultural and demographic whiteness of music studies, programs like "Daughters" provide a new model of humanities-based sound-oriented work that explicitly invites underrepresented demographics to participate in the social and intellectual culture of the university. According to the Department of Education's data for 2016, 66.3 percent of music degrees were awarded to white students, 11.1 percent to Hispanic students, 6.9 percent to Black students, 5.5 percent to Asian students, 4.2 percent to multiracial students, 5.5 percent to students of unknown race/ethnicity, 0.3 percent to Native students, and 0.1 percent to [Pacific] Islander students.[57] With regard to gender, the Department of Education's data for 2016 indicate that 56.3 percent of degrees in music were awarded to men; nearly twice as many degrees were awarded to men as were awarded to women at the Berklee College of Music, which focuses on contemporary music with a national reputation in jazz and popular music studies.[58]

As Georgina Born and Kyle Devine have documented, gendered and racial barriers in music spaces do not necessarily correlate and are further structured by class in complicated ways. Their research shows that technology-oriented music degrees overwhelmingly attract and admit male applicants, but these student populations are more ethnically and socioeconomically diverse than those of traditional music degrees, which, however, show a significantly more equitable gender balance.[59] In the case of "Daughters," we hoped that by having high school students engage with faculty, alumni, and students at Columbia, participants would get a sense of the people and the work going on inside the walls of Columbia and Barnard, which might spark students' interest in eventually applying.

Coda: Transposing "Daughters" and Futures

We hope that the "Daughters of Harlem" project will have many futures. In addition to establishing the workshop as an annual event, we are considering creating a free summer program for high school students that would offer an intensive daily program over several weeks, responding to a request from the participants who enthusiastically suggested in their exit surveys that we should hold workshops more frequently. After word of "Daughters of Harlem" began to circulate, we were contacted by a number of colleges and universities, from small liberal arts colleges to public research universities, about how to bring a version of the workshop to their campuses. We hope that our work will encourage others to consider developing the "Daughters" initiative at their own institutions as a way of bridging public-facing music scholarship and community engagement. In order to assist this process of translating the workshop to other local contexts, we may present this project at a national conference, perhaps on a panel that addresses possibilities for public musicology / music theory, and to offer our experience as a resource from which others may draw ideas and a possible template for their own workshops.

Further, we hope to develop courses from our experience in conceiving and implementing the workshop. A graduate seminar could explore how research in the academy can be harnessed to advance equity; the course would explore texts such as DeNora's in providing a theoretical basis for the work, discuss the ethics of organizing, and provide practical information about how to write grants, locate applicants, and plan and implement a daylong or more extended workshop.[60] A course designed for undergraduate students might focus on music and arts instruction in public schools; segregation and poverty in school systems like the one in New York City; action that can be taken by parents, students, and community members to address the inequities in urban public education; and incorporation of student participation in a capstone end-of-semester workshop.[61]

The "Daughters" initiative is rooted in our concern with enacting social justice and is fundamentally site-specific and collaborative. That is, our work evolved from our interest in learning about and responding to the historical and current spatial and political contexts of our university and the surrounding community and from recognizing the resource gaps that demarcate this relationship. Like ethnomusicologist Holly Wissler, we trusted that a small-scale applied music project rooted in collaboration might be an especially effective, and intellectually and ethically responsible form of response.[62] Any offshoots of the "Daughters" project should thus similarly stem from its home institution's local context, and involve—on the part of the organizers—some amount of study of institutional and local history, and a review of the realities of local public education. Participants will already have empirical experience with the effects of this local history, and learning about the specific institutional and municipal actions that structure their lives can offer reference points for their life experience and potentially for their sound work. Just as we (as organizers) studied the historical, institutional, and educational contexts, organizing a workshop for high school students required reflection upon how we might advance equity through research in a meaningful, age-appropriate way. Thus, shaping the project collaboratively—not only in conversation with the co-organizers and workshop leaders, but also with advice from local organizations working with youth and students and faculty who had experience working with high school students—was instructive to us. It is in this sense, too, that the "Daughters" initiative also fulfills the "R" (Research) pillar of its original funder, CAETR: it invites a dynamic response to the intersection of local contexts and lived experiences, bridging campus and community through sound.

Notes

1. For providing seed funding for this project through the Collaborative to Advance Equity Through Research (CAETR), we thank Farah Jasmine Griffin and Alondra Nelson. "For the Daughters of Harlem" received funding from Humanities New York and the following departments and programs at Columbia University: Society of Fellows and Heyman Center for the Humanities, Center for Science and Society, Department of Music, Louis Armstrong Jazz Performance Program, Department of Sociology, Institute for Research on Women, Gender, and Sexuality, and Women Making Change/Center for the Study of Social Difference. We also extend our thanks to Africana Studies and Women's, Gender and Sexuality Studies at Barnard College. For additional support, we are grateful to Brad Garton, Yvette Christiansë, Laura Ciolkowski, Patricia Dailey, Aaron Fox, Eileen Gillooly, Jack Halberstam, Marianne Hirsch, Janet Jakobsen, Shamus Khan, George E. Lewis, Reinhold Martin, Ana M. Ochoa Gautier, Shanny Peer, Pamela Smith, and Chris Washburne. We thank workshop leaders David Adamcyk, Courtney Bryan, Kamari Carter, Seth Cluett, Zosha Di Castri, Rachel Devorah Rome, Miya Masaoka, Matthew D. Morrison, Ebonie Smith, and Sondra E. Woodruff II; graduate coordinators Laina Dawes and Finola Merivale, designer Brandon Sugiyama, and photographers Maria Fantinato Geo de Siqueira and Kevin Jiang. For their kind assistance, we thank Teresa Aguayo, Khadija Belly,

Laura Ciolkowski, Ryan Grubbs, Akemi Kochiyama, Alex Kutler, Catherine LaSota, Jenny Lee, Erica Lockhart, Johanna Lopez, Yulanda McKenzie, Alicia Hall Moran, Jenny Navasky, Mark Nomadiou, Beth Pratt, Michelle Rowland, Gabriela Kumar Sharma, Michèle Solá, Vina Tran, and the late Anne Gefell. Ellie Hisama would like to thank Nalini Ghuman, Elizabeth Gould, Peng Liu, Carol Matthews, and Allison Sokil; the students and faculty at her keynote address "Lost Voices, Found Histories: On Silences and Soundings" delivered at the conference "Music and Culture of the Americas," Butler School of Music, University of Texas at Austin (April 2019); and the audience at her Kenneth H. Peacock Lecture at the University of Toronto's Faculty of Music (March 2019) for their encouraging responses to this work. Lucie Vágnerová would like to thank Kate Galloway and students in Galloway's graduate seminar in applied ethnomusicology at Wesleyan University (spring 2019) for their helpful comments.

2. The project's website, which houses a gallery of photographs from the workshops, is https://daughtersofharlem.wordpress.com/ and the project report for the April 2018 workshop is available at https://daughtersofharlem.wordpress.com/report1/

3. Collaborative to Advance Equity through Research (CAETR), http://wgssc.columbia.edu/she-rises, accessed June 20, 2020.

4. Women's, Gender, and Sexuality Studies Council, "She Rises in the Sunshine: The Collaborative to Advance Equity through Research at Columbia University," http://wgssc.columbia.edu/she-rises, accessed June 20, 2020.

5. In a *New York Times* op-ed, Kimberlé Williams Crenshaw observes that My Brother's Keeper, "a five-year, $200 million program that will give mentorships, summer jobs and other support to boys and young men of color, most of them African-American or Hispanic . . . amounts to an abandonment of women of color." See Crenshaw, "The Girls Obama Forgot," *New York Times,* July 29, 2014. CAETR receives material support from the institutions that have signed onto the collaborative, which include Columbia University, and not from a foundation or central funding source.

6. Giovanni Russonello, "Inside Sonny Rollins's Jazz Archive, Headed Home to Harlem," *New York Times,* May 29, 2017.

7. Tia DeNora, *Music in Everyday Life* (Cambridge: Cambridge University Press, 2000).

8. The institutional history of the CMC/CPEMC is overwhelmingly white and male in most retellings. Elizabeth Hinkle-Turner notes that even Pril Smiley and Alice Shields, each of whom acted as associate director at different points, are seldom mentioned in these roles, and "neither woman was ever named a faculty member" in spite of doing most of the teaching (and even picking up the teaching loads of Bülent Arel and Vladimir Ussachevsky). Their categorizations as "clerk" and "Science Technician II" in the employment record are testament to their "relatively poor treatment" at the center. See Elizabeth Hinkle-Turner, *Women Composers and Music Technology in the United States: Crossing the Line* (Burlington, VT: Ashgate, 2006), 21. Lucie Vágnerová explores the histories of women working in sound technologies including at the CMC in "Sirens/Cyborgs: Sound Technologies and the Musical Body" (PhD diss., Columbia University, 2016). The symposium Unsung Stories: Women at Columbia's Computer Music

Center, which took place on April 9–10, 2021, helped to illuminate the hidden history of women, BIPOC, and LGBTQ+ composers at the CMC/CPEMC.

9. Appendices 1 and 2 contain biographies of the workshop leaders and discussants, as well as a list of the students who participated in the workshops and the schools they attended.

10. The School of General Studies at Columbia University was "created specifically for returning and nontraditional students." See website of School of General Studies, Columbia University, https://gs.columbia.edu/, accessed June 20, 2020.

11. Sondra Woodruff, e-mail message to the authors, January 30, 2019.

12. Pamela Z, "A Tool Is a Tool," in *Women, Art, and Technology*, ed. Judy Malloy (Cambridge, MA: MIT Press, 2003), 356.

13. Sam Bloch and Kate Taylor, "In New York High Schools, the Sound of Music is Muted," *New York Times*, May 13, 2018.

14. Jeff Nussbaum, "The Night New York Saved Itself from Bankruptcy," *New Yorker*, October 16, 2005.

15. Tyleah Hawkins, "Will Less Art and Music in the Classroom Really Help Students Soar Academically?," *Washington Post*, December 28, 2012; Bloch and Taylor, "New York High Schools."

16. New York City Department of Education, "Arts in Schools Report 2017–18" (2018), 45, https://infohub.nyced.org/docs/default-source/default-document-library/arts_in_school_report_17-18.pdf?sfvrsn=34ec35f9_2

17. New York City Department of Education, "Arts in Schools Report 2017–18," 41–43.

18. New York City Department of Education, "NYC School Survey Citywide Results," August 2018, 9, https://infohub.nyced.org/docs/default-source/default-document-library/2018-citywide-analysis-of-survey-resultsfbf5c93b49d9464aa516910b95543d26.pdf

19. John Kucsera and Gary Orfield, "New York State's Extreme School Segregation: Inequality, Inaction and a Damaged Future," in *The Civil Rights Project / Proyecto Derechos Civiles* (Los Angeles: UCLA, 2014), 19–23.

20. Eliza Shapiro, "Only 7 Black Students Got into Stuyvesant, N.Y.'s Most Selective High School, Out of 895 Spots," *New York Times*, March 18, 2019.

21. NYC Department of Education, "Stuyvesant High School," *2017–2018 School Quality Snapshot* (2018), https://tools.nycenet.edu/snapshot/2018/02M475/HS

22. Stuyvesant High School, Music program (n.d.), https://stuy.enschool.org/m/pages/index.jsp?uREC_ID=126961&type=d&pREC_ID=253554

23. Ellie M. Hisama chronicles the principles in organizing the 2015 symposium "Women, Music, Power," which supported payment to student workers and gave participants access to childcare and lactation rooms. See Hisama, "Power and Equity in the Academy: Change from Within," *Current Musicology*, special issue *Sounding the Break: Music Studies and the Political* 102 (Spring 2018): 81–92. https://journals.library.columbia.edu/index.php/currentmusicology/article/view/5365. For more information about the symposium "Women, Music, Power: A Celebration of Suzanne G. Cusick's Work," visit the website http://www.womenmusicpower.com/

24. The first "Daughters" workshop on April 28, 2018, coincided with a strike of Graduate Workers of Columbia (GWC), now GWC-UAW Local 2110, the union for research and teaching assistants at Columbia University. All students working on the "Daughters of Harlem" workshop stated to the workshop organizers that they felt that their involvement did not constitute breaking the strike or crossing picket lines because of the public-outreach nature of the initiative and the budgeting of hourly pay for graduate students. For more information about GWC-UAW Local 2110, visit https://columbiagradunion.org/

25. Robert Branch, "Daughters of Harlem Teaches Local Young Women to Record and Produce Their Own Music," Columbia News Video (2018), https://vimeo.com/294854021; Eve Glasberg, "Daughters of Harlem Teaches Local Young Women to Record and Produce Their Own Music," *Columbia News*, December 17, 2018, https://news.columbia.edu/daughtersofharlem

26. DeNora, *Music in Everyday Life*, x.

27. DeNora, *Music in Everyday Life*, 53.

28. DeNora, *Music in Everyday Life*, 47.

29. "The Banneker Institute summer program at Harvard is a full-time, ten-week research and study experience. We prepare undergraduate students of color for graduate programs in astronomy by emphasizing research, building community, and encouraging debate and political action through social justice education." Website of Banneker Institute, https://bannekerinstitute.fas.harvard.edu/, accessed April 28, 2019.

30. Emma Buzbee, "New Faculty Diversity Data Shows Stagnation in Percentage of Black, Latinx Faculty," *Columbia Spectator*, September 13, 2018, https://www.columbiaspectator.com/news/2018/09/13/new-faculty-diversity-data-shows-stagnation-in-percentage-of-black-latinx-faculty/

31. Khadija Hussain, "Off the Radar: At Public Schools Where Columbia Doesn't Recruit, Applicants Face Uphill Battle," *Columbia Spectator*, September 20, 2018, https://www.columbiaspectator.com/news/2018/09/20/off-the-radar-at-public-schools-where-columbia-doesnt-recruit-applicants-face-uphill-battle/

32. Courtney Bryan, "The Power of Representation," in *Remembering Geri Allen (1957–2017)*, ed. Ellie M. Hisama, memorial booklet distributed at Feminist Theory and Music 14, San Francisco State University, July 29, 2017, https://projects.iq.harvard.edu/files/geri-allen-symposium/files/geri_allen_tributes_booklet_ftm_july_2017.pdf

33. Branch, "Daughters of Harlem."

34. Branch, "Daughters of Harlem."

35. For the Daughters of Harlem Participant Survey, April 2018.

36. Courtney Bryan, personal communication, February 20, 2019.

37. Courtney Bryan, e-mail message to Ellie Hisama, October 11, 2018.

38. Bryan, e-mail message to Ellie Hisama, 2018.

39. Daughters of Harlem SoundCloud, 2018, https://soundcloud.com/user-353254380

40. Group C, Daughters of Harlem SoundCloud.

41. Group B, Daughters of Harlem SoundCloud.

42. Group B, Daughters of Harlem SoundCloud.

43. With the recording running and the table percussion continuing, one of

the participants broke into singing "Shine bright like a diamond" (the first line of "Diamonds" by Rihanna), and the rest of the group spontaneously joined in unison, embodying the community-building power of music described by DeNora, and recasting self-love in yet another way. Group B, Daughters of Harlem SoundCloud.

44. Group C, Daughters of Harlem SoundCloud.

45. Anne Balsamo, *Designing Culture: The Technological Imagination at Work* (Durham, NC: Duke University Press, 2011), 254.

46. Matt Ratto and Stephen Hockema, "FLWR PWR—Tending the Walled Garden," in *Walled Garden*, ed. Annet Dekker and Annette Wolfsberger (Rotterdam: Virtueel Platform, 2009), 52, https://criticalmaking.com/wp-content/uploads/2009/10/2448_alledgarden_ch06_ratto_hockema.pdf

47. The older brother, Thomas Kanewakeron Gray, shared his hope with a journalist that he would "get a doctorate in music to start his own school and become a music therapist." See Niraj Chokshi, "Native American Brothers Pulled from Campus Tour after Nervous Parent Calls Police," *New York Times*, May 5, 2018.

48. According to the New York City Department of City Planning, Population Division, using data from the US Census Bureau, residents of Manhattanville in 2010 who were of Hispanic Origin (Any Race) were 62.8 percent; Black/African American 26.8 percent; White 7.45 percent; Asian 2.2 percent; Some Other Race 0.33 percent, Native Hawaiian and Other Pacific Islander 0.02 percent; American Indian and Alaska Native 0.3 percent. See New York City Department of City Planning, "Total Population by Mutually Exclusive Race and Hispanic Origin New York City Neighborhood Tabulation Areas, 2010," March 29, 2011, https://www1.nyc.gov/assets/planning/download/pdf/data-maps/nyc-population/census2010/t_pl_p3a_nta.pdf

49. Branch, "Daughters of Harlem."

50. Historian Rosalind Rosenberg notes the small numbers of Black students in the 1920s through the 1950s at Barnard, an all-women's college, and Columbia, which first admitted women in 1983, compared to the population in the community. She notes that "there do not seem to have been more than five [African American students]" at Barnard per class into the 1950s, slightly higher than other Seven Sisters colleges, "where two black students per class remained the norm." See Rosenberg, *Changing the Subject: How the Women of Columbia Shaped the Way We Think about Sex and Politics* (New York: Columbia University Press, 2004), 239. She comments on the marginalization of women in Students for a Democratic Society (SDS). In an interview with Rosenberg, Rusti (Carolyn) Eisenberg, the only woman on the strike-coordinating committee during the occupation of buildings at Columbia in 1968, observes the "very macho behavior" of men on the committee, and noted that "if you didn't have a loud voice, you did not get heard" (240). See Christiane Crasemann Collins, *A Storm Foretold: Columbia University and Morningside Heights, 1968* (n.p.: EbookBakery Books, 2015); and Rosenberg, *Changing the Subject*, 239–40.

51. Collins, *A Storm Foretold*; and Sam Roberts, "Christiane Collins, Scholar Who Fought a Columbia Gym, Dies at 92," *New York Times*, May 8, 2018.

52. See Rosenberg, *Changing the Subject*, 239. Over two decades later, New

York City Department of Parks and Recreation turned the initial excavation site into a small pond with a waterfall. See City of New York Department of Parks and Recreation, "A Conceptual Master Plan for Morningside Park," prepared by Bond Ryder Wilson and Quennell Rothschild Associates, July 1985.

53. Steven Gregory, "The Radiant University: Space, Urban Redevelopment, and the Public Good," *City & Society* 25, no. 1 (2013): 47–69.

54. Manhattan Country School, Martin Luther King, Jr. Commemorative March Newsletter (2019), https://www.manhattancountryschool.org/news-events/publications

55. Jeff Todd Titon, "Section 1. Applied Ethnomusicology: A Descriptive and Historical Account," in *The Oxford Handbook of Applied Ethnomusicology*, ed. Svanibor Pettan and Jeff Todd Titon (New York: Oxford University Press, 2015), 4.

56. Eric Martin Usner, "United States Ethnomusicology and the Engaged University," in *Applied Ethnomusicology: Historical and Contemporary Approaches*, ed. Klisala Harrison, Elizabeth Mackinlay, and Svanibor Pettan (n.p.: Cambridge Scholars Publishing, 2010), 76–95; emphasis ours.

57. DATAUSA: Music (n.d.), https://datausa.io/profile/cip/5009/#demographics, accessed April 28, 2019.

58. DATAUSA: Music.

59. Georgina Born and Kyle Devine, "Gender, Creativity and Education in Digital Musics and Sound Art," *Contemporary Music Review* 35, no. 1 (2016): 2.

60. Kate Galloway devoted a session to the "Daughters of Harlem" project in her spring 2019 graduate seminar at Wesleyan University in Applied Ethnomusicology. Via Skype, Vágnerová talked about the project and answered questions on April 26, 2019.

61. Kavitha Mediratta, Norm Fruchter, and Anne C. Lewis, "Organizing for School Reform: How Communities are Finding Their Voices and Reclaiming Public Schools," New York: Institute for Education and Social Policy, Steinhardt School, New York University, October 2002, https://files.eric.ed.gov/fulltext/ED475909.pdf

62. Holly Wissler, "Andes to Amazon on the River Q'eros: Indigenous Voice in Grassroots Tourism, Safeguarding, and Ownership Projects of the Q'eros and Wachiperi Peoples," in Pettan and Titon, *Oxford Handbook of Applied Ethnomusicology*, 399.

APPENDIX 1
Biographies of workshop leaders and discussants

David Adamcyk is a composer, electronic musician, and sound engineer who teaches composition at the Manhattan School of Music and Columbia University. He holds a doctorate in composition from McGill University. Adamcyk creates musical works for the concert hall as well as for the theatrical stage. His interest in technology has pushed him to explore various ways to combine electronic devices with acoustic instruments.

Courtney Bryan is a composer and pianist and the Albert and Linda Mintz Professor of Music at Tulane University. She holds a DMA in composition from Columbia University. Bryan's award-winning music draws on jazz and other types of experimental music, as well as traditional gospel, spirituals, and hymns. She was awarded the 2018 Herb Alpert Award in the Arts and the 2019–20 Samuel Barber Rome Prize, and is a 2020 United States Artists Fellow.

Kamari Carter is a producer, performer, sound designer, and installation artist primarily working with sound and found objects. Carter's work has been exhibited at Automata Arts, MoMA, Fridman Gallery, Lenfest Center for the Arts, and Issue Project Room. Carter holds a BFA in music technology from California Institute of the Arts and an MFA in sound art from Columbia University.

Seth Cluett is a composer and artist, assistant director of the Computer Music Center and Sound Art Program at Columbia University, and artist-in-residence at Nokia Bell Labs, where he researches spatial audio and multisensory communication. He holds a PhD in music composition from Princeton University. Cluett's work addresses issues of attention and listening to critique the role of media in society.

Zosha Di Castri is a composer, pianist, and Francis Goelet Assistant Professor of Music at Columbia University, where she completed a DMA in composition. Di Castri works with instruments, electronics, installations, and collaborations with video and dance. She received the Jules Leger Prize for New Chamber Music in 2012, was a fellow at the Institute for Ideas and Imagination in Paris in 2018–19, and was commissioned to open the 2019 BBC Proms.

Miya Masaoka is a composer and sound artist, associate professor of professional practice, and the director of the Sound Art MFA Program, Columbia University. She is a Fulbright scholar, and has been named a Studio Artist by the Park Avenue Armory. Her work has been exhibited at MoMA PS1, the Venice Biennale, and ICA Philadelphia, and her compositions have been performed by the BBC Scottish Symphony, Bang on a Can, and Jack Quartet. Her work crosses disciplines and employs metaphors and modes of listening and perception.

Matthew D. Morrison, a native of Charlotte, North Carolina, is a musicologist, violinist, and assistant professor of music, New York University, Tisch School of the Arts. He obtained his PhD in musicology from Columbia University in 2014, and in 2018–19 he was a Hutchins Fellow at the W. E. B. Du Bois Research Institute, Harvard University. His research explores race and performance, and he is working on a book titled *Blacksound: Making Race & Popular Music in the U.S.*

Rachel Devorah Rome is a sound artist and feminist technologist, assistant professor of electronic production and design at the Berklee College of Music, and the 2018–19 Adrian Piper Foundation Berlin Fellow. She holds a PhD in music composition and computer technologies from the University of Virginia. Rome's work engages the poetics and politics of their specific contexts.

Ebonie Smith is an award-winning music producer, audio engineer, and singer-songwriter; founder and president of Gender Amplified, a nonprofit organization that celebrates and supports women and girls in music production; and producer at Atlantic Records. Smith is an alumna of Barnard College, Columbia University, and New York University, Steinhardt School. She is a *Forbes Magazine* 30 Under 30 nominee and was assistant engineer for *Hamilton (Original Broadway Cast Recording).*

Sondra E. Woodruff II graduated from Columbia University's School of General Studies in 2019. As vice president of Campus Life, she worked to bridge resource gaps in the Columbia community. Woodruff is a recording artist, majored in music, and has taught audio production. She works as Producer, Engagement & Social Impact, at the Kelly Strayhorn Theater in Pittsburgh.

APPENDIX 2
Student participants (and where they describe growing up)

J'Lanee Acevedo
Kristen Ackon, the Bronx
Rachell Alejo, New York
Lara Buchan, Scotland and NYC
Jadebelle Buday, Harlem and the Bronx
Michelle Cabrera, the Bronx*
Assaitia Camara
Yaya Camara, the Bronx
Leandra Castillo
Mercedes Clark, the Bronx
Leila De la Rosa, the Bronx
Ndeye Diop, NYC
Carys Dixon-Cabo, the Bronx
Ashanti Espiritusanto, Harlem*
Amanda Felix, Lower East Side
Alaura Flynn, Riverdale, the Bronx
Maia Gambrell, Harlem
Faith Lee, Queens and the Bronx
Avery Palmer, NYC
Anell Ramos, Washington Heights*
Fiona Robinson, Jamaica
Katelyn Walnord-Scott

*Participated in fall and spring workshops

Represented Schools

Art and Design High School, New York
Columbia Secondary School, New York
Cornerstone Academy for Social Action, Bronx (a public middle school)
Humanities Preparatory Academy, New York
Institute for Collaborative Education, New York
Landmark High School, New York
Manhattan Early College School for Advertising, New York
Mott Hall II, New York
The Young Women's Leadership School of the Bronx, Bronx

SIX | The Law of Returns

MUHAL RICHARD ABRAMS AND VIJAY IYER IN CONVERSATION

Introduction by Vijay Iyer

On June 11, 2017, at the Ojai Music Festival in Southern California, I was one of several hundred witnesses to one of the final performances of pianist-composer Muhal Richard Abrams (1930–2017).[1] Abrams was appearing in trio with two longtime colleagues, multi-instrumentalist Roscoe Mitchell (b. 1940) and trombonist/electronic musician George Lewis (b. 1952); all three were members of the Association for the Advancement of Creative Musicians, a long-standing aggregate of African American composer-performers formed in 1963 on Chicago's South Side.

In this trio's music-making, as evidenced across numerous performances from 2003 to 2017 as well as on disc, a guiding aesthetic invariably revealed itself: a profoundly committed ethos of rigorous listening, plaintive sonic inquiry, and elemental construction.[2] That morning in Ojai, as the music proceeded in what initially appeared as irresolvable clumps, the three men carried themselves with an uncanny composure, displaying a faith in some mysterious process. Musical acts were conjured in real time, seemingly from scratch but somehow with great foresight: fragments and shards of sound from Mitchell's soprano saxophone, plangent clusters and raw gestures from Abrams's piano, digitally processed and multiplied drones from Lewis's trombone. The music grew steadily more significant, as each new bit of material revealed new coun-

Figure 6.1. Muhal Richard Abrams (right) and Vijay Iyer reflected in a dusty mirror backstage at the Skopje Jazz Festival, Skopje, Macedonia, October 23, 2011

terpoints and conjunctures, and the gently ebbing episodes stirred up subtle energies. In just under an hour, as this calm, resourceful enactment of musical interdependence drew to a close, the entire Libby Bowl audience solemnly held onto the gravity of the moment, before erupting in an ecstatic ovation. Part of me wanted to preserve and examine this ineffable feeling that brought audience members to our feet, many of us in tears. How had these elemental sonic maneuvers come to *matter?* How had small moments of intention/invention become *events,* and how had those events become form? How, when, and where did an affective register open up in this formal enterprise? What did this music *do?*

In full disclosure, I am very well acquainted with each of this trio's members; Lewis was one of my dissertation advisers in the 1990s, Mitchell employed me as a pianist in his ensembles in the early 2000s, and all three continue to exert a significant influence on my life, music, and thought. But in the years since this performance, I've found myself revisiting various conversations I'd had with Abrams over two decades.

What I remember most is how his language—condensed, poetic, sage-like utterances—could gently dismantle one's standpoint on an issue. In

1996, in one of our earliest encounters, he asked what I was working on, and I fumbled through a synopsis of my graduate studies in music cognition. He responded with a query: "Are you your mind?" I didn't have an answer (and indeed barely understood the question), so he asked it again, and again: "Are you your mind?" Eventually he answered his own question with an allusion to Buddhist and yogic traditions, which were among the many esoteric topics he had studied in great depth: You are also *the one who observes* your own mind. I was left wondering what this distinction might suggest for music. The implication of the disunity of the self, and the suggestion that "mind" might be but a facet of who and what we are, seemed to run counter to prevailing perspectives on "music cognition" or the then-common phrase, "the musical mind"; and these views might further imply that music cognition is not a straightforward, unified, or complete process either. Soon afterward I found my way into perspectives on embodied cognition that were also influenced by Buddhist perspectives, and eventually, perhaps not fully aware of the impact of Abrams's intervention on my own line of inquiry, I developed a dissertation's worth of ideas about embodied music cognition.[3]

I am reminded almost daily of another potent Abrams utterance from those years. In his description of composer-pianist Thelonious Monk, Abrams stated, with a Monk-like repetition: "Monk was always creating—*always creating*." I'd considered myself a Monk devotee at the time, but Abrams's statement here has, over time, brought me multiple significant and ongoing epiphanies on Monk's music. This phrase dismantles the tiresome composition-improvisation dichotomy, in its assertion that for Monk, even a repetition is not a repetition; rather it is the same idea formed again—created anew. As I listened for this quality in Monk's music, I started to hear it in others as well: Roy Haynes, Zigaboo Modeliste, Alice Coltrane, Betty Carter, Roy Hargrove, Tyshawn Sorey—and Muhal Richard Abrams.

After graduate school, at the end of 1998, I made a beeline for New York City. Since the early 1980s, Abrams had lived in an apartment in Manhattan Plaza (New York's famous Midtown West apartment complex with dedicated housing for artists) with his wife Peggy and daughter Richarda. Their family welcomed me into the community of New York musicians, treating me with kindness and generosity.

By fall 1999 I had started to perform regularly in town with my ensembles and collaborators. One such group, the first incarnation of the collaborative trio Fieldwork with Aaron Stewart and Elliot Humberto Kavee, played a set at The AlterKnit, a claustrophobic thirty-five-seat basement room at the Knitting Factory on Leonard Street. Abrams came with fellow former Chicagoans, the legendary composer-performers Andrew Hill and Henry Threadgill. These three elder masters sat directly in front of the band, on metal folding chairs around a tiny table. I was nervously encouraged by their presence, yet mortified that they had to see us in such undignified surroundings. After the set, Abrams came up to me with some encouraging words. I thanked him and said, "We're just trying to get out of this room." Abrams replied, "Well . . . just *play your way out.* That's all." And he said it again: *Play your way out.* In that moment I was caught up in my own frustration about the vagaries of an indifferent music business, but Abrams handily dispelled my qualms in one simple, resonant utterance. Hearing it from him, the phrase carried a lifetime of perspective: music, when handled with care, attention, and commitment, contained the ingredients for growth, transformation, even liberation. Music-making itself would, quite literally, carry us somewhere higher.

On September 5, 2012, I had the chance to interview Abrams for a podcast for the occasion of his receipt of an award from the Mid-Atlantic Arts Foundation. We sat together for an hour in a bare boardroom at the offices of Chamber Music America. In our exchange you hear him caring about words and their impact, contrasting my word choices with his, and always unpacking the resonant, significant *musicalities* of each utterance. He knows what they can do, not just their sounds and their senses but their timing and their formal relationships, their emphases, energetic contours, and patternings. What he seems to aim to do with his words, as he did for a lifetime with his music, is activate more growth, more individuation, more forms of human life.

In beginning with the above anecdotes, I realize that I might appear to the reader as a nonobjective acolyte or devotee of some kind. But I chose to set up this chapter in this manner with the hope of setting it apart from the genre of "jazz oral history." In a stretch, this chapter *could* be called an interview, if only in the original sense of that term: *entrevoir,* to see each other. More to the point, it might best be understood as a collaborative endeavor of knowledge construction, in the genre of a Socratic dialogue or a Buddhist sutra. This conversation is not particularly about jazz, nor is it a straightforward oral history; instead it is one link in a decades-long chain of interactions between two people, in a tradition of inquiry into music-making, humanity, and to use Abrams's preferred encapsulation in this period, "individualism."

This term deserves comment, since it "holds a problematic but central position in jazz narratives," as Fumi Okiji has noted, and yet acquires central importance in our conversation.[4] Similar remarks from Abrams on a separate occasion prove pivotal to Okiji's reconsideration of Adorno's writings on jazz.[5] As will also become clear in our dialogue, Okiji has observed that

> Abrams's "individual" is encoded with heterogeneity and distinction. True individualism cannot occur in isolation. It is not captured by mere tolerance of difference. In fact, it goes beyond a virtuous embrace of the best examples of multiculturalism. It involves an awareness of the individual's dependence on what it is not. An individual cannot reach truth alone, "the information" being distributed across each and every one. . . . Abrams's nuanced, very particular understanding of individualism helps us to see what is lost in shorthanded parlance.[6]

In what follows, I offer a glimpse of an ongoing practice of research, speculation, experimenting, assessing, and theorizing that has long pervaded Black creative cultures.[7] As Wadada Leo Smith writes, "Artists are the best explainers and models of what they do. Their views, reflections, and contemplations are closer to the truth and more authentic than any other view concerning the music-objects they create."[8] When Abrams asks, "*What did the music do?*" he is also posing a fundamental question about how we hear across difference, and his clear-minded insights about a phenomenon of *mutual resonance* ("a bell within them that was already there") come from decades of practice, study, and observation. Our conversation, while reflecting our own differences (forty-one years separated us in age, and equally substantial distance in culture and history), exemplifies this reciprocal process of bell-ringing. I have kept the dialogue largely intact, with its repetitions, fragments, and rapid interchanges, in hopes of evoking the temporal flow of Abrams's presence: his way of hearing and relating to others, his vivid thought process, and his gentle, resolute intellectual guidance.

MUHAL RICHARD ABRAMS: Hello, I'm Muhal Richard Abrams.

VIJAY IYER: Hi, this is Vijay Iyer. We're speaking to you from New York City. I'm honored to converse with this major figure in American music: someone I've admired for decades, since as long as I knew anything about Creative Music and the whole Creative Music movement. Mr. Abrams, you come from Chicago, and you are one of the founders for the Association for the Advancement of Creative Musicians, and you are a composer and pianist of international stature and have had a huge impact on the world of music over the last five decades. So I don't want to spend too much time on biographical stuff because I think anybody who wants to know can find that. I mean, that's well documented. But I was wondering if you might talk a little bit from a personal perspective about what were the beginnings of this path for you, in terms of *choosing* a life in the arts, a life in music, and what were the steps that led you to that decision?

MRA: Well, first let me thank you for the compliments. . . . I think it *chose me.* And I think that's the case with most continuous musicians, people that come into the world of the arts and they stay. It becomes part of their life. But I think, to answer your question, I think it just chose me. There came a time when I felt I should just do it. And I guess it had chosen me long before, and then it came to a point where I *heard it,* I mean [chuckles], and that's really, in terms of any sort of path—

VI: Yeah, how old were you, would you say, when that realization struck?

MRA: Oh, I don't know, sixteen or seventeen.

VI: But music was in your life before that?

MRA: Uhh, no: sports. Now, let me say this: The answer is yes, in terms of my being attracted to music, in terms of listening to it, you know? And I would always, it would always stop me. If I heard some music I would just *stop.* I would just notice it. There was a curiosity. But not a curiosity in the earlier times that gave me the feeling I wanted to act in any certain way in terms of pursuing it. And, at some point, it just, it *called.* That's about it—I stepped in.

VI: And it was the piano first?

MRA: Yeah.

VI: Because you've played a number of instruments in your life.

MRA: The clarinet.

VI: Yes.

MRA: Definitely clarinet, violin, cello, stuff like that.

VI: Now, Chicago has such a rich musical legacy, a history that must have been all around you at that time.

MRA: Oh, long before I stepped in it was *there* [chuckles], that's right, yeah.

VI: So what were your first opportunities that you remember, playing piano?

MRA: Oh, I don't know. It would be hard to pin something like that down. I mean, I just started to participate in things, you know? And study. And learn. Any specific *event*, in terms of playing the piano, right now I couldn't really give you; there were so *many*, you know.

VI: Right, I'm sure. It's been reported that you were self-taught on the piano.

MRA: I am self-taught, sure.

VI: And so, what did that mean for you?

MRA: [Taken aback, with humor] What do you mean?

VI: How does one teach oneself?

MRA: [Shifting gears, more earnest] One teaches oneself because that's a natural phenomenon, in terms of your individuality.[9] You can teach yourself anything if you respect the fact that you have to study, *seriously*, in terms of gathering the proper kind of information. It's a process that, of course, had a lot of trial and error in it.

VI: Yes, of course.

MRA: But you know, the fact that you *stick with* a situation: you soon learn from your mistakes and your accomplishments together.

VI: Yeah. I mean, as you know, I ask that question from a perspective of sympathy [laughter] or mutual understanding. So I can attest to what you've said in the sense that it's a process, and it's sort of a *lifelong* process. In particular, you know, often it's said that people pass through a kind of imitative phase before getting to a point of true creativity, or—

MRA: Well, I would have said it a little differently. But I don't disagree with you.

VI: Though I've always had the sense from your work and your perspective that you were never not a creative musician, in the sense that creativity was always part of the process for you. And so, I guess what that says to me is that there are creative forms of imitation. In the way that you might digest the work of another artist, you can do that in a way that's empowering.

MRA: Yes, you could say it in the way that you're saying. I would say it differently, but you could certainly say it.

VI: How would—please, how would—?

MRA: No, it's OK, it's OK, it's OK. Because, you know, I can take that because we all have different concepts. That's how we learn from each other, because there are many approaches to the same thing, and then ways of saying the same thing, you know, so it's OK. But back to when you say it's like "imitation"—well, we all pass through imitative stages, because that is wise and healthy, if you are imitating what you consider to be masters at what you want to do, like Art Tatum, master at playing the piano, you know what I mean?

VI: Right.

MRA: Well, like Bud Powell. Or *Horowitz*, you know? Then that's healthy. But the thing is, I've always felt that I wanted to do things, I wanted to create music—*original* things—you know, I've *always* felt that way, when I first started. That's all I wanted to do, was to do it *my way*. But first I had to learn *how* to do it. So this [followed], the imitation, the studying of literature or music, studying individuals who appeared to me to know what they were doing, *listening* to them, you know what I mean? And then I came in contact, of course, on the scene, with musicians who were accomplished. And I had to equip myself to perform with them. So all of that was a part of a learning experience, you know.

VI: On-the-job training [laughs].

MRA: Yes, because, you know, you didn't get to the stage with certain people until you developed your abilities to where you could hold your own, you know, and so all of that. And *Chicago*, I mean, you know, *that* school [laughs] was quite demanding, but fair!

VI: [Laughter] That's good to know!

MRA: No,[10] it's *fair*, but it's *demanding!* Because you know, after all, if you work hard to do something, put a lot of hours in and things like that, then you want to be performing with people who respect that, because they've done a similar type thing. So you're among your peers in that sense. Yeah, so it's fair.

VI: Yes. Now, if we look at the beginnings of the AACM, the organization that you were one of the founding members of, and if I understand right you convened the first meeting, is that fair to say?

MRA: Oh yeah.[11]

VI: So, you know, this was a collective of African American musicians from the South[12]—

MRA: An *association.*

VI: [Pauses] An association—

MRA: *Not* a collective.

VI: Oh, OK.

MRA: An *association.*

VI: Well, what's the distinction there?

MRA: [Dryly] Well, the two words are different. You can analyze those words and there's a distinction there. [A pause, then with more warmth] But, to give you what I mean, an *association* is, like, *respect for the other individual.* It's not a collective in the sense of what a collective would be.

VI: Is there an implication with the word "collective" that individual identity is maybe downplayed or suppressed?

MRA: Well, I don't want to belabor that, but it was an *association.* That says, you know, because it's not—I mean, when people call a grouping a "collective," they have a certain thing in mind when they say "collective." And some people just like to apply the word "collective," rather than any other word. But, we said the *Association* for the Advancement of Creative Musicians. And that's what it is and that's what it was then when we started: we *associated* with each other.

VI: So, you moved freely in the world as individuals—

MRA: That's right.

VI:—and yet there's an affiliation that you cultivated amongst yourselves at the same time.

MRA: Well, we were already performing and associating with each other as Chicago musicians. And so, the AACM was developed to create a forum for these musicians, who were associating with each other, to express their individualism through original work.

VI: Right.

MRA: Follow me?

VI: Yes.

MRA: And that was the whole key.

VI: That's what I wanted to ask you about.

MRA: The whole purpose.

VI: Yeah. That was in the original—

MRA: Purpose!

VI: Yeah, that was something that you laid out in the beginning: that original music was the utmost priority.

MRA: It *was* the priority. That was *it.* That was it.

VI: Did that pose a challenge for some people who felt that maybe that wasn't their own orientation?

MRA: No. When you're dealing with individualism, individuals have a right to do what they feel they should do. If they didn't agree, if any musician didn't agree with what we set out to do, they were free to go do what they wanted to do, you know, because the respect for one's individualism was primary to what we were doing—respect for the individual. All individuals, whether they were a part of the association, the AACM, or not, they were still individuals who pursued their own path. So we *respected* that, and we respected the fact that we wanted to create original music through composition and improvisation and theater and, you know, other related type of activity. But the main point is the respect for the individual. It's *much bigger,* the idea is *much bigger* than the AACM. Respect for the individual because we were expressing that in terms of *life itself,* you see? You respect the ditchdigger, you respect the great musician, you respect the hairdresser, you respect the swami. You respect people, you know what I mean? You respect the rabbi. You respect *people,* whoever they are. You respect the fact that they *have a right to choose.* That is what went into the AACM, as you know yourself, in the first wave of AACM musicians, and it still goes on now, but I'm speaking of the first wave because I was closely associated in that grouping. All of those people are distinct individuals—what they do. Now, how did that happen?

VI: Yeah [laughs], that's a good question!

MRA: It happened because of what I'm telling you. It was there, not to *interfere* with anyone, but to *assist*—in this association—to *assist* each of us. We *assisted* each other in developing the individual pursuit, in terms of, in our case, producing and improvising music.

VI: And, as I understand, teaching was a major part of the work that AACM was doing.

MRA: Oh yeah.

VI: It seemed that there was a desire to broaden everyone's and deepen everyone's perspectives on music. Did everybody participate as teachers? Or—

MRA: Everybody.

VI: Yeah.

MRA: Well, let me say something. You just said something that I would put it a little differently.

VI: Yes.

MRA: The individuals broaden their *own* horizons. There was no *process* that broadened their horizons. The association and each person—each individual—had many opportunities to produce, for instance, a concert of theirs. So therefore they broadened their horizons through *that*: the opportunity to express and learn from their trial and error with whatever they wanted to do.

VI: Yes.

MRA: *That's* how they broadened their horizons. I mean, at *no point* was there anything that interfered with the individual. You gotta understand that.

VI: So then, what teaching did was just put people in contact with *information*, is that what you're saying, without a kind of—

MRA: No, no, no, no. No no, no no. The teaching was mostly done by young aspiring musicians who we would take in to teach.

VI: I see. So then the students, the participants, were younger people from your community—

MRA: Community.

VI:—from the community, yes.

MRA: Yeah, now, when you associate with other musicians, you automatically learn from their individualism.

VI: Right.

MRA: That took place automatically. You follow me?

VI: Yeah.

MRA: Because the thing about individualism, primary to humans, is the sense that we're all different. Each one of us are individuals. Whether we function like that or not, that's another question, but we're individuals. We're individuals. Now, why is it that humanity is constructed like that?

VI: Uh, well—

MRA: Why is that?

VI: The answer I would give is that what we carry are memories of our experiences in the world—basically our record of the paths we take through life. So, you know, what makes us different are our experiences. And of course, what makes those experiences different is many, many forces.

MRA: Well the first thing that makes your experience different is choice: your choice. You decide to do something. That's why it's different. You made a choice. Now, why don't we make the same choice? We can make the same choice by imitating; I don't mean that. You come in and you have a particular way that you want to do things—each one of us. Why is that? That's what I'm asking. Because, let's say it this way: *All of the information was not put in one place.*

VI: Right.

MRA: You understand?

VI: Yeah.

MRA: You could explain it this way. There's many ways of expressing or explaining individualism, you know, and it doesn't have to all be from the same perspective. One thing I've learned about individualism is that all of the information that humans need to know is not in one place. It's not in one country. It's, you know, you can just expand it. It's like raising things to powers, you know what I mean? And the reason for that is because: *we* can *learn* from each other. You understand? There's a *reason* for that, it gets much *deeper* even, why humanity is constructed like that. You know, I didn't really expect an answer from you when I asked you to tell me about individualism!

VI: [Laughter]

MRA: 'course, I mean, it's really too complex—

VI: Yes.

MRA: —*but,* the thing is, I've noticed we actually learn from each other. Your way of doing something is quite different from mine. And so, when you act, I can say, "Oh, it can be done *that* way." Or if I act, you say, "Hmm, it could be done *that* way." *That's why. That's why.* Now, that's not the reason, but that certainly is a very noticeable aspect of the reason. And so, when we talk about the AACM: *that's what happened.* When you talk about the teaching: *that's* what happened.

VI: It's about choices?

MRA: Well, you can take any of them musicians—and you know most of them—

VI: Yeah, we were talking about Henry Threadgill and Anthony Braxton—

MRA: —they're all distinct individuals.

VI: Yes.

MRA: There's *no similarity* or *nothing*—

VI: It's true! [Laughs] It's *alarming*, actually.

MRA: —between *any* of us.

VI: Considering how many of you grew up together.

MRA: But we collaborated and associated with each other every day for years.

VI: Yeah.

MRA: *Every day*—

VI: Yeah.

MRA: —*for years!* You see? But that process was a human process.

VI: Right.

MRA: It was a human process, you know, *but*, with the emphasis on respect for the individual and the individual's right to *pursue* his or her direction, and in our case, again, in terms of composing and performing music.

VI: This music, then, proceeded, in the years that followed, to be heard around the world—in many ways *changed* the world, if you ask me. It had such a profound influence across so many communities. And that, to me, is—in a way it's perhaps easier to assess in retrospect. This is a strange question, but what did that feel like?

MRA: [Smiling] What did *what* feel like?!

VI: [Laughs] The realization—I mean, in a way, perhaps, what you're saying is that you knew all along because you were basically on to some very *human* questions. You know, at some level, it was through music, you were doing these things that were ultimately *not just* about music.

MRA: Right.

VI: So as that work then traveled and propagated—you know, for example, as you found yourself leaving Chicago and performing internationally and seeing this music *work* in different contexts. It was born in such a focused context; and yet, it then resonated outward. And so *that's* what I'm asking: What did you notice as, say, for example, performing in Europe in a cultural context that was very different from the circumstances in which a lot of the work was born? What did that *feel like*, interacting with those communities and those audiences and also other artists from that space?

MRA: Well, the fact that they, in Europe, the fact that they were like, they *welcomed* it, you know what I mean, then, it *expanded* the information that one would have about humanity itself.

Because, *what is it in them* that they could understand about what we were doing? [Whispering intensely] *The individual part of it. That's what I'm telling you, you understand?* [Normal voice] *It's much bigger* than this phenomenon we're talking about, "music." It's much bigger than that. You see? Individualism is a very *elusive* phenomenon. But yet we could go to Europe and pique someone's interest who knew nothing about the environment that we functioned in before we expanded, in terms of travel and whatnot like that. *And the reason is because on a human level, we rung a bell within them that was already there.*

VI: Yeah.

MRA: You see?

VI: I do.

MRA: Not that we set out to do that. But that's what happened. But then it was vice versa now. Wait a minute—see? They also rung a bell for *us*. It also enlightened *us*. You follow me?

VI: Yeah, I do.

MRA: Now we're getting closer to more information, in terms of individualism, you understand? And humanity.

VI: I mean, it's something I've learned—especially in the last few years, because I've had opportunities that I'd never had before—in fact, as you know, we ran into each other—

MRA: Oh, yeah, yeah. Nice concert.[13]

VI: —more than once, out there. We got to do a wonderful double bill in Macedonia.

MRA: Mm-hmm, mm-hmm.

VI: And it's like [Henry] Threadgill said to me once—that you learn things out there that you won't learn anywhere else, in terms of, in the course of performance, in particular, because it's—especially performance of this sort that we're talking about where choices are being made every step of the way.

MRA: Right.

VI: Every moment is a choice—

MRA: Exactly.

VI: —and so, those decisions, like you say, those choices, those are, on some level, that's you. Right?

MRA: Oh, it's you!

VI: Yeah.

MRA: It's you. You know—well, I don't mean to cut you off. You through?

VI: Well, I guess what I was just going to say is that what I find is that I'm listening to the audience. You know, they come to listen to us, but I'm there to listen to them.

MRA: It's an exchange, of course.

VI: So it sort of just amplifies what you were just saying, in the sense that, yes, "They rang a bell in me."

MRA: Of course—it's an exchange. Anyway, there seems to be a consistent—I'll call it a *law*—consistent law that pervades human activity. . . . It can be characterized in many ways, but I'll just say it's *the law of returns*, you know what I mean? You breathe out and you breathe in. In fact, breathing is a very great example of that law. Inhale and exhale? Well that's the whole thing: it's pulsating. Push the wind that way and then it comes back this way. That law is *consistent* throughout all humanity. There's no other law that's consistent like that throughout humanity. No other law. Some people say: reap what you sow. The boomerang. Know what I mean? So—

VI: Or karma.

MRA: Karma. *Of course.*[14] When we do this music, know what I mean, we have a responsibility. The first move is a selfish move: here's what I want to do—I want to do this, I want to do that, I want to play this now—it's a selfish move, you know what I mean?

VI: Yes.

MRA: But the consequences of that move, or the effect of that move, we don't think about. So we come to these audiences; *then*, we get what the effect was. What did it do? This exchange, you know, what did it do? *What did it do?* We've had conversations with people—if five people walk up here, they all say different things about what they heard you do on the stage!

VI: They do, they really do.

MRA: But what they say is pretty, you know, *serious*. That individualism, I think, is a direct—and there's different types of individualism, of course: a guy could be playing bebop and playing it real good. You understand what I'm talking about? *He's a messenger, too.* You understand?

VI: Of course.

MRA: His individual way of expressing bebop, his individualism comes through *that*. Instead of a completely composed work that would be of his making, you know what I mean? But the thing in his individualism, his very strong individualism is going to come through, especially if he's accomplished from hard work and study, know what I mean? A respect for what it is that he's doing, of course.

VI: Yeah, you can always hear traces of that kind of discipline—

MRA: *Sure.*

VI: —no matter what they're doing.

MRA: Right, right. You hear it because if they really respected that, they usually can do it pretty well.

VI: [Laughs]

MRA: Of course they respected it! You know what I mean? And so, they spent a lot of hours, you know, developing. But that individualism comes through like that because when you hear the person, you say, "Oh, that's so-and-so." How can you say that? You *know* it's so-and-so.

VI: Right.

MRA: Because you know so-and-so's individualism: the way so-and-so approaches what he or she does. Now, it's not always as easy to discern, especially in new music, or people doing just straight-out original music, it's not as easy to discern because, well, it's changeable.

VI: Well, the choices—

MRA: It may never come up the same way because there's no formula. So, you know, you can't pin it down like that. Although you get used to hearing some individual, you say, "Oh, it sounds like so-and-so" because you could hear it.

VI: I guess to me what makes it challenging is when you don't really know what the parameters of expression, like, where are the choices being made, essentially. And what you're hearing is the person's individual nature—

MRA: Right.

VI: —*resounding.*

MRA: *Right.*

VI: Right.

MRA: And there, we hear, well, we hear possibilities in any area. But certainly, we hear the possibilities that do not have formula as we know it—formulae, or however you want to say it, as we know it. So therefore, enlightened *or repelled,* in a different way, this process is *constantly going on*—constantly going on. Why the AACM people were chosen, *and we were chosen,* to do what it is that we've done and continue to do—*who knows?* Who knows? But, if it helped or enlightened someone as it further enlightened us at the same time, then that's great.

VI: It is [laughs].

MRA: That's great. [Chuckles] You know what I mean? Because, for me, just to continue doing what I do—I'm already rewarded. I'm already rewarded. The fact that I can do what I want to do—that's my reward itself.

VI: It really is.

MRA: I don't need any other reward. I don't need praise. I don't need anything. That's it right there. It's all in the one package, you know what I mean? Because, if I can continue to do it and continue to visualize and *imagine* further growth and whatnot like that, you know what I mean, then *that's the reward itself.*

VI: It is [laughs].

MRA: Yeah. You know, *that's it.*

VI: I mean, this conversation is in the context of you being *presented* with an award. And you've been—

MRA: Well now, now, of course—

VI: [Laughs]

MRA: —now, here, let me say, let me say, with due respect to that: if someone feels they want to show an appreciation for something I've done, I'm grateful. I'm very grateful. Of course, it has nothing to do with *my continuum,* know what I mean? But I'm grateful, because I made contact with someone.

VI: Right.

MRA: That's gratifying. I mean, you know, it encourages me to keep going.

VI: It means that you've been heard, basically.

MRA: Well, well, well the thing is, I *made human contact.* Know what I mean?

VI: Yeah. It's more than being heard.

MRA: *It's more than the music.* There's human contact, because, you know, people, you know, when they really say what it is that caused the attraction, you usually end up talking about something other than music [laughs].

VI: I hear you. So let me ask you this. I mean this is the kind of, in a way, an absurd, or I guess the word is *preposterous*—it's a preposterous question. But I feel you can answer it [laughs] because when you speak this way, it leads me to ask—and many other things have led me to ask this: *why do we have music?* Because you're talking about questions that, as you say, are beyond music, and truths that are beyond music. So then: *what is music?* And *why do we have it?*

MRA: Well, music is harnessed sound. Like you harness something?

VI: Yes.

MRA: Sound comes first. Sound is the raw material. Music is, you say, "Let me take some of this raw material and put it in a glass." It's harnessed. Now there it is. But sound is everywhere—it's still there.

VI: It is.

MRA: You just took a little sound, and you're treating it with this shape, here, you know what I mean? So you say, "Hmm, uh, let me pour it into this vessel." Now it's taking this shape. Because sound takes the shape that you can successfully put it in. That's not always easy to treat sound in that way; but sound is—well, sound can be—well, sound is sound, I mean, it can take whatever your imagination can accomplish. Sound can give you that. You're stopping it. So that's what music is: you've stopped this sound, you know, or you've *ordered* it—put it in a certain order. And that's all of the music: placed in a certain order, whether it's improvised or written. So you've harnessed some sound. So we call it music because we can hear it, and, well, you could say, oh that's, you say, "*de de de de de de, de de de de de*"—it's *harnessed.* That, for me, is the real focus—you're asking about the beginnings, you know—the focus on sound. Even when I didn't realize, that was the focus: on *sound. Sound.* And the fact that you can harness and organize sound *over and over,* repeatedly, over and over, in different ways, from your own individual perspective, of course. But you can do it over and over, and never get the same thing, except your own habits [laughs]. That's what you—you're gonna get that!

VI: Yeah.

MRA: But other than that—

VI: So that music is then something that we do. It's not something that we discover or find, but it's something that we *make.*

MRA: [Agreeing] You *make* it.

VI: Yeah.

MRA: You make it. But you make it *out of sound.*

VI: Yes.

MRA: You make it out of sound. You take that recorder. You hear that sound? We could take that recorder, go out there and get five minutes of it, take it back, put it in a piece. Well, now it's not the same as that anymore. Of course, you're going to run it—you've got five minutes. And you could repeat that over and over: [imitating sound of loop] *mmmmmm ti mmmmmm ti* . . .

VI: [Laughs]

MRA: And you could do that over and over because you got five minutes of that; but you don't have *that*.

VI: Yeah, yeah.

MRA: And that's what it is.

VI: So it's something about intention? The fact that when someone hears it, they hear the vestige of intention that was put into it—that, somehow, somebody made this.

MRA: Yeah, they hear the individual's choice—what makes them individual.

VI: And so somehow we also as individual listeners are kind of recognizing that part of ourselves that might have done that too perhaps.

MRA: That's a possibility. It depends on how the person takes it, you know? Certainly the listener's imagination is *piqued*, and the listener could imagine something completely different from what the individual intended when the individual harnessed the sound to make music. You know, usually that's the case, you know what I mean? But then, it brings us to the fact that *the purpose of it is to excite all these different perspectives.* Because when the person comes and tells you, "*Oh*, when I heard your concert, it made me think about so-and-so and so-and-so," and you say, "What?" Because—you know what I mean?

VI: Yeah, yeah.

MRA: But there's a perspective that you wouldn't have even thought about, know what I mean? The act of doing it caused a reaction of that sort.

VI: Yes. Now you mentioned earlier theater, and I know also that you worked in visual art as well.

MRA: Still do.

VI: And still do. And is it all related for you?

MRA: Oh yeah.

VI: As you move across—

MRA: Yeah.

VI: —what are traditionally called disciplines, do you find that you're bringing the same sensibility to these investigations? Like, are you the composer also you the painter? Or do you find that—

MRA: *Yes.*

VI: —painting reveals something new?

MRA: It's all sort of one thing, because, you know, as you know, you can associate color and rhythm to music and painting. You know what I mean? If you want to imagine it that way you could just do that. That's what I do. Because, from looking at painters and listening to musicians, I find, to analyze it for my own purposes so I remember, I say, "Well, that's what they're doing."

VI: Yes.

MRA: So—

VI: It is.

MRA: —you know, I say, "That's what they're doing."

VI: Do you find that there's something analogous to composition and improvisation in painting, in the construction of visual art?

MRA: It could be, in the sense that improvisation has two processes going. It has improvisation *and composition* going at the same time. It's all at the same time—I'm composing and I'm performing at the same time. *I'm composing and I'm performing at the same time.* It's all the same! So with the painting it's the same thing. It's the same thing, you know. I think one time you asked me—[smiling] *you asked me* when I went on the stage—you asked me, you asked me, you said, "What do you do? Do you have a theme or something or do you have something?"—didn't you, you asked me that one time when we were in Italy.

VI: [Remembering] Uh-huh! When you played solo.[15]

MRA: Yeah, you asked me. And I think I told you—I *did* tell you: I said no.

VI: [Laughs]

MRA: I said, "I go up and I drop my hand down and when I hit a note, that's it." *I'm composing and performing at the same time.*

VI: Basically, the process has begun.

MRA: Right.

VI: And then, from there, it's all choices.

MRA: *Yes.*

VI: So why are these terms useful then—composition and improvisation?

MRA: Well . . .

VI: Or are they? [Laughs]

MRA: That's an interesting question, *Are they useful?* [Laughs]

VI: [Laughing] I mean, they get hung on lots of things, but . . .

MRA: Well, the thing is, I think it depends on who's using them, because how can you talk about something like that, because, one thing . . . going back to the individualism idea again: each of us has a *right* to *connotate,* you know what I mean, what a thing is, or what a word is, you know—

VI: Yeah.

MRA: —semantically, or whether it's necessary to apply to certain things, like you're suggesting here. When you say "composition," what does it mean to you? What does it mean to me? What does it mean to him? I can only say what it means to me. If I'm composing, I'm harnessing sound in a certain way, perhaps with a pencil, you know what I mean? I'm harnessing this sound with this pencil. So like, the pencil is useful for *architectural* purposes, know what I mean, in terms of the shaping, uh, graphic. But now, I call that composing. And I also call it improvisation because I'm improvising also. I'm improvising also.

VI: But, at the same time, to me, and this is actually something you said once, and in fact you said it at Columbia that time, in that symposium.[16] You said that "improvisation is a human response to necessity."

MRA: *Right.*

VI: Which gives a sense of there's something irreversible about that.

MRA: Well, just take a look at humans. Not just musicians.

VI: Yes, of course.

MRA: *Any* human.

VI: In fact, when you said that, you weren't specifically talking about music.

MRA: I wasn't. I was talking about *people.*

VI: Right.

MRA: Because *everybody* here: the lady that's cooking in the kitchen, she's cooking food, so she needs three eggs, she only has two, you understand? So she says, "Hmm, only got two eggs, gotta make this thing, so, OK, it calls for three eggs, tell you what I'll do, uh, eggs now, uh . . ." She might imagine, she says, "Well, if I take this milk and this cheese . . ." [Laughs]

VI: Right, yeah.

MRA: You know . . . [Laughs loudly]

VI: [Laughs] The color might be right, anyway.

MRA: Right, "I take the milk and this cheese, and I'll just *put it in there.* Hmm, that might be *nice.*"

VI: Yeah.

MRA: So she improvises. You know, it doesn't have to be that extreme, but she *improvises.* So people improvise all the time.

VI: Yeah, of course.

MRA: You know what I mean? They improvise *all the time,* because it becomes *necessary* to improvise in order to do what it is that they want to do. That's why I made that statement, because it's been my experience, in observing humans and myself, that that's pretty consistent: everybody improvises.

VI: Yeah, of course.

MRA: *Everybody improvises.*

VI: There's nobody who doesn't.

MRA: Right! You know.

VI: [Laughs]

MRA: You improvise because you just . . . it will become necessary. Sometimes during the day it will become necessary for you to improvise, in some way.

VI: Well, to me it's like we're born doing that.

MRA: Right. Exactly.

VI: I mean, that's what we are.

MRA: That's right. You have the capacity to go *beyond* what your base state is. If it becomes necessary to go beyond that, you go beyond. Now what is that phenomenon? You follow? You just say, "Oh, OK, well uh, so-and-so and so-and-so-and-so, tell you what, this thing, just let me turn this table upside down, and I think we can address this stuff a little bit better." Just like that, you just turn it upside down. So, you know . . .

VI: Yeah [laughing].

MRA: It's very consistent. Music, in terms of improvisers, might be an area that *specializes* in a certain form of improvisation. But it is not the only area; it doesn't start in music. It starts in human life, you know what I mean? Music gives one a chance to be more *extreme* [laughs].

VI: Yes [laughs].

MRA: Or painting, you know, it depends.

VI: Whether it's presence or absence, I suppose—the extreme in either way.

MRA: Yeah. But, the thing is, it's very difficult to talk about this thing that we're talking about!

VI: [Laughs]

MRA: Because it's, well, you know . . .

VI: [Uncertain] Well, I guess, the only reason I—

MRA: No, you OK!

VI: Yeah, I mean, not even to make an excuse. But when you spoke of using a pencil, I mean, you can erase what you write with a pencil, right?

MRA: *Yes, you can.*

VI: So what I meant is that composing seems, in the sense it is used in the West, which is basically where the term was invented, there is a sense that it's something that is being prepared to be executed.

MRA: Well, OK. You're talking about a certain concept of composing.

VI: Right, I mean look, I suppose we could go all day, talking about stuff like this! [Laughs]

MRA: Well, you see!

VI: I'm down, but I know that—

MRA: *But* the plotting of a continuum is done all over the world, in all cultures, the plotting of a continuum, *which is composing.* It's composing. Now, I think the fact that one area does not want to use the language that another area uses does not change the fact that they're doing the same thing. Don't use the language. *Don't use that language.* I mean, use the language of your area. But, on a human level, when the plotting of this continuum goes, *there's a calculation going on* of some sort, because humans must *finally have order* even if it's very abstract. The system must have order, in the sense that it is, it *could be* doing that, but it's doing *that,* you understand? It has its order—it's *doing that.*

VI: Right, right.

MRA: Use any word, "chaotic," whatever—*it has its order.* You follow me? It's deliberately doing this. So it gets random stuff, and this, that, and the other, you know what I mean—but it's deliberately doing that. It's consistent in that. For instance, in your country: raga. Raga. You know what I mean? There's a *system* to the raga. It *means* something. *It means something.* It *means* something. You know. It means something.

VI: It does.

MRA: There's certain emphasis and things that occur, and it occurs there all the time. Follow what I'm talking about?

VI: Yup.

MRA: Even though the whole situation is being improvised in a way also. So it's the combination of so-called composition or whatever—we don't have to use those terms, though, when we're talking about that, though, because those terms don't fit, you follow me, because there's another focus, see?

VI: It's a set of priorities or principles.

MRA: *Right.* You follow me? And you take . . . you go to China—[laughs, abandoning that idea]. But the thing is, this harnessing of sound—and that's the great part about the individualism, you understand? Why do we all have all these different languages? And these different so-called musical systems? Why?

VI: Well, I suppose, I would say that they emerge in mutual isolation over many years, centuries, millennia, based on the choices of individuals in a community, And customs that develop over time, and norms, and I guess you end up having a certain kind of continuity. But then there may also be ruptures or, say, hybridizations or invasions or different things that happen.

MRA: Well, you're telling me about development, but you didn't answer my question. And I don't expect you to answer it.

VI: [Laughs]

MRA: I wouldn't put that on you. But you're telling me—

VI: *Is* there an answer?

MRA: Right, so you're telling me about development, but what I'm talking about is *humankind*, you follow me? There's this phenomenon that pervades humankind that allows you to say "bread" in your language, the way you would say it in an Indian language, and it allows me to say it as a Black person in America. It allows him to say it, you know, from his base. You follow what I'm talking about?

VI: Yeah.

MRA: We say the same thing, but, the tongue organizes the situation quite differently, you follow what I'm talking about? But the fact that we're talking about the same thing and can say it in different tongues—that's worth investigating as to why. *What's the purpose of that? What's the purpose of it?* Well, I'll tell you one thing: the rhythmic difference is fascinating. What produces that phenomenon? Why would it produce a phenomenon like that? You know what I mean? So my investigation, or my interest, not investigation but my interest—I suppose it is an investigation, too—but my interest or my focus is like that. I'm curious about why is this great phenomenon so basic. It's so *basic* but yet *so elusive.* My quest to, like, create in this area where we are, *music* and whatnot like that, you know what I mean, it's, like, all one thing. Back to what we were talking about: the improvisation and the composition are the same. And I believe it's the same in *every* community. See, because improvisation and composition, being the *one* process, came *before the pencil.*

VI: Right.

MRA: [Laughs]

VI: Sure did.

MRA: [Laughs] It came before the pencil!

VI: Before, yes, before any writing instrument.

MRA: It came before *any* recording of the situation. It came *long before it.* Right?

VI: Yeah.

MRA: *Long* before it. The whole idea of it having significant *spiritual* meaning came *long* before the *secular* display that we engage in [laughs].

VI: [Laughs] Right.

MRA: But it's all great because it's never beyond humanity. It's never beyond humanity. Some people like rap music. Some people like—

VI: A lot of people do! [Laughs]

MRA: It's OK!

VI: [Laughs]

MRA: Some people like hard rock, you know what I mean? Some people like rhythm and blues. Some people like bebop. Some people like, you know, the so-called new approaches to music, you know what I mean? So you have people at every turn, regardless to what it is, you have people at every turn. Why? Because the way it seems to me is that each one of us gets our message from different perspectives, see, so, and it all just comes out of the very thing that we're talking about [slyly] and *not* talking about, because obviously we don't know what we're talking about! [Laughs]

VI: [Laughs] Well!

MRA: In the sense of, you know, how it applies to the phenomenon of *humanity itself.*

VI: Yeah. I've always just been so inspired by your—I mean it's not this is only your approach—but your way of treating music as a line of inquiry into these basic human questions. I know that you identify with a community and at the same time you also—in a way this is one of the gifts of the AACM, is to assert a certain kind of global relevance of something that seems so specific at the same time. And I guess I just want to thank you, for that has been [MRA laughs] such a profound inspiration to me and to many, many of my peers and comrades, and many people across many generations, many communities around the world. And, you know, this is the kind of work that can only inspire. And you've dedicated to this pursuit, and it's been of utmost impact in the world.

MRA: Well, I thank you for that. But I'll have to pass it on to the real receiver. I'm a *vessel,* you know what I mean? And I accept what you've said. But I'm receiving as a representative, in the sense that the power that saw fit to release us all into this individual firmament and yet leave us basic to the human principle of—what should I say, it's very difficult to talk about these things—well, to the human principle of just *being a part of that law of return that I spoke about,* you know what I mean? Being a part of that law of return, that force, you know what I mean. I think, I'll have to pass the appreciation to that force and yet accept it myself on a human level. And I must compliment you for being *consistent* in what *you* do.

VI: Well, thank you.

MRA: You know because I appreciate that. I appreciate that. You've been quite consistent, and I appreciate that.

VI: Well, it's come from, as I said, being inspired by the examples that you and your peers have set forth. I'm just glad to get to participate in the same conversation.

MRA: Well, I'm delighted and happy to speak with you, you know, because I don't do much talking [laughs].

VI: [Laughs] You don't do this?

MRA: I mean, I'm *capable* of doing a lot of talking, but I just don't *do* a lot of talking.

VI: Well, I guess, I feel like what's been evident even in this—however long we've spoken is—it's a phrase that you used once years ago when you were talking to me about [Thelonious] Monk.

MRA: Mmmhmm.

VI: I think it was about fifteen years ago.

MRA: Mmmhmm.

VI: You said that *Monk was always creating.*

MRA: [Whispering] *That's right.*

VI: And that phrase has really stuck with me. I think about it all the time. And I think *you* are always creating. I mean, I think it's a perfect encapsulation of the kind of work you do. Because, you know, when we talk about all those distinctions and parsing words and what's composition and isn't and so on—none of that matters because it all is essentially *that*, you know. And it's all that ongoing and endless process.

MRA: Right. I think it all should be respected, though, because *individuals* are doing it. If a guy likes to do mainstream things—great. Do it well. You know, that's all that matters. Just do it well. Do it with respect. You know what I mean? I'll be cheering for you [laughs].

VI: [Laughs]

MRA: Whatever it is—just do it well. If a cat can rap real good, I mean, really do it *real* good, you know what I mean—do it well—*I like it.* You know what I mean?

VI: Yeah.

MRA: I like it because you *respect* it, you know what I mean? You do it well, you know what I mean? I think that's great.

VI: Yes.

MRA: Because people can trust that. A guy that works hard to really perfect it. The audience can come and they can *trust* that person. You know? And that's important because, after all, they're, like, *wide open*, and they can be harmed.

VI: Right. That's how vulnerable they are . . . So, it's a half-century, basically, of activity from the AACM.

MRA: Oh yeah, it's been quite a while. But, here in New York since '83.

VI: Yeah.

MRA: 'bout '83.

VI: Congratulations on a profound—I mean, again, this isn't just to praise you for its own sake or anything—but, *seriously*, I commend you for this amazing legacy and for continuing to push boundaries and create and inspire us all.

MRA: Well, thank you, and I'm also inspired by your activities. You know, you can believe that. I mean, we *really learn* from each other, you know. That's the great part. So I appreciate that and I appreciate your comments.

VI: Thank you.

Afterword

Abrams's law of return(s) consists of the understanding that the vaunted "individual" exists only in relation, that for this reason we respect the ditchdigger, the musician, the hairdresser, the swami. Any individual's actions resonate, as clearly as a bell, within others, provoking a wide, endless, unpredictable range of individual responses; the special purpose of music-making is "to excite all these different perspectives" in their polyphonic resonance, through which, reciprocally, music-makers also hear a bell clearly being "rung . . . for us." We might call it a sonorous ethics, but we can also detect within it a personal practice of freedom: "For me, just to continue doing what I do—I'm already rewarded."

Such Abrams utterances—"Are you your mind?" or "Play your way out" or "the law of return(s)"—often do more than narrate or teach. On impact, as delivered in Abrams's signature echoic fashion, such phrases become new and permanent fixtures of your person; they lodge themselves in the ear and the mind, remaining alive to you, like a new and useful part of the body, or like benevolent earworms, calling from within. Such language can reactivate in key moments, mantra-like, and recondition an experience in the present. Because of them, you are able to do more, see and hear further, imagine more vividly and to greater effect. These words inspire and animate: they propel the spirit and motivate action. They are phrases of change.

This resonant, antiphonal musicality with language exemplifies gospel music scholar Braxton Shelley's theorization of sacred words. Invoking the "new materialism" of Jane Bennett and others, Shelley writes, "Yes, gospel is a discursive tradition, but its primary discourse is believed to have 'thing-power.' The thing-power of sacred words moves mountains, soothes sickness, and grants blessings. If one listens to gospel songs and sermons, it becomes apparent words are believed to act on the material world."[17] While Abrams did not situate himself directly in the communities of belief whose medium is gospel music, he did state in our interview, "The whole idea of [music] having significant *spiritual* meaning came *long* before the *secular* display that we engage in." Moreover, he did make consistent use of this Black esoteric tradition of crafting new musicalities with words, so that they might continue to act on the material world well beyond their moment of utterance.[18] Might we suppose something similar about music-making—that for a community of believers, musical acts might live on in the world, like the long resonant tail of a rung bell? Might we therefore accept that belief becomes the socially cohesive force that facilitates and organizes this process? Perhaps belief is the hinge on which hangs our very notions of musicality: how we call to others, and how we are called; how we decide who or what has the power to speak or sing, to us or for us; how we ring bells within others, and how bells within us are rung in return.

In March 2018, five months after Abrams's passing, fellow composer-pianist Craig Taborn and I recorded a duo concert of spontaneous two-piano creations in Budapest.[19] On the ensuing live album, we dedicated the most substantial piece to Abrams, a towering influence on us both. We titled it "Clear Monolith," to invoke Abrams's favorite bell-like parting salutation: *Stay clear!*

Acknowledgments

Thanks to Joshua Kohn, the Mid-Atlantic Arts Foundation, and Phillip Golub for help with the transcription, and an inexpressible gratitude to my collaborator, the late Muhal Richard Abrams.

Notes

The definitive source on Abrams's life is the substantial work of historical musicology by one of his former pupils: trombonist, composer, electronic musician, and scholar George Lewis's comprehensive history of the Association for the Advancement of Creative Musicians, *A Power Stronger Than Itself: The AACM and Experimental Music* (Chicago: University of Chicago Press, 2007). Abrams's presence permeates nearly every page of this landmark book. The reader is also directed to Abrams's own website, https://www.muhalrichardabrams.com/. Later interviews with Abrams include "Steve Smith Interviews Muhal Richard

Abrams and Roscoe Mitchell," Ojai Music Festival, June 10, 2017, https://www.youtube.com/watch?v=YRWEgK6J6b0; Ted Panken, "For the 84th Birthday of Muhal Richard Abrams, Two Downbeat Articles (2006, 2010), one Jazziz Article (2011), and a Profile for All about Jazz (2007)," in the blog *Today Is the Question: Ted Panken on Music, Politics and the Arts,* September 19, 2014, https://tedpanken.wordpress.com/2014/09/19/for-the-84th-birthday-of-muhal-richard-abrams-two-downbeat-articles-2009-2010-and-one-jazziz-article-2011/. Due to their availability elsewhere, I won't rehearse further biographical details here except as they emerge in our discussion.

1. I served as music director for this iteration of the festival and curated this performance. The concert was captured on video and can be viewed at https://www.youtube.com/watch?v=Bp9MoWVWkjo

2. Muhal Richard Abrams with Roscoe Mitchell and George Lewis, *Streaming,* sound recording, New York: Pi Recordings, 2006.

3. See, for example, Francisco Varela, Evan Thompson, and Eleanor Rosch, *The Embodied Mind: Cognitive Science and Human Experience* (1991; Cambridge, MA: MIT Press, 2016); Vijay Iyer, "Microstructures of Feel, Macrostructures of Sound: Embodied Cognition in West African and African American Musics" (PhD diss., University of California at Berkeley, 1998).

4. Fumi Okiji, *Jazz as Critique: Adorno and Black Expression Revisited* (Stanford, CA: Stanford University Press, 2018), 5.

5. "AACM Panel Discussion," Stanford University, May 12, 2014, https://www.youtube.com/watch?v=HuT8r8D0w3Q

6. Okiji, *Jazz as Critique,* 6.

7. See, for instance, Eric Porter, *What Is This Thing Called Jazz? African American Musicians as Artists, Critics, and Activists* (Berkeley: University of California Press, 2002); Arthur Taylor, *Notes and Tones: Musician-to-Musician Interviews* (New York: Da Capo Press, 1977).

8. From Smith's back-cover blurb for William Parker, *Conversations* (Paris: RogueArt, 2011).

9. Here is the first of many instances of this idea: *individuality, individualism,* or *the individual.*

10. This is an instance of something that Abrams and others of his region and generation employed often in speech: a "no" that is intended as an *affirmative* interjection.

11. This meeting was recorded, and a transcript appears in its entirety in Lewis, *Power Stronger Than Itself,* 2007.

12. I intended to say, "South Side of Chicago."

13. We are referring to a festival in October 2011 in Skopje, Macedonia, where my working trio performed on a double bill with his aforementioned trio with Mitchell and Lewis.

14. The "of course" was evidently intended as a nod to my Indian heritage.

15. He is referring to our backstage encounter before his 2005 solo performance at Ai Confini tra Sardegna e Jazz, in Sant'Anna Arresi, Sardinia.

16. "The Conversations Series: Improvisation in Everyday Life," September 25, 2007, Columbia University. "The guiding premise of the series, co-sponsored by the Center for Jazz Studies at Columbia University, is that the study of impro-

visation can present a new animating paradigm for scholarly inquiry in the humanities, arts and the social, political and natural sciences." The dialogue included Abrams, George Lewis, Yusef Komunyakaa, Patricia Williams, and Margo Jefferson. https://worldleaders.columbia.edu/events/conversations-series-improvisation-everyday-life

17. Braxton Shelley, *Healing for the Soul: Richard Smallwood, the Vamp, and the Gospel Imagination* (New York: Oxford University Press, forthcoming). The phrase "thing-power" cites Jane Bennett, *Vibrant Matter: A Political Ecology of Things* (Durham, NC: Duke University Press, 2010), 2–3. To my knowledge Shelley is one of the only scholars as of this writing to apply the influential idea of thing-power back onto language, in a way that complements notions of performativity, signifying, call-and-response, and other common framings of Black discourse.

18. His album titles reflect this creative, poetically layered approach, including esoteric phrases (*Levels and Degrees of Light*, 1967, *Young at Heart / Wise in Time*, 1969, *Things to Come from Those Now Gone*, 1972, *Vision towards Essence*, 2007) and neologistic portmanteaus (*Afrisong*, 1975, *Sightsong*, 1975, *LifeA BlineC*, 1978, *Spihumonesty*, 1978).

19. Vijay Iyer and Craig Taborn, *The Transitory Poems* (Munich: ECM Records, 2019).

The Politics of Historiography

SEVEN | White Noise

Historiographical Exceptionalism and the Construction of a White American Music History

GLENDA GOODMAN AND SAMUEL PARLER

One of the pervasive themes of twentieth-century American exceptionalism was the belief that only those who came to the United States from certain parts of Europe belonged there. We are witnessing a resurgence of this xenophobic ideology today. With this in mind, we start with a proposition: in Americanist music historiography, the effort to distinguish US music scholarship from the Eurocentric musicological mainstream has resulted in an assertion of American distinctiveness that is often predicated on constructing and maintaining musical categories based on racial difference. These categories can all too easily be mobilized into hierarchies that support white supremacist tenets. Some of the most vibrant areas of US music scholarship are those that document and celebrate musicians of color, sometimes to uplift a narrative of distinctive melting-pot pluralism, and sometimes as a self-conscious critique of a discipline still beholden to the repertory and values of dead white male composers. Nevertheless, much of US music historiography remains mired in a defensive exceptionalist claim to greatness that privileges white subjects.[1]

This historiographical tendency in US music studies reflects similar trends in the long history of US immigration. For instance, a backstop of settler colonial belonging can be found in Massachusetts governor John Winthrop's "city on a hill" sermon, which in 1630 claimed for English settler colonists a divine justification to seize inhabited territory, and simultaneously celebrated and warned Englishmen and women to live up to the expectation that they would do good there. Native Americans existed, for English settler colonists, first as essential lifelines but quickly as foils against which an idealized, Christian, civilized, and white dominion could be forged.[2] Ensuing decades saw a hardening of racial regimes; we might take as a second backstop the 1790 naturalization law, which dictated US citizenship as the purview of whites—a framing that required, of course, a belief in essential racial difference. The twin forces of welcome and exclusivity, of claiming immigrant exceptionalism as a blanket ideal and applying it in practice only to a select segment of the population, invests rhetoric about belonging with racial meaning. The specific composition of that racial meaning changed over time. As Matthew Frye Jacobson and others have argued, the whiteness of citizenship was a moving target, opening up to some and closing off others based on other economic, sociocultural, and political factors.[3] However, one enduring point must be underscored: accompanying the celebration of immigrant diversity in the United States is the fact that, for some, diversification brought severely harmful consequences. For those who were forced to migrate in chains, and for those whose land was seized, the spread of US sovereignty did not just diversify America; it bleached and stripped the cultural landscape.

The bluntness of this evaluation is purposeful, for we wish to suggest that, to a large extent, US-focused musicology has not disentangled itself from exceptionalism and its attendant racial ideologies. Scholars seldom regard or evaluate white composers and musicians as representatives of a more generalized racial outlook, yet such an approach is common when writing about their nonwhite counterparts. Furthermore, when scholars themselves are white, racial identification with a white historical subject can unconsciously encourage an imagined familiarity, even when the historical circumstances for author and subject are vastly different, such that the implications of whiteness go unexamined. Alternatively, authors perceiving racial difference from their subject may be bound to reproduce that difference in the written word.[4] As W. E. B. Du Bois suggested, double consciousness is rare among whites, because their experiences are the norm against which difference is defined. Indeed, what has been considered instead is the extent to which white composers' music represents their unique experiences and identity—an expression of unexamined privilege if ever there was one, for what is more validating than to consider a person as an individual rather than as a representative of a larger group? This chapter takes aim at the indelible whiteness of historiographical exceptionalism, which has not yet been fully diagnosed and analyzed.

Identifying the privilege of whiteness may help contain it. We do so through case studies of two iconic figures in US music history: eighteenth-century hymnodist William Billings and twentieth-century country musician Gene Autry. In juxtaposing these two figures, we are not endorsing a direct parallel between their experiences and contributions; the periods in which they lived were radically different, as were the specific politics of race in which they must be situated. The asymmetries between these two case studies permit a conversation about whiteness more broadly across historical periods.[5] Moreover, we are not asking how these white men represent white men generally (for collapsing the individual into the whole would only replicate the problematic analyses to which minority composers have been treated), but to contest the universality of whiteness by examining how it was constructed historically and musically.

In what follows we submit that the connection between American exceptionalism and whiteness is evident in two ways. First, it is established through difference, with whiteness representing civilization and racialized "Others" suggesting barbarism and savagery. Second, these false binaries feed tacit and explicit exclusion, whereby nonwhite peoples are historiographically sidelined by lack of attention in scholarship. Our decision to focus on two white male figures might seem counterproductive for this second claim, but our contention is that, in addition to acknowledging the music and cultures of nonwhite peoples, it is also necessary to recognize canonic white figures as racialized subjects and as being in dialogue with nonwhite subjects. To move beyond historiographic exceptionalism, whiteness itself must be actively and deliberately deconstructed. By thematizing settler colonists' land seizure as a triumph of whiteness over savagery, these musical traditions at once exemplify and excuse the violence that was inherent to the construction and naturalization of whiteness. Ironically, however, whiteness itself has been precarious, its contours and privileges constantly policed and renegotiated as the nation's racial profile shifted. As these case studies reveal, assertions of whiteness have helped these men to escape other negative class identities—a topic to which we return at the end of the chapter.

The "Native" American Composer Billings

Because William Billings witnessed the formation of the United States and wrote patriotic Protestant sacred music, scholars have routinely interpolated historic events into assessments of his life and works. He is presented as a maverick mold-breaker whose life and works represent American values of liberal individualism. Gilbert Chase, for instance, claimed Billings's famous statement, "I think it best for every *Composer* to be his own *Carver*," found in the preface to the *New-England Psalm-Singer* (1770), was a "personal 'declaration of independence.'"[6] In fact, Billings's astoundingly voluminous and distinctive output does set him apart from what came before. No one in British North America had published a single-author book of newly composed sacred music before Billings did so in 1770. Billings's political affiliation with prominent patriots, among them Samuel Adams and Paul Revere, further bolsters the association between the composer and the Revolutionary cause. The originality of his compositions, his zest for paraphrasing sacred lyrics to make them applicable both for religious and for political interpretation, and his skill with crafting rhythmically energetic tunes, earned him a deserved place in the nation's musical canon.[7]

Yet it is how Billings is presented in that canon that matters. However noteworthy his accomplishments, placing Billings at the beginning of a "maverick tradition" helps to create a canon based on reductive binaries—innovators versus conformists, provincial versus cosmopolitan—which set up a logic that makes it hard to see the blanketing whiteness of the tradition's norms.[8] Moreover, the standard interpretation of Billings masks several ways in which his music reifies whiteness by evacuating New England of Native Americans. The strategy of literal and figurative dispossession of Indigenous people of their land and their place in history was not necessarily conscious on Billings's part; in fact, it is the implicit assumption that his position of primacy can be asserted in the context of an otherwise virgin (musical) landscape. This occurs in two ways. First, Billings is repeatedly framed, by himself in his own words and works as well as by others in writings about him, as the first "native" American composer.[9] Second, in his own compositions he thematized exclusive white citizenship, initially through his presentation of Revolutionary patriotism, then later through thanksgiving hymns and anthems. It is important not to be seduced into normalizing the settler colonial logic of eliminating Indigenous peoples.[10]

Several small clues tying Billings to Native exoticism and erasure surface once we think to look for them. Some are circumstantial, such as the fact that the men who staged the Boston Tea Party used the office of Billings's first printers, Benjamin Edes and John Gill, to don their "Indian" costumes.[11] Given that Billings's closeness to patriots Samuel

Adams and Paul Revere is taken to indicate his political beliefs, further confirmed by his compositions, the cultural trope of "playing Indian" as a form of rebellion should be added to the contextualizing evidence for Billings.[12] He would have been familiar with such masquerading, even if he himself did not take part. Other ways in which Billings is "nativized" are more explicit. For example, in their landmark biography of William Billings, Richard Crawford and David McKay note the composer was deemed important because of "priority or local color," meaning that he represented a "first" in US music history and was uniquely tied to New England.[13] More than a century earlier, Nathaniel Gould made much the same claim in his important book on church music in New England, claiming that before 1770 "no native American had attempted to compose and publish a single tune, that we can ascertain."[14] Billings was indeed the first to publish a single-author collection of hymns. However, claims about his primacy and nativeness indicate one way in which his life and works have been turned to foster whiteness: in the guise of a quasi-patriotic celebration of an American-born composer, Billings-the-"native" becomes a cypher for settler colonialism.

Claims of belonging that reinforced settler colonial priority in New England are evident in the material record of Billings's publications, particularly in the ubiquity of New England place-names. The title page of the *New-England Psalm-Singer* labels Billings as a "native of Boston." The word "native" used here indicates his place of birth (Billings was in fact born in Boston), and is striking because tunebook title pages did not conventionally acknowledge the composers' places of origin. Inside the covers of this book, the many instances of place-names as titles to hymns might have, as Crawford and McKay claim, given his readers a pleasurable jolt of recognition. Perhaps these place-names, including "Brookline," "Nantucket," and "Hampshire," reminded colonists of their regional identity, while generic titles such as "Freedom," "Liberty," and "Union" conjured abstract political ideals that were growing as discontent with the metropole intensified. Yet also undeniable, though little commented on, is the fact that such place-names confirmed the *re*naming that had been underway for over a century, as English towns crowded out Native Americans. Some titles, such as "Swanzey," a contested and embattled site in King Philip's War (1675–76), may have reminded colonists of the bloody contests over specific areas that had been carried out in wars between the English and local nations in previous generations.[15] This is not to say that Billings's claim to Boston as his home was hollow. One of his most affecting pieces, "Lamentation over Boston" from *The*

Singing Master's Assistant (1778), paraphrases a lamentation in Psalm 137 and passages from Jeremiah to express the deep remorse and pathos of expulsion from a homeland.[16] Billings's hymn is about the British occupation of Boston in 1775–76, and with its sensitive setting of the lyrics he depicted the utter dejection of loss. The opening, with its repeated phrases of "we wept" separated by pauses and its melismatic setting of "weeping," evocatively expresses emotional devastation.[17] Billings's sincerity is not the question, however; instead, it is the authority with which he claims to speak, like his confederates, as a "native" of the area who had special and exclusive claim to the land.

Themes of belonging are further developed in Billings's final publication, *The Continental Harmony* (1794). Unlike Billings's previous publications, thanksgiving looms large in this tunebook.[18] This could be because the publication was funded through subscription by his friends and supporters in the hopes of alleviating the composer's poverty—reason enough to express gratitude, although this reason is not explicitly highlighted in the pieces themselves. Thanksgiving is also a long-standing theme for Congregationalists, apparent in the first generations of Puritan colonists, who regularly called for days of fasting and of thanksgiving as they grappled with interpreting the signs from God about their progress toward becoming a society of visible saints.[19] Generic praise for God is found in "St Enoch, for a Thanksgiving, after a Victory" and "Universal Praise: An Anthem for Thanksgiving, taken from Psalm 149."[20] Billings also included several anthems specifically for days of thanksgiving, which although still containing generic praise and gratitude, indicate an investment in a historical claim to belonging in New England.[21]

These claims are furthered in anthems that explicitly thematize the English landing in Plymouth and the dispossession of Native land. One, labeled "Suitable to be sung on the anniversary of our Fore-fathers' landing, and for Thanksgiving," attributes the successful conquest and colonization of New England to God's plan with lyrics from Psalm 44 that begin: "We have heard with our ears, and our fathers have told us, / How thou didst drive out the heathen before them, and planted them, / for they got not the land by their sword, nor by their bow, / But [by] thy right hand and holy arm."[22] Lyrics that deliver an Old Testament message about a covenanted people struggling to make headway in a land of "heathens" take on a different connotation in the context of New England, where Puritan colonists believed they had a mandate from God to convert Native Americans and, in doing so, dispossessed them of their land. Another piece, "New Plymouth, for Pilgrims' landing anniversary," develops similar themes.[23] The title is followed by an indication that it is "Suitable to be sung on the Anniversary of our Forefathers' landing in New England, Nov. 20th. Anno Domini 1620," recalling unequivocally a starting date to English claims to legitimate belonging. The lyrics, though from the Tate and Brady psalter and thus composed in England, take on a strongly colonialist valence in New England, with phrases such as "How thou to plant them here didst drive / The heathen from this land, / Dispeopl'd by repeated strokes of thy avenging hand." To place the responsibility for "dispeopling" the land of Native Americans in order to make way for English Christian colonists on God's shoulders not only absolved Englishmen and women of any whiff of doubt about whether the depopulation and dispossession that attended colonialism was justified, it also thematized the necessity of the demographic transformation of New England.

The thematization of nativeness and belonging found in Billings's compositions indicates one mode through which whiteness was constructed in early American hymnody. By representing New England as a Protestant country, colonized with divine authorization, Billings erased Native Americans from the landscape. The same logic that called Billings "native" also underwrote white landownership, a cornerstone of the construction of white identity.[24] Yet the possession of property was only tenuously held by Billings himself, whose social position was periodically precarious. While his music exemplifies confidence in the supremacy of white Christians in the face of so-called savages, his personal experiences demonstrate how precarious claims to white privilege were.

Billings's Insecurity and the Vulnerability of Whiteness

Although Billings is much celebrated as a progenitor of American originality, his biography reveals that his actual life was marked by precariousness. In particular, his money troubles, in which he was not alone in the tremendously volatile economic period following the Revolution, made him financially vulnerable. Music historians highlight this fact, although rarely with sufficient context to elucidate his unexceptionality in this regard—many people lost a lot of money. Economic security and the ability to secure property, which Billings managed to achieve, were keyed to race; after all, enfranchisement was limited to those who were white, male, and propertied. Thus, Billings's biography presents an opportunity to question how money helped to construct difference, and whether one who lost money might have also seemed to slip in other sorts of status. For although poverty is by no means predictive of future renown (and indeed, is integral to stereotypes about so-called starving artists), the historiographical treatment of Billings's hardship has reinforced his exceptional status by marking him as particularly disadvantaged.

For much of his life, Billings earned his keep not just through music but as an artisan and menial worker. His father died when Billings was fourteen, and like many boys in families whose fortunes dropped dramatically, Billings became an apprentice. He learned the trade of leather tanning, which was messy and smelly work. As his biographers note, he learned music through singing schools and by studying tunebooks, and himself became a singing master. With the publication of the unrefined but astonishingly inventive *New-England Psalm-Singer* in 1770 and the more sophisticated *Singing Master's Assistant* in 1778, Billings became well known in New England as a premier psalmodist as well as the singing master in fashionable Boston churches.[25] He was able to marry, buy a house on a posh street in Boston, and buy a church pew—all achievements that confirmed his success. Social class was not established by financial resources alone, however, and Billings's rise in prominence did not coincide with an elevation of his social position in the eyes of the elite.

Billings either did not know the rules of polite society, failed to adequately abide by them, or did not wish to; whatever the case, his comportment was distinctly uncouth, according to both his critics and his admirers.[26] His biographers have attempted to make sense of the contradictory evidence that he was popular, even famous, but also maligned. With varying degrees of defensiveness, they have commented on how he behaved when confronted with what one calls "class bias."[27] Indeed, nothing about Billings's behavior or appearance aligned with eighteenth-century ideas of civility. Civility depended upon one's knowledge and physical self-control: the ability to make amusing conversation, possessing polite bodily habits (such as refraining from blowing one's nose in public, or making the correct kind of bow in greeting), and knowledge of social protocols (such as how to take tea) were just a few of the myriad rules governing polite society.[28] Billings came into conflict with these rules when he tried to start a belletristic magazine titled the *Boston Magazine.* He managed to publish one issue of it before a group of prominent Boston clergymen and other gentlemen conspired to take over the periodical. At fault was Billings's distinct lack of taste; although he intended the magazine to be "improving" and to appeal to gentlemen of "learning and leisure," the results were unintentionally crude both in content and execution. The quality of printing was poor, and the literary materials he chose were sensational (particularly a gruesome story about a cannibalistic Scottish family). No reflections on art or higher sentiments could be found in the pages. Prominent men in Boston gossiped about the ill-conceived effort, swapping notes with each other ridiculing the periodical and Billings. How exactly the transfer of editorship transpired is unclear, but the following month they issued their own *Boston Magazine*, displaying the influence of British models such as the *Spectator* rather than the sensational muckrakers, and repudiating Billings's previous effort.[29]

Billings was marginal to elite society in Boston, and his physical appearance was partially responsible for his social status. Two historical sources mention Billings's body: a diary kept by William Bentley, a contemporary of Billings, and Nathaniel Gould's *Church Music in America*, published in 1853 but based on accounts from a person who saw Billings. From these two sources we know that Billings had some sort of disability. The two accounts agree that he was blind in one eye and that one of his legs was shorter than the other. Gould also claims that the composer had a "somewhat withered" arm. We might speculate about the cause of his impairments (perhaps Billings suffered an accident with the caustic materials used to tan leather, resulting in his partial blindness), but what is most noteworthy is how these physical differences were perceived. Both descriptions tie his appearance to his general temperament and character, indicating that his disabilities were of a piece with his general maladaptation to polite society. Bentley, who had met Billings in person, noted in his entry about Billings's death that the composer "was a singular man," who not only was "short of leg, with one eye," but who also was "without any address, & with an uncommon negligence of person." Bentley's reflection suggests that Billings's inability to present himself well was of a piece with his physical differences. It was not *because* Billings was disabled that his presentation was poor; rather, his disability was just one sign of his broader shortcoming. Thus, the ambiguous description "without any address" becomes especially telling, suggesting both his homelessness and his poverty of manners. As Bentley wrote, sympathetically, "He died poor & neglected & perhaps did too much neglect himself."[30]

Bentley's description of Billings highlights a general attitude toward physical differences in the eighteenth century. As historian Jennifer Van Horn notes, commonly held beliefs of the era were that "physical disabilities were the outward manifestations of internal moral failure. In medical texts and politeness manuals, authors maintained that handicaps—referred to in the period as 'defects' and 'deformities'—were God's retribution for the person's sins or the result of sustained ill behavior."[31] Yet when many men lost limbs fighting in the Revolution, the association of disability with immorality was challenged; without limbs it was hard to be self-sufficient, as well as display masculine tropes of civility and virility, but prostheses (particularly for lower limbs) helped to compensate for these losses. No prosthesis would have served Billings's blindness or adequately compensated for his visible difference, for his was not only a matter of a missing limb but of an overall lack of civility.

Gould's account of Billings's appearance emphasizes this point. In a section titled "Billings' [*sic*] Voice, Personal Appearance and Habits," he labeled the composer "somewhat deformed in person," and in addition to adding the possibility of an impairment in his arm, he claimed that these disabilities were matched by "a mind as eccentric as his person was deformed." Implying not just that Billings was impolite and lacked civility, Gould suggested eccentricity on the path to mental illness or drug addiction. Billings was in the habit of taking enormous quantities of snuff, Gould wrote. Even this drug habit was not done in the correct manner: "Instead of taking it in the usual manner, with thumb and finger, would take out a handful and snuff it from between his thumb and clenched hand." Thus Gould attaches Billings's body to his temperament, as did Bentley, but takes it steps further in terms of moralizing and sensationalizing the composer, hitching physical disability to a general "deformity of his habits."[32] Eventually historians would use Billings's disability part and parcel with what they saw as his ineptitude as a composer, as Charles Perkins and John Sullivan Dwight did when they labeled Billings the "American Cyclops."[33]

On several fronts, Billings failed or was unable to meet the standards of embodied and enacted civility required for his acceptance into mainstream ideas about genteel masculinity in the early American republic. His social background, modes of earning an income, disastrous attempt to engage in polite letters, and physical appearance marked him as marginal to polite society. While music historians have noted his unusualness in terms of his compositional style, these social factors also mark him as an outsider. His marginality co-constituted the whiteness of early American hymnody. If Billings's hymns exemplify whiteness presaged on the logics of settler colonialism that sought to remove nonwhite people from the land and replace them with those who upheld the cultural and political goals of European civilization, his biography showcases the precariousness of that white supremacy.

Whiteness was fragile on an individual basis, as Billings shows. But it was also unstable discursively, for eighteenth-century ideas about race held that racial categorizations were mutable. Environmental theories of race argued that skin color and cultural attributes were flexible, could be changed based on exposure, and thus whiteness was at risk of darkening.[34] For example, Samuel Stanhope Smith's *An Essay on the Causes of the Variety of Complexion and Figure in the Human Species* (published in Philadelphia in 1787 and warmly received on both sides of the Atlantic) argued that the environment determined race, listing anecdotal evidence of whites who, after spending time as captives among Native American groups, assimilated not only culturally but racially.[35] Such immediate amalgamation was fearful: if race was mutable within one generation, then the acquisitions of white privilege could be lost quickly, just as an economic crisis could (and did) wipe out financial resources. This racial fear was deep-seated in late eighteenth-century North America, where the construction of hierarchical racial difference was necessary to make sense of the enslavement of African-descended women and men and the genocide of Native Americans. As historian Joyce Chaplin argues, the belief that whites were superior stemmed from the contrast of European health in the face of massive Native American deaths from disease (diseases that, of course, were transmitted by Europeans).[36] In the post-Revolutionary period, as the United States was being formed as a nation of white citizens, concerns about the deleterious racial effect of exposure to nonwhite peoples, particularly on the contested borderlands at the western edges of white-claimed territory, gave rise to defensive proclamations about the durability of whiteness. Thomas Jefferson's *Notes on the State of Virginia* (1784) denigrated African Americans as natural slaves, claiming that people of European, especially Anglo-Saxon, descent would remain superior in the New World. Jefferson's scientific racism belied an overarching insecurity about white identity; whiteness had to be protected, and white privilege was ensured through laws, social structures, and cultural forms such as hymnody.

Thus far, this chapter has sought to point out the ways in which William Billings has been exceptionalized in historiography, while also assessing the historical particularities of his life and works that did indeed make him unusual. After all, Billings lived through the American Revolution, an unprecedented event in which the possibility of political sovereignty shared by a confederation of semiautonomous states was rendered into reality. He witnessed the violent and devastating reality of war and celebrated the underlying principles that drove many people to withstand hardship for the sake of a new nation. As we shall see, the nationalism of Gene Autry's period was of a different order, for it no longer stemmed from the novelty of differentiating from an imperial power but *as* an imperial power that was also undergoing substantial demographic change among its inhabitants. The territorialism of nationhood, noteworthy in Billings's titles, persists across time periods, and surfaces in Autry's work in its emphasis on the western frontier. That is, aspects, such as the religiosity of Billings's work, become sublimated to an assumed Protestantism that need not be explicitly stated in Autry's case. But for both Billings and Autry, historiography has also on some level linked their exceptionalism to a marginal class status that challenged and was ridiculed by the established, elite order. The difference is that Autry, unlike Billings, succeeded in scaling the social hierarchy within his own lifetime, witnessing the celebration of his repertory as part of the US music canon.

From Mavericks to Hillbillies to Cowboys

The ideology of white supremacy that underwrote land seizures and enslavement in the early republic morphed throughout the nineteenth and into the twentieth centuries, but the foundational premise that white cultural creations were preeminent, and that white artists should receive the lion's share of critical attention, remained largely unchanged. As the western frontier closed and chattel slavery gave way to new forms of racial subjugation, the popular music industry served to articulate anew the same national and racial hierarchies. When the commercial recording industry emerged in the early decades of the twentieth century, it advertised its products according to a set of invented genre labels that mapped onto perceived racial, class, and national markers. The development of niche "foreign music" and exoticist genres (such as Hawaiian music) allowed record companies to expand into international markets. At the same time, these recordings satisfied demands for exoticism among US consumers.[37] As with Billings, US musical nationalism during this era was defined in part by difference. Furthermore, these recordings echoed the capitalist exploitation of settler colonialism, depending upon an expansionist US imperialism that sought to extract material and cultural wealth from subjugated peoples, especially in the Pacific and Latin America. The proliferation of "foreign" and "ethnic" novelty songs and recordings during these decades, which often presented ethnic Others in a comic or hypersexualized light, reflected anxieties about the unprecedented waves of immigration to the United States around 1900.[38] Increasingly restrictive immigration laws, most notably the Johnson-Reed Act of 1924, likewise sought to assuage such nativist anxieties.[39] At the same time, US folklore studies emerged as a form of cultural nationalism that was largely Eurocentric in its outlook, locating the nation's cultural origins in the ostensibly "pure" whiteness of the British Isles.

Contrasted with "foreign" music, record companies in the 1920s and 1930s began marketing "American" popular music according to three categories. US vernacular roots music was divided into two genres according to the race of the performer, despite considerable stylistic and audience overlap; the "hillbilly" genre signified music by and for a white, mostly southern, rural underclass, while so-called race records were by African American performers. This "musical color line," to use Karl Hagstrom Miller's formulation, reproduced the racial privileges of Jim Crow; white performers could traverse the line into blues and other ostensibly Black repertories and styles, but Black musicians were expected to hew closely to a narrowly defined set of racialized styles or else be denied professional opportunities.[40] These two genre categories were defined in contrast with mainstream pop, a racially unmarked category that tacitly served white, middle-class audiences. Mainstream pop entrepreneurs, such as the established composers of Tin Pan Alley, often wielded the classed language of respectability politics to distinguish their work from hillbilly and race musicians. Thus, white country musicians of the era found themselves in the middle of a classed and racialized hierarchy.

Beginning in the 1920s and 1930s, the commercial country music industry seized on both folkloric language as well as minstrelsy's racial slippages to establish and fortify its claims to whiteness.[41] "Singing cowboy" Gene Autry was an early beneficiary of this system, and his career trajectory offers striking parallels with that of Billings. Both participated (wittingly or not) in the establishment of white identity through racial difference from Native American populations, which gave their whiteness a distinctly American tint. Both also produced music that elite critics initially disparaged, often for reasons of class bias, but their idiosyncrasies have since come to be regarded as part of US musical exceptionalism. Yet Autry is distinguished from Billings in several important respects. Most obviously, Autry was involved in commercial popular music, an industry that had roots in early US music publishing, but with multimedia expansions that transformed it past all recognition from Billings's day. Simply put, Autry's agency was more diffused across a vast network of songwriters, performers, record producers, film directors, and other industry figures. The recordings, films, and other media attributed to Autry—and thus their messages regarding national and racial identities—were shaped by this network and cannot and should not be viewed as necessarily representing Autry's singular artistic will or political outlook, at least not his alone. Rather than the musical maverick status later ascribed to Billings, Autry proved musically and ideologically flexible in order to appeal to a wider mainstream listenership. Autry's generally personable demeanor allowed him to navigate rarefied social settings more easily, while Billings's apparent unlikability and disability inhibited social mobility. And while Billings's compositions merely alluded to Native populations in passing, Autry's work across various media sought to represent them visually and sonically. In so doing, his work highlighted racial difference much more strongly, which served to make his own music—country music—appear whiter than it had previously, ultimately working to its commercial advantage.

As the country music industry began to coalesce in the late 1920s, it was dogged by negative class stereotypes, embodied most emphatically in the figure of the hillbilly. While some country institutions clung to the hillbilly image as a matter of working-class and regional pride, the established popular music industry remained gleefully disdainful toward this class- and race-marked figure.[42] Writing for *Variety* in 1926, Abel Green taunted:

> The "hillbilly" is a North Carolina or Tennessee and adjacent mountaineer type of illiterate white whose creed and allegiance are to the Bible, the chautauqua, and the phonograph. The talking machine's relation to the show business interests most. The mountaineer is of "poor white trash" genera.[43]

Green's "poor white trash" epithet echoed other critics who coupled the genre's working-class identity with a racially marked whiteness—one that distinguished country audiences from the unremarkable whiteness of middle-class pop listeners. A 1930 article in *Metronome* elaborated on the hillbilly stereotype: "a *browned* and bearded individual in overalls, straw hat and a piece of hay protruding from his mouth."[44] Class disdain thus became a distinction of color, as outdoor labor rendered white people brown, literally and figuratively. Another epithet, "redneck," also gained currency beginning in the late nineteenth century to describe the suntanned necks of white southern farmers, whose labor transformed them into a physically marked, lower class of white.[45] Deployed by the mainstream music industry, "hillbilly" and its synonyms served to valorize pop audiences as possessing the normative and desirable type of whiteness.

For country music entrepreneurs, the hillbilly figure presented a barrier to audience expansion. Entrepreneurs thus sought new performative models that would maintain country's aura of rustic authenticity while also projecting a stronger sense of middle-class respectability. By the mid-1930s, the cowboy emerged as the most viable candidate to combat the negative stereotypes facing country music.[46] A romanticized, heroic figure, the cowboy seemed to embody distinctly American ideals of rugged individualism and self-reliance, offering audiences a masculinist, class-independent alternative to the hillbilly while simultaneously easing the socioeconomic anxieties unleashed by industrialization and the Depression.

Not coincidentally, the cowboy myth also presented an unblemished whiteness compared to the hillbilly's racial ambiguities. Although the historical cowboy performed outdoor labor, and indeed the industry's labor force was racially diverse, in the popular imagination the cowboy was idealized as white and was seemingly not subject to the same racial transformations endured by rural southern farmers.[47] Instead, the cowboy's race was defined via contrast with American Indians, an exoticized Other whose apparently insurmountable racial difference made cowboys appear whiter. At the same time, academic folklorists and popular media both began promoting a narrative of Anglo-Saxon origins for cowboy song repertory, which compounded the cowboy's racial identity as white. The cowboy thus appeared as a uniquely American cultural hero linked almost exclusively to a western European racial background. For the cowboy singers who achieved popularity via this new heroic image, most notably Gene Autry, the cowboy's Americanized whiteness proved to be an avenue of social uplift, avoiding the class-based stigmas faced by other country performers of the era.

Autry's image drew heavily upon the previous generation of cowboys in popular culture as well as on the work of cultural historians from the first decades of the twentieth century. While dime novels and silent western films established the cowboy's commercial viability and penchant for spectacle, academic folklorists gave the cowboy a veneer of respectability and cultural authenticity. As the frontier "closed" in the late 1800s, the cowboy narrative emerged as a lucrative genre that romanticized and whitewashed the history of western expansion, stoking nationalist pride at the seeming fulfillment of Manifest Destiny. Dime novels featuring cowboy heroes began to emerge shortly following the Civil War.[48] Buffalo Bill Cody's Wild West show likewise imagined the cowboy's foundational role in the creation of a new America.[49] Owen Wister's *The Virginian*, published in 1902, elevated the genre to middle-class readership, selling fifty thousand copies within two months.[50] The western novel declined in popularity with the introduction of silent westerns in the early 1900s, but this change in media did little to undermine the nationalist implications of the cowboy or to blunt its appeal.[51]

At the same time, academics and other cultural custodians used the cowboy to shore up the nation's racial identity. During a period of increasing immigration, authors depicted the cowboy as a white, Anglo-Saxon figure distinct from not only African Americans and Native Americans, but also from southern and eastern Europeans. (Of course, these assertions of the cowboy's ethnicity did not match historical realities). Theodore Roosevelt championed the cowboy in his 1896 book *Ranch Life and the Hunting Trail*, contrasting the rugged, self-reliant manliness of the Anglo-Saxon cowboy with Indians and Mexicans, described as physically weak and untrustworthy.[52] Owen Wister made Anglo-Saxon supremacy explicit, writing in 1895 that "to survive in the clean cattle country requires spirit of adventure, courage, and self-sufficiency; you will not find many Poles or Huns or Russian Jews in that district."[53]

Folk song collectors began to turn their attention to cowboy repertory around this time, and they tended to echo these messages of white supremacy. Folk song collection was intimately bound up with questions of cultural nationalism.[54] In the United States, many nineteenth-century collectors were fervently engaged in debates over the scope and meaning of the nation's folk music, in particular how the US might distinguish itself from European counterparts; as demonstrated by the landmark 1867 collection *Slave Songs of the United States*, the racial contours of US folk song were strongly contested.[55] One of the first collections of cowboy songs, *Songs of the Cowboys*, was published by N. Howard "Jack" Thorp in 1908.[56] A former cowboy, Thorp's methods as a collector were mixed, presenting material from the field alongside original compositions and songs previously published elsewhere. However, Thorp's volume provided little historical context for the repertory and avoided overt racial rhetoric, even as the cowboy's whiteness was perhaps assumed.[57]

Thorp's collection was eclipsed two years later by the publication of *Cowboy Songs and Other Frontier Ballads*, compiled by folklorist John A. Lomax. Boasting an academic pedigree that included Harvard and the University of Texas, Lomax yoked white supremacy and US exceptionalism more explicitly. The collection opens with a congratulatory letter from Theodore Roosevelt, to whom Lomax dedicated the volume. Roosevelt's panegyric is followed by a preface in which Lomax praises the rugged independence and hard work of the cowboy, linking his repertory to "the Anglo-Saxon ballad."[58] Lomax thus followed in the footsteps of British ballad hunters like Francis James Child and Cecil Sharp, who heard in the oral tradition of the peasant class the truest expression of national identity.[59] In valorizing white origins, Lomax pushed strongly against competing multiracial perspectives on US musical nationalism, promulgated by prominent composers like Dvořák and in later folk song collections documenting African American vernacular repertories.[60] The authenticity of Lomax's collection—that is, the possibility that nineteenth-century cowboys performed much of this repertory—is dubious. Likewise, Lomax's methods, and his claims that cowboy repertory can be reliably traced to British antecedents, have been thoroughly critiqued.[61] Nevertheless, *Cowboy Songs and Other Frontier Ballads* proved immensely popular, selling thousands of copies and appearing in an expanded edition in 1938. In the words of Mark Fenster, Lomax thus "helped to define both the repertoire and the romantic nature of the singing cowboy figure that was to follow in the mass media."[62]

In the ensuing decades, Autry and his publicity machine drew upon Lomax's work to give his cowboy persona a veneer of intellectual legitimacy. Song folios, interviews, and other promotional material appeared to crib freely from *Cowboy Songs and Other Frontier Ballads*, emphasizing the music's American identity, democratic spirit, and whiteness. One Autry song folio, sensitive to the class upheavals of the Depression, described cowboy society in utopian terms:

> The most significant thing about cowboy music is its innate democracy. Except for the *Boss* or Foreman, there are no definite class distinctions on a ranch. Everybody, from the *straw boss* down to the *cook* and humblest *wrangler*, are on *equal terms*. The isolation from *conventional society* caused by their particular sort of work breaks down any barriers among them.[63]

These comments tracked closely with the preface in Lomax's collection:

> A trip up the trail made a distinct break in the monotonous life of the big ranches, often situated hundreds of miles from where the *conventions of society* were observed. The ranch community consisted usually of the *boss*, the *straw-boss*, the cowboys proper, the horse *wrangler*, and the *cook*—often a negro. These men lived on *terms of practical equality*.[64]

That Autry and his promoters felt the need to emphasize class equality reveals the nagging anxiety of being called a hillbilly. Especially during the Depression, Autry's popularity depended largely upon the cowboy mythology promoted by Lomax, which denied class distinctions in favor of racial, gender, and nationalist ideologies that uplifted white working-class audiences.

Sounding Whiteness

The cowboy rhetoric surrounding Autry's repertory belied its eclecticism, derived from multiple racially ambiguous sources, including Lomax ballads, minstrel songs, and Tin Pan Alley compositions. This apparent diversity was reconciled through rhetoric claiming a white national heritage for the music as well as through homogenizing, pop-oriented performance strategies. Over a career of nearly thirty years, Autry's recordings increasingly tended toward middle-class pop styles in both form and delivery, elevating the country genre in the process.

To be sure, much of Autry's repertory dealt with cowboy themes like boots, saddles, and cattle drives, and advertising took pains to establish the authenticity of this material as white folk song. A handful of Autry's recordings, such as "Home on the Range" and "The Old Chisholm Trail," had appeared in Lomax's *Cowboy Songs and Other Frontier Ballads* and would have been familiar as folk songs to the record-buying public. Seeking to further burnish the authenticity of this repertory, songbooks and other publicity touted the songs' supposedly Anglo-American roots. A rodeo program from the 1940s included a testimonial, ostensibly written by Autry, claiming that "better than anything else, yes, even better than the Negro spiritual, the American cowboy song typifies this great, young country of ours." Later, the program suggested that most cowboy repertory derived from "Elizabethan England."[65] A lengthier testimonial explained:

> A lot of Texas cowboys were southerners who drifted to the Southwest after the Civil War. They brought with them the old time romantic southern tunes and the ancient English folk songs. Some of the boys were Irish and, with the Celtic love for story and song, added greatly to the fast-growing fund of word-of-mouth ballads that the cowboys passed on to each other.[66]

Such publicity reinforced the whiteness of Autry's repertory—one transformed through a uniquely American experience into a distinctive national form of folk song. Newly composed cowboy songs, such as "Back in the Saddle Again" and "Take Me Back to My Boots and Saddle," could escape charges of commercial inauthenticity by falling back on this same racially coded nationalist discourse.

So dominant was this narrative in Autry's publicity that his eclectic repertory never threatened to undermine his cowboy persona. It perhaps helped that many of these other repertories were likewise viewed as thoroughly American. The music of Stephen Foster, for example, proved a consistently popular choice in Autry's films; Foster's "Oh, Susanna!" and "De Camptown Races" appeared with striking regularity.[67] Other musical repertories included blackface minstrel songs, Tin Pan Alley ballads, comic novelty songs, and cover versions of "hillbilly" performers like Jimmie Rodgers.[68] This diversity of styles and musical sources mirrored that of the early country music industry overall, which worked mightily to transform all of these styles into a singular race- and class-marked genre steeped in nostalgia and rusticity.[69] In so doing, the industry arguably asserted a set of canonical US vernacular styles that subsequent generations of country musicians could exploit as an ideological and musical reservoir. Thus, for listeners already engaged with country music across recordings, radio, film, and other media, there was no need to resolve the apparent racial inconsistencies and style anachronisms in Autry's repertory. Rather, Autry's output in these various media worked synergistically to reinforce the repertory's shared American heritage. Publicly, Autry remained always a cowboy, an image that effectively transformed all of his performances into performances of an uncontroversial whiteness.

Further aiding this transformation were deliberate changes to Autry's performance style. In accordance with both his own musical preferences and the direction of his musical collaborators, Autry increasingly sought to mimic the sounds of mainstream popular music in order to capture a broader, middle-class audience. Like the rhetorical shift from hillbilly to cowboy, these self-conscious stylistic changes implied a move from a marked to an unmarked whiteness—one again defined by white, middle-class values. Most notable was Autry's early turn from a twang-filled singing style to a smoother crooning delivery. In his earliest recordings, Autry worked as a Jimmie Rodgers sound-alike, emphasizing nasality that indexed the vocal timbre of white southerners.[70] These recordings did not reflect Autry's usual singing voice, however; he intentionally added the twang. Autry's first national hit in 1935, "That Silver-Haired Daddy of Mine," marked his switch to crooning, closer to the style of middle-class white singers like Al Jolson and Rudy Vallée, whom Autry cited as influences.[71] In addition to smooth vocal delivery, Autry's recordings throughout the 1930s and 1940s increasingly relied on more elaborate written arrangements that could involve string sections, trumpet, or clarinet, rather than the guitar, fiddle, and banjo more typical of early country ensembles.[72]

By uniting these disparate but popular musical repertories and filtering them through his signature vocal style, Autry expanded the stylistic scope of "country" as a genre. And where country audiences had previously been confined to a regional, mostly working-class identity, Autry's films presented alternative possibilities and helped to place them in the national mainstream. The potentially "inauthentic," emotionalist, even effeminizing effects of moving from twang to croon, as well as the adoption of more pop-oriented arrangements, were mitigated in Autry's case by the white, masculinist, and Americanist discourses surrounding the cowboy figure.[73] As we will see, this became the standard against which nonwhite characters would be tacitly compared in Autry's films.

Staging Others

The utopian nationalism of Autry's cowboy image was built on a rejection of class hierarchies that also typically avoided acknowledging racial conflicts. Despite country's historical links to minstrelsy, Autry's repertory rarely engaged in representations of racial Others.[74] Within Autry's films—over ninety were produced between 1934 and 1953—this strategy effectively positioned whiteness as a normative identity, denied nonwhite characters any notion of interiority, and glossed over the politics of racial representation, even as it avoided overt evidence of racial intolerance. Any nonwhites were peripheral, seldom seen or heard. Black actors occasionally appeared as servants or medicine show entertainers, while

Latinx characters cropped up in a handful of "south of the border" films as an alluring exotic Other.[75] Indians were depicted as the racial group most likely to disrupt the white social order—especially for films set in the American Southwest. Representations of Indians drew upon stereotypical nineteenth-century historical narratives of violent Native/white encounters, even though film plots were typically set in the present day.

Autry's films worked to highlight Indian/white racial difference through dramatic and musical means, which served to sharpen the contours of whiteness while erasing class differences among white characters. In dozens of formulaic plots, Indians were almost always villainous extras, often nameless, depicted as prone to irrational violence and moral depravity. Their deaths were relentless, remorseless, unremarkable—collateral damage in larger narratives pitting Autry against powerful white villains who are in cahoots with the duped Indians. The 1950 film *Indian Territory* included a texted prologue that underscored both the notion of Indian inferiority and their propensity to exploitation by immoral whites: "Whole communities were left to the merciless Apaches and the lawless whites, for there was little or no civilian law enforcement on the frontier. In order to control and loot these unprotected areas, unscrupulous white men did not hesitate to use the Indian tribes in their greedy attempts to halt the slow march of law and order."[76] Such formulations underscored racial difference and valorized white cowboy figures like Autry as heroic civilizing agents in US westward expansion—in other words, exceptional figures in the nation's history. The Indians' supposed irrationality was further articulated by nondiegetic music that contrasted sharply with Autry's country pop music, relying not on tonality, AABA song structures, and smooth vocals, but on drums and chants. While Autry performed several songs over the course of each film, diegetic musical performances by Native characters were exceedingly rare, and in fact Indians rarely spoke in most of Autry's films. Their voices remained silent except for the stereotypical war-whoop of battle—not merely sound but an inarticulate, menacing noise.[77]

Orchestral scores during Indian attack scenes fell back on conventional primitivist signifiers—parallel fifths, drones, modal melodies, and an emphasis on woodwinds and drums.[78] Consistent with industry practice, such stock scores were frequently repurposed from one film to another.[79] The reuse of scores and stock footage was born of budgetary expediency, but it also reflected apathy among some film collaborators toward the representation of Indian characters. Rather than crafting new music for each film to give Indian characters a greater sense of complexity and specificity, the presence of generic scores across multiple films could create the impression of a homogenized, static Indian. These sonic distinctions between whites and Indians not only robbed Indian characters of the possibility for meaningful subjectivity, but also served to amplify the whiteness of Autry's cowboy, deflecting the racially ambiguous, class-determined hillbilly figure that country music sought to escape.

Through musical, narrative, and other means across an array of media industries, Autry developed a durable, respectable image of the cowboy as American hero—an image predicated in part on racial difference that would prove lucrative and culturally resonant. Dozens of cowboy acts, such as Roy Rogers and the Sons of the Pioneers, would follow in the wake of Autry's model, furthering both the cowboy image and the country music industry.[80] Although major film studios were initially reluctant to embrace the western film genre, by the late 1940s Autry and his cohort had convinced studio heads of the western's financial and dramatic potential; well-funded, prestigious films like *High Noon* (1952) and *The Searchers* (1956) soon followed, largely replicating the exceptionalist mythology of the white American cowboy. By the end of his entertainment career, Autry had amassed a personal fortune unprecedented in the world of country music; through savvy business investments, he would later become one of the few entertainers to regularly make the *Forbes* list of the four hundred wealthiest Americans.[81] Late in life, Autry became the primary benefactor of the Autry Museum of the American West, a research center opened in Los Angeles in 1988. As articulated in both its mission statement and its archival collections, the museum is dedicated to the study of "all peoples of the American West," particularly through collection and preservation of artifacts from American Indian cultures.[82] Ironically, wealth built upon a narrative of white American exceptionalism would come to fund a revisionist historiography that seeks to critique it.

Race, Recognition, and the Future of Americanist Musicology

Our comparison of Billings and Autry is in many ways unexpected: it is diachronic and cross-genre, features contrasting geographic circumstances, and engages multiple modalities of embodied difference. While we do not mean to suggest a neat one-to-one correlation between their careers or the role that whiteness played, such a comparison provides insights about the construction of whiteness in US music history. Scholars (and fans) recognize both figures' significance, but the centrality of racial privilege to their accomplishments has gone largely unacknowledged. Racial privilege manifested in various ways: for Billings, as a (temporarily) property-owning white man, he possessed enfranchisement; he could make financial and legal decisions on behalf of his entire family; he could expect to receive remuneration for his musical and other forms of labor. All of these were freedoms that were not available to all in the late eighteenth century. Together, they positioned Billings historically as an autonomous individual, and for posterity, as a composer whose works can be gathered together, evaluated on aesthetic merits, and canonized. In Autry's case, Jim Crow laws conferred upon Autry access to spaces and resources unavailable to most musicians of color, while it also gave legal sanction to social hierarchies based around race. Within the context of the Hollywood film industry of the 1930s and 1940s, Autry also enjoyed more professional opportunities and rewards: he played heroic leading men rather than stereotyped extras, he received greater compensation, and he exercised greater control over contracts and the direction of his career. Greater recognition of such racial privileges and how they have shaped our understanding of the field is, we believe, imperative for Americanist musicology. In the spirit of this edited collection, which seeks not only to reflect on the current state of US music studies but to chart new paths of inquiry, we highlight here a few common themes and their implications for future research.

The first is a need to attend to other facets of identity within the racialized category of whiteness. This requires first a forthright acknowledgment that many of the composers and performers that constitute our musical canon and research subjects were regarded as white. This racial identity is not simply incidental or irrelevant but instead fundamental to how audiences and scholars have conceived of their musical value and historical significance. And yet this whiteness is not monolithic but shaded according to other aspects of identity, especially class and labor status, but also gender, ability, geography, and nationality. Even as Billings and Autry sought to turn white identity to their advantage, these other categories yielded hierarchies of whiteness within which these white men could still be regarded as less than. Billings's upper-class critics seldom referenced his literal skin color but focused intensely on his physicality. For Autry, the proliferation of racialized labels pertaining to geography and class (hillbilly, cowboy) likewise demonstrates the complexity of race within a broader network of identities. Both figures occupied privileged spaces of maleness and whiteness, yet this whiteness was mutable, its benefits not always secure. In time, both men in one way or another were rescued from class disdain through assertions of whiteness coupled with rhetoric over their exceptionalist "American" identity. But to claim whiteness as an advantage equally bestowed upon its owners is a mistake. Rather, certain advantages were conceivable, if not realized, for both. For scholars, it is not enough to simply observe that a performer was (regarded as) white and thus benefited from racial privilege. That privilege must be assessed as a contingency amid a host of other historical and personal factors.

Beyond the particulars of the individual racialized subject, we also note the need to historicize US whiteness and to investigate the agents involved in its construction across historical periods. Only select members of each generation in the United States have been empowered to define whiteness, and they have done so differently over time. Operating from a position of greater authority, economic and cultural elites have controlled the boundaries of whiteness, applying or denying it to Billings and Autry as was most beneficial to themselves. In Billings's day, these elites included members of the religious establishment and wealthy landholders. Autry and his music were initially disparaged by Hollywood and Tin Pan Alley insiders like Abel Green, who found the music and its audience insufficiently white, and who relented only once Autry's music proved too lucrative to dismiss. At the same time, cowboy repertory was granted intellectual and cultural legitimacy through the efforts of early academics like John Lomax, who staked the music's worth in large part on its status as a specifically Anglo-American repertory. That both Billings and Autry have since been heralded as exemplars of American music should give us pause, for there seems to be here an uncomfortable conflation of American identity with whiteness. Across historical periods, what do elite cultural agents have to gain in asserting Americanness—a term that obscures rather than erases racial ideologies? In these two case studies, at least, labeling music as "American" made it more salable and serious, and whiter.

This question of authority and inclusion becomes perhaps even more acute as we approach the present day and investigate persistent biases within the musicological discipline. In its earliest decades, Americanist musicology was marginalized within a larger field that still privileged the model of the white, male European composer. For those invested in scholarly study of US music, Billings could fit more or less comfortably into that model, his idiosyncrasies as a composer making him just different enough from European counterparts to serve as a celebrated fountainhead of US classical composition. At some level, Billings's whiteness helped to legitimate him as an object of serious scholarly study. Meanwhile Autry, for multiple reasons, but especially as an avatar of critically maligned, commercial country music, remained beyond the scope of midcentury musicology. His time would come only as US popular music made its first tentative steps into the academy, again under a problematic banner of cultural nationalism that regarded racial and stylistic diversity as part of US exceptionalism but that largely elided the politics of whiteness. As musicological scholarship has more recently embraced multicultural perspectives and sought to diversify the canon, whiteness has too often remained unmarked, unremarkable, perhaps even taboo—a tacit category against which musicians of color are compared. Attending to musical whiteness as actively constructed, historically dynamic, and deployed strategically for purposes of social inclusion and exclusion, makes us question how ideologies of whiteness might still linger in our present scholarship.

Notes

1. Establishing the field of US music studies in the twentieth century required robust advocacy on behalf of its relevance, particularly in the face of its dismissal by musicologists who focused on the European canon. A well-known example of such a dismissal is Joseph Kerman's address to the American Musicological Society in 1964, followed by his article, in which he wrote: "Unfortunately, American music has not been interesting enough, artistically, to merit from us that [scholarly] commitment." Kerman, "A Profile for American Musicology," *Journal of the American Musicological Society* 18, no. 1 (Spring 1965): 68. Also see the responses: Edward E. Lowinsky, "Character and Purposes of American Musicology: A Reply to Joseph Kerman," *Journal of the American Musicological Society* 18, no. 2 (Summer 1965): 222–34; Joseph Kerman, [Letter from Joseph Kerman], *Journal of the American Musicological Society* 18, no. 3 (Autumn 1965): 426–27; Donald M. McCorkle, "Finding a Place for American Studies in American Musicology," *Journal of the American Musicological Society* 19, no. 1 (Spring 1966): 73–84. Examples of scholarship that promotes the relevance of Americanist musicology more broadly can be found in H. Wiley Hitchcock, *Music in the United States: A Historical Introduction* (Englewood Cliffs, NJ: Prentice-Hall, 1969); Richard Crawford, *The American Musical Landscape* (Berkeley: University of California Press, 1993). Unlike Black music studies, white music studies has not undergone a process of critical self-reflection. See, for example, Guthrie P. Ramsey, Jr., "Who Hears Here? Black Music, Critical Bias, and the Musicological Skin Trade," *Musical Quarterly* 85, no. 1 (Spring 2001): 1–52; Kira Thurman, "Singing Against the Grain: Playing Beethoven in the #BlackLivesMatter era," *Examined Life*, issue 17 (September 29, 2018), https://thepointmag.com/examined-life/singing-against-grain-playing-beethoven-blacklivesmatter-era/

2. We use "Native American," "American Indian," and "Indian" interchangeably when not referring to a specific nation or group.

3. Matthew Frye Jacobson, *Whiteness of a Different Color: European Immigrants and the Alchemy of Race* (Cambridge, MA: Harvard University Press, 1998); Grace Elizabeth Hale, *Making Whiteness: The Culture of Segregation in the South, 1890–1940* (New York: Pantheon Books, 1998).

4. As two white scholars collaborating on this chapter about whiteness, we have become acutely aware of this tendency. One goal of this chapter is to encourage a greater awareness, discussion, and critique of whiteness among white scholars, even as we acknowledge the racial privileges and epistemological blind spots of our own subjective position. On white epistemologies, see Tom Perchard, "New Riffs on the Old Mind-Body Blues: 'Black Rhythm,' 'White Logic,' and Music Theory in the Twenty-First Century," *Journal of the Society for American Music* 9, no. 3 (August 2015): 321–48; Veronica Watson, *The Souls of White Folk: African American Writers Theorize Whiteness* (Jackson: University Press of Mississippi, 2013).

5. Our collaborative method entailed conversations and shared reading to develop the questions and critical framework of this project. Conversations about the two individuals we decided to profile led to fruitful comparisons, in which we identified ways in which they engaged similar questions. We then wrote the two case studies independently (Goodman wrote Billings, Parler wrote Autry), which allowed us to capitalize on our different areas of expertise. Reading through each other's sections and offering comments followed, and finally we drafted the introduction and conclusion.

6. Gilbert Chase, *America's Music, from the Pilgrims to the Present*, 3rd ed. (Urbana: University of Illinois Press, 1987), 115. Gender also plays a significant role in this framing. See Elizabeth B. Crist, "'Ye Sons of Harmony': Politics, Masculinity, and the Music of William Billings in Revolutionary Boston," *William and Mary Quarterly* 60, no. 2 (2003): 333–54.

7. Billings's canonicity was achieved thanks to the publication of his complete works, a catalog raisonné, a major biography, and a prominent position in American music history textbooks. See Karl Kroeger and Hans Nathan, eds., *The Complete Works of William Billings*, 4 vols. (Charlottesville: University Press of Virginia, 1977–90); Karl Kroeger, comp., *Catalog of the Musical Works of William Billings* (New York: Greenwood Press, 1991); David P. McKay and Richard Crawford, *William Billings of Boston: Eighteenth-Century Composer* (Princeton, NJ: Princeton University Press, 1975).

8. Michael Broyles, *Mavericks and Other Traditions in American Music* (New Haven: Yale University Press, 2004), 2.

9. The use of lowercase in "native" marks an important, though uncommented upon, distinction in historians' use of the designation. Billings was not Native, and his reception makes no claims to his membership in a Native (Indigenous) community. Nevertheless, placing Billings figuratively in the category of "native" works to eliminate Native Americans from the discourse.

10. On the tendency in New England histories to claim "nativeness" for white settler colonists see Jean O'Brien, *Firsting and Lasting: Writing Indians Out of Existence in New England* (Minneapolis: University of Minnesota Press, 2010), 51.

Also see Patrick Wolfe, "Settler Colonialism and the Elimination of the Native," *Journal of Genocide Research* 8, no. 4 (2006): 387–409.

11. McKay and Crawford, *William Billings of Boston*, 65.

12. The assumption of Native American personae to express political discontent was not new in this instance. As Philip Deloria notes, "playing Indian" was an established mode through which British colonists confronted the establishment. Philip J. Deloria, "Patriotic Indians and Identities of Revolution," chap. 1 in *Playing Indian* (New Haven: Yale University Press, 1998).

13. McKay and Crawford, *William Billings of Boston*, 216.

14. Nathaniel Gould, *Church Music in America* (Boston: A. N. Johnson, 1853), 41.

15. William Billings, *The New-England Psalm-Singer* (Boston: Printed by Edes and Gill, 1770), 72.

16. Murray Barbour, *The Church Music of William Billings* (East Lansing: Michigan State University Press, 1960), 8–12.

17. William Billings, *The Singing Master's Assistant* (Boston: Printed by Draper and Folsom, 1778), 33–38.

18. This refers not to the annual secular US holiday of Thanksgiving, but to a Protestant religious practice of periodically offering gratitude to God in an effort either to stave off or respond to challenges. On the history of Thanksgiving as a holiday, and its significance for Native Americans in southern New England in particular, see David Silverman, *This Land Is Their Land: The Wampanoag Indians, Plymouth Colony, and the Troubled History of Thanksgiving* (New York: Bloomsbury, 2019).

19. Edmund S. Morgan, *Visible Saints: The History of a Puritan Idea* (New York: New York University Press, 1963).

20. Billings, *The Continental Harmony* (Boston: Printed by I. Thomas and E. T. Andrews, 1794), 67, 97–104.

21. These thanksgiving-day anthems include "An Anthem. For Thanksgiving Day Morning," "Thanksgiving day anthem, psalm 149," and "An Anthem. Psalm 108. For Thanksgiving Day morning." Billings, *The Continental Harmony*, 70–75, 97–104, 176–84.

22. Billings, *The Continental Harmony*, 84–85.

23. Billings, *The Continental Harmony*, 169–70.

24. Aileen Moreton-Robinson, *The White Possessive: Property, Power, and Indigenous Sovereignty* (Minneapolis: University of Minnesota Press, 2015).

25. Billings worked at Brattle Street Church, Old South Church, First Church, and Stone Chapel.

26. Billings was aware that he and his compositional style were being closely observed; see his satire of critics in *Singing Master's Assistant*, 16–17 (discussed in McKay and Crawford, *William Billings of Boston*, 81–82). On his admirers, more below, but chiefly Bentley's diary.

27. On "class bias," see Gillian B. Anderson, "Eighteenth-Century Evaluations of William Billings: A Reappraisal," *Quarterly Journal of the Library of Congress* 35, no. 1 (January 1978): 51. McKay and Crawford have a more balanced take on Billings's coarseness, noting that if he wanted to be refined, he failed, but that he might not have wanted to.

28. David S. Shields, *Civil Tongues and Polite Letters in British America* (Chapel Hill: University of North Carolina Press, 1997); Dallett C. Hemphill, *Bowing to Necessities: A History of Manners in America, 1620–1860* (New York: Oxford University Press, 1999).

29. McKay and Crawford quote a disparaging private letter sent from Rev. John Eliot to Rev. Jeremy Belknap about *Boston Magazine*, which shows how the Boston elite rallied against Billings (*William Billings of Boston*, 128–29).

30. September 28, 1800, entry, William Bentley, *The Diary of William Bentley*, vol. 2 (Salem, MA: Essex Institute, 1907), 351.

31. Jennifer Van Horn, *The Power of Objects in Eighteenth-Century British America* (Chapel Hill: University of North Carolina Press, published for the Omohundro Institute of Early American History and Culture, 2017), 353.

32. Gould, *Church Music in America*, 46.

33. Charles C. Perkins and John S. Dwight, *History of the Handel and Haydn Society of Boston, Massachusetts*, vol. 1 (Boston: Alfred Mudge & Son, 1883), 22.

34. Roxann Wheeler, *The Complexion of Race: Categories of Difference in Eighteenth-Century British Culture* (Philadelphia: University of Pennsylvania Press, 2000), 6. Also see Van Horn on the use of cosmetics to mask skin color, making darker-skinned people appear whiter. *The Power of Objects*, 316.

35. Samuel Stanhope Smith, *An Essay on the Causes of the Variety of Complexion and Figure in the Human Species* (Philadelphia: Robert Aitken, 1787).

36. Joyce E. Chaplin, *Subject Matter: Technology, the Body, and Science on the Anglo-American Frontier, 1500–1676* (Cambridge, MA: Harvard University Press, 2001).

37. On "foreign music," see David Brackett, "Foreign Music and the Emergence of Phonography," chap. 2 in *Categorizing Sound: Genre and Twentieth-Century Popular Music* (Oakland: University of California Press, 2016).

38. For example, see discussions of Chinese American musical representation in Charles Hiroshi Garrett, "Chinatown, Whose Chinatown? Defining America's Borders with Musical Orientalism," chap. 4 in *Struggling to Define a Nation: American Music and the Twentieth Century* (Berkeley: University of California Press, 2008).

39. See Mae M. Ngai, "The Johnson-Reed Act of 1924 and the Reconstruction of Race in Immigration Law," chap. 1 in *Impossible Subjects: Illegal Aliens and the Making of Modern America*, rev. ed. (Princeton, NJ: Princeton University Press, 2014).

40. On hillbilly and race records, see Karl Hagstrom Miller, *Segregating Sound: Inventing Folk and Pop Music in the Age of Jim Crow* (Durham, NC: Duke University Press, 2010).

41. On folkloric and minstrelsy paradigms in 1920s and 1930s popular music, see Miller, *Segregating Sound*, 6–13.

42. In the 1920s and 1930s, the Grand Ole Opry radio program was a primary exponent of "hillbilly" identity. See Pamela Fox, "Reluctant Hillbillies: Rube and Blackface Performance in the Barn Dance Era," chap. 2 in *Natural Acts: Gender, Race, and Rusticity in Country Music* (Ann Arbor: University of Michigan Press, 2009); and Charles K. Wolfe, *A Good-Natured Riot: The Birth of the Grand Ole Opry* (Nashville, TN: Country Music Foundation Press and Vanderbilt University Press, 1999).

43. The language in this quotation is unorthodox, but it is replicated accurately. Abel Green, "'Hill-Billy' Music," *Variety*, December 29, 1926. Quoted in Archie Green, "Hillbilly Music: Source and Symbol," *Journal of American Folklore* 78, no. 309 (July–September 1965): 221.

44. Emphasis added. Doron K. Antrim, "He Found Pay Dirt on the Farm: Carson Robison, American Balladist," *Metronome* 46, no. 6 (June 1930), Carson J. Robison Collection, 1903–1988, Oversize Box F246, Special Collections and University Archives, Leonard H. Axe Library, Pittsburg State University.

45. An etymology of the term "redneck" is given in Patrick Huber, "A Short History of *Redneck*: The Fashioning of a Southern White Masculine Identity," *Southern Cultures* 1, no. 2 (Winter 1995): 146–48.

46. A fuller history of these two archetypes appears in Bill C. Malone, *Singing Cowboys and Musical Mountaineers: Southern Culture and the Roots of Country Music* (Athens: University of Georgia Press, 1993).

47. Long neglected in historiography, the history of African American cowboys has been the subject of much scholarship in the last twenty years. See, for example, Bruce A. Glasrud and Michael N. Searles, eds., *Black Cowboys in the American West: On the Range, on the Stage, behind the Badge* (Norman: University of Oklahoma Press, 2016); and Michael K. Johnson, *Hoo-Doo Cowboys and Bronze Buckaroos: Conceptions of the African American West* (Jackson: University Press of Mississippi, 2014).

48. Mark Fenster, "Preparing the Audience, Informing the Performers: John A. Lomax and *Cowboy Songs and Other Frontier Ballads*," *American Music* 7, no. 3 (Autumn 1989): 264–65.

49. On Cody, see Beth E. Levy, *Frontier Figures: American Music and the Mythology of the American West* (Berkeley: University of California Press, 2012), 10–13.

50. Fenster, "Preparing the Audience," 264.

51. On silent westerns, see Peter Stanfield, "Liberty's Cuckoos: Cowboys of the Silent Screen," chap. 2 in *Horse Opera: The Strange History of the 1930s Singing Cowboy* (Urbana: University of Illinois Press, 2002).

52. Stanfield, "Liberty's Cuckoos," 12–13.

53. Owen Wister, "The Evolution of the Cow-Puncher," *Harper's Monthly*, September 1895. Reprinted in Ben Merchant Vorpahl, *My Dear Wister: The Frederic Remington-Owen Wister Letters* (Palo Alto, CA: American West, 1972), 80. Quoted in Stanfield, "Liberty's Cuckoos," 15.

54. Johann Gottfried Herder (1744–1803) is often cited as a founding figure of this field in Europe. For translation of and commentary on Herder's work, see Johann Gottfried Herder and Philip V. Bohlman, *Song Loves the Masses: Herder on Music and Nationalism* (Oakland: University of California Press, 2017); and Matthew Gelbart, *The Invention of "Folk Music" and "Art Music": Emerging Categories from Ossian to Wagner* (New York: Cambridge University Press, 2007).

55. William Francis Allen, Charles Pickard Ware, and Lucy McKim Garrison, *Slave Songs of the United States* (New York: A. Simpson & Co., 1867).

56. N. Howard Thorp, *Songs of the Cowboys*, with an introduction by Alice Corbin Henderson (Boston: Houghton Mifflin, 1921).

57. In her introduction to the 1921 reprint, Henderson commented upon the similarity between cowboy repertory and Irish and "Celtic" ballads. Thorp, *Songs of the Cowboys*, xix.

58. John A. Lomax, *Cowboy Songs and Other Frontier Ballads* (New York: Sturgis and Walton, reprint 1911), xvii.

59. On nationalist ideology in the work of Child and Sharp, see Benjamin Filene, "Setting the Stage: Identifying an American Folk Heritage, 1900–1930," chap. 1 in *Romancing the Folk: Public Memory & American Roots Music* (Chapel Hill: University of North Carolina Press, 2000). The collection by Olive Dame Campbell and Cecil J. Sharp, *English Folk Songs from the Southern Appalachians* (New York: G.P. Putnam's Sons, 1917), likewise sought to link US national identity with Anglo-Saxon origins.

60. Dvořák's thoughts on US musical nationalism are discussed in John C. Tibbetts, ed., *Dvořák in America, 1892–1895* (Portland, OR: Amadeus Press, 1993), among many other publications. African American folk song collections include Natalie Curtis Burlin, *Negro Folk-Songs*, 4 vols. (New York: G. Schirmer, 1918); and Maud Cuney-Hare, *Negro Musicians and Their Music* (Washington, DC: Associated Publishers, 1936). See also Burlin's work on Native American music, *The Indians' Book: An Offering by the American Indians of Indian Lore, Musical and Narrative, to Form a Record of the Songs and Legends of Their Race* (New York: Harper and Brothers, 1907).

61. Regarding the authenticity of cowboy folk song, see Ted Gioia, "The Big Roundup: John Lomax Roamed the West, Collecting Classic Songs from the Cowboy Era," *American Scholar* 74, no. 2 (Spring 2005): 101–11. On Lomax's ethnographic methods, see Austin E. Fife and Alta S. Fife, eds., *Cowboy and Western Songs: A Comprehensive Anthology* (New York: C. N. Potter, 1969); and D. K. Wilgus, *Anglo-American Folksong Scholarship since 1898* (New Brunswick, NJ: Rutgers University Press, 1959).

62. Fenster, "Preparing the Audience," 261.

63. Emphasis added for purposes of comparison. Attr. Gene Autry, "Cowboys n' Ballads" (song folio clipping), n.d., Autry Scrapbook T87-36-43, Gene Autry Personal Papers and Business Archives, 1900–2002, on loan from Mr. and Mrs. Gene Autry, Autry National Center, Los Angeles; MSA.28.

64. Lomax, *Cowboy Songs*, xviii.

65. Attr. Gene Autry, "Cowboy Songs: Familiar Tunes of the Trail Herders Important Contribution to American Folk Music," in David B. Whalen, ed., "Gene Autry's Flying 'A' Ranch Stampede," Official Program [ca. 1940s], photocopy, Jesse Austin Morris Collection Box I.1, Center for Popular Music, Middle Tennessee State University.

66. Autry, "Cowboys n' Ballads."

67. For "Oh, Susanna!," see the films *Tumbling Tumbleweeds* (1935), *Oh, Susanna!* (1936), and *Rancho Grande* (1940). For "De Camptown Races," see *The Singing Vagabond* (1935) and *Oh, Susanna!*.

68. For an example of a comic number, see Smiley Burnette's performance of "Heebie Jeebie Blues" in *Public Cowboy No. 1* (1937). For a Tin Pan Alley love song, see "I'm Mad about You" in *The Big Show* (1936) and "Dinah" in *Round-Up Time in Texas* (1937). Rodgers's "In the Jailhouse Now" appears in both *Back in the Saddle* (1941) and *Prairie Moon* (1938).

69. For the standard account of country music's stylistic and commercial ori-

gins, see Bill C. Malone and Tracey E. W. Laird, *Country Music USA*, 50th anniversary ed. (Austin: University of Texas Press, 2018).

70. Don Cusic, *Gene Autry: His Life and Career* (Jefferson, NC: McFarland, 2007), 23. Examples of Autry's Rodgers impersonation include "Dallas County Jail Blues" and "T.B. Blues." Autry also recorded several tributes to Rodgers after his death in 1933, such as "The Life of Jimmie Rodgers."

71. On Vallée, see Cusic, *Gene Autry*, 24. On Jolson, see Holly George-Warren, *Public Cowboy No. 1: The Life and Times of Gene Autry* (New York: Oxford University Press, 2007), 28–29. A fuller account of crooning appears in Allison McCracken, *Real Men Don't Sing: Crooning in American Culture* (Durham, NC: Duke University Press, 2015).

72. Jonathan Guyot Smith specifically cites Autry's October 11, 1937, recording session in Los Angeles as the moment when Autry switched to more elaborate musical arrangements. Jonathan Guyot Smith, "The Brilliant Artistry of Gene Autry," *DISCoveries*, December 1993, photocopy, Jesse Austin Morris Collection Box I.1.

73. This masculinist figure, however, provided room for ambivalence. As Stephanie Vander Wel explains, "Autry's musical imagery shaped the singing cowboy into a sentimental figure who underscored the vulnerability of men in the 1930s." Stephanie Vander Wel, "The Lavender Cowboy and 'The She Buckaroo': Gene Autry, Patsy Montana, and Depression-Era Gender Roles," *Musical Quarterly* 95, nos. 2–3 (Summer–Fall 2012): 244.

74. Country's minstrelsy connections are explored in Fox, "Reluctant Hillbillies," chap. 2.

75. Films featuring prominent Latinx characters or themes are *Rootin' Tootin' Rhythm* (1937), *South of the Border* (1939), *Mexicali Rose* (1939), *Down Mexico Way* (1941), *Twilight on the Rio Grande* (1947), and *The Big Sombrero* (1949).

76. For further examples of such alliances between Indians and white villains, see Autry's films *The Singing Vagabond* (1935), *Ride, Ranger, Ride* (1936), *Apache Country* (1952), and *Winning of the West* (1953).

77. Only in a series of late-career, "pro-Indian" films were Indian characters given substantial speaking roles. These include *The Last Round-Up* (1947), *The Cowboy and the Indians* (1949), and *Apache Country* (1952).

78. On orchestral representations of American Indians in the early twentieth century, see Michael V. Pisani, *Imagining Native America in Music* (New Haven: Yale University Press, 2005). Few scores survive for specific Autry films, but the following examples of generic Indian music appear to have been used interchangeably across films: Mischa Bakaleinikoff, "Indian Tom-Toms #1 (Fast)" and "Indian Tom-Toms #2 (Slow)" (single sheet scores, no folder), Mischa Bakaleinikoff Collection, USC Libraries Cinematic Arts Library. For scenes in which such exoticist tropes appeared, see *Ride, Ranger, Ride* (1936) at the 47:20 mark; *The Last Round-Up* (1947) at 55:10; *The Cowboy and the Indians* (1949) at 5:55; *Indian Territory* (1950), opening credits; *Apache Country* (1952), opening credits.

79. Boyd Magers, *Gene Autry Westerns* (Madison, NC: Empire, 2007), 246.

80. Earlier in their career, the Sons of the Pioneers appeared with Autry in

The Old Corral (1936), *The Big Show* (1936), and *Call of the Canyon* (1942). Rogers got his start at Republic Pictures as a substitute for Autry while Autry was serving in the army during World War II. For more on Rogers's career, see Roy Rogers and Dale Evans, with Jane Stern and Michael Stern, *Happy Trails: Our Life Story* (New York: Simon and Schuster, 1994). Discussion of Rogers's career at Republic can be found on pages 97–117.

81. On the *Forbes* list in 1985, see "The Forbes 400: Walton Tops List of Richest Americans," *Los Angeles Times*, October 15, 1985; for the 1990 list, see Cusic, *Gene Autry*, 186.

82. "What Is the Autry?," Autry Museum of the American West, https://theautry.org/about-us. For further information about the history of the museum and its attempts to promote a more inclusive history of the American West, see Louise Pubols, "The Singing Cowboy and the Professor: The New West at the Autry National Center," *Public Historian* 31, no. 4 (November 2009): 71–76.

EIGHT | Exceptional Matters, Exceptional Times

A Conversation about the Challenges of US Music Scholarship in the Age of Black Lives Matter and Trump

JOSH KUN AND ALEJANDRO L. MADRID

The two of us—one based in musicology and Latina/o studies, the other in communication and American studies—convened for a conversation about the divergent approaches to studying US music within each of these disciplines. Our goal was to explore questions about the intellectual and social relevance of music studies today, not only within the humanities and social sciences but also in society at large. This concern has motivated much of our scholarship for several years and has brought us together several times to collaborate on different projects.

This particular conversation unfolded in late 2018, early 2019, and again in mid-2020, in direct response to the extreme polarizations within the current political moment in the United States and the continuous invocation of cultural values rooted in xenophobia, hate, anti-Black racism, and the general normalization of cruelty. We are hopeful that this difficult and harmful conjuncture in US political life—while rooted in histories of the United States that date back to the nation's founding in inequality, white supremacist thought, and racial subjugation—will soon be a sad and distant memory and thus do not want to make it the sole target of our discussion. Instead, we take it as a point of entry into questioning a series of issues that we believe have been central in defining American identity as an exceptionalist project and thus have also been at stake in shaping the trajectory of US music studies as an essentialist endeavor. Here, our discussion of exceptionalism is informed by both the conventional understanding of the word—something that is extraordinary—as well as the political ideology that, in the particular context of US history, has claimed a unique and superior character for the US nation state as an excuse for imperialist expansion and ethnic domination. In doing this we dwell on the aesthetic, pedagogical, and political configurations at the intersection of the two concepts and how they have positively and negatively informed political and academic projects: the US national fantasy and musicology in this case.

We have structured the conversation around four axes: the transhistorical US dystopia; exceptionalism, broadly defined; the possibility or desirability of a more unified field of US music studies; and the need to develop postnationalist agendas at the intersection of music and politics. Thus, first, we explore the continuities of some of the dystopian practices that have surfaced in US everyday life in recent years—white supremacy, xenophobia, anti-intellectualism, trans- and homophobia, among others—with practices of discrimination and imperial expansion at the core of the American experience. In doing so, we ponder the question of whether the Trump era is in fact a truly exceptional one in the history of the United States. Second, drawing a parallel between musicology's exceptionalist claims about music—which has often relegated music scholarship developed in other disciplines as inconsequential and even irrelevant—and the discourse of exceptionalism that has characterized the US nation-building project, we seek to generate a dialogue between the critical interventions of American studies scholarship and the ongoing transformations and disruptions of musicology, in an attempt to question the role of critical theory broadly—and critical theories of difference, transnationalism, diaspora, and social change more specifically—in generating a more open, dynamic, and interdisciplinary field of US music studies. Third, we try to imagine what such a field would look like, what kinds of questions it would privilege, and how it could engage an activism that articulates the kind of transformation from below that projects like the Movement for Black Lives / Black Lives Matter or the Occupy movement entail. Finally, we propose that instead of reacting by seeking refuge in the replication of old supremacist fantasies about how the country and its people should be, the time is ripe for an approach to the study of US music that questions these values and furthers new, critical, more inclusive—but also more decolonial—perspectives and narratives about Americanness that center the experiences of exploitation of the many constituencies included in, and excluded from, the category of "American."

As this book moved from the editing stage toward production in the spring of 2020, many of the issues discussed below took on even greater urgency. Notably, the global crisis generated by the COVID-19 pandemic and the mass nationwide Black Lives Matter protests that engulfed the country after the police killings of George Floyd, Breonna Taylor, and Ahmaud Arbery ignited critical conversations, social and political policy revisions, and large-scale activism for structural change. In music studies, the discussion about race and white supremacy hit the Society for Ethnomusicology particularly hard when an open letter by Danielle Brown detailing her experience as a Black member of the society generated a heated debate that confronted systematic practices of racial erasure and white supremacy that many in the association had failed to identify and address effectively.[1] We hope that our conversation speaks to these recent events in both broad and specific ways, and we trust that readers will make connections between the issues discussed here and the political moments that have no doubt continued to unfold since the spring of 2020.

AM: During the fall 2016 semester I was teaching an undergraduate seminar about the musics of Latinx communities in the United States that met only once a week. I taught that class the afternoon of the day of the presidential election. Needless to say, when I came back home that evening and learned about the result I felt that something truly tragic had just taken place. I started wondering how to talk about it with my students since many of them were first-generation Latinx in college and the anti-immigration rhetoric of the campaign had touched them on a very personal and emotional level. But in the end, even for the white students in the class, the election results seemed to validate a type of hate speech that most of them probably had never experienced. I was in shock for a while but as the days went by I started remembering my childhood at the US-Mexico border in the 1970s, my experience as a young adult in New England and New York when I moved there to study music in the 1990s, and the kinds of aggressions and microaggressions I experienced and would often dismiss with "They just do not know better." In 2016, I realized that my anxiety about entering a new dark age in US public life was somehow based on an illusion created in the last decade or so of the United States as a truly progressive society. The fact is that the ugly side of the United States that somehow surprised us during the months leading up to the 2016 election had always been there: it was nothing new for people of color. So when I faced my students a week later I listened to their fears, their concerns, and their stories; we talked about ways to navigate a moment of increased intimidation toward those who are different or think differently; but I also made a point of letting them know that for folks of color this scary underbelly of the United States was nothing new and that looking at the historical experiences of African Americans, Latinxs, Asian Americans, and Native Americans may help us define or identify strategies to struggle against it. I think we feel so anxious about the age of Trump because it brings to the fore some of the basic contradictions at the core of US identity. That is, it puts at odds the realities of exceptionalism, white supremacy, and imperialism, which are central to the political foundation and social organization of this country, in relation to the utopian idealism and optimism about democracy, freedom, and equality that are also essential to understanding the US experiment.

JK: Those two currents were always at odds and in some ways can't exist without each other. The historian Edmund Morgan once famously described it as the American paradox of freedom and slavery, the existence of the former required the existence of the latter.[2] The country was founded on a commitment to freedom that required a commitment to slavery, a belief in a religion of racial capitalism in which freedom was not only reserved for white men but was the economic system they profited from and that systemically reinvested in them. The pursuit of happiness required the pursuit of racial terror. The abstract glory of democracy was always contingent in principle; like justice, it belonged to the few, not the many. Music has played a central role in voicing, exacerbating, and pushing back against these tensions, whether in the way Du Bois used sorrow songs to frame his arguments in *The Souls of Black Folk* (1903) or in the way the symphony functioned as the model for both the melting pot and the concept of cultural pluralism, two key early twentieth-century theories of cultural order that both resulted in sameness and consensus more than difference and dissonance.[3] I mean, one way to tell the history of Black music in the United States—as Frederick Douglass, Amiri Baraka, Angela Y. Davis, Saidiya Hartman, and so many others have argued for well over a century—is that it evolves precisely out of (or as) the constant possibility of Black freedom in a political and social system determined to prevent the achievement of that freedom through control, capture, policing, and enclosure (for example, the "minor key" revolutions and "riotous refrains" of the early twentieth-century Black women that Hartman writes about).[4] Similarly, you can also say that there is a paradox of freedom and empire, or freedom and settlement, in which the free movement of a population (westward ho and all that) and a nation founded on the expansionist myth of the open road require the removal of that free movement for others, whether the brutal enclosures and disappearing of Native populations or the drawing of the border with and against Mexico in the name of a divinely sanctioned Manifest Destiny. All of these historical forces have never stopped buzzing and circulating and flowing; the current political moment may feel exceptional in many ways, but its reliance on these long-circulating currents is key: new orange wine in old casks. If history often rhymes, as Twain said, then we are living in a rhyme fest, bludgeoned by couplets.[5]

I'm typing these words at the end of 2018, a year in which eight of the ten most watched music videos on YouTube (globally) were in Spanish and the top two are reggaeton tracks featuring Latinx artists from the United States, Puerto Rico, and Colombia; a year in which—as Latinx music critics Suzy Exposito and Isabelia Herrera have been consistently pointing out and parsing—the music of African American and Latinx artists continued to dominate Billboard and Spotify charts in the United States and a Bronx-born Dominican-Trinidadian rapper (Cardi B) was an inescapable, top-grossing presence across genres.[6] When Colombia's J Balvin popped up in the middle of Beyoncé's Coachella set to perform their remix of his song "Mi Gente," it marked the onstage meeting of two of the world's most bankable and brandable pop stars, their music united in the digital recombination of African rhythms. "Lift up your people," Beyoncé sang (over a track originally produced in France by the son of Mauritian Creole immigrants, Willy Williams, as "The Voodoo Song"). "From Texas, Puerto Rico / Dem islands to Mexico," she continued. This is a geography impossible without the violent circulation of slavery's financial capital, without the flows of the African diaspora, and without the land grabs, enclosures, and labor markets—the multilevel colonial shaping—of what we now call Latin America. This is a geography of hurricanes and deserts, a geography of Black and Brown *gente* whose demographic power and political power and consumer power are just some of the reasons the president—and a now shuttered but successful GoFundMe campaign of independent fear-mongering donors ready to donate millions—want a wall where a wall already exists, want an empty monument to oppression and restriction where oppression and restriction already flourish.

The filmmaker and multifaceted artist Arthur Jafa officially debuted his piece *Love Is the Message and the Message Is Death* in 2016, during the same month Trump won the election, and it still haunts the unfolding political moment. A seven-minute collision of repurposed YouTube clips, watermarked images, cell phone videos, and television broadcasts, *Love Is the Message* interprets Black joy and Black death within a historical framework of Black struggles for justice and the pulsating freedoms of everyday pleasure. It's all cut to Kanye West's "Ultralight Beam," which adds sonic layers to history's rhymes across slavery and the Civil War, across Trayvon Martin and Serena Williams, across the gospel church, Auto-Tune futurism, and breakbeat salvation.[7] An audiovisual American mash-up of freedom and slavery, love and death, fugitivity and capture, the piece edits together images and shouts of bodily pain and bodily prowess and exuberance all haunted by the possibility that, to borrow the title of Kepla and DeForrest Brown Jr.'s 2018 album, the wages of being Black is death.[8] There was an important Latinx companion to these interventions by Ecuadorian-Floridian-Brooklynite Helado Negro (Roberto Carlos Lange) in that same fateful 2016 year. On the album that also launched the new Latinx/queer/feminist anthem "Young, Latin, and Proud," Lange included "It's My Brown Skin," in which he counters the racial profiling and the wages of visual racism against Brown skin with self-care and self-protection, a skin that "glows in the dark" and "shines in the light." Brownness holds him tight. The song ends with him chanting, "It'll keep you safe," like a spell that, if you just say it enough times, will make that promise of safety come true.

In 2019, the Alabama artist and singer Lonnie Holley released one of my favorite songs inspired by this/that political moment, "I Woke Up in a Fucked-Up America." Holley, born in 1950 in the Jim Crow South, knows many fucked-up Americas, but the one he "dreamed" he woke up in is unmistakably the one unfolding now, "a human fightin' industry" full of "computer misusin'" tech vampires. It's a song haunted by cages and shackles, by the gold generated from the trapping and tracking of human flesh, and by "A wall, a wall / All about the wall, all about the wall / Arguin', boxin', and fightin' about the wall / All the way up a wall, I dreamed." I find it so interesting that Holley calls this a dream and not a nightmare. It's a song of horror but also of a certain hope. He dreams that he wakes up, but then he wakes up from the dream, in a fucked-up America that he has not dreamed, yet he is still committed to dreaming as a way out. This is a new song, but its historical rhymes are ancient. It's the sound of the exception as not so exceptional.

AM: It's also interesting that at the end of the song Holley sings, "I woke up in a dream / in a dream, in death's dream / Please go / let me out of this dream," almost like the dreamer finally realizes the maze they are in is a surreal space where they dream of themselves in a dream about themselves dreaming and finally want to break out of it to find themselves somehow floating in a white vacuum. I could read that also as the realization that the dream turns into a nightmarish maze for folks of color because it is a dream that is not meant for them. It is a more pessimistic interpretation, but I like that it opens the door to speak about the relation that oppressed people have with the instruments of their oppression. In other words, it provides a moment to speak about the symptom, that almost mystical term that offers a space for the intersection of dreams and commodities as understood by Lacan and Marx respectively.[9]

One of the processes that concerns me in the current political moment is the ability of the ruling political and economic elites to co-opt legit concerns by marginalized groups across color lines regarding the trajectory and direction of globalization and who is really reaping the benefits of neoliberal capitalism. We can see this phenomenon in how Trumpism in the United States or Brexit in the UK (just to mention a couple of examples) have been able to successfully rechannel social unrest and anxiety about globalization to their advantage. I believe this co-option is possible because of people's inabilities to properly identify the source of their marginalization; and that inability in turn is possible because they bought into discursive fantasies about the nation state, racial superiority and racial difference, liberal democracy, and the rule of law as sources of their individual uniqueness—their perceived exceptionalism, so to speak. In the case of the United States, maybe more than in any other nationalist agenda, those myths are central to our national identity and to understanding ourselves as Americans. The asymmetric access to the promises of these ideas in a society as unequal as the United States promotes fragmentation and prevents the recognition of shared experiences of exploitation across class, ethnic, and racial lines. A fragmented social fabric that has been further corroded by anti-intellectualism and intolerance provides fertile ground for xenophobic fear-mongering and nativist paranoia. So it seems to me that it is all about the symptom: ideology not as false consciousness but as reality itself. In that sense maybe my reading of Holley's final words in "I Woke Up in a Fucked-Up America" is not as pessimistic as I may have first thought. If, as you say, his rhymes are the sound of the exception as not so exceptional, maybe they index that fissure, that logic of exceptionalism that Žižek believes is crucial in subverting the type of universalist bourgeois notions that the American fantasy is based on.[10] Maybe that is one of the positive aspects of living in a political moment as polarized as today's: the potential to realize what Holley's lyrics suggest, that the dreams we live in and in which we are required to play very particular roles are not reality but just an ideological web. I wonder if these realizations might provide the foundation not only for a globalization from below but also for transethnic, transracial, and transclass political and aesthetic alliances. In terms of musical style, production history, and target audience, could songs as different as "I Woke Up in a Fucked-Up America," Luis Fonsi and Daddy Yankee's "Despacito," and Cardi B's "Money" provide the soundtrack for a decolonial globalization? Or maybe a decolonial globalization has already started and these songs are simply indexing it?

JK: I've been thinking a lot about these very questions in my current writing and research. On the one hand, I certainly believe the current global music-scape is full of material ripe for experiencing decolonized or decolonial globalization, shaped through and because of global markets and music industries. In a sense this would be a twenty-first-century version of what Michael Denning so brilliantly explored in his book *Noise Uprising* (2015), a "decolonizing of the ear" that happened in the early twentieth century as the recording industry opened up outposts all over the world, especially in port cities and sites where migrant labor was a key feature of local economic life. The market for records produced a soundtrack to a polylingual, migrant world that foregrounded local accents, languages, and experiences that, as Denning argues, prefigure the great anticolonial movements of the twentieth century.[11] There is certainly something like this afoot right now when the world's loudest musical voices are not necessarily in English, but in Spanish, Mandarin, and Arabic, and when, as I'm trying to show in my own new work, the popular music of the twenty-first century is virtually impossible without shared global experiences of migration and displacement due to war, climate change, economic collapse, and gender violence, among other factors. In the intervening century, monolithic recording empires have been decentralized into new, still corporate and perhaps still imperial, platforms like Soundcloud, Bandcamp, and Spotify and into more free-form online "open airwaves" radio ecologies like NTS, Dublab, Cashmere Radio, and Radio Alhara. These transformations are crucial factors in complicating, diversifying, and proliferating listening experiences rooted in diaspora, exile, and displacement.[12] On the other hand, it is crucial to make sure—as so many have argued, from Hito Steyerl to Richard Iton—that we don't confuse cultural enfranchisement for political enfranchisement, cultural visibility and cultural presence for political rights and social freedoms.[13] We shouldn't confuse nonhierarchical musical platform ecologies with an overturning of neocolonial hierarchies of belonging and recognition, the legal flow of music by migrants online and the offline illegalization of migrant populations. Thus we should also be doing work on the more fundamental notion of sonic rights, of the very relationship of sound and music to human rights. Hannah Arendt famously argued, from a twentieth-century position of displacement and exile that echoes into our own century, that politics is the space of appearance and the legislation of a right to appear, but also the right to speak and be heard—politics as the space of sounding/music-making, as the legislation of a right to sound, sing, and play. In a project I did in 2017 in San Francisco that used the music of the city to explore issues of eviction, gentrification, and the forced removal of communities of color, I framed these questions using the metaphor of the hit parade—whose songs are hits and who gets hit? The degree to which these musical exclusions so often echo larger social and political exclusions can be tracked, especially in urban histories of cities like San Francisco and Los Angeles. The hit parade of a city can be the inverted mirror of social marginalization and exclusion.[14]

It's been interesting, and from my increasingly more vintage and seasoned viewpoint (there's an emoji that belongs here), it is encouraging to watch as the scholarly legacies and interventions of postcolonial and decolonial thought leave their mark on music studies broadly but on ethnomusicology and musicology specifically, and to see how these concerns and urgencies are taken up across different scales. Linda Tuhiwai Smith has argued that "decolonization once viewed as the formal process of handing over the instruments of government is now recognized as a long-term process involving the bureaucratic, cultural, linguistic, and psychological divesting of colonial power."[15] How can we divest music of its colonial power? What does colonial divestment sound like? This is where I think our work as music students, scholars, and fans ought to be focused right now—on picking apart and historicizing what Rolando Vazquez writes about as "listening-power," the long-standing link between music and sound and colonial power.[16] This is where I think we take some concrete steps as scholars and teachers, interrogating music through the ear of coloniality, attuned to how colonialism has long shaped the contours of musical life and musical markets. By listening differently, we teach ourselves and our students new ways of documenting and understanding the evolution of music and musical politics in the United States. To take an obvious example, you can't teach US music, or the notion of America through music, if you don't begin with the premise of empire and colony, with the foundational violences of Native death and population control and African enslavement. I'd contend that all music made in the United States follows from those (ongoing) historical moments and is joined with them through both direct market and ideological links as well as indirect influence of various kinds. Similarly, no history of US music should omit a consideration of what my late mentor Mike Rogin called "The American 1848," that nineteenth-century convergence of telecommunications, imperial war with Mexico, and westward expansion to "settle" and "tame" the American West.[17] Every corrido on the radio and on today's Billboard charts stems from this moment.

Or to pick up on another history that Raúl Fernández and Gaye Theresa Johnson have both researched in depth: the 1884 World's Industrial and Cotton Centennial Exposition in New Orleans, which celebrated the one-hundred-year anniversary of the cotton industry in the United States and the central role of New Orleans as a cotton capital.[18] With the end of the Civil War, the agricultural fate of New Orleans was up in the air, and the exposition was seen as a cure and a lure. Among the many countries that participated, none had as much of a lasting impact as Mexico. Beyond its lavish pavilion, Mexico introduced the Eighth Cavalry Mexican Band to the people of New Orleans. A massive seventy-six-member all-brass band dressed in full military regalia played regular concerts of Mexican, Cuban, and local New Orleans songs to enraptured audiences in Audubon Park. The music of "The Mexican Band," as they became known, seeped into the local repertoires of New Orleans, and soon Mexican songs like "Sobre las olas," renamed "Over the Waves," were given new lives in the instruments of local US bands. Some of the Mexican musicians never left New Orleans and later reemerged as local music teachers. As jazz began to take shape in the years following the exposition, many of these songs of the Mexican Band—"Over the Waves" especially—became early jazz standards, and the local Mexican music teachers taught some of jazz's earliest pioneers. The songs would soon travel west to cities like Los Angeles in the songbooks of migrant jazz musicians.

It may seem obvious, but we have to teach US music through histories like this one. To think through a contemporary decolonized or decolonial musical globalization is vital, and so is the retelling of American music history with a decolonial attunement, an ear for the uneven distribution of sonic rights. What is US music if not the story, to borrow from Fred Moten, of dispossession as a form of belonging? This past year I've been constantly returning to a passage from Moten's contribution to *The Freedom Principle: Experiments in Art and Music 1965–Now*, the catalog for an exhibition on the ongoing traditions of African American musical radicalism and experimentation at the Museum of Contemporary Art in Chicago. Moten writes that jazz "emerges from our dispossession, not as compensation but rather as a critique of possession. . . . How could the transformative power we know the music has, that we know is held in music, be held there unless it's upheld there, held out from there, out of there, disbursed and dispersed? . . . It runs away from being held and it's held out to be given away."[19] He is talking about a specific genealogy born of specific historical events, but I think there is a lot to be learned from this in terms of how to rethink the teaching of what US music is: a chronic, defining struggle between the sounds of running away from being held and of the holding outward to be given away—of captivity, fugitivity, and enclosure—alongside alliance, radical relationality, and the breaching of borders. One's possession always linked to another's—and one's own—dispossession.

AM: It is very important to remain suspicious about some of the most uncritical and celebratory scholarship about the anticolonial power of music. Denning's work is crucial in moving music studies beyond certain fossilized paradigms about aesthetic value and production into a true attempt to listen to music's anticolonial potential; but it is also important that young scholars take his work as a point of departure for more critical theorizations. I am thinking of recent scholarship by Sergio Ospina-Romero, who explores how the decolonization of the ear and the globalization of local sounds, as chronicled by Denning, also provoked the implementation of new political and economic networks as well as the development of new consumer markets that not only reproduced old imbalances of colonial power but also facilitated the furthering of neocolonialist and cultural imperialist projects.[20] This is also something I find problematic in the celebratory tone of sound studies, what Jonathan Sterne termed its "audiovisual litany."[21] In my recent work, I have questioned whether this shift from visuo-centric to audio-centric culture truly challenges old colonial structures—such as what Ángel Rama called, in the Latin American case, the "Lettered City."[22] Who controls the circulation of and access to these sounds? Who decides which bodies can move beyond borders to accompany the sounds they produce and which sounds will be experienced in a disembodied fashion? What are the power imbalances that these dynamics perpetuate and generate? What kinds of listening practices do these dynamics generate? Who shapes these listening practices?

All of this connects to your concerns with the intersection of human rights and sonic rights. I'm reminded here of Alex Rivera's *Sleep Dealer* (2008), a movie that shows a dystopian future in which bodies are technologically separated from their labor so that corporations can maintain the profit this labor produces while being spared of the physical presence of the racialized bodies that generate those profits. In the realm of music this could be a metaphor for the flow of sound and its commodification against the attempt to contain the flow of the bodies connected to making these sounds. That is a central question when imagining the imbalances and inequalities potentially (re)produced by new decolonial or critical globalization music projects. Because it speaks of difference, this question is also central to the very processes of identification at play when we try to determine what Americanness is or could be. I would argue that the media rhetoric at stake when speaking about the border and the bodies that corrupt the United States by penetrating it is informed by questions of difference that are central to identity. Furthermore, I believe that this emphasis on difference also connects to the dynamics of identity politics that led to the type of radical cultural and political polarization that gave us Trump. If identity politics played an important role in empowering marginalized communities, it has also served as a fracturing device that often prevents the establishment of transethnic alliances—that is, it inhibits people from identifying shared experiences of marginalization and therefore being able to act against the source of that marginalization. In that sense, I have suggested elsewhere that the time may be ripe to productively revisit Paul Gilroy's *Against Race* (2000), a book that unfortunately, in my opinion, has not been as influential as his previous work about diaspora and double consciousness in *The Black Atlantic* (1993).[23] Gilroy's concern with how the notion of race could be turned around from the emancipatory rhetoric of race theory into the racist discourse of fascism is similar to my own concern with how identity politics provide a fertile ground for the kind of social fragmentation that may backfire against marginalized groups and individuals. I have suggested an emphasis on critical sameness. In doing so, I am aware that one should be very careful to avoid the rhetorical trap of those who criticize the Black Lives Matter movement by countering with the motto "All Lives Matter," which erases, misidentifies, and trivializes the particular histories of oppression experienced by people of color.

So what I propose with critical sameness is a project that may help us move away from spectacles of identity into processes that help articulate shared experiences of oppression beyond our own identitarian groups. What do disenfranchised white people have in common with oppressed communities of people of color? I believe that finding answers to this question—and doing so without losing sight of the ways in which different ethnic and racial communities experience these processes of disenfranchisement differently—could open a space for productive empathy and political change. In talking about the critical teaching of US music, I do so from the perspective of a scholar trained as a musicologist who became an ethnomusicologist by academic choice but also by practical necessity—in response to how academia misrepresents a person like me, studying the many different musics I have studied throughout my career. I would like to see an approach that furthers this project by subverting the commodification of marginalized musics—musics that have remained marginal in the academic canon privileged by musicologists and ethnomusicologists—as well as that of marginalized groups and subjects. An expanded, more-inclusive canon might end up simply reproducing the supremacist values at the core of musicology's mainstream canon. In other words, I do not want to see discussions of African American or Latinx music that end up reproducing deeply ingrained stereotypes about these communities or that simply use their musics to reinforce canonic values that accept them as marginal. Instead, I would like to see discussions of these musics that highlight the shared experiences of exploitation beyond color lines, experiences that have been rendered invisible by the white supremacist values at the core of the canonic fantasy. I am advocating for discussions aimed at corroding the exceptionalist character of the canonic fantasy.

Regardless of the growing presence of progressive musicologists in the last thirty years, I still feel a sense of rejection or apprehension of these ideas from the musicological mainstream, which often tunes them out. It is funny you mentioned the presence of influential Mexican musicians in New Orleans at the turn of the twentieth century. A chapter of *Danzón* (2013) deals precisely with that phenomenon as well as with the presence of Afro-Caribbean performance practices at the core of early jazz improvisation.[24] When Robin Moore and I wrote that book we expected that chapter was going to make waves among US music scholars because it basically provides a very strong critique of the essentialist Black-white dichotomy that characterizes much of what has been written about the birth of jazz—a view in sync with the equally nearsighted essentialist take on race in the United States that dominates popular culture. We were proposing a musical lineage that completely challenged this ideology. Nevertheless, it has remained largely ignored within US music scholarship. It is almost as if dealing with Latin American and Caribbean music prevents the book from entering discussions about US music.

Moving scholars out of their comfort zone is very difficult. Musicologists tend to be protective of their individual areas of study in a way that often betrays a type of academic exceptionalism. In fact, I feel that this exceptionalism is something that characterizes the field at large. I remember when you and I met back in the early 2000s. I was a PhD student and you came to Ohio State to present your research about audiotopias at a moment when I was feeling very disappointed with the field of musicology and its exceptionalist attitude—sometimes arrogant and sometimes defensive, but mostly dismissive of what scholars in other fields could say about music. I felt that the attitudes of musicologists prevented them from actually asking intellectually relevant questions about music or the musical experience.[25] At the time I had encountered performance studies through the work of Jill Lane and Barry Shank, and I was fascinated by how scholars in cultural studies were studying music to ask questions about affect and emotion that resonated across many intellectual disciplines. But I felt that most musicologists still neglected to engage with these theorizations. To me it felt like two completely different worlds, and I was excited to wonder about the possibilities that these approaches outside of musicology could bring to my own scholarship. Yet it was sobering then to hear you say something unexpected when asked whether musicologists had anything relevant to say about music. You answered with an example of how a certain musicological discussion about the tonal and melodic structure of a given song had actually opened your ears and provided a new way of listening. That made me think of how the old formal analytical tools of musicology might still be relevant as long as they help us answer the right questions, as long as they are part of a larger intellectual project beyond a particular arrangement of pitches and chords on the piano keyboard, the guitar fretboard, or the music sheet. At any rate, I always remember that moment when thinking about the differences between how musicologists and American studies' scholars approach music and when pondering the potential of each field to further questions about the relevance of music to better understand affective, social, and political responses to our everyday life.

JK: I'm not surprised to hear that your attempt to stir the pot went unnoticed. As you say, Latinx music still does not tend to register much in wider debates and canons concerning race and culture in "American" music (you wrote about aspects of this with great clarity in your 2017 essay in the *Journal of Music History Pedagogy*).[26] It never fails: when I teach my survey course on popular music and culture in the United States and include multiweek units on corridos, mambo, tejano, salsa, and reggaeton, I get complaints. "Why do you have to include so much music in Spanish?" A couple years ago I remember people on social media celebrating that year's Coachella lineup for finally being diverse, and yet there were only two Latinx acts on a three-day bill, in Southern California, in the middle of the Coachella Valley, in a Mexican-dominant city shaped by the labor of farmworkers. Music connected to Latin America, to Spanish-speaking populations in the Americas, is foundational to the history of music in the United States—inseparable from it—and yet it is perennially marginalized. It is at the center always, remarginalized always—a virtual deportation. Some of this bias, of course, has to do with deeply rooted xenophobia and ingrained racism that are equally as foundational to the United States, and some of it is about the incurable fear of the Spanish language. As I have said before elsewhere, English-speaking audiences will sell out the Hollywood Bowl to listen to the Icelandic band Sigur Rós sing in a language that does not exist and yet will be slower to go see a band sing in Spanish. Spanish-dominant artists in the United States—no matter the various success stories we can point to—all feel some pressure to sing in English. It's a mandated cultural assimilation that even markets do not bear out. All that said, though, there are vital shifts in this landscape with the mercurial and magnetic rise of Bad Bunny, whose popularity and influence seem to know no bounds and has landed him on the cover of *Rolling Stone* in a piece by Suzy Exposito, the first cover feature ever written by a Latinx woman in the magazine's history.[27] You and I both keep coming back to the relationships between music markets and social populations, commodified sounds and cultural (dis)enfranchisement. How is the commitment to keeping Latinx music from the center of "American music" a tool for keeping Latinx populations from the center of US political culture? As we have been witnessing with Trump's attacks on birthright citizenship and his desire to denaturalize populations, Latinx music is so easily reframed as "foreign" and "other," just as people and communities so central to US culture, politics, and economics are always available for possible excision from the national body—forever undocumented, forever potentially illegal, forever deportees in waiting.

I do think that more dialogue between musicologists and ethnomusicologists and the traditions of scholarship under the American studies umbrella—music-studying historians, feminist theorists, queer theorists, sociologists, and political scientists, among others —is important to bear witness to and understand the complex and dense role that music plays in constituting and reimagining the social fabric. I remember that visit to Ohio State University, and I remember our conversation. Luckily a lot has changed since then; the divides are not as deep and the disciplinary structures not as entrenched. When I was in graduate school at UC Berkeley in the 1990s, I was rebuked so many times by prominent musicologists who made me feel my work was unworthy and misguided (no tea will be spilled here) that it became a badge of honor, and I was forced to find other models for thinking about music that went beyond aesthetic formalism and colonial ethnography. When I began teaching at UC Riverside, I was lucky to have the extraordinary musician, conductor, and musicologist Phillip Brett as a colleague; he was so generous with his knowledge and so committed to helping me think about musicology as I began writing my first book. He broke down lots of walls that I was keeping up around me, and he opened me up to traditions of listening—in European classical and art music specifically—that I felt I had no right to engage with given my training. I still seek out these kinds of encounters because I know how vital they are for doing the kind of work I want to do. I have always appreciated (and learned from) your work, for example, because your expertise moves across these divides. When we were both writing about Nortec and the electronic music scene of Tijuana, I was always appreciative of the ways you listened to the music that I just didn't have the chops for.[28]

Like you, I worry about the formulas of automatic opposition and resistance that some cultural studies scholarship can produce, a tendency I have certainly fallen prey to myself. I don't know if you have spent much time with it, but Chris Waterman and Larry Starr's textbook, *American Popular Music* (2003), does a pretty fantastic job of moving between musicological and sociological/cultural approaches.[29] When we use it in my survey class, it forces us nonmusicians to think about musical forms, while it challenges classically trained musicians to think about politics and identity in ways perhaps outside their experiences. I'd like to see even more of that kind of work. The changes are also happening, of course, within traditional academic spheres in music. There have been important overhauls and interventions in ethnomusicology through postcolonial and decolonial thought, and music departments are beginning to do some necessary restructuring of curricular models to disrupt the "possessive investments" in both whiteness and Western classical music.[30] The 2017 shake-up at Harvard is perhaps the best example of beginning to reimagine starting points, question accepted centers, and interrogate the politics of inclusion.

One of the people whose lead I follow in all these areas is composer, musician, scholar, and teacher Vijay Iyer, who is of course part of this new era at Harvard.[31] He has been a real model for me in approaching music aesthetically and formally—with tremendous care, training, and obvious joy alongside deep political commitment—while always refusing to treat music autonomously and essentially. He engages openly in critical thinking heavily rooted in traditions of Black radicalism, critical ethnic studies, and social justice organizing. He's done this in his recordings (his 2017 sextet recording, *Far from Over,* is a recent and particularly powerful example); his interviews and essays on improvisation, cognition, and cities; and his collegiality, advocacy, and commitment to collective creation (in the spirit of the Association for the Advancement of Creative Musicians). Something he wrote in program notes during his turn as music director of the 2017 Ojai Music Festival—the first of the Trump era—is very relevant to what we are talking about here: that is, the difference between a more common understanding of *music as resistance* and a less common and potentially more promising and productive understanding of *resistance as music.* Connecting his festival choices to Judith Butler's then-recent book on the politics of assembly, he said that he was interested in music as the representation of preexisting community—tribes of players, teachers and students, allies, common travelers, families and friends, unions, community groups—but also music as a force and practice for imagining new kinds of community, unexpected and unscripted gatherings of new bodies with new bodies, the formation of new tribes and new kinships (what other art form than music better gives expression to the move, signaled by Edouard Glissant, from the filial to the relational?).[32] In terms of political agency and political opposition, there is the music we readily identify as protest music and then there is *resistance as music* itself "because all music is social, born of collective human action; that listening to musical performance is no less than a process of empathy; that given time and listening with care, anyone can make music together, even across what may seem like chasms of difference; and that essentially, this phenomenon that we call music begins not with sound, not with rhythm, but with our shared personhood."[33]

I have had many informal conversations about these ideas with one of Iyer's colleagues and coconspirators, the extraordinary flautist and experimentalist Claire Chase, whose ears and spirit are about as open as anyone I've ever met. Over the past couple of years, we have talked a lot about music as a form of social action that does not just reflect social truths or experiences but is the very ground and the process through which the social is imagined, with never predictable results. Claire has encouraged me to keep thinking about these ideas, which I started playing with in my San Francisco project (2017). I asked a group of musicians who didn't know each other and had different trainings to come together, without rehearsal, and figure out how to play a piece of music they were handed on the spot in front of local audiences at branches of the San Francisco Public Library. The goal was rather simple: to see what nonmusicians can learn from how musicians play together in the name of solving a common problem, to see how musicians negotiate the individual with the collective, and to see how they perform difference within a collective setting that depends on collective action. At a conference that Claire and I both attended recently, I ended my talk—after prefacing it by reminding the audience I was not a singer or a musician—by singing a song that the musicians played during that project. When it was over Claire told the room that I was wrong, that in fact I was a musician. I almost died. Learning how she approaches the lifeworlds of music has been a boon to my own growth as a thinker. The work I am doing now contains a spirit of performance and musicality that I don't think would have been possible without these kinds of encounters.

AM: Your mention of the ambivalent place of Latinx and Latin American music in the development of US music—both central and marginal—reminded me of Dean Martin's release of "Sway" in 1954. This is a song that came to epitomize Martin's lounge act; it became an anthem of the King of Cool's coolness. But regardless of the fact that the song remains a vague signifier of Latin or Hispanic culture, its origins are usually obscured. In fact, "Sway," composed in 1953 by Luis Demetrio and Pablo Beltrán Ruiz as "¿Quién será?," is a song of Mexican origin that was a hit there before making its way north of the border in Dean Martin's famous version. Instead, its place of origin was rendered invisible and refashioned as a sort of pan-Latinx index by the race machine of the US entertainment industry. "Sway" is not the only case in which Mexican music or expressive culture have been embraced inadvertently by audiences who would otherwise despise more visible expressions of Mexicanness. Earlier you mentioned Juventino Rosas's "Sobre las olas," which in the 1890s became immensely popular in the United States and Europe as "Over the Waves" or "Über den Wellen," and, although his music came to represent amusement parks and trapeze acts worldwide, Rosas's name was somehow lost in translation and the Mexican origin of the waltz was largely forgotten. If you were Mexican, it was not uncommon in the 1960s and 1970s to change your name or disguise your ethnicity in order to be able to enter the mainstream US entertainment industry. Thus, Richard Steven Valenzuela became Ritchie Valens, Florencia Bisenta de Casillas became Vikki Carr, and Baldemar Garza Huerta became Freddy Fender, just as decades earlier actors such as Antonio Rodolfo Quinn Oaxaca had become Anthony Quinn, and Jo Raquel Tejada had become Raquel Welch. In the 1970s, Linda Ronstadt and Lynda Carter became icons of Americana with few knowing they were of Mexican descent. These are instances of what I call the invisible Mexican among us: the unacknowledged and often neglected element of Mexicanness that has been always central in the configuration not only of American identity but also of the very geographic space that occupies the American nation state with its history of erasure and dispossession. Of course, these processes become more problematic when Mexicanness is extended to other Latin American ethnicities in mainstream US culture, thus subjecting them to the same dynamics of erasure. The pervasiveness of these processes throughout US history makes it necessary to approach them from transdisciplinary perspectives and to keep in mind the historicity as well as the anthropological and sociological specificity of these processes.

Unlike you, I have never had a chance to teach a survey of US music; thus, I am only superficially familiar with Starr and Waterman's *American Popular Music*. However, I am not surprised that it took the collaborative efforts of a musicologist and an ethnomusicologist to find the right way to flow between musicological interests in aesthetic value and sociological concerns with the cultural coordinates that give meaning to that aesthetic focus. Nevertheless, as much as I am in favor of these kinds of intradisciplinary collaborations, I would also like to see musicologists and ethnomusicologists collaborating with scholars in other disciplines. That could be the most efficient way of dismantling some of these fundamentally misleading biracial narratives about American music that even Starr and Waterman reproduce: Tin Pan Alley versus Broadway and race records versus hillbilly music, among others. In them, Latinx, Asian Americans, and members of other ethnicities continue to play marginal roles—or, at best, central roles only at the margins—of these essentialist historical narratives. I have to say that I have learned the most from my collaborations with people like Ignacio Corona (literary studies), Ramón Rivera-Servera (performance studies), and Pepe Rojo (science fiction writer), who do not come from music studies. Working with them there was always an "Ah!" moment that changed my way of listening and enjoying music and that helped me move in new directions. So I am a true believer that this kind of collaborative writing is necessary to break away from the constraints of our academic training—and that is the only way to move forward into new and exciting territory.

I agree with you that a lot has changed in musicology as a discipline since the early 2000s. I notice these changes not only in the kind of work that many musicologists are doing but also in the recent programs of the American Musicological Society's annual conference. I think there is a sincere effort within the discipline to become more inclusive in terms of geography, methodology, and disciplinary orientation. I believe that many of these changes have been inspired precisely by the intellectual relevance of some of the scholarship about music produced by scholars outside of musicology and by the fact that these fields (cultural studies, American studies, African American studies, performance studies, ethnic studies, etc.) have embraced scholars of color who had not found musicology to be welcoming. So, in a way, musicology is reacting positively to broad-based pressures to make itself more intellectually relevant and truly inclusive. The Harvard curricular shake-up, which was a radical response to changes previously explored and put in place at UCLA, the University of Virginia, NYU, and Cornell, among others, is an example of this. Of course, the purely scholarly aspect of this shift should be traced back to the efforts of musicologists like Susan McClary, Suzanne Cusick, Philip Brett, Samuel A. Floyd, Jr., Ruth Solie, Gary Tomlinson, and Richard Taruskin, among others, as well as ethnomusicologists like Gerard Béhague, Philip Bohlman, Judith Becker, Georgina Born, Mellonee Burnim, Jocelyne Guilbault, Bruno Nettl, Christopher Small, and Thomas Turino, among others. But I do not think it could have been possible without the fundamental work from beyond the walls of musicology by scholars like Frances Aparicio, Philip Auslander, Barbara Browning, Tia DeNora, Simon Frith, Anahid Kassabian, José Limón, George Lipsitz, and many others. Furthermore, the advent of sound studies and the aural turn have had a significant impact on more recent developments in the field especially the move to decenter the ideology of master composers and masterworks into a focus on listening as a locus of musical meaning. That being said, I also frequently encounter music colleagues who remain trapped in old paradigms, who continue to think of ethnomusicology as the study of non-Western musics, as opposed to the ethnographic study of any type of music, including Western European classical music, or who believe that the role of musicology is to prepare the next generation of classical music audiences. Even more tragic is the degree to which they are still influencing young scholars to buy into these misconstrued ideas. This kind of thinking is deeply rooted in the exceptionalist beliefs that gave musicology its raison d'être throughout the twentieth century (music scholarship as propaganda for Western European classical music) and that finds a lifeline in the split between schools of music and music departments in US academia. By contrast, I love your experience with Claire Chase; it is a humble reminder, by a master musician trained within the Western art music tradition, that Christopher Small was right when he acknowledged that there were many ways of making and experiencing music, and that we, as music scholars, should open our ears to them.[34]

JK: I am so tempted to go down a "Sway" wormhole and get into what happens when a Mexican song is rewritten into an English hit that is then rewritten in Spanish as an Afro-Cuban mambo and released as its own hit by Pérez Prado and Rosemary Clooney on a 1959 album that sends the song back to Mexico via US jazz and Cuban dance music on an album named *A Touch of Tabasco,* which took the name of a Louisiana hot sauce that in turn was named for a Mexican state. Then that widely circulated Mexican version was sampled by Erick Sermon and Redman on an album they dedicated to New York. Instead I will quickly say that the "invisible Mexican" haunting US popular music is a major theme, and it is increasingly being paid attention to. In a recent collection of essays that I edited with a series of scholars, musicians, and journalists, we explored both the "invisible Mexican" and the "invisible Latina/o" in the musical history of Los Angeles—how Latinx musicians are ghosts in the machine of Los Angeles musical modernism.[35] We use the case study of L.A. to make the argument that much as Robert O'Meally has written of the "jazz cadence of American culture" there is also a "Latin American cadence of American culture."[36] As O'Meally notes, Ralph Ellison—when writing about Ernest Hemingway and Stephen Crane—suggested that America was "jazz-shaped," but isn't it also mambo shaped, clave shaped, and mariachi shaped?[37] You mention Richard Valenzuela becoming Ritchie Valens, but on the way, he billed himself in live gigs as "Little Richard of the Valley," the son of Mexican immigrant parents who grew up wanting to be Little Richard. While I was researching the book, the percussionist and bandleader Alberto López tipped me off to the story of his uncle Johnny Richards, who was one of the great jazz arrangers and bandleaders of the post–World War II era. He recorded with Dizzy Gillespie, Sonny Stitt, Harry James, and Stan Kenton, arranged a slew of his own hyper-sophisticated big-band LPs in the 1950s and 1960s, and wrote "Young at Heart" for Sinatra. Turns out Richards was actually Juan Cascales, born in Mexico, and he changed his name once he immigrated to the United States to avoid discrimination and land more arranging jobs. His Mexican identity was largely not discussed by his collaborators and ironically in some circles he became known as a gringo with an expertise in Latin music.

This kind of requisite invisible visibility and these kinds of coerced accommodations still exist of course—across identities—but, as we have been discussing, they are becoming less and less the norm. One important shift that I want to highlight is who the scholars are now, who the writers are now. A new generation of scholars of color, women academics, queer and trans scholars, as well as a new generation of music critics of color, women critics, and queer and trans critics are actively eroding earlier structures of musical discourse, research, and criticism and doing so in important ways; they are setting the terms of the debates and shaping the content of criticism. We've been having parts of this conversation as dream hampton's *Surviving R. Kelly* series has been airing, and it's been a powerful reminder of how much gender inequality and sexual violence against Black women specifically and all women generally have been centerpieces of US music culture and the US music industry historically. The work that connects contemporary iterations of #MeToo to the long history of sexual violence against women in the music industry is now being written en masse.[38] This will be, and should be, a vital rewriting of what anyone means when they refer to American music or US music in the future. It's a reckoning that is long overdue.

Notes

1. Danielle Brown's open letter can be found here: https://www.mypeopletellstories.com/blog/open-letter. She posted it to the Society for Ethnomusicology electronic list (SEM-L) on June 12, 2020, sparking animated discussion on the list and beyond.

2. Edmund S. Morgan, "Slavery and Freedom: The American Paradox," *Journal of American History* 59, no. 1 (1972): 5–6.

3. See W. E. B. Du Bois, *The Souls of Black Folk* (1903; Minneapolis: Lerner, 2016), 206–16; and Horace Kallen, *Culture and Democracy in the United States: Studies in the Group Psychology of the American People* (1924; New York: Arno Press and New York Times, 1970), 125.

4. Saidiya Hartman, *Wayward Lives, Beautiful Experiments: Intimate Histories of Riotous Black Girls, Troublesome Women, and Queer Radicals* (New York: Norton, 2019) 263–86, 346–53. See also Amiri Baraka, *Black Music* (1968; New York: Akashic, 2010); and Angela Y. Davis, *Blues Legacies and Black Feminism* (New York: Pantheon Books, 1998).

5. "History doesn't repeat itself, but it often rhymes" is a phrase attributed to Mark Twain.

6. A new generation of Latinx music writers, arguably led by Exposito and Herrera, have been instrumental to writing about these shifts with great insight. See, for example, https://slate.com/culture/2018/10/latino-music-new-american-songbook-spanish-language.html and https://www.rollingstone.com/music/music-latin/bad-bunny-new-album-x100pre-latin-grammys-interview-770180/

7. For some of the many takes on the piece, see essays by Christina Sharpe and Greg Tate in Arthur Jafa, *Love Is the Message and the Message Is Death* (New York: Gavin Brown Enterprises, 2016); and Helen Molesworth, "Arthur Jafa: Love Is the Message and the Message Is Death," https://www.moca.org/arthurjafaessay, accessed June 15, 2019.

8. They explain the album this way: "an exhausted and defeated audio documentation of the alienation—and eventual distillation—of the Black Body as a subject and content of the social sphere." https://purpletapepedigree.bandcamp.com/album/the-wages-of-being-black-is-death

9. See Slavoj Žižek, *The Sublime Object of Ideology* (London: Verso, 1989), 1–55.

10. See Žižek, *Sublime Object of Ideology*, 16.

11. See Michael Denning, *Noise Uprising: The Audiopolitics of a World Musical Revolution* (London: Verso, 2015).

12. Music critic Liz Pelly has been tracking these evolutions well in a series of pieces, for example, https://frieze.com/article/age-lean-back-listening-does-spotify-have-neocolonial-ambitions and https://thebaffler.com/downstream/streambait-pop-pelly. I thank another music critic, Julyssa Lopez, for alerting me to Pelly's work.

13. For example, Hito Steyerl, "Gaps and Potentials: The Exhibition 'Heimat Kunst': Migrant Culture as an Allegory of the Global Market," *New German Critique*, no. 92 (Spring–Summer 2004): 159–68; and Richard Iton, *In Search of the Black Fantastic: Politics and Popular Culture in the Post Civil Rights Era* (New York: Oxford University Press, 2010).

14. For more on the hit parade, see https://publicknowledge.sfmoma.org/hit-parade/ and https://www.sfmoma.org/watch/hit-parade-josh-kun/

15. Linda Tuhiwai Smith, *Decolonizing Methodologies: Research and Indigenous Peoples* (New York: Zed Books, 2012), 98. See also Luis Chávez and Russell P. Skelchy, "Decolonizable Spaces in Ethnomusicology," *SEM Student News* 12, no. 2 (Winter 2016): 20–21, https://cdn.ymaws.com/www.ethnomusicology.org/resource/group/dc75b7e7-47d7-4d59-a660-19c3e0f7c83e/publications/SEMSN12.2.pdf

16. Rolando Vázquez and Bhavisha Panchia, "Listening as Critique: Rolando Vázquez in Conversation with Bhavisha Panchia," in *Buried in the Mix*, ed. Bhavisha Panchia (Memmingen: MEWO Kunsthalle, 2018), 39–50.

17. Michael Paul Rogin, *Subversive Genealogy: The Politics and Art of Herman Melville* (Berkeley: University of California Press, 1985), 102–54.

18. Raúl Fernández, *Latin Jazz: The Perfect Combination* (San Francisco: Chronicle Books / Smithsonian Institution, 2002); Gaye Theresa Johnson, "'Sobre las Olas': A Mexican Genesis in Borderlands Jazz and the Legacy for Ethnic Studies," *Comparative Studies* 6, no. 3 (2008): 225–40.

19. Fred Moten cited in *The Freedom Principle: Experiments in Art and Music, 1965 to Now*, ed. Naomi Beckwith and Dieter Roelstraete (Chicago: MCA Chicago, 2015), 191.

20. Sergio Ospina-Romero, "Recording Studios on Tour: The Expeditions of the Victor Talking Machine Company through Latin America, 1905–1926" (PhD diss., Cornell University, 2019).

21. Jonathan Sterne, *The Audible Past: Cultural Origins of Sound Reproduction* (Durham, NC: Duke University Press, 2006), 15.

22. Alejandro L. Madrid, "Landscapes and Gimmicks from the 'Sounded City': Listening for the Nation at the Sound Archive," *Sound Studies* 2, no. 2 (2016): 119–36. See also Ángel Rama, *The Lettered City* (1984), ed. and trans. John Charles Chasteen (Durham, NC: Duke University Press, 1996).

23. Paul Gilroy, *Against Race: Imagining Political Culture beyond the Color Line* (Cambridge, MA: Harvard University Press, 2000); Paul Gilroy, *The Black Atlantic: Modernity and Double Consciousness* (Cambridge, MA: Harvard University Press, 1993). See also Alejandro L. Madrid, "Listening from 'The Other Side': Music, Border Studies, and the Limits of Identity Politics," in *Decentering the Nation: Music, Mexicanidad, and Globalization*, ed. Jesús Ramos-Kittrell (Lanham, MD: Lexington Books, 2020), 211–30.

24. Alejandro L. Madrid and Robin D. Moore, *Danzón: Circum-Caribbean Dialogues in Music and Dance* (New York: Oxford University Press, 2013), 117–49.

25. See Josh Kun, *Audiotopia: Music, Race, and America* (Berkeley: University of California Press, 2005).

26. Alejandro L. Madrid, "Diversity, Tokenism, Non-canonical Musics, and the Crisis of the Humanities in U.S. Academia," *Journal of Music History Pedagogy* 7, no. 2 (2017): 124–29. Also: Madrid, "American Music in Times of Postnationality," in "Studying U.S. Music in the Twenty-First Century," ed. Charles Hiroshi Garrett and Carol J. Oja, *Journal of the American Musicological Society* 64, no. 3 (Fall 2011): 699–703.

27. Suzy Exposito, "Bad Bunny in Captivity," *Rolling Stone*, May 14, 2020.

28. Josh Kun, "They're from Where? Nortec through U.S. Ears," in José Manuel Valenzuela Arce, *Paso del Nortec: This Is Tijuana!* (Mexico City: Trilce, 2004), 312–16; Josh Kun, "File Under: Post-Mexico," *Aztlán* 29, no. 1 (2004), 271–7; and Alejandro L. Madrid, *Nor-Tec Rifa! Electronic Dance Music from Tijuana to the World* (New York: Oxford University Press, 2008).

29. Larry Starr and Christopher Waterman, *American Popular Music: From Minstrelsy to MP3* (New York: Oxford University Press, 2010).

30. See George Lipsitz, *The Possessive Investment in Whiteness: How White People Profit from Identity Politics* (Philadelphia: Temple University Press, 1998); and Loren Kajikawa, "The Possessive Investment in Classical Music: Confronting Legacies of White Supremacy in U.S. Schools and Departments of Music," in

Seeing Race Again, ed. Kimberlé Crenshaw Williams, Daniel Martinez HoSang, and George Lipsitz (Berkeley: University of California Press, 2019), 155–74.

31. Chapter 6 of this volume features Vijay Iyer in conversation with Muhal Richard Abrams.

32. Edouard Glissant, *Poetics of Relation* (Ann Arbor: University of Michigan Press, 1997).

33. Vijay Iyer, program notes, *71st Ojai Music Festival* (Ojai Festivals, Ltd, 2017), 95.

34. Christopher Small, *Musicking: The Meanings of Performing and Listening* (Middletown, CT: Wesleyan University Press, 1998).

35. Josh Kun, "Introduction: The Tide Was Always High," in *The Tide Was Always High: The Music of Latin America in Los Angeles*, ed. Josh Kun (Berkeley: University of California Press, 2017), 5. In the same volume, see also Brian Cross's essay on the Brazilian influence on L.A. jazz and funk, Martha Gonzalez's essay on the *son jarocho* influence in L.A., and Betto Arcos's interviews with leading Latin American session musicians who have played on thousands of influential R & B, rock, folk, and pop albums.

36. Robert G. O' Meally, ed., *The Jazz Cadence of American Culture* (New York: Columbia University Press, 1998).

37. Ralph Ellison, *The Collected Essays of Ralph Ellison* (New York: Modern Library, 2003), 586; Ellison cited in O'Meally, *Jazz Cadence*, xi.

38. See, for example, NPR's "Turning the Tables" project, https://www.npr.org/series/538009815/turning-the-tables; Marc Hogan, "Music and #MeToo," *Pitchfork*, December 19, 2018, https://pitchfork.com/features/article/why-the-mainstream-music-industry-is-still-struggling-to-address-metoo/; Hanif Abdurraqib, "The Slow Road to Music's #MeToo Moment," *Billboard*, December 13, 2018, https://www.billboard.com/articles/events/year-in-music-2018/8489958/metoo-movement-music-industry-year-in-music-2018; Jessica Hopper, "It Was Us against Those Guys: The Women Who Transformed *Rolling Stone* in the Mid-70s," *Vanity Fair*, August 28, 2018, https://www.vanityfair.com/style/2018/08/the-women-who-transformed-rolling-stone-in-the-mid-70s

NINE | Music, Travel, and Circuitous Reflections of Community

MONICA A. HERSHBERGER AND SARAH SUHADOLNIK

A Point in Time, a Moment in Place

Justice for Mike Brown is justice for us all
Which side are you on, friend?
Which side are you on?

On Saturday, October 4, 2014, protesters disrupted the carefree chatter of intermission at the St. Louis Symphony to sing a requiem for Michael Brown, an unarmed Black man shot to death in Ferguson, Missouri, by Darren Wilson, a white police officer, approximately one month prior.[1] The St. Louis Symphony was performing the Brahms Requiem. The localized movements of however many performers, production staff, and patrons—seemingly made static by the ritualized activity of Western symphonic orchestra concert programming—were suddenly set in motion again. Although media coverage was quick to identify a "disturbance" in Powell Hall, the seemingly impromptu demonstration could also be viewed as a fitting addition to the planned musical program. From this vantage point, the orchestra's display was paired with the coordinated activity of the assembled protesters, who sang iteration after iteration of the "Which side are you on?" refrain, orchestrating their own requiem of sorts.[2] Eventually, they simply began to chant: "Black lives matter," as those positioned in the balcony unfurled banners. "Racism Lives Here," one read.

In this chapter, we investigate this spontaneous protest as one possible site, or source, of a more inclusive framing of the music of the United States: that is, the special interplay of music and movement that existed in Powell Hall in St. Louis in 2014. Powell Hall houses activity that routinely highlights the transplanted nature of some US musical traditions, such as a performance of the Brahms Requiem, while excluding the sounds of others. On October 4, 2014, the venue also acted as a resonating chamber for US music that often communicates most urgently en route. A cell phone video of the 2014 event, later posted to YouTube and embedded in Robert Samuels's article for the *Washington Post,* shows an audience member or two stand up and join the demonstration. Others applauded. Still others looked bewildered and slightly irritated. One woman appeared openly hostile. Several members of the St. Louis Symphony, seated on the stage, turned to listen to and then applaud the singers.[3] In sum, the often impromptu performance of *Which Side Are You On?*—as staged, in this instance, in a place reserved for scheduled musical activity and during a moment traditionally reserved as a break—enlisted passive listeners in the work of musical protest, making for a contentious atmosphere. The tensions this suggests between dueling processes of musical identity formation drive much of what we consider to be the history of music in the United States. With this in mind, one could say that this added musical movement—specifically that which exists outside the ritualized activity of symphonic music—also made for a more unqualified view of US musical traditions. While the Brahms Requiem arguably rooted those assembled in the exclusive world of the Western concert hall, *Which Side Are You On?* evoked the experiences of the marginalized—forcing the change in perspective we explore in this chapter.

We decided to follow this song, *Which Side Are You On?*, as opposed to the more "traditional" and more extensively documented musical activity that passes through the walls of Powell Hall, to open up the historical dimensions of such musical movement. Indeed, the song the St. Louis protesters chose to sing has a long history, stretching back to a community geographically removed from Ferguson and St. Louis, and to a very different political and social conflict. Rather than fragment its perceived national identity, the travels of *Which Side Are You On?* through the nation have only expanded the range at which this work can resonate as music of the United States.[4] Elisions of otherwise illuminating notions of US performance practice(s), "folk" histor(ies), and evolving political discourse(s) often preserve cultural relevance at the expense of a clear, linear, historical progression. Moreover, collisions across different stylistic boundaries and spheres of commercial activity correspond to moments—like the one captured in St. Louis in 2014—of raised awareness of a national US music at the same time that they call attention to a multiplicity of musical expressions of it.

In dialogue with myriad iterations and works that have charted equally significant, albeit circuitous paths through US music, *Which Side Are You On?* both asks and answers questions at the heart of twenty-first-century studies of US music history. In short, how do we best account for the contributions of musical works that historically "disturb" the now dominant narratives that first allowed a diverse population of US musicians, citizens, and historians to claim a musical past of their own? In this chapter, we pursue answers to such questions by approaching *Which Side Are You On?* less as a single, diachronic arc for examination than as a means to examine music in motion, putting various renditions of this song—including Ani DiFranco's 2012 remake—into conversation with each other, and, to a limited extent, with entirely different works such as Duke Ellington's *A Drum Is a Woman.* The result allows us to broadly consider these different, intertwining trajectories of music and movement as the beginnings of a more inclusive framing of the music of the United States.

How does music *move* people in the United States, literally and metaphorically, "then" and "now"? In terms of *travel*—predictable and unpredictable patterns of physical, cultural, and political movement—the music of the United States might be understood in the following ways.

- The music of the United States is rooted in musical traditions that largely originated elsewhere, regardless of genre or genre expectation.
- The music of the United States moves across all parts of the nation with varying degrees of historical documentation.
- The music of the United States is both defined and redefined by an ability to somehow represent a constantly changing nation, which lacks a single, shared ethnicity, both at home and abroad.

Closer attention to the cultural work accomplished by the different types of musical movements listed, which we address generally as *travel* in this chapter, affords ample opportunity to address the negotiation of the movable sonic and social lines of demarcation drawn around musical experience(s) inside and outside the United States with broader frameworks for understanding music in motion. Building on the perceived slippage of time and space that underpins the so-called spatial turn in humanities research,[5] we adopt a broadly inclusive position on *musical travel* in this comparative and collaborative study of *Which Side Are You On?* as a means of better understanding the role of social movement in the definition of musical and cultural identity.[6] The movements of *Which Side Are You On?* record a range of compelling possibilities, informed by the different levels at which *travel* informs public conceptions of US music. To this end, we synthesize a vocabulary of movement between "centers" (i.e., traditional locations of power) and "margins" (i.e., ad hoc sites of resistance) in historiography, musical analysis, and cultural history as a model for moving toward more inclusive histories of US music.

On the Margins

In the summer of 1931, songwriter Florence Reece (1900–1986) was living in Harlan County, Kentucky, a coal-mining community located in the southeast corner of the state.[7] It was there that she penned *Which Side Are You On?* to document the bitter labor battle in which coal miners and their families found themselves embroiled. After learning that their already meager wages would be cut by 10 percent in February 1931, many Harlan miners, encouraged by the United Mine Workers (UMW), went out on strike. The strike proved a colossal failure, and by May 1931, the UMW had withdrawn from Harlan County. The more radical National Miners Union (NMU), associated with the Communist Party of the United States of America, quickly moved in to take up the cause.

A miner named Sam Reece joined the NMU's efforts in Harlan, which brought his wife Florence to the area. The Reeces had been run out of Tennessee for their interest in union representation for coal miners, and they discovered that the struggle for unionization in Kentucky would prove just as difficult as in Tennessee. Indeed, Harlan County quickly earned the nickname "Bloody Harlan."[8] With *Which Side Are You On?* Florence Reece documented this dangerous chapter in Harlan's history, putting forth her stance on the struggle; in one verse, for example, she referenced the tactics used by armed deputies ("gun thugs") to intimidate striking miners and their families. Reece knew these tactics all too well, as she and her children were terrified when deputies shot through the walls of her family's cabin when her husband was away:

If you go to Harlan County
There is no neutral there
You'll either be a union man
Or a thug for J.H. Blair.[9]

For a refrain, she posed her now-famous question:

Which side are you on?
Which side are you on?[10]

Like professional, and canonized, US composers such as Aaron Copland, who set "Into the Streets May First" to music in 1934, as well as professional folk singers and US cultural icons such as Woody Guthrie and Pete Seeger, Reece sought to call attention to labor issues through song, painting a vivid picture of what was at stake. She believed that listeners could be for workers and their families or against them. Even in 1975, she held fast to this assertion, explaining, "You *have* to be on one side or the other. Some people say, 'I don't take sides—I'm neutral.' There's no such thing."[11] Calls for action can echo widely across time and space. In St. Louis in 2014, Derek Laney, a community organizer for Missourians Organizing for Reform and Empowerment, stated similarly that "you have to make a choice . . . it's not all right to just ignore it."[12] Such powerful resonances are not always as thoroughly documented in the history of US music as we might think or hope. For example, despite some significant similarities, the recorded history of *Which Side Are You On?* differs greatly from the history of a song like "This Land Is Your Land," which Guthrie, in response to "God Bless America," famously penned (and repenned) in the 1940s to the tune of the Carter Family's "When the World's on Fire." Unlike Guthrie, Reece is barely remembered in or for *Which Side Are You On?* By 2014, she had been deceased almost thirty years, yet both her song and her belief continued to *travel*—arriving over eight decades later in that partial political and social space in St. Louis. How do we best acknowledge this disconnect? Where a scholar could search for a linear, or strictly diachronic, chain of events that explains how Laney became aware of Reece's song, we argue that the more substantive connection lies elsewhere. Simply put, then and now, the impact of *Which Side Are You On?* hinges on movement for or against locations of power, and a propensity to elicit this mode of *travel* is what has allowed this work to continue to *travel* today.

Feminist theorist bell hooks has written extensively about such locations of power and the significance of movement between them. Throughout this chapter, we draw heavily on hooks's theory of marginality, embracing Reece's *Which Side Are You On?* as an opportunity to consider the musical equivalent of what hooks addresses as "the possibility of radical perspective from which to see and create, to imagine alternatives, new worlds."[13] Like Reece, hooks had experience in a deeply divided Kentucky town, yet whereas Reece, a white woman, defined divisions solely in terms of social class, hooks, a Black woman, took an intersectional perspective, defining divisions in terms of race and class.

Recalling her childhood in Hopkinsville, a town in the southwest corner of the state, nearly three hundred miles from Harlan County, hooks described the experience of crossing the railroad tracks, that "daily reminder of our marginality."[14] Black Kentuckians could cross the tracks to enter the white world, the so-called center, to work "in a service capacity"; however, hooks writes, they "had always to return to the margin, to cross the tracks to shacks and abandoned houses on the edge of town."[15] Hooks parlays this transformative experience physically traveling to and from identified margins into a theoretical model for a kind of reflexive subject position. She argues that by "living as we did—on the edge—we developed a particular way of seeing reality. We looked both from the outside in and from the inside out. We focused our attention on the center as well as on the margin. We understood both."[16] As spaces that accommodate fluctuating geographical mapping and ad hoc identity formation, hooks thus defines "the margin" as doubly reflexive: space(s) of exclusion and space(s) "where one is able to redeem and reclaim the past, legacies of pain, suffering, and triumph in ways that transform present reality."[17] By adopting hooks's terminology, we leverage what she identifies as "a site of creativity and power" as a historiographical space where we might, as she puts it, "recover ourselves" and where we might "move in solidarity to erase the category colonized/colonizer."[18] This "place," or reflexive view of marginality, thus engages the ideas of encounter at the heart of humanistic studies of *travel*, and encourages us to similarly scrutinize our own movements as listeners, researchers, and scholars acting in and around what we call music of the United States.

Travelogues of Identity Formation

The recuperative value of the proposed framework—a means of relating *travel* to hooks's view of marginality—can be demonstrated in multiple ways. Our discussion of Reece can and, to a certain extent, does operate as a means of recovering the contributions of a musician largely forgotten by the movements of her most popular song. Over the course of her life, Reece also moved physically, from Tennessee (where she was born) to Kentucky and back again, but she moved across marginalized social spaces as well. She worked as a wife and as a political activist, yet she did not embrace the latter role in a particularly public way. Unlike other musical organizers from eastern Kentucky, including Aunt Molly Jackson (1880–1960) and Sarah Ogan Gunning (1910–1983), Reece did not travel to places like New York City to spread her music and activism. She did not perform alongside professional singers like Guthrie or Seeger, and she probably never expected or intended for *Which Side Are You On?* to reach the ears of those beyond her immediate community. In 1971, Reece told Ron Stanford that she sang *Which Side Are You On?* "for neighbors mainly, not crowds," countering the widely held view of the US balladeer as a public figure—singing to and for "the masses."[19]

Reece's seemingly tenuous relationship with dominant histories of US folk music, however, belies the long-term impact of *Which Side Are You On?*, a song that has fulfilled the promises of US folk music for decades. Reconciling Reece's personal *travels* with those of her musical work thus creates space to reexamine the access, social mobility, and powers of (re) definition that "folk" musicians have been able to exercise in reinterpreting Reece's work. This is treated as recuperative here because the reflexive view of the music in question makes room to consider the historical arcs of both music and musician, which, at the expense of a little-known figure like Reece, don't unfurl entirely in tandem. Again, we need not search for contemporary connections to Reece and her past to recognize the influence her music has had in motion. As we will see, however, we do need to take careful note of the movements of her work to preserve her memory.

Equally intriguing are the methodological implications of comparing the "travelogues" of works that resonate in similar ways. If, in other words, the legacy of *Which Side Are You On?* is rooted in how it historically elicited movement, it follows that other works of US music may operate similarly. Such a comparison—particularly one that exists across limiting notions of tradition and performance practice—could more fully access the processes of identity formation at work in narrative-defying collisions (like that made visible at the 2014 Black Lives Matter protest in St. Louis). Through the identification of comparable locations of power, and associated positions of marginality, this type of comparative analysis can help scholars take stock of a fuller range of significant musical motion, like the historic *travels* of Reece and her work, and thus adopt a more nuanced view of US music. If nothing else, this allows for a more holistic view of musical activity that "disturbs" dominant musical narratives—past and present—addressing gaps in various archives with greater care and compassion.

Before undertaking the more difficult work of traversing the sonic and social boundaries that exist between works that share similar travelogues, we begin with an illustration of what can be gained when a figure like Reece, who left little historical footprint outside of her influential work, is given more of her due. Without this added consideration—or acknowledgment of the role Reece's personal experiences played in the creation of a song that has traveled so far without her—she quickly becomes marginalized. For example, in 1967, Guthrie wrote that *Which Side Are You On?* "was composed in 19 and 31 by the two children of Sam Reece, two little girls. They're grown up now but one was nine and the other eleven then. It was made up from the condition of their father, who was organizer in Harlan County."[20] On another occasion, Alan Lomax supposedly described Reece as "a shy, towheaded Kentucky miner's daughter" who composed *Which Side Are You On?* "at the age of twelve when her father was out on strike. She sang it to me standing in front of the primitive hearth of a log cabin in the backwoods of Kentucky in 1937, and it has since become a national union song."[21] Much of the information contained in these anecdotes, often repeated in the popular press and blogosphere without proper citation, is incorrect. Reece was the daughter of a Tennessee miner and wife of a Tennessee-turned Kentucky miner named Sam; additionally, Reece's lyrics clearly refer to Harlan County in the 1930s, not Fork Ridge, Tennessee, where her father had gone on strike in 1912. Lomax's supposed words, however, could suggest that Reece carried what she witnessed in Fork Ridge with her to Harlan County. As she officially wrote *Which Side Are You On?* in 1931, she may have been writing through a struggle that had characterized her entire life. Indeed, in the song's final verse, she references her father:

> My daddy was a miner
> He's now in the air and sun
> He'll be with you fellow workers
> Till every battle's won.[22]

To be "in the air and sun" was to be blacklisted and without a job. Yet in 1931, Reece's father was no longer blacklisted: he had been dead for almost twenty years. Reece may have been recalling his struggle; or, she may have first sung these words as a child, thus composing *Which Side Are You On?* over the course of her life.

The omissions, or limitations, of Guthrie's and Lomax's accounts stack up quickly, demonstrating the haziness of the historical record and the need to allow Reece to speak for herself. In 1971, Reece recalled her compositional process to Stanford, explaining that in 1931, she had set her words to the hymn "I'm Going to Land on That Shore."[23] In 1975, she cited another old hymn tune, "Lay the Lily Low," as her melodic model.[24] To this day, folklorists do not agree on Reece's source material. But according to Timothy P. Lynch, "Regardless as to the particular song used as the model, it was a song in the mountain tradition familiar to the people."[25] This resonates with Reece's own thoughts on the matter, as she herself noted that she grew up in a community that relied on song to cope with "the troubles" of poverty.[26] She claimed that from the time she was born, "there was always singing."[27] Her mother, for example "always sang hymns."[28] Perhaps this is where Reece heard the tune, showing us where and how she may have found her voice to protest. We will likely never know for sure, and by attempting to "collect" Reece and *Which Side Are You On?* in the tradition of a ballad collector, we miss an opportunity to understand the broader utility of this music.

Guthrie's and Lomax's depictions of Reece, moreover, seem to freeze her in a particular time and place, ultimately denying her, and us, the opportunity to "imagine the alternatives" viewable from the margins of history she represents. According to Lomax, Reece was a child, "a shy, towheaded Kentucky miner's daughter." Yet in 1937, the year in which Reece supposedly sang for Lomax, she would have been almost forty years old! Thus for all that Lomax's supposed words may begin to illuminate about the history of *Which Side Are You On?*, they refuse to travel through that cumulative history, obscuring the transformative movement of Reece's work, particularly as the song traveled seemingly without her.

Historicizing Musical Travels

As a musical "travelogue," *Which Side Are You On?* documents many, if not most, of the types of musical movement defined at the beginning of this chapter as examples of *musical travel.* The ability to mine such moments of encounter requires the kind of reflexive view we take from hooks and her theory of marginality. Those engaged in the analysis of historic travelogues—meaning journals and other prose expressions of how people in motion have interpreted their destinations—often employ the limited terminology of "native" and "foreigner." In his work, anthropologist James Clifford uses the more inclusive terms "dweller" (marginalized subject) and "traveler" (centered subject), which, as a more inclusive frame for such analysis, both operates outside of the sociopolitical situations in which hooks formulated her notion of marginality, and calls attention to the fluidity that may also exist between these differing subject positions for viewing life in motion. He characterizes this work as involving "attempts to trace old and new maps and histories of people in transit variously empowered and compelled."[29] Indeed, Clifford's "dweller"/"traveler" framework more explicitly accounts for time, yielding the equally reflexive concepts of "travels" and "contacts" as "sites of unfinished modernity," which become viewable through Clifford's notion of marginal space—"dwelling in travel."[30]

The idea of "dwelling in travel" points toward the kind of interdisciplinary collaboration we think furthers the increasingly expansive aims of US music studies in the twenty-first century. One might imagine that reframing US music in the ways we have advocated would preclude a singular notion of US music as a disciplinary field of study. On the contrary. In her study of the travels of nineteenth-century composer Felix Mendelssohn, Celia Applegate identifies four musical means of relating to one's nationality in music (two more than typically accommodated by dominant narratives of US music history). After the "patriotic" (or "chauvinistic") and "cosmopolitan," Applegate considers the movements of musicians who, when in motion or *traveling*, also represent a kind of "distilled version of their nationality" or engage with a "definite consciousness of national identity."[31] Reece and her song have arguably been treated and mistreated as examples of the musician (and their music, presumably) who works as a "distillation of their nationality." Reece, at present, is not a US musical figure who is well-documented by conventional historical methods, despite the continued performance of *Which Side Are You On?* as a musical means of expressing community solidarity—most recently in connection with Black Lives Matter. Remarkably, the one archived performance of Reece singing *Which Side Are You On?*—captured by film director Barbara Kopple in her Academy Award–winning documentary of the 1973–74 Brookside strike in Harlan County—would seem to belie Reece's absence.[32] After largely disappearing from the history of *Which Side Are You On?*, Reece suddenly reappeared to sing at a union rally in Harlan County. Standing before the crowd of Brookside miners and their families, Reece explained that she was about to sing a song she had written in the 1930s. She admitted that she no longer sang "very well," yet she delivered the song with confidence and conviction, enlisting those gathered to join her chorus. Just as soon as Reece reemerged in the historical narrative, however, she seemed to vanish again.

In 1972, a year before Reece returned to Harlan County, folklorist Archie Green noted that it had been "nearly forty years since 'Which Side Are You On?' emerged from a dissident [National Miners Union] setting to become a general labor song, shorn of its sectarian coloration."[33] In fact, the song quickly moved beyond the classification of "labor song" altogether. The Freedom Singers adapted the ballad to the civil rights movement in the 1960s, writing new words to all the verses to tell their story of racial struggle. In 2014, St. Louis protesters went a step further, completely remaking the song by moving away from the conventions of the ballad. Protesters had only to add the name of Mike Brown to Reece's tune, insisting that justice for him represented justice for everyone in the United States. They did not retell the story of his death. In 2015, rapper Talib Kweli sampled some of the St. Louis protesters at the beginning of *Which Side Are You On?*, the first track on his hip-hop album *Indie 500*. Thus labor, Reece, and the expectations of the lionized ballad tradition all slipped away from proximal definitions of *Which Side Are You On?* but were arguably still evoked for the participants in the protests by the movement(s) the music elicited. As an extension of community action—imagined communities "made real"—this type of musical activity, in Applegate's words, "illuminate[s] one way in which national communities t[a]k[e] shape and function through cultural exchange," and make the traveling musician "an especially potent representative of national identities."[34] Thus, it is only through *motion*—only when we follow the work into new situations, and across easy genre classifications—that the full reach and impact of *Which Side Are You On?* as US music can be properly gauged.

Ani DiFranco's *Which Side Are You On?* arguably mistreats Reece and her anthem. The critique is doubly significant to the goals of this chapter, as it is rooted in approaching DiFranco as an example of a musician who works with a "definite consciousness of national identity," while also reasserting the recuperative value of the outlined analytical framework for approaching the study of US music as music in motion.[35] The American singer-songwriter and commercial record label owner began singing an updated version of *Which Side Are You On?* in 2009, in part because she had been asked to perform the song at Pete Seeger's ninetieth birthday concert.[36] In 2012, she released her version on her seventeenth studio album, entitled *Which Side Are You On?* Positioning her work as a reflection on US politics since the Reagan era, DiFranco shaped the contemporary political message of *her* track in terms of a long-standing tradition of repurposing tried and true folk tunes, what DiFranco herself referred to as the "folk process" in a 2010 webcast performance.[37] Although DiFranco does engage in the same creative work of crafting her own lyrics that the 2014 St. Louis demonstrators did, and other artists like them, DiFranco's take on *Which Side Are You On?* is made more permanent by her mode of musical engagement with it and thus warrants special consideration.

Indeed, the limitations of medium—DiFranco's *Which Side Are You On?* is carefully preserved on her album, unlike other such renditions composed through the "folk process"—can offer further warning against what can be lost when other possible "radical alternatives," or "unfinished modernities," are entirely lost to history. DiFranco's lyrics cover a lot of contemporary political ground, including an extensive reflection on the state and meaning of US feminism. At the same time, DiFranco's remake might give us a certain amount of pause, particularly in terms of the way she sought to write feminism into a song written by a woman unacknowledged on both the Pete Seeger ninetieth-birthday concert program and the DiFranco studio release, and marginalized by the dominant historical narratives of US folk music we have sketched. Did DiFranco know anything about Reece, this woman who was arguably a feminist before the term "feminist" existed and who struggled against the political and economic margins throughout her entire life? The answer is unclear. In concert performances, DiFranco tends to refer to the song *Which Side Are You On?* as an "old labor song from the 1930s."[38] DiFranco's record label, Righteous Babe Records, advertises the album *Which Side Are You On?* as featuring "11 new songs alongside a radically reworked rendition of the classic title song, famously popularized by the one and only Pete Seeger nearly five decades ago, but no less relevant today."[39] This product description is not incorrect—Seeger, beginning with his days in the Almanac Singers, was instrumental in helping to popularize the song—yet in harkening back only as far as Seeger, a strictly diachronic view of the work's history, the characterization is incomplete.[40] The lack of attention DiFranco devotes to the broader *musical travels* of Reece's work weakens the result.

On the surface, DiFranco—with her clear ties to the US folk music community—would appear best positioned to take up *Which Side Are You*

On? for twenty-first-century audiences. DiFranco's adaptation, unlike some of the other adaptations of the song discussed in this chapter, pulls the song not so much across margins but into a center, perhaps *the* center of US folk music. Yet this is precisely where the notion of genre DiFranco employs to frame her revamped chronicle of US politics falls short. *Which Side Are You On?* is more than an "old labor ballad" popularized by Pete Seeger. It is a song in constant motion, and an example of a musical work that moves us to pursue more inclusive frames for US music history. One might argue that Righteous Babe Records is simply attempting to capitalize on Seeger's more recognizable name, yet this move contradicts DiFranco's own description of Righteous Babe's mission as "a people-friendly, sub-corporate, woman-informed, queer-happy small business that puts music before rock stardom and ideology before profit."[41] From this perspective, the fraught decision to freeze *Which Side Are You On?* in place as "famously popularized by the one and only Pete Seeger" calls attention to the push and pull of *musical travels*, and the recuperative work that can be done in the process of excavating them. Following Celia Applegate in this regard, we argue that the activity of such liminal spaces is what best articulates the "capacity of musical travel to define and strengthen national communities by traveling among them."[42]

Looking further afield stylistically for an additional test case, Edward Kennedy "Duke" Ellington's *A Drum Is a Woman* (1957) can be read through a similar lens. As a work with a comparable "travelogue" to *Which Side Are You On?*, Ellington's "jazz allegory" tells the story of jazz as an "American" musical tradition from the vantage point of both "traveler" and "dweller"—forcing an equally reflexive view of the music's past, present, and future.[43] In practice, Ellington's narration follows Madam Zajj, "a personified drum who symbolizes jazz," as she moves in and out of colorful tableaus set in and beyond New Orleans.[44] Ellington's colorful free-form orchestrations feature tight ensemble playing, loose improvisation, and fully composed song, bringing Madame Zajj's movements to life at the expense of an easy-to-categorize musical approach.

Nowhere is the work's reflexive view of US jazz history clearer than in the Congo Square scene. "You can almost smell violence and fear," Ellington tells us, describing the "congregated crowd" before Madame Zajj finally arrives. Where, in performance, Reece's pointed refrain typically forces the listener to consider their actions in "real time," Ellington's immersive, spoken-word narration forces the listener into a through-composed historical space. "They may be afraid to be there, they may be afraid not to be there," he says, distancing both himself and the singer/dancer that plays Zajj from the assembled audience before moving to the subject position of the audience for the narration of the main event. This engages the privileged position of the entertained "traveler" as a point of departure, priming the listener/audience to be displaced—ultimately forced to hear the scene as exploitative spectacle. Ellington continues: "The stage is set, we await the rising of a curtain that is not down, or even there." The sensuous dance and drum beats of Madame Zajj generate "waves of desire in the crowd" until, "suddenly, a monstrous man leaps out of nowhere, snatches up [Madame Zajj] bodily, and carries her out of the clearing."

Beginning and ending with the perspective of the crowd congregated around Madame Zajj, Ellington as narrator brings the listener with him as he moves about Congo Square. Transported by the music between center and margin, the listener comes to see their historic role, or subject position, in a new way. The discomfort that settles in as the scene draws to a close thus plays upon the "dweller" status of the US listeners reflexively approached as "travelers," which is to say that US audiences would, or should, knowingly respond with horror when the specter of slavery appears in this recounting of a jazz origins story. Although comparable in some respects to earlier programmatic works by Ellington (e.g., *Black, Brown, and Beige*), the spoken word narration woven throughout the album-length *A Drum Is a Woman* thus makes the composer's commentary on African American music, culture, and experience more immediate. Who does the listener see as personifying jazz? Where? How? Where do they see themselves in the story of jazz? How does it feel to be a gawking onlooker?

In short: which side are you on?

Richard Crawford, in his foreword to the revised third edition of Gilbert Chase's *America's Music: From the Pilgrims to the Present*, credited Chase with engaging in both "diachronic" and "synchronic" views of time as a means of fully recounting the kaleidoscopic landscape of US music. According to Crawford, "American music's long history, Chase knew, needed to be studied diachronically, but its diversity demanded synchronic treatment. Only by mastering both concepts of time and interweaving them, he concluded, could he, as a historian of American music, do full justice to his subject."[45] Against this historiographical backdrop, we see an approach to US music history that could accommodate a comparative view of Reece's *Which Side Are You On?* and Ellington's *A Drum Is a Woman*—works that raise equally provocative questions about

US music in motion through the equally reflexive views of US music and culture they evoke—as an opportunity to do full(er) justice to the diversity of voices that have helped to make the varied landscape of US music what it is. Where the iterations of Reece's work over time arguably double as a living record of how the song has been transformed by the people it has moved (often in protest), the circulation of Ellington's *A Drum Is a Woman* as both a commercial record release and a promotional television broadcast has since inspired critics and scholars alike to reflect on how jazz travels with a "definite consciousness of national identity" (à la Applegate). Neither of our case studies presents a comprehensive view of a national musical tradition, but both together begin to articulate the sounds of the United States in terms of community movement and collective action.

There are many other instances of US music in motion that we might consider as well. Although the activity we have defined as *travel* refers most directly to musicians who routinely moved between social worlds for the work of their music, it easily could be expanded to address music traveling through virtual worlds as well. Consider, for instance, the popular Acapella App musical collage—an increasingly common means of experiencing "live" music in the United States that now travels extensively beyond its original inspiration, intentions, and conventions.[46] Indeed, both at the time of this writing in the midst of a global pandemic, and in retrospect, collaborative displays of artistic talent convened for performances of everything ranging from school fight songs to classical masterworks have resonated first and foremost because of the unrestricted movement and social connection enabled by virtual networks. Following the travels of US music in all of these ways offers rewarding opportunities to join a growing field of scholars who treat such movement—physical, cultural, and political—as integral to the study of the history of music.

We also contend that the identification of key sites, and routes, of travel can provide further help to the scholar to identify the moves—physical, rhetorical, and metaphorical—that work to replicate one's own worldview in otherwise unfamiliar cultures and contexts. This is, in turn, an opportunity to make effective use of the more reflexive models of encounter that characterize *travel* studies. As Clifford asserts, "Cultural centers, discrete regions and territories, do not exist prior to contacts, but are sustained through them, appropriating and disciplining the restless movements of people and things."[47] Although separated in some respects by differing disciplinary objectives, we too want to discover what else we can see and hear, for we believe the results yield productive contributions toward the disciplinary push across US music studies for more inclusive scholarship. While daunting at first, embracing the perpetual motion of music of the United States allows us to apprehend the unfinished state of US music as a subject, a field, and a community. By honing in on the processes of becoming and re-becoming that pull together the experiences of stylistically removed works across discrete historical periods, we can better understand both the music of the United States and the choices that we make in defining that history.

On Being Ourselves (circa 2018)

We drafted much of this chapter over the course of several intense days in June 2018. Sarah flew from Iowa to New York and hopped a train (via car from her childhood home to the train station) to Connecticut, where we proceeded to think, talk, write, and discuss in coffee shops, by the pool, on the balcony, and in the safety and security of each other's company and friendship. Outside the cocoon we created for ourselves, it seemed like the United States fell into even more disarray. The reality of a Supreme Court suddenly set in flux by a retirement, just after the court voted to uphold Trump's ban on travel from several predominantly Muslim countries, reiterated for us the significance of thinking about travel in a new way.[48] The result was an early iteration of this chapter, in which we focused on the ideas and activities of what we have defined in terms of "musical travel." It is worth noting that Reece's comment that people can only "be for themselves or against themselves"—pulled from a 1971 interview and as the inspiration for our chapter—also holds up a mirror to our own personal and professional "travels," which have only continued to evolve since this point. Every career opportunity, it seems, throughout graduate school and beyond, has also become a choice about what to be—move away from home(s) or stay stagnant, advance through increasingly unclear career milestones or fall behind. Develop more professional skills with less time. Work at the expense of reinforcing the crumbling infrastructure of higher education and without the same job security. In this way, Reece's evocative phrase is for us reflective of both movement in a historical sense and the processes of becoming and re-becoming we have undertaken in joining the field of US music studies in our own lifetimes.

We privilege the idea of "being" in our engagement with travel as a way to emphasize the dual character of this project. This is not strictly a scholarly endeavor for us, in the sense that this framework also speaks to the realities of our shared positions in life. As two junior women scholars trained and tested in the move from the optimism of the Barack Obama presidency into the pessimism of the so-called Donald Trump era, the project of diverse scholarship is one of basic survival. New interdisciplinary models of scholarly inquiry within our field also reflect, for us, more livable notions of expertise. We both emerged from our shared writing process thinking we could never have undertaken a project like this on our own. Moreover, we find, as we have in the dialogic motion of this chapter itself, that there is community and space for inclusion in the perpetual motion of our twenty-first-century academic lives. Even now, as our lives change even more, our conversations with each other will continue to impact the ways in which our scholarship works in dialogue with that of others. Overall, our collaboration very much resembles the work we feel it would take to recuperate the unfinished project of the collaborative, though "circuitous," community relationships that build our nation, make our music, and chronicle our past.

Notes

1. Wilson shot and killed Brown on August 9, 2014, prompting weeks of protests. On November 24, the St. Louis County prosecutor announced that a grand jury had decided not to indict Wilson, fueling another wave of protests. In March 2015, the US Department of Justice declared that Ferguson had engaged in constitutional violations and called on the city to overhaul its criminal justice system. Protesters who gathered to sing a requiem for "Mike" Brown (rather than Michael Brown) likely sought to fit Brown's name to the preexisting tune, discussed later in this chapter, that they referenced.

2. Throughout this chapter, we italicize the title of *Which Side Are You On?* (rather than use quotation marks) to underscore the significance of the musical moments in time and place documented by this song's circuitous history. We also seek to trouble the hierarchy of genre, wherein song titles are conventionally placed in quotation marks and symphonies, opera, and other large works in italics.

3. Robert Samuels, "Protesters Interrupt St. Louis Symphony With 'Requiem for Mike Brown,'" *Washington Post,* October 5, 2014, https://www.washingtonpost.com/news/post-nation/wp/2014/10/05/protesters-interrupt-st-louis-symphony-with-requiem-for-mike-brown/?utm_term=.73dc4cc627a1. See also https://youtu.be/T_7ErkQFduQ. The cell phone video was first posted by Rebecca Rivas, reporter/video editor for the *St. Louis American.*

4. The contemporary reverberation of the phrase "Which side are you on" also echoes in Cheryl Townsend Gilkes's reflection in chapter 4 of this volume.

5. In 2011, musicologist Robert Fink framed this disciplinary turn in music research as an "epistemic shift" in which "*Time,* the original structuring prin-

ciple of musicological inquiry, is making room for a new organizing framework based on the phenomenology of space." See "File Under: American Spaces," in "Studying U.S. Music in the Twenty-First Century," ed. Charles Hiroshi Garrett and Carol J. Oja, *Journal of the American Musicological Society* 64, no. 3 (2011): 708–9. Through his use of Henri Lefebvre's theories of social space construction, maintenance, and representation, Fink also delineates the effects of the experience of "time-space compression" that David Harvey has theorized as part of the "postmodern condition." See "Time-Space Compression and the Postmodern Condition," chap. 17 in *The Condition of Postmodernity: An Enquiry into the Origins of Cultural Change* (Cambridge: Blackwell, 1989).

6. For examples of other works that approach the idea of *musical travel* in a similar way, see Marie Jorritsma, "The Significance of Small Journeys: Travel and the Congregational Music of Kroonvale, South Africa," *Nineteenth-Century Music Review* 16, no. 2 (2018): 1–19; Linda Phyllis Austern, Candace Bailey, and Amanda Eubanks Winkler, eds., *Beyond Boundaries: Rethinking Music Circulation in Early Modern England* (Bloomington: Indiana University Press, 2017); Gordon E. Slethaug, ed., *Music and The Road: Essays on the Interplay of Music and the Popular Culture of the American Road* (New York: Bloomsbury Academic Press, 2017). See also Arjun Appadurai, *Modernity at Large: Cultural Dimensions of Globalization* (Minneapolis: University of Minnesota Press, 1996). Appadurai does not engage with music or travel as explicitly, but scrutinizes the ideas of cultural flow that underpin the relative definitions of "centers" and "margins" that we evoke here.

7. Reece recounted her life story to both Ron Stanford and Kathy Kahn. See "'Which Side Are You On?': An Interview with Florence Reece by Ron Stanford," *Sing Out!* 20, no. 6 (1971): 13–15. See also "They Say Them Child Brides Don't Last: Florence Reece, Ellistown, Tennessee," in Kathy Kahn, *Hillbilly Women* (Garden City, NY: Doubleday, 1973), 27–38.

8. Historian John W. Hevener has examined this chapter in Harlan's history. See *Which Side Are You On? The Harlan County Coal Miners, 1930–39* (Urbana: University of Illinois Press, 1978).

9. J. H. Blair was the sheriff in Harlan County.

10. See the lyrics for *Which Side Are You On?* in Stanford, "Which Side Are You On?," 14. Reece's song is quoted and discussed in several studies of US protest music. See Timothy P. Lynch, *Strike Songs of the Depression* (Jackson: University Press of Mississippi, 2001): 66–68; Guy Carawan and Candie Carawan, *Voices from the Mountains* (New York: Alfred A. Knopf, 1975), 119; John Greenway, *American Folksongs of Protest* (New York: Octagon Books, 1970), 169–71; Alan Lomax, Woody Guthrie, and Pete Seeger, *Hard Hitting Songs for Hard-Hit People* (New York: Oak Publications, 1967), 176–77.

11. Reece, quoted in Carawan and Carawan, *Voices from the Mountains*, 119.

12. Derek Laney, quoted in Samuels, "Protesters Interrupt St. Louis Symphony."

13. bell hooks, *Yearning: Race, Gender, and Cultural Politics* (Boston: South End Press, 1990), 150. See also bell hooks, *Feminist Theory: From Margin to Center* (New York: Routledge, 1984).

14. hooks, *Yearning*, 149.

15. hooks, *Yearning*, 149.

16. hooks, *Yearning*, 149.
17. hooks, *Yearning*, 147.
18. hooks, *Yearning*, 152.
19. See Stanford, "Which Side Are You On?," 15. Reece went on, however, to perform her song in a formal public setting on at least one occasion; in 1973, when Harlan miners found themselves forced to strike yet again, she sang at a union rally.
20. Guthrie, in Lomax, Guthrie, and Seeger, *Hard Hitting Songs*, 176.
21. For example, see Blake Skylar, "Today in Labor History: Songwriter, Activist Florence Reece Is Born," *People's World*, April 12, 2013, https://www.peoplesworld.org/article/today-in-labor-history-songwriter-activist-florence-reece-is-born/. According to Skylar, "Lomax wrote in his book, 'Florence Reece, a shy, towheaded Kentucky miner's daughter, composed this song at the age of twelve when her father was out on strike. She sang it to me standing in front of the primitive hearth of a log cabin in the backwoods of Kentucky in 1937, and it has since become a national union song.'" Skylar does not identify Lomax's book, and we have been unable to locate the quotation in any of Lomax's publications. According to William Serrin, journalist and author of *The Company and The Union: The "Civilized Relationship" of the General Motors Corporation and the United Automobile Workers*, Guy Carawan and Candie Carawan were the first to record Reece singing *Which Side Are You On?* in 1980 at Reece's home in Fountain City, Tennessee. See "Labor Song's Writer, Frail at 83, Shows She is Still a Fighter," *New York Times*, March 18, 1984.
22. See the lyrics for *Which Side Are You On?* in Stanford, "Which Side Are You On?," 14.
23. See Stanford, "Which Side Are You On?," 15.
24. See Carawan and Carawan, *Voices from the Mountains*, 119.
25. Lynch, *Strike Songs*, 142.
26. Reece, quoted in Stanford, "Which Side Are You On?," 13.
27. Reece, quoted in Stanford, "Which Side Are You On?," 15.
28. Reece, quoted in Stanford, "Which Side Are You On?," 15.
29. James Clifford, *Routes: Travel and Translation in the Late Twentieth Century* (Cambridge, MA: Harvard University Press, 1997), 2.
30. Clifford, *Routes*, 2.
31. Celia Applegate, "Mendelssohn on the Road: Music, Travel, and the Anglo-German Symbiosis," in *The Oxford Handbook of the New Cultural History of Music*, ed. Jane F. Fulcher (New York: Oxford University Press, 2011), 232–33.
32. *Harlan County, USA*, directed by Barbara Kopple, 1976, New York, Cabin Creek Films, DVD.
33. Archie Green, *Only a Miner: Studies in Recorded Coal-Mining Songs* (Urbana: University of Illinois Press, 1972), 429.
34. Applegate, "Mendelssohn on the Road," 229, 230.
35. Applegate, "Mendelssohn on the Road," 232–33.
36. As DiFranco recalled in a later concert, singers participated in "a folk fiesta" for Seeger's ninetieth birthday concert at Madison Square Garden on May 3, 2009. See Ani DiFranco performing *Which Side Are You On?* at the Clay Center for the Arts and Sciences in Charleston, West Virginia: https://youtu.be/MzQ-n4RLMC4

37. See Ani DiFranco performing *Which Side Are You On?* on the Ex'pression Web Cast, June 24, 2010, https://www.youtube.com/watch?v=wnFfg_u9wQo

38. See Ani DiFranco performing *Which Side Are You On?* on the Ex'pression Web Cast.

39. See Righteous Babe Records, "Ani DiFranco—Which Side Are You On?," product description, https://www.righteousbabe.com/products/which-side-are-you-on?variant=31351197770

40. According to Serrin, Pete Seeger learned *Which Side Are You On?* from "Tillman Cadle, a coal miner then living in New York. In 1941, it was recorded by the Almanac Singers, of which Mr. Seeger was a member . . . This version made the song famous." See "Labor Song's Writer."

41. See Righteous Babe Records, "About Us," https://www.righteousbabe.com/pages/about-us

42. Applegate, "Mendelssohn on the Road," 231.

43. Critics in 1957 labeled *A Drum Is a Woman* everything from "musical fantasy" and "jazz-tinged opera-cum-ballet" to "a musical history of jazz."

44. "'Drum Is a Woman' on CBS Television," May 1, 1957, press release circulated by Columbia Records. On file at the Institute of Jazz Studies at Rutgers University–Newark.

45. Richard Crawford, foreword to Gilbert Chase, *America's Music: From the Pilgrims to the Present,* 3rd ed. (Urbana: University of Illinois Press, 1987), xx.

46. *Acapella* is an app by Mixcord that allows the user to craft a multitrack recording, which takes the form of a multiframe music video. In the midst of the 2020 COVID19 pandemic—a moment in which many people living in the United States were confined to their homes (unless forced to work because of financial need or essential worker status)—*Acapella* collages allowed US musicians to perform virtually in public and build community.

47. Clifford, *Routes,* 3.

48. At the time, "Trump travel ban" was shorthand for Executive Order 13769, titled "Protecting the Nation from Foreign Terrorist Entry into the United States."

Reaching Outward as Teachers and Scholars

TEN | Pedagogies of Music, Politics, and Race in US Music Studies

LOREN KAJIKAWA AND DANIEL MARTINEZ HOSANG

> Acts of accompaniment and improvisation can set in motion processes that produce new practices and as a result, new kinds of people, new social relationships, and new social imaginaries.[1]

In their recent book *Insubordinate Spaces: Improvisation and Accompaniment for Social Justice*, Barbara Tomlinson and George Lipsitz explore political resistance within a variety of contemporary contexts, including the neoliberal university. They encourage those of us working in higher education to recognize and embrace the liberatory potential of our work. Despite constant reminders that our respective institutions seem to prioritize brand building and individual ascension of select academic stars over community building and collective justice, they argue that the university's "residual commitments" to democratic education and the public good might offer alternatives to an otherwise relentless fixation on market logic and material gain.[2] This chapter considers the challenges and possibilities of remaking US music studies through innovations in pedagogy, drawing from a three-year team-taught course at the University of Oregon that focused on the intersection of music, politics, and race in the United States.

Even in interdisciplinary formations, such as ethnic studies or American studies, it is common to have some courses focus on social problems and histories of oppression, while others explore the literature, art, or creative practices of subordinated groups. Such divisions are particularly acute when it comes to music, a discipline whose course offerings are traditionally organized around particular genres (opera, rock, etc.) and historical periods (medieval, twentieth century, etc.). Although scholars have long recognized what Lipsitz describes as music's ability to allow people to "rehearse identities, stances, and social relations not yet permissible in politics," it can be difficult to teach about the material dimensions of inequality and, at the same time, incorporate discussions of artistic practices separate from or subordinate to the formal realm of politics.[3] Drawing on particular examples from our course, we center interdisciplinarity not only in course content but also in structure—finding ways of getting music studies out of its marginalized box as "just vibrations" (to borrow William Cheng's term) and into greater dialogue with projects whose purpose is to challenge systemic inequality.[4]

Such engagement can be difficult because music departments occupy institutional spaces far removed from the social sciences. Our team-taught course, Music, Politics, and Race, made it possible for a faculty member in Ethnic Studies / Political Science, appointed in the College of Arts and Sciences, to work closely with a musicologist from the School of Music and Dance. These academic units rarely collaborate, and our partnership reflected sustained efforts to prioritize interdisciplinary work.[5] Stemming from a shared interest in California history and our location on the West Coast of the United States, our course was predicated on a commitment to two principles: first, there are some things about music we can only learn from sustained attention to politics; and second, there are some things we can understand about politics only by considering music. This orientation forced us to bring together diverse bodies of knowledge, leading to new insights that we have applied in our teaching and research. We found that team teaching opened up new possibilities for collaboration, helping us to rethink what might be achievable, especially with respect to social justice commitments.

We are not suggesting that political topics are somehow new to the music classroom. Musicologists regularly use politics as a lens for understanding and teaching about music. Politics provide important context for particular works as well as the lives of musicians and composers. In surveys of Western classical music, for example, we teach our students to appreciate the dramatic ending of Dimitry Shostakovich's Fifth Symphony and the controversy surrounding it by explaining what life was like under Stalin's oppressive regime. And in popular music courses, we help students understand the violent imagery in N.W.A's infamous song "Fuck Tha Police" by characterizing it as a response to the war on drugs and the Los Angeles Police Department's heavy-handed policing of Black communities.

Although contextual cues can aid students in interpreting music and thinking about it historically, our team-taught class sought to do more than demonstrate how music reflects political conditions. Instead, we placed music at the center of our narrative as a world-making practice that engages the profound demographic, material, and ideological shifts of twentieth- and twenty-first-century California. Doing so meant considering some musical forms and practices that are not regularly found in music history courses, moving away from a sustained focus on canonical genres and artists. It also involved engaging scholarship produced outside of music disciplines, asking what musicologists could both learn and contribute to these conversations. By framing music as a mode of expression, a sedimentation of history, and a way of creatively envisioning possible worlds, the course allowed students to gain critical insights about how imagination and performance shape political realities in the Golden State.[6]

This chapter is organized around three interrelated themes that emerged from our course and came to serve as an organizing framework for the syllabus and its broader pedagogical commitments: (1) the culture of politics; (2) performance and play; and (3) identity as relational. In the first year that we offered the course, these themes were all present but implicit. Only through teaching together and being open to unanticipated convergences did they emerge as more explicit principles. Through acts of improvisation and accompaniment in the classroom, our discussions led us in new and generative directions. By sharing examples of listening assignments and other forms of creative engagement, we hope to inspire others to develop new approaches to teaching about music, politics, and race in both team-taught and more traditional individual-taught courses.

The Culture of Politics

The lights dim in a room of about 150 students, with eyes straining toward the screen. The video begins. As an ominous bassline thumps in the background, the narrator warns sternly: "They keep coming. Two million illegal immigrants in California. The federal government won't stop them at the border, yet requires us to pay billions to take care of them." We see grainy footage of figures dashing through traffic at a border crossing in San Diego, offered as indisputable proof of the lawlessness said to be overtaking the international border. The thirty-second ad concludes with an austere white male candidate, speaking directly to voters, promising to protect those "who work hard, pay taxes and obey the law." He declares sternly, "Enough is enough."[7]

This political ad was not the work of 2016 presidential contender Donald Trump, or any of the hundreds of candidates for federal, state, and local office who have run recently on a platform of immigration restriction. The piece was instead produced in 1994 by the campaign of California's incumbent Republican governor, Pete Wilson, who had historically held quite moderate positions on immigration but had fallen behind in his reelection bid. His poll numbers plummeting, Wilson tied his fortunes to the ascent of a statewide ballot measure, Proposition 187, that promised to deny a broad range of health, education, and social services to those who could not prove their lawful immigration status. The measure also required tens of thousands of nurses, social workers, schoolteachers, and other public employees to become de facto immigration officers, obligated to verify the immigration status of the individuals and families they serve and to report suspected violators to federal authorities. A large majority of California voters statewide cast ballots in favor of Proposition 187 (though courts would ultimately block its implementation), and Wilson won reelection handily.[8]

This ad might be shown in any number of undergraduate courses in political science, history, sociology, or ethnic studies related to racial politics, immigration policy, or social inequality. It helps to illustrate the recurring patterns of inclusion and exclusion that have long marked US nationalism in general and California political history in particular. Relying solely on the ad and a discussion of nativism, however, gives little agency to the people, communities, and social practices of those understood as the target of Proposition 187—recent immigrants and longstanding Californians alike—whose Mexican identity was constructed as a social problem.[9]

Following a lecture and discussion about the Proposition 187 campaign, the room quiets again. We hear the opening bars of a ranchera titled "Un Indio Quiere Llorar," the brass section shining over a waltzlike rhythm. Released in 1992 by the group Banda Machos, based in the Mexican state of Jalisco, the ballad tells a story of unrequited love between a solitary figure ("un indio") and an upper-class woman in the city. The lyrics, shown on the screen in Spanish and translated into English, describe his pain and loneliness, culminating in the cry "ese indio yo soy" (this Indian is me), marking his rejection as one that is both individual and social, shared by the singer and audience alike.

The class turns to a discussion of the banda and norteño craze that swept across the radio stations and dance halls of California in the early 1990s, making artists like Banda Machos and Los Tigres Del Norte household names in Spanish-speaking communities. After a review of some of the central themes, rhythms, and instrumentation of the music and its emergence across the US-Mexico border, we take up George Lipsitz's chapter "Banda: The Hidden History of Greater Mexico."[10] Lipsitz documents the extraordinary commercial success of banda on radio stations like La Equis (KLAX 97.9), which became the number one station in Los Angeles in the early 1990s by attracting more than a million listeners at any given time.[11] Lipsitz emphasizes the central role that banda, and the many dozens of quebredita dance clubs that spread throughout Southern California in the 1990s, played in response to the intense social dislocation brought about by neoliberal trade policies. As economic forces pushed Mexican farmers from rural communities into low-wage industrial jobs and set off waves of migration toward the United States, regional genres like banda and norteño became a "songbook of migrancy."[12]

Banda and quebredita clubs fostered emergent identities that rejected the stigmatization and subordination undergirding the Proposition 187 campaign. Some songs, such as Los Tigres del Norte's "Jaula de Oro" ("The Golden Cage") addressed explicitly political themes, including the conditions of vulnerability and fear marking life for unauthorized immigrants, thus building on a long history of corridos documenting the plight of migrant workers in the United States.[13] Many others had no explicit political references. Yet the communal relations forged in the dance halls and on the radio were very much political, challenging long-standing hierarchies of citizenship and cultural value. Indeed, in October 1994, at the height of the Proposition 187 campaign, an estimated seventy thousand people marched from East Los Angeles to the downtown area to protest the initiative and Governor Wilson in one of the largest demonstrations in the city's history.[14] The action, organized in just a few days, was promoted almost entirely through Spanish-language radio, community organizations, and print media, with the dance halls quite literally spilling into the streets.

Teaching about banda, norteño, and quebredita dancing apart from this historical and political context would be equally as limiting as addressing the political themes without attending to these cultural formations. Genre-based music courses might only make passing references to these racialized dimensions, emphasizing instead the more formal elements of rhythm, instrumentation, and regional signifiers. Yet by putting the Proposition 187 campaign ad into direct dialogue with popular music and dance, students generate new insights about how music and politics often help constitute one another by populating the social field with ideas, images, sounds, and feelings.

In addition, our unit on banda enabled us to make our own discoveries as teachers. Thinking about the music's role as a catalyst in political formation, for example, caused us to rethink the prioritization of stylistic innovation in music history courses. In traditional period or genre-based classes, lectures often hinge on exploring noteworthy developments in style and/or the traits that make critically acclaimed works seem exceptional. Doing so helps to give narrative shape to our courses, while tacitly propagating the notion that the most meaningful (i.e., political) music is *always* that which defies the status quo. Yet banda's success—and its contribution to political formation and resistance—depended precisely on its most commonplace features. Its danceability, its lyrical simplicity, and its broad commercial appeal were all qualities that enabled it to be accepted in countless everyday contexts. The music's story suggests that our bias toward "disruptive" artists might impede our ability to recognize the social and political importance of everyday sounds and practices.

The Politics of Performance and Play

On a Tuesday afternoon in early spring, dozens of students begin making their way into the classroom again and take their seats. Their conversations compete with a pounding bassline and synthesizer track emanating from the room's speakers: an excerpt from DJ Larry Levan spinning live at the Paradise Garage in lower Manhattan in 1979, selected to anticipate and cue the day's theme. A slide at the front of the room frames the planned lecture and discussion: "Can disco change the world?"

The title is meant to be provocative but not facetious. On the same slide, we see a snapshot taken in 1978 of Harvey Milk, seated and smiling, his head resting lightly against that of the singer and disco star Sylvester (figure 10.1). Milk had recently won a seat on the San Francisco Board of Supervisors, becoming the first openly gay elected official in California history. The same year, Sylvester's "You Make Me Feel (Mighty Real)" dominated disco clubs and radio charts in dozens of countries. And when Milk was assassinated just a few months later by Dan White, a fellow supervisor, it was Sylvester's sold-out performance at the San Francisco War Memorial Opera House (during which he was presented a key to the city by new mayor Dianne Feinstein) and his performance at the San Francisco Gay Freedom Parade in June 1979 that helped the city's gay community regain its bearings.

Figure 10.1. Sylvester with Harvey Milk at Milk's 1978 birthday party just months before his assassination. Photograph courtesy of Dan Cuny.

Although disco is commonly stereotyped as apolitical and shallow, the sense of freedom and pleasure that Sylvester helped to shape on the dance floor was central to the political formation of the Castro, the San Francisco neighborhood that both Milk and Sylvester called home and shared with thousands of other gay men and women for whom it represented a place of possibility, if not liberation.

Sylvester James was born in the Black working-class community of South Los Angeles in 1947 and grew up singing in a local Black church. As a teenager, he joined a crew of friends called the Discotays, a group of cross-dressing and gender-bending queens who performed at local parties (they called it "masquerading"). It was a time of intense state repression of queer life: police raided gay and lesbian bars and social spaces constantly. But as students learn from sociologist Joshua Gamson's brilliant book *The Fabulous Sylvester*, the spaces inhabited and formed by Sylvester and the Discotays became subversive and politically generative precisely because of their performativity.[15] Their gender-bending, sex-positive brand of opposition—to state authority and violence, to norms of sex and gender regulation—became key tactics in the struggle for freedom.

Sylvester would eventually leave Los Angeles in the early 1970s for the Haight-Ashbury District of San Francisco, arriving as the foment of the counterculture was at its height. Students watch clips of Sylvester and a drag performance troupe he joined called The Cockettes, described by one observer as a "hippie, glitter, genderfuck troop."[16] The performances are chaotic and sometimes nonsensical—animated in equal parts by patriarchal rebellion and hallucinogens. And yet as the social theorist Benjamin Shepard argues, "a spirit of liberatory play coursed through" the social movements of the 1970s with groups like The Cockettes, "infusing pleasure and fun into world-making practices supporting social and sexual freedom as well as cultural resistance." Shepard notes that "notions of play interact magnetically with efforts focused on emancipation, social protest, and pluralistic democracy."[17] Working with this framework, students began understanding the role of disco music and gay dance clubs as an articulation of a queer politics that, Shepard explains, "rejected the politics of prohibition in favor of the politics of pleasure, authenticity, and social connection."[18]

Sylvester rarely made overt political statements, but as Gamson explained in a guest lecture to our class, "Some of the most radical change in society comes from people who aren't even trying to make change."[19] These relations of solidarity and mutuality did not emerge because people were circulating petitions within dance clubs or making political speeches from the stage. Sylvester's world, the world of San Francisco's nightclubs, was one of fantasy. His attention to fashion and his musical commitment to singing in a high falsetto foregrounded the creation of new possibilities through what Shepard describes as "liberatory play"—a mode of improvising social identities and relations that resist hegemonic constructions of race, gender, and sexuality. Offered little room to be who he wanted to be in the world he inhabited, Sylvester helped his fans imagine a new and better world for themselves, allowing them to fashion new forms of agency and solidarity.

The case of Sylvester and disco asks us to think carefully about how artistic practices mobilize creativity and pleasure in ways that ultimately effect material change. Theorizing performance thus became a crucial component of the class. We emphasized different ways of understanding music and cultural production as critical sites from which to evaluate wide-ranging dynamics of power and social formation, highlighting the concept of liberatory play as a rubric for understanding music as a world-making practice with material consequences. For nonmusic scholars with experience teaching about social inequality but little practice teaching about music, this focus means taking what musicians do seriously *as music*, not simply as a reflection of sociopolitical realities.[20]

Although often dismissed as frivolous and ephemeral, music has the ability to offer a taste of another way of being that can have profound consequences for how people see themselves and how they expect to be treated. As semipublic/semiprivate spaces, gay discos provided a key liminal space in the struggle for gay rights. As performance theorist David Román explains, "Something was happening across America in the late 1970s that was drastically shifting life for lesbians and gays and it was palpable in dance clubs and in the music that filled these public spaces." "Dance," he explains, "signaled not the promise of gay liberation but its practice."[21] Similar to the case of banda, the identities and social networks forged in San Francisco's nightclubs eventually found their way into the streets. The feelings of acceptance and community fostered throughout the disco scene helped embolden gay men and women who turned out in droves for political rallies and gay freedom parades, which were themselves spectacular and creative displays of gender-bending nonconformity.[22] More than simply a response to political realities, our course challenged students to understand music and dance as political acts that can help chart new paths toward freedom.

Focusing on pleasure and performance also presented us with an opportunity to make connections to other musical genres and historical moments that might seem untenable in other courses. Our students' extensive engagement with Sylvester through the framework of liberatory play provided a foundation for the next unit of the class on West Coast gangsta rap. In a typical hip-hop history course, for example, one might approach the iconic Los Angeles–based group N.W.A chronologically, tracing their influences from Ice-T back to East Coast rappers like Schoolly D and KRS-One. Yet when we placed N.W.A in dialogue with Sylvester, our students' attention was drawn to a new set of questions and concerns related to gender performance that enriched our discussion and made it more intersectional than it might have been otherwise. We discussed gangsta rap in the context of the war on drugs and the dramatic expansion of the carceral state and its regulation of Black life, as might typically be the case in a hip-hop history course. But instead of viewing N.W.A as simply an angry response to these conditions, or as street reportage (to use a popular metaphor), students were prepared to discuss gangsta rap as a mode of performance. They could see how the group's members were participating in a form of self-fashioning, making creative decisions about how they presented themselves to the world, that was strikingly similar to what Sylvester had been doing in disco.

Figure 10.2. Album covers for World Class Wreckin' Cru, *Rapped in Romance* (1986) and N.W.A, *Straight Outta Compton* (1988)

For example, N.W.A cofounder Dr. Dre began his music career with an L.A. electro group called World Class Wreckin' Cru. Los Angeles's postdisco electro scene was a world of fantasy and sexual pleasure, and Dr. Dre rapped and worked the turntables wearing shiny sequined jackets and a stethoscope around his neck. Joining forces with N.W.A, however, meant leaving the flamboyant and more gender-expansive world of electro behind and moving toward a new intensified performance of Black masculinity associated with the sartorial style and roughneck imagery of Los Angeles street gangs (figure 10.2).[23]

Getting to gangsta rap through Dr. Dre's origins in dance club culture allowed students to appreciate how N.W.A's critique of the criminalization of Black youth and the LAPD's oppressive policing tactics depended on how the group manipulated tropes of race, gender, and

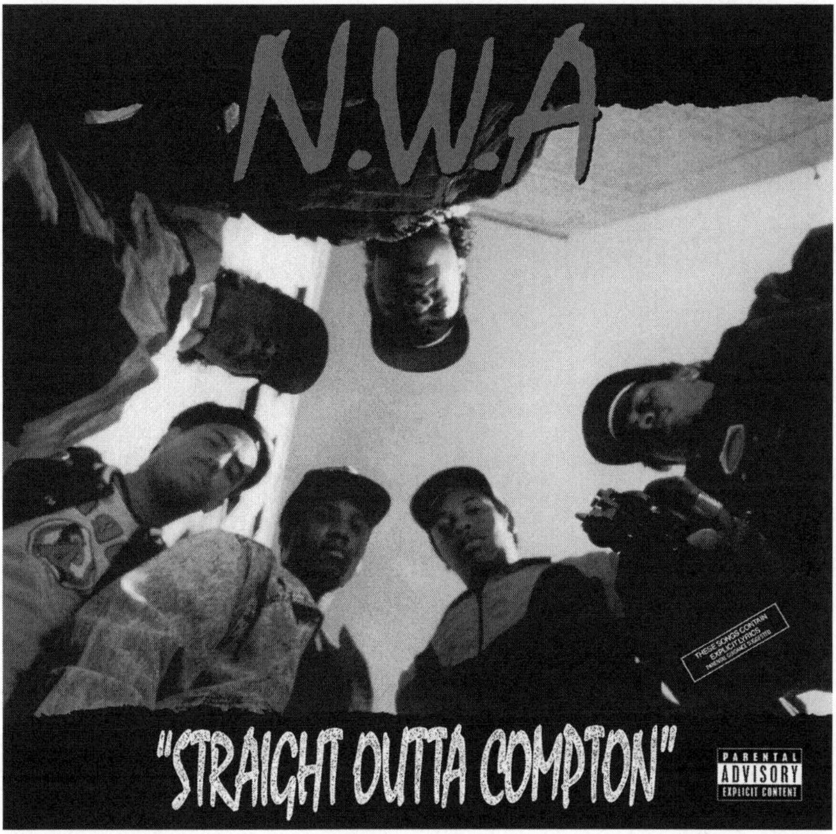

sexuality. Their most famous track, "Fuck Tha Police," includes lyrics that condemn police brutality using homophobic language: "I don't know if they're fags or what; search a nigga down and grabbing his nuts."[24] Following our unit on disco, this rhyme jumped out at our students, who had come to empathize and identify with Sylvester and his fans in a way that might not have been the case in a class focusing more strictly on hip-hop. We found that the main benefit of pairing Sylvester and N.W.A, however, was not simply that it allowed us to call attention to homophobia and masculine self-fashioning in hip-hop. Instead it was how our students came to recognize all of the things that N.W.A and Sylvester have in common.

Both Sylvester and the members of N.W.A grew up in South Los Angeles having to negotiate a segregated social world with limited opportunities for success. Both found ways to achieve stardom by crossing racial lines and appealing to broad audiences. And both did so by taking the things that stigmatized them—that should have held them back—and transforming them into precisely the things that allowed them to succeed. Sylvester was a cross-dressing Black man with a hit record in 1978. It is easy to imagine that he should not have been a star. By the same token, the members of N.W.A were young Black men coming from South Central Los Angeles and Compton in an era when those neighborhoods were feared and associated with drugs and gangs.

Rather than downplay those aspects of their identities, however, both Sylvester and N.W.A deployed them as strategic advantages. Sylvester and N.W.A succeed not in spite of the social forces aligned against them but because of the way they playfully manipulated those forces. The concept behind N.W.A's infamous song "Fuck Tha Police" is a mock trial. The song stages a courtroom scene that inverts the status quo by casting the LAPD as defendants on trial for police brutality with members of N.W.A serving as the judge, prosecuting attorney, and expert witnesses. Given the humor and creativity in this example, we asked students to discuss how N.W.A's music might count as a form of liberatory play. Our focus on this theme allowed us to think creatively across genres and historical contexts, theorizing together about the political work music can do.

Relational Formations of Race

A middle-aged Asian man sits at the grand piano, alone on the stage of Beall Concert Hall at the University of Oregon. As the audience, including about one hundred students from Music, Politics, and Race, leans forward in anticipation, he begins playing the "Butterfly Lover's Song," a Chinese folk melody that was popularized in the years following the Cultural Revolution.[25] His solo piano playing renders the song's melody in shimmering octaves that evoke the sound of the Chinese hammered dulcimer (yang-kin). The pentatonic melody, played with expressive rubato, gives the performance a plaintive character. After stating the melody once, the pianist begins improvising on it, embellishing its clear pentatonic lines with chromatic tones and scalar runs that strain against the song's original form. About two minutes into the performance, he abruptly changes the song's rhythmic and harmonic texture. The doubled-octave in the right hand gives way to a bluesy melody supported by rich dominant-seventh chords and a syncopated "in the pocket" groove. In an instant, the pianist sends the "Butterfly Lovers" into flight as a rousing gospel tune.

Figure 10.3. Jon Jang performing at Beall Concert Hall at the University of Oregon on January 20, 2015. Photograph by Loren Kajikawa.

The day before his performance for our students, San Francisco–based pianist and composer Jon Jang visited the class to talk about his life as a musician and political activist. Jang showed slides of 1960s jazz giants John Coltrane, Charles Mingus, and Archie Shepp and discussed the profound influence of Amiri Baraka (Leroi Jones) on his identity as a young Asian American. He spoke about his days as a union organizer in the San Francisco Bay Area during the early 1980s, and how he was inspired by the Black Arts movement, which led him to embrace music full time as his contribution to the era's radical politics. Turning to a discussion of Loren Kajikawa's chapter "The Sound of Struggle: Black Revolutionary Nationalism and Asian American Jazz," we asked students to consider the role of African American culture in the formation of Asian American identity, and how musicians like Jang, in collaboration with African American colleagues, produced a sound and a practice of multiracial solidarity.[26]

Jang's classroom visit and piano performance helped the students understand racial formation as fundamentally relational; racial meaning, identity, and power are coproduced and coconstitutive. Students used Jang's life and music to critique common understandings of race that celebrate difference as static and bounded, assumptions often implicit in frameworks of multiculturalism that imagine racial and ethnic groups as distinct entities, and which often portray Asian Americans and African Americans as diametrically opposed minority groups. Jang's music and guest lecture demonstrated instead the ways that Asian American political organizing and collective identification was produced in relationship to Black music and political struggle. Their musical movement grew out of their proximity to and engagement with African American culture, a process that the scholar activist Vijay Prashad describes as "polyculturalism."[27]

The notion that racial formation and identity is relational informed many class discussions. For example, in our unit on Los Angeles's Central Avenue and Boyle Heights neighborhoods, we showed a series of animated maps produced by the historian Phil Ethington that chart the city's changing racial demographics over time.[28] These maps reveal patterns of residential segregation that were enforced by racially restrictive covenants, redlining, white homeowner activism, and real estate agencies. Students examine copies of restrictive covenants and real estate flyers advertising "all white" communities to prospective home buyers.[29] Returning to the animated maps that begin in the 1940s and continue through the early 2000s, students directly see the effects of these exclusionary practices and how Black residents (coded blue) were confined to South Central Los Angeles and how Mexican American residents (coded red) were concentrated in East Los Angeles. As more immigrants from Mexico and Central America came to the United States in the 1970s and 1980s, however, parts of Los Angeles that were blue turned purple and then, eventually, red.

Understanding these patterns of discrimination and segregation is critical, particularly in a state that has long prided itself on being progressive, forward-thinking, and inclusive. At the same time, the maps representing these patterns of segregation, which show firm borders around the neighborhoods where Black and Brown Angelenos were permitted to rent and buy property, conceal as much as they reveal. Visually, the segregated neighborhoods of South Los Angeles and East Los Angeles are often read as places of desperation, failure, and social death, particularly for students who only know those places through popular media depictions. At best, they evoke a paternalistic sympathy; at worst a racialized fear of danger and violence.

But what happens if we redraw the maps to also foreground areas of musical and artistic production and political mobilization? If you listen to Lionel Hampton's hopping 1940 track "Central Avenue Breakdown," a tribute to the famed jazz district that was at the heart of Black Los Angeles, you get a much different perspective on the lifeworlds that flourished even during this period of exclusion. At the same time as racially restrictive housing covenants were taking hold of the region, Central Avenue was a thriving hub for African American artists performing for multiracial audiences. Hampton was part of a long tradition of innovative, diverse, and influential musicians rooted in Los Angeles's Black communities that have had a profound effect on the city's life and identity.

Similarly, we see that the city of Pacoima in the northwest San Fernando Valley—for decades the only city in the Valley where many Black and Brown people were permitted to buy or rent homes—was also home to the famed rock-and-roll musician Richie Valens. Valens's parents were Mexican, and he grew up in a multiracial urban space, listening to and playing mariachi music, flamenco guitar, R & B, and jump blues. Valens's most famous hit, "La Bamba," was a rock 'n' roll adaption of a folk song from Veracruz, Mexico's son jarocho tradition. We introduce the class to Valens's recording as an expression of the hidden history of multiracial Los Angeles and then return to the song in a more contemporary recording by the East L.A.-based Las Cafeteras titled "La Bamba Rebelde." In the video for the song, group members carry their instruments, including the tarima (a wooden platform for dancers) to different parts of the city. Instead of visiting established Los Angeles landmarks, such as Hollywood Boulevard or Venice Beach, they stage impromptu performances in cafés, backyard parties, parks, and even a freeway overpass. Moreover, the locations they choose—Boyle Heights, downtown, Chinatown, and the San Gabriel Valley—represent the predominantly Latinx and Asian American eastside of Los Angeles. Adding new lyrics to the song that proudly proclaims, "We don't believe in borders; we cross them," Las Cafeteras presents an inclusive view of community that unites "La Bamba's" multiracial past with the present moment.[30] To build on these themes, we assign excerpts from Gaye Theresa Johnson's *Spaces of Conflict, Sounds of Solidarity: Music, Race, and Spatial Entitlement in Los*

Angeles to help students deepen their understanding of how music has served as a site of resistance to exclusionary practices.[31]

We also play a 2009 music video by an artist named Don Cheto, who is not a real person but the fictional alter ego of Los Angeles radio personality Juan Carlos Razo. Portrayed by Razo as a loud-mouthed sixty-five-year-old man, Don Cheto hosts a radio and television show, and he even appears as a character in the *Grand Theft Auto* video game series. Through his entertaining on-air persona and musical parodies, he has become an icon for Spanish-speaking immigrant communities. The video for "La Crisis," released in the aftermath of the 2008 financial crash, blends the sounds of banda music with hip-hop, and Don Cheto raps in Spanish about being out of work. His rhymed lyrics cast a humorous light on his predicament, explaining unabashedly that he'll do whatever he can to survive, making a meal out of samples at the supermarket or stealing packets of sugar, plastic utensils, and even toilet paper from McDonald's.

Students immediately grasp how Don Cheto establishes a connection to working class communities by offering a humorous take on their shared struggles. But by thinking about this music video in the context of the city's changing demographics and history of racial segregation, they begin to understand how these musicians and musical forms are interconnected historically through what George Lipsitz calls popular music's "long fetch."[32] In fact, Don Cheto is speaking to audiences in South Los Angeles neighborhoods where Black and Brown communities have intersected for decades. The forces of racial segregation that shaped Los Angeles throughout the twentieth century brought Spanish-speaking immigrants into predominantly African American neighborhoods, providing a larger context for understanding Don Cheto's musical blend of banda and rap. A final example that we share after discussing Don Cheto is Ryan Lowery, an African American singer from Compton who goes by the stage name El Compa Negro (The Black Friend). Growing up immersed in the music and culture of Latino immigrants, Lowery learned to speak Spanish and sing with a banda group, forging his own vision of hybridity and polyculturalism.

These examples help emphasize that structures of segregation and subordination are continually subjected to challenge and reimagination, that—as the common saying goes—it's not where you're from, but where you're at. Thinking about musical and cultural hybridity as the "growing together" of cultural practices that emerge from the intersection of various communities and their shared material realities provides an important corrective to views of race and culture as static and separate.[33]

Appreciating the dynamic nature of popular culture as a site of resistance, survival, and celebration helps emphasize that these segregated areas on the map are not just zones of failure and oppression, but places from which important new technologies emerge for living in an increasingly globalized world.

The Challenge and Promise of Cross-Disciplinary Teaching

This three-year venture at the University of Oregon was one of the most rewarding and intellectually stimulating experiences of our respective careers. Yet team teaching is often discouraged by deans and department heads who too often equate academic labor with generating student credit hours, known colloquially as "butts in seats." Existing budget models, which distribute tuition dollars to academic units based on the number of students they serve, lead administrators to view team teaching as an inefficient use of faculty resources. Having two instructors devoted to a shared class can seem wasteful, even if planning and executing team-taught courses leads to new insights and experiences for students that would be unavailable in already established classes.

To anticipate and overcome potential objections, we used two main strategies. First, we developed Music, Politics, and Race as part of a larger campus initiative geared toward curricular innovation. Our team-teaching proposal was approved in part because it was tied to a campus-wide initiative to rethink what general education courses could look like. Second, and perhaps more importantly, we crafted a memorandum of understanding (MOU) between the School of Music and Dance and the Ethnic Studies Department that split the student credit hours for the course evenly regardless of whether students enrolled in our course through the MUS (music) or ES (ethnic studies) prefix. This ensured that all revenues generated from the course would be shared equally, and we were able to assure our supervisors that there would be no loss of revenue to participating departments. In fact, by combining forces it is possible that we actually enrolled more students than we might have otherwise.

The true benefits of team teaching, however, extended beyond the classroom space that we were fortunate enough to share. Team teaching fostered moments of reflection and collaboration both during and after classroom lectures that led to new insights and prompted further action. In solo-taught courses, we often find ourselves preoccupied with thinking about the next thing to say: the next fact to share, the next question to ask. The team-teaching environment provided more opportunities for us to listen, to reflect, and to be open to new perspectives. These changes were noticed by our teaching assistants and students, and our experiences in Music, Politics, and Race led to additional collaborations outside of the classroom. Through a series of public events, including music concerts, lectures, and teach-ins, we helped to foster new forms of solidarity between the School of Music and Dance and the Department of Ethnic Studies.

Live performances and class appearances by guest artists were highlights of each course and reinforced the key theme of music and politics as coproductive and codependent. During the winter of 2016, we organized a series of events featuring Martha González and Quetzal Flores, the lead singer and founder, respectively, of the Grammy Award-winning Los Angeles–based band Quetzal. González and Flores visited our class, a class in the Dance Department, and conducted a songwriting workshop for first-year students of color (figure 10.4). Drawing on a range of musical practices and experiences, from community fandango performances to collective songwriting workshops to collaborations with son jarocho musicians based in Veracruz, Mexico, they demonstrated the synergy between music and politics. They showed, for example, the ways that the tarima, the portable wooden platform around which fandango events are centered, enacts a "reciprocity between community and art."[34] Students also attended a large Quetzal concert, featuring all five members of the group, that was also well attended by faculty, staff, and members of the general public.

Although opportunities such as these can be time-consuming and costly to organize, our team-taught course provided an anchor for funding requests and ensured a built-in audience for each event. We began planning and fundraising nearly a year in advance of such visits, and we relied on many diverse sources for revenue, including the School of Music and Dance's "World Music Concert Series" organized by our ethnomusicology colleague Ed Wolf, as well as the Office of Student Affairs, which at the time was looking for programming to support and enhance the experience of students of color. These class visits and performances—which in other years included jazz bassist Tatsu Aoki performing together with dancer and choreographer Lenora Lee as well as pianist Jon Jang, whose visit was discussed previously—continually emphasized course practices, concepts, and articulations.

The course also benefited from guest lectures by faculty in Ethnic Studies, as well as other interdisciplinary scholars who have centered

Figure 10.4. Members of the group Quetzal meet with dance students at the University of Oregon on February 25, 2016. Photograph by Loren Kajikawa.

music in their scholarship on political and racial formations. The team-taught course provided a platform to bring speakers to our class who might otherwise not be invited to a music-speakers' series. These guests included folklorist Lisa Gilman discussing her research on the listening habits of US servicemen deployed in Iraq and Afghanistan; political science professor Joseph Lowndes discussing the relationship between country music, populism, and the "southern strategy"; women's and gender studies faculty Shoniqua Roach analyzing 1990s R & B artists Erykah Badu and Destiny's Child to explain the policing of Black women's sexuality in the context of welfare reform; ethnic studies scholar Paula Ioanide drawing from her 2015 monograph *The Emotional Politics of Racism* to show how the group La Santa Cecilia uses music videos and social media to counter anti-immigrant sentiment; and writer and activist Jeff Chang and professor of Black studies James Braxton Peterson sharing the stage to discuss the role of music in the Ferguson uprising and the broader Black Lives Matter movement.[35]

We used the model of thinking and teaching about music and politics as coconstitutive in a series of successful campus teach-ins organized in the aftermath of the 2016 presidential election of Donald Trump.

Afterward, a number of instances of racist intimidation and threats were reported on the University of Oregon campus. The Ethnic Studies Department, in collaboration with Kajikawa and the School of Music and Dance, organized five campus-wide teach-ins in order to provide political and historical context as well as a space for shared inquiry and engagement to students, faculty, and staff. Each teach-in began with a musical performance, and the audience was asked to consider the connections between the music and the subject being discussed. For example, before Professor Ibram X Kendi led a teach-in on the history of the Black student movement that took root at hundreds of college campuses in the 1960s and 1970s, an ensemble comprising students from the jazz studies program performed a rendition of Art Blakey and the Jazz Messengers' "Moanin'" and invited the audience to contemplate the central role that musicians and other artists played in the Black freedom struggle. Another teach-in on the histories of progressive organizing in rural areas in Oregon featured a folk music performance by the Low Tide Drifters, a local duo specializing in labor-related anthems and protest songs, which foregrounded the legacies of antiracist social movements in areas often characterized as "Trump Country." The teach-ins collectively demonstrated the ways that the pedagogies of music, politics, and race developed in the classroom could resonate in other spaces and prompt political engagement.

Music scholars can sometimes feel like interlopers when venturing into political waters. Disciplinary norms in political science and music, respectively, often encourage us to think of music and politics as two separate worlds. Policy debate, party affiliations, and polling data can appear to have little to do with the artistic forms and practices of musicians. Yet as our course attempted to make clear, contemporary politics, including debates about immigration, LGBTQ rights, and economic inequality, rely on cultural production to shape and mobilize public thoughts and feelings. In the music classroom of the twenty-first century, we have an opportunity to help students develop an enhanced understanding of music's role in these processes, recognizing musicking as a social force and appreciating the role of performance in struggles for freedom. Doing so might help imbue the specialized knowledge produced in music programs with new direction and resonance while simultaneously challenging conventional frameworks in the study of politics that marginalize music and other forms of cultural production from the realm of meaningful focus and theorization.

Notes

1. Epigraph: Barbara Tomlinson and George Lipsitz, *Insubordinate Spaces: Improvisation and Accompaniment for Social Justice* (Philadelphia: Temple University Press, 2019), 30.

2. Tomlinson and Lipsitz, *Insubordinate Spaces,* 189.

3. George Lipsitz, *Dangerous Crossroads* (New York: Verso, 1994), 137.

4. William Cheng, *Just Vibrations: The Purpose of Sounding Good* (Ann Arbor: University of Michigan Press, 2016).

5. We first conceived the course as part of a University of Oregon–sponsored effort to rethink general education requirements. The College of Arts and Sciences (CAS) had called for faculty members to propose clusters of group-satisfying courses from different departments centered around particular themes. With the support of colleagues in Political Science, Sociology, Ethnic Studies, and Women and Gender Studies, Daniel HoSang drafted a proposal for a cluster of courses focusing on social inequality. As an initiative sponsored by CAS, however, the competition was not open to faculty from the School of Music and Dance (SOMD). Fortunately, Loren Kajikawa's status as a participating member of the Ethnic Studies Department, and his record of cross-listing his music history courses with Ethnic Studies, enabled him to participate as a member of the cluster. He was the only SOMD faculty member to participate in the GE initiative.

6. We are indebted to Alejandra Cebreros, Sam Golter, and Sarah Ray Rondot, who served as teaching assistants and provided valuable real-time feedback on the course. We are especially grateful to Sam Golter, a graduate student in music at the time, who served the course for three consecutive years and helped us to reflect on the course's contributions, especially with respect to its difference from more traditional music offerings.

7. "Pete Wilson 1994 campaign ad on illegal immigration." Available at https://www.youtube.com/watch?v=lLIzzs2HHgY

8. See Daniel Martinez HoSang, "'They Keep Coming!' The Tangled Roots of Proposition 187," chap. 6 in *Racial Propositions: Ballot Initiatives and the Making of Postwar California* (Berkeley: University of California Press, 2010).

9. Leo R. Chavez, *The Latino Threat: Constructing Immigrants, Citizens, and the Nation* (Stanford, CA: Stanford University Press, 2013).

10. George Lipsitz, *Footsteps in the Dark: The Hidden Histories of Popular Music* (Minneapolis: University of Minnesota Press, 2007).

11. Lipsitz, *Footsteps in the Dark,* 55–56.

12. Gustavo Lopez Castro, as quoted in Josh Kun, "California Sueños," *Boom: A Journal of California* 1, no.1 (Spring 2011): 63.

13. As early as 1929, Los Hermanos Bañuelos recorded "El Lavaplatos" ("The Dishwasher"), a corrido recounting the indignities suffered by a Mexican migrant worker in Los Angeles. Kun, "California Sueños," 63.

14. Patrick J. McDonnell and Robert J. Lopez, "L.A. March against Prop. 187 Draws 70,000: Immigration Protesters Condemn Wilson for Backing Initiative That They Say Promotes 'Racism, Scapegoating,'" *Los Angeles Times,* October 17, 1994, https://www.latimes.com/archives/la-xpm-1994-10-17-mn-51339-story.html

15. Joshua Gamson, *The Fabulous Sylvester: The Legend, the Music, the Seventies in San Francisco* (New York: Picador, 2005).

16. Benjamin Shepard, "Play and World Making: From Gay Liberation to DIY Community Building," in *The Hidden 1970s: Histories of Radicalism*, ed. Dan Berger (New Brunswick, NJ: Rutgers University Press, 2010), 179.

17. Shepard, "Play and World Making," 177–78.

18. Shepard, "Play and World Making," 178.

19. Joshua Gamson, guest lecture in Music, Politics, and Race, University of Oregon, May 15, 2017.

20. Interdisciplinary scholars of music and politics, such as Robin D. G. Kelley and Tricia Rose, have long cautioned against treating Black music, hip-hop in particular, as a mere reflection of sociological realities. Getting students to understand hip-hop as music is vital in an era when rap lyrics are being introduced as evidence in criminal prosecutions and when rap continues to be used to scapegoat Black youth for their disproportionate share of poverty and incarceration. See Erik Nielson and Charis E. Kubri, "Rap Lyrics on Trial," *New York Times*, January 13, 2014, https://www.nytimes.com/2014/01/14/opinion/rap-lyrics-on-trial.html; William Cheng, "Black Noise, White Ears: Resilience, Rap, and the Killing of Jordan Davis," *Current Musicology* 102 (Spring 2018): 115–89.

21. David Román, "Dance Liberation," *Theatre Journal* 55, no. 3, Dance (October 2003): 381.

22. We are grateful to musicologist Louis Niebur for sharing his research on the musical politics of gay communities in the 1980s, especially the "San Francisco Sound" of independent labels, including Moby Dick Records and Megatone Records.

23. After Dr. Dre terminated his relationship with N.W.A, his former bandmate Eazy-E verbally attacked his past with the World Class Wreckin' Cru. Eazy-E called him out for wearing mascara and eyeliner and even featured an old publicity photo of Dre from his Wreckin' Cru days on one of his album covers as a way of questioning Dre's masculinity and authenticity as a rapper. Eazy-E, *It's On (Dr. Dre) 187um Killa*, Ruthless Records 88561-5503-2, 1993.

24. N.W.A, "Fuck Tha Police," *Straight Outta Compton*, Ruthless Records SL 57102, 1988.

25. *The Butterfly Lovers' Violin Concerto* was written in 1959 by two Chinese composers, He Zhanhao (何占豪, b. 1933) and Chen Gang (陈钢, b. 1935). Recordings of Jon Jang's jazz interpretation can be found on multiple albums, including *Self Defense!*, Soul Note 121203-2, 1992; *Tienanmen!*, Soul Note 121223-2, 1993; and *Two Flowers on a Stem*, Soul Note 121253-2, 1996.

26. Loren Kajikawa, "The Sound of Struggle: Black Revolutionary Nationalism and Asian American Jazz," in *Jazz / Not Jazz: The Music and Its Boundaries*, ed. David Ake, Charles Hiroshi Garrett, and Daniel Goldmark (Berkeley: University of California Press, 2012), 190–216.

27. Vijay Prashad, *Everybody Was Kung Fu Fighting: Afro-Asian Connections and the Myth of Cultural Purity* (Boston: Beacon Press, 2001).

28. Phillip Ethington, "Segregated Diversity: Race-Ethnicity, Space, and Political Fragmentation in Los Angeles County, 1940–1994 (2000)," Final Report submitted to the John Randolph Haynes and Dora Haynes Foundation.

29. For examples of these primary documents see Ryan Reft, "How Prop 14

Shaped California's Racial Covenants," *KCET City Rising*, September 20, 2017, https://www.kcet.org/shows/city-rising/how-prop-14-shaped-californias-racial-covenants; and HoSang, *Racial Propositions*, 2010.

30. Las Cafeteras, "La Bamba Rebelde," https://www.youtube.com/watch?v=9xv-FjbXaqk

31. Gaye Theresa Johnson, *Spaces of Conflict, Sounds of Solidarity: Music, Race, and Spatial Entitlement in Los Angeles* (Berkeley: University of California Press, 2013).

32. Lipsitz, *Footsteps in the Dark*, vii–viii.

33. Lisa Lowe, "Heterogeneity, Hybridity, Multiplicity: Asian American Differences," chap. 3 in *Immigrant Acts: On Asian American Cultural Politics* (Durham, NC: Duke University Press, 1996).

34. Quetzal Flores, as quoted in Rob Rosenthal and Richard Flacks, *Playing for Change: Music and Musicians in the Service of Social Movements* (New York: Routledge, 2010), 243.

35. See Lisa Gilman, *My Music, My War: The Listening Practices of U.S. Troops in Iraq and Afghanistan* (Middletown, CT: Wesleyan University Press, 2016); Joseph Lowndes, *From the New Deal to the New Right: Race and the Southern Origins of Modern Conservatism* (New Haven: Yale University Press, 2009); Shoniqua Roach, "Black Respectable Currency: Reading Black Feminism and Sexuality in Contemporary Performance," *Journal of American Culture* 42, no. 1 (March 2019): 10–20; Paula Ioanide, *The Emotional Politics of Racism: How Feelings Trump Facts in an Era of Colorblindness* (Palo Alto, CA: Stanford University Press, 2015); Jeff Chang, *Who We Be: The Colorization of America* (New York: Macmillan, 2014); and James Braxton Peterson, *The Hip Hop Underground and African American Culture: Beneath the Surface* (New York: Macmillan, 2014).

ELEVEN | Finding Success inside and outside the Academy

MICHAEL SY UY AND NAOMI ANDRÉ

The demands and needs of universities have changed substantially over the past century, as have those of musicologists. The 2008 global financial crisis was another wake-up call, after decades of stagnation and decline in the humanities, reminding the musicological field that it still faces a jobs dilemma, with the number of available tenure-track jobs paling in comparison to the number of qualified applicants. The 2008 crisis was not simplistically a turn from "good times" to "bad times"—the state of the humanities has always been at risk and to varying levels—but the musicological field confronted yet another set of realities as a result of the economic downturn, including a widening "gig economy" of contingent labor. Thus, highly educated academic job seekers increasingly faced the prospect of delaying graduation or finding postdoctoral fellowships and/or adjunct teaching. With the recent experience of COVID-19, beginning in early 2020, additional reshaping of the financial and career landscapes is, to say the least, happening once again.

Many other employment opportunities exist outside of academia, however, and a shift in the production of certain kinds of knowledge and the development of particular marketable skills during doctoral training is becoming a critical need. Those seeking jobs in the "real world" are translating their expertise and talents while at the same time, the "ivory tower" is asking its inhabitants to open up their research to wider audiences. Working as a musicologist in the institutional environment of early twenty-first-century America therefore requires new ways of thinking about one's work and career.

In this chapter, we aim to bring together intertwining threads about the current and evolving job markets for PhDs in musicology, which have usually been kept separate: quantitative data, traditional perspectives vis-à-vis new directions within a discipline, and personal stories. We take a capacious view of the discipline of musicology as embracing both historical musicology and ethnomusicology, and encompassing research degrees that incorporate written publications as well as newer directions in musical scholarship.[1] We integrate numerical data that outlines trends in the broader humanities, and specifically, academic opportunities in music scholarship; we connect this statistical analysis with information about placement inside and outside of academia, as well as examining measures of professional and personal satisfaction for both groups; and we incorporate our personal experiences to offer two voices behind these numbers, which help to contextualize the details and qualitative trends that shape the data.

This chapter—like many in this book—draws on a collaboration between two musicologists and friends. It was originally conceived by Michael at the workshop organized by Carol Oja and Charles Hiroshi Garrett at the Radcliffe Institute in spring 2017, but quickly became a labor of love for two people who first met as professional colleagues at an American Musicological Society (AMS) conference in San Francisco in 2011. Throughout our writing process, we exchanged drafts and sections via e-mail and Google Docs, and we met and discussed our work at meetings of the AMS and the Society for American Music (SAM) from 2017 to 2020. This collaboration has been immensely rewarding—a thought-provoking and honest dialogue about our identities, our experiences, and our thoughts about the state of our field. It is a dialogue that has been influenced by many other colleagues—especially those of color—and we hope that the discussion continues.

The State of the Job Market

We begin our story by recounting the challenges those completing graduate studies in the humanities have faced over multiple decades, providing an essential context for the job market in musicology today. The precarious state of the larger humanities job market is hardly a surprise for anyone who has been in the academy recently, or in fact, since the mid-twentieth century. The situation is doubly compounded by the problems of attrition during graduate studies as well as the poor placement of those who do finish. It is not an exaggeration to say that, for many years now, an extraordinary number of extremely talented graduate students across the humanities have completed the PhD but left academia after failing to secure a university or college position. And they have often done so without having a strong idea about what comes next.

In response to this landscape, and with aspirations to decrease graduate student attrition and lower the amount of time for a student to complete a doctoral degree, the Andrew W. Mellon Foundation initiated two significant studies, the Graduate Education Initiative (GEI) and the Graduate Education Survey (GES), which gathered important benchmarking data. The GEI (1991–2000) collected and analyzed data from fifty-four departments and programs at ten universities; it included thirty thousand students and cost over $85 million.[2] Its goal was "to achieve systematic improvements in the structure and organization of PhD programs in the humanities [including musicology] and related social sciences."[3] Additionally, the Mellon Foundation implemented the GES to "obtain the views of all doctoral students who began their study in the departments participating in the GEI and in control departments between 1982 and 1997," with a high response rate of 74 percent.[4]

The authors of the study observed that there had been "three large-scale developments affecting graduate education in the humanities" during and since the GEI, which were "(1) the deteriorating job market, (2) the intensification of competition among graduate departments for students deemed most promising, and (3) changes in financial-aid regimes."[5] Debates among faculty members in each department centered on "the place of theory in graduate education, on what the humanities were for, what students should know, what skills they should command, and whether 'the canon' should survive and if so, how it should be constituted."[6]

The study found that the number one reason for leaving a humanities PhD program was a change in career goal (56 percent), while the next most common reasons were being dissatisfied with the department (52 percent pre-, 45 percent postcandidacy), and health or family issues (41 percent pre-, 44 percent postcandidacy). A major occupational employment category for humanities "leavers" was "administration, executives, and managers" (17.1 percent, as of the survey date), with a third of those gaining employment in higher-education administration. Others who left became artists, writers, public-relations specialists, and broadcasters (13.5 percent as of the survey date).[7] Therefore, the authors concluded that "the vast majority [of leavers were] not trapped in menial, low-level jobs and that they in fact received a payoff from their investment in doctoral education."[8]

One of the most important conclusions determined by the Mellon studies concerned their data on tenure-track jobs in the pre-2008 market. Even before the financial crisis, the situation was not optimistic. The foundation found that only 30.2 percent of graduating humanities PhDs in the 1998–2000 cohort were employed in tenure-track positions at four-year colleges and universities six months after graduation. The rate did increase three years after graduation, with just slightly more than half, or 52 percent, of the cohort employed in a tenure-track position. On the one hand, the higher rate indicates that there was mobility between non-tenure-track positions (57.8 percent of the cohort after the first six months) to tenure-track ones and that more than half of PhDs from elite schools eventually landed a position.[9] On the other hand, three years is a long time to be working in the contingent labor market (often with very low pay and minimal—if any—benefits). Furthermore, there were still large numbers of PhDs (that is, the other 48 percent) who did not move into tenure-track jobs.

It is finally worth reemphasizing that while these sobering statistics summarized Mellon's analysis of the top humanities programs in the country, they were not representative of the entire field of the humanities. These elite programs conferred only 15 percent of all humanities PhDs. As Robert Townsend corroborates separately in his study of the discipline of history, there is a high relative proportion of full-time faculty teaching at liberal arts colleges and universities who obtained PhDs from the top graduate programs.[10] Roughly three out of five history faculty at *U.S. News and World Report* top 25 schools received their PhDs from the top 10 programs. As a proportion of PhDs, however, top 10 programs only conferred 28 percent of degrees in the discipline of history. Thus, the outlook for those PhDs who did not graduate from a top 10 school is perhaps twice as difficult. The current situation is no better in the field of musicology.

The State of Musicology: Completing the PhD

The two Mellon-funded GEI and GES studies confirmed the slow rate of employment into tenure-track positions for humanities doctorates overall before 2008. The particular case for musicology PhDs pre-2008 and into the next decade emerges from an analysis of a larger consortium of foundation work included in Humanities Indicators, a project of the American Academy of Arts and Sciences, in tandem with data from the NORC Survey of Earned Doctorates (SED).[11] Analysis of employment data before and after the 2008 financial crisis is crucial to understanding the crisis's impacts as well as the current state of the higher education field. Humanities Indicators uses US Department of Education (previously Office of Education) records on postsecondary degree completions to provide "comprehensive trend data" and "statistical information on the condition of the humanities."[12] An additional source of data comes from the NORC SED, a federal agency survey conducted by the National Science Foundation and five other agencies.[13]

According to Humanities Indicators, doctoral degree completions in the humanities in all graduate programs across the country have experienced a steady rise over the past three decades, from 3,206 PhDs in 1987 to 5,891 PhDs in 2015. Humanities doctorates under the category "Study of the Arts" (which includes musicology PhDs) have also more than doubled, from 192 in 1987 to 454 in 2015. As a percentage of all advanced doctoral degrees conferred, however, the humanities have fallen, from 9.4 percent in 1987, to a high of 11.1 percent in 2000, a low of 7.9 percent in 2007, and 8.7 percent in 2015.

In 2013, musicology was included in the Humanities Departmental Survey, which polled approximately fourteen hundred four-year college and university humanities departments in the United States.[14] With these results we can examine the state of doctoral studies in our own field. According to the data, in fall 2012, there were roughly 1,200 graduate students in musicology at primarily research universities (a Carnegie classification), with eighty departments averaging 15.6 graduate students each. Of those 1,200 graduate students, 1,065 were at research universities where the highest degree offered was a doctorate (fifty-two departments, averaging 20.5 graduate students each).[15] The same year, there were only seventy new hires for "tenured, tenure-track, or permanent faculty positions" (relative to roughly 650 full-time faculty members in the field).[16] If we assume that an average length of study for a doctoral degree is seven years, then of the 1,065, there are roughly 150 new musicology PhDs graduating each year from primarily research universities, which means that more than half of those, or 80 of 150, would be unable to land a tenured, tenure-track, or permanent faculty position. The percentage is even bleaker when you take into consideration that new PhDs would likely not be in a position to apply for a senior "tenured" faculty position, thus diminishing the available spots even further.

The most recent source of information comes from the NORC SED. Its data from the aggregate years 2013 to 2016 is especially useful because unlike the Humanities Departmental Survey, it shows PhDs in musicology and ethnomusicology (grouped together) and music theory

Table 11.1. NORC Survey of Earned Doctorates (SED) in Music, 2013–16

	American Indian	Asian	Black and African American	Hispanic and Latino	White	Other or unknown	Total known race
Musicology/ ethnomusicology	1 (0.2%)	23 (5.4%)	18 (4.2%)	25 (5.9%)	357 (84.2%)	6 (1.4%)	424
Music theory and composition	1 (0.3%)	9 (3.0%)	5 (1.7%)	18 (6.0%)	268 (89%)	3 (1.0%)	301
Total	2 (0.3%)	32 (4.4%)	23 (3.2%)	43 (5.9%)	625 (86.2%)	9 (1.2%)	725

Table 11.2. NORC Survey of Earned Doctorates (SED) in Music, 2016

	American Indian	Asian	Black and African American	Hispanic and Latino	White	Other or unknown	Total known race
Musicology/ ethnomusicology	0 (0%)	8 (7.2%)	7 (6.3%)	5 (4.5%)	85 (76.6%)	6 (5.4%)	111
Music theory and composition	0 (0%)	2 (2.7%)	1 (1.3%)	4 (5.3%)	62 (82.7%)	6 (8%)	75
Total	0 (0%)	10 (5.4%)	8 (4.3%)	9 (4.8%)	147 (79%)	12 (6.4%)	186

and composition (also grouped together).[17] For further reference, we include the data for the specific year 2016.

Not only does the NORC SED data confirm that roughly 150 musicology PhDs are graduating every year (the difficulty is distinguishing musicology, ethnomusicology, music theory, and composition), but it also provides a breakdown by racial category in the field of musicology that the Humanities Indicators does not include. Despite marginal interyear differences, it is clear from these numbers that American Indian, Asian, Black/African American, and Latinx students are largely underrepresented among graduating music PhDs, relative to US census data from 2010.[18] In this regard, the underrepresentation of minority graduate students in musicology parallels trends more broadly in the humanities, and those tendencies have not changed substantially over the past two and a half decades.

Experiences of Minority Graduate Students in the Humanities

The percentage of humanities doctoral degrees awarded to members of traditionally underrepresented racial/ethnic groups has generally remained under 10 percent for the past twenty-five years.[19] The US Department of Education's definition of "underrepresented racial/ ethnic groups" includes African Americans (non-Hispanic), Hispanics, and American Indians/Alaskan Natives. While the US Department of Education's definition does not include Asians or Pacific Islanders, other data sources, such as the GEI, GES, and Humanities Indicators, do so. In this chapter, we consider Asians and Pacific Islanders as people of color and, thus, historically marginalized racial groups in our field. We also use the terms "minority" and "underrepresented" to refer to all of these groups in aggregate, acknowledging that, historically, there have been different names and categories applied to each of these groups. In 1995, when data was first collected, 6.1 percent of humanities PhDs were conferred to traditionally underrepresented racial/ethnic groups; in 2015, the figure was at 10.5 percent.[20]

In addition to underrepresentation as humanities graduate students, racial minorities also face greater challenges during their PhD careers. One concrete example of this difference is a lower completion rate. The Mellon Foundation's GEI and GES demonstrated that minority US citizens studying humanities PhDs "are more likely to have left [their program] and less likely to have graduated than their white U.S.-citizen counterparts."[21] Not only race, but intersectional identities also have an

Table 11.3. Racial/Ethnic Distribution of 2015 Doctoral Degree Recipients in the Humanities

	Doctoral Degree Recipients in Humanities	Percentage of Total
African American, non-Hispanic	208	3.5
American Indian or Alaska Native	27	0.46
Asian or Pacific Islander	230	3.9
Hispanic	385	6.5
White, non-Hispanic	3,528	59.9
Other/unknown race and ethnicities	574	9.7
Temporary resident	939	15.9
Total	5,891	100

Note: Data for this table derives from Humanities Indicators. According to US census data from 2010, the following percentages are those for the listed categories: Black or African American (12.6%), American Indian and Alaska Native (0.9%), Asian, Native Hawaiian, and Other Pacific Islander (5%), White non-Hispanic-identifying (56%), Hispanic (16.3%), Other races (9.1%). In order to compare these percentages with those in Table 1, the number of "Temporary Residents" should be factored out. Since we do not know the racial composition of temporary residents, then we unfortunately cannot precisely redistribute the 939 doctoral recipients into the racial categories. https://factfinder.census.gov/faces/tableservices/jsf/pages/productview.xhtml?pid=DEC_10_DP_DPDP1&src=pt

impact on these graduate students' experiences, including citizenship, socioeconomic background, religion, and gender identity.

In terms of academic job placement for graduate students of color, we note that there are some *positive effects* of being an underrepresented minority US citizen, with the probability of obtaining a tenure-track position at six months (20.8 percent more likely to be employed) and three years (20.1 percent more likely to be employed). This difference reflects efforts to diversify faculty by hiring PhDs of color.[22] Nevertheless, the improved effects of being a US-citizen minority *disappeared* when it came to securing tenure.[23] Instead, the only statistically significant segment of the population that did better in attaining tenure was married men with children, who were 10.3 percent more likely to achieve that goal.[24] Thus, the data demonstrates that US-citizen minorities might be more likely to get a junior faculty position but no more likely to get tenure. A foot in the door—or really, a toe in the door—did not translate to a seat at the table.

Another compounding factor must be added to the equation: that is, the publication rate among scholars of color in the humanities. On the one hand, the Mellon GES data suggests that among US citizens, minority academics in the humanities were less likely to have published (65 percent versus 72 percent non-minorities) either during their doctoral programs or during their first three years after receipt of the PhD—that is, scholars of color were generally publishing less.[25] On the other hand, however, minority PhDs in the humanities who *had* published during this same early stage of career produced slightly *more* scholarship than nonminorities.[26] Thus, while the overall percentage of early-career minority scholars who published was lower, the productivity of those who did publish was higher than for their nonminority counterparts. Comparing the higher percentage of productivity by minorities to the lower rate at which they achieve tenure exposes another discrepancy. These numbers suggest that scholars of color are working hard to publish while not gaining more success at achieving tenure. Clearly, the academic pipeline is in need of fixing, especially if we are considering the issue of faculty diversity.

Who We Are: Our Own Experiences

Our discussion of data on the tenure-track employability of new doctorates in the humanities and musicology is grim—no matter who you are. In this section, we try to bring alive this quantitative data by relating our own experiences. Our time in graduate school was marked by some key similarities, both of us being first-generation college students of color (and first-generation PhDs), as well as some differences, such as when we began searching for jobs, where we are today, and how other aspects of our identity have shaped our experiences. We share these personal reflections in an attempt to have a transparent dialogue about the state of our field as seen from the vantage point of both a young and a newly senior scholar.

One unifying aspect of our graduate experience was how we had to navigate our PhD programs at an elite Ivy League university as the first members of our family to go to college. The son of Chinese immigrants from the Philippines, Michael went to a large public undergraduate university before completing a two-year MPhil in England and a PhD in historical musicology in 2017. Naomi attended a Seven Sisters college with a very strong music undergraduate program and then attended graduate school in historical musicology in the early to mid-1990s, graduating in 1996. As an African American first-generation college student, Naomi notes that she lacked an awareness of the nuances regarding how advanced degrees and academic labor worked. She came from a single-parent family that viewed the prestige of university positions from a distance. While we both had strong and invaluable mentors who helped advise us through our programs, we also had few—practically no—tenured faculty-of-color role models who could speak to our different experiences and identities. As first-generation students, we needed to learn quickly what the norms of academia and our discipline were (sometimes referred to as the "hidden curriculum"), but we also did not always know what, or whom, to ask.

Not only did we lack role models of color, but our experience as racial minorities was also marked by similar feelings of disbelonging. Each of us has been often isolated as one of the very few scholars of color in the musicological room. As an Asian American, Michael has experienced the all-too-familiar trope of foreignness, especially in institutional settings and at national scholarly conferences—of questions about his belonging or his right to enter a space; of furtive looks that are at times bemused, at times hostile; of implicit or explicit challenging of his ability to speak or write in English; of being confused for, or casually interchanged with, different people of color as if we were the same person; of attributing a natural proclivity toward introversion as being antisocial or uninteresting or uninterested.

Sometimes, questions about race, class, or other belonging emerge from a place of well-meaning: folks are curious, they want to know more, they want to extend what they think is a helping hand, or they want to try to rationalize and categorize in a world of great complexity. But unreflective and misinformed words and actions can feel, at a minimum tiresome, and at their worst, alienating or prejudicial. Not every underrepresented minority, for example, wants the burden of educating others of their experiences, especially when a plethora of narratives and resources is readily accessible.[27]

Naomi feels she has had to prove herself on multiple levels in academia, and that continues to be the case. Certainly, everyone faces challenges to their academic and discursive knowledge, but scholars of color, especially Black and Latinx scholars, also have to navigate the changing climate around support of, and hostility to, affirmative action. She has experienced others immediately assuming that she had received a "handout" and that she did not really belong. Some try to overcompensate for any opposition to affirmative action by seeing her as being overly heroic and having some "magical Black knowledge" that combined the tough grit of Queen Latifah and the poetic wisdom of Maya Angelou.

Even as Michael and Naomi have been surrounded by a community that is notorious for being "independent university thinkers," possessing a range of personal experiences that make them quite sophisticated and urbane, there have still been many who have had no idea how to relate to us. Because of barriers to entering higher education, very few of us come from the horrors of ghettoized life. Just as well, the liberal pursuit of universalizing cultural equivalents is just as invalid in the way it erases unique contributions and differences.

"Sameness" has never been the full story; the white norm contained many minorities who "passed." At the same time there are vast socioeconomic and cultural differences existing among white students. "Passing" allowed those who embodied something outside the norm to appear to fit in. However, passing was never an ideal situation since it did not genuinely bring people together; rather the fear of being found out reinforced the boundaries that kept people apart.[28] Whereas the complexities and pain of passing around race, especially for very light-skinned Black people passing as white during slavery up through Jim Crow and segregation, has received the most scholarly attention, the metaphor (and very real practice) of "passing" for an oppressed group into the hegemonic majority is relevant in this study among several other parameters. Hiding and protecting the truth about one's sexual preference and gender expression, one's family background and economic circumstances, one's religion and ethnic heritage, one's national and legal status, one's physical and mental health—all these factors add even more layers of outsiderness. This list exposes a past that was unfair and often quite brutal to those who were excluded. With the changing demographics of the United States, we hope that our colleagues and students will increasingly meet Black women outside of service positions, know more than a single gay Latinx uncle by marriage whom they see at holidays, and be acquainted with more Southeast Asians than the few enrolled in a required undergraduate course.

Many disciplines in the academy, including musicology, are moving toward the first critical mass of scholars of color. This changing reality means that those in the academy (students, other professors, staff, administrators) must become more used to seeing people of color as graduate students and professors, and we need the cultural and racial competence to understand and interact with one another across racial boundaries. Standard narratives about diversifying the academy often leave out a fundamental point: the rules have been very different for people of color than they have been for those who are considered as "traditional" graduate students and professors. Moreover, not all people of color have the same stories, despite attempts to stereotype the ghetto child, model minority, or illegal alien. Not all Black people have the same story even if many of us have very similar overlapping experiences. By the same token, Asian Americans have some stories that overlap with the experiences of African Americans, while both groups also have experiences that are quite different from one another.

With regard to our personal experiences on the job market, we were both fortunate to land where we have. Even by the standards of the mid-1990s, Naomi notes that her path to a tenure-track job was remarkably smooth. When a position for a scholar who could teach both Western historical and world musics opened up, she was invited to apply and received an offer from a music school in a Big Ten university. Given the development of her academic research in gender, race, and cultural studies in opera, she found welcoming homes in that university's liberal arts college. As the most recent of the two scholars to enter the job market, Michael remembers the constant pressure throughout his graduate years of watching his peers seek academic jobs, even from the moment he arrived on campus. Older students asserted year after year that applying for positions was a part-time job in itself, and many of them had to apply for multiple years before getting the "coveted" tenure-track professorship. In addition to grants and awards, there were also the constant worries of producing conference presentations and publications. Successful students were both venerated and envied. The department newsletter regularly published their accomplishments, and faculty reported them at meetings, with minutes later distributed to everyone. What his department lacked, though—which is true, actually, of nearly all musicology graduate programs, as we will soon discuss—was recognition of, and support for, exploring career paths outside of academia.

In his dissertation completion year, Michael applied to selected tenure-track jobs but not to every job that was posted. He searched for the elusive balance between work and life, focusing on jobs and universities in cities where he could see himself living and being happy, in addition to other family and personal factors. He was not invited for any interviews. Fortunately, however, he was offered a full-time job in a half-administrative, half-teaching position at the university from which he obtained his PhD. Outside of academia, he also applied to, and interviewed for, positions with a large philanthropic institution, Top 3 management consulting firms, and the US Department of State. He admits that he felt that apart from his student peers, not many people in his department understood what it was *really* like to be applying for gainful employment outside the traditional academic track.

Both of us are glad now to take part in the discussion on the job market on a wider scale, and we recognize our privilege writing from the security of the other side.

Challenges We Face Today, Part 1: Musicologists as Adjunct Faculty in the Gig Economy

As we demonstrated in the earlier section, "The State of Musicology," there aren't enough jobs in academic fields to accommodate all of our graduating PhDs. Graduate programs are producing roughly 150 to 180 musicology PhDs a year, yet in recent years there have only been some seventy job postings for tenured, tenure-track, or permanent faculty musicology positions (as found in the Humanities Departmental Survey). The category "musicology" is self-reported in NORC and does not distinguish between musicology and ethnomusicology. Many graduating students will thus need to find work beyond their domain-specific academic expertise. Unfortunately, one rapidly growing trend in higher education is the increasing reliance on adjunct faculty for teaching college and university courses. As a result, PhDs and even predoctoral candidates increasingly serve as contingent labor, usually without benefits such as health insurance or retirement contributions. The academic gig economy is by no means isolated to the discipline of musicology, as the *Chronicle of Higher Education* documents in its series the "Freelance Academic," where contributors discuss the practical realities of part-time, adjunct positions. One former contingent faculty employee, Katie Rose Guest Pryal, writes candidly that as a freelancer, she never knows how much money she'll receive in a given month. Sometimes she "strikes it big—relatively speaking," but "basically, working as a freelancer can be exhausting because it can feel like you're always on a roller-coaster."[29]

Challenges surrounding the gig economy occupy musicology as well. At the 2018 SAM conference, a panel was hosted by the Forum for Early Career Professionals with facilitators Sarah Gerk and Kate Galloway.[30] Gerk and Galloway presented recent data from the Gig Economy Survey Report, initiated the year prior, to better understand contingent labor within the discipline and especially among doctoral graduates.[31] While a third of the participants in the report remarked on how the gig economy offered them flexibility, independence, teaching experience, and opportunities for creative work, many others commented on its negative impacts. Twenty-seven of forty-three talked about financial insecurity, and twenty of forty-three reported physical, emotional, or family hardships from contingent employment. Others described needing food stamps, Medicaid, and help from parents, other family members, and friends. Furthermore, many respondents expressed concerns about having limited opportunities for professional advancement, feeling undervalued and underrespected, and possessing insufficient time to conduct research. Similarly, the 2018 AMS conference hosted several panels and workshops on the topic of adjunct teaching and the contingent labor market.

We are not arguing that PhD students need to give up on academia or even that we need to banish all forms of contingent labor. Some may choose to teach class-by-class because it affords them the most independence and flexibility. What we are trying to say, though—which is really not that revolutionary—is that there are many career options for musicology PhDs and that departments and faculty members could do a better job exposing students to these possibilities, rather than doubling down on a system that is clearly constrained from both the supply and demand sides.

Higher-education professionals have noted that the expertise of the PhD goes beyond the specific content knowledge of a discipline. The skills learned during PhD training (excellence in writing, teaching, and managing large projects—to name just a few) are quite transferrable and leave the degree holder poised for strong performance in multiple areas. In any case, the one-career job path has become less common for all employed adults—not just academics. Perhaps another way of reframing the discussion is to think again, as musicologists and ethnomusicologists, about the purpose of the doctorate and the dissertation in a labor market that encompasses not just academic writing and publishing, but also many other jobs and opportunities.

Challenges We Face Today, Part 2: New Paradigms in Music Scholarship Including Applied and Engaged Musicologies

As the sister disciplines of historical musicology and ethnomusicology come closer together in their use of sources (written and oral), different forms of media, and theoretical approaches to cultural context, we outline two directions that address the inclusivity of what is studied, who are the people doing the research, and where the impact of this scholarship reaches. The first comes originally from "applied" work in the field of ethnomusicology; the second comes from an interdisciplinary historical model of "engaged musicology."

"Applied" work, also known as public-sector, active, or practice-based scholarship, has had a long history in ethnomusicology but heretofore not as large of an impact in musicological studies on European and North American topics.[32] The Applied Ethnomusicology Section of the Society for Ethnomusicology defines it as "ethnomusicology that puts music to use in a variety of contexts, academic and otherwise, including education, cultural policy, conflict resolution, medicine, arts programming, and community music."[33] Taking this basic definition further, for some scholars, applied work is explicitly a mission of advocacy or social justice. Daniel Sheehy argues that applied ethnomusicology is a "conscious practice" evident in a scholar's "implacable tendency first to see opportunities for a better life for others through the use of musical knowledge."[34] Svanibor Pettan defines it as "the approach guided by principles of social responsibility . . . toward solving concrete problems and toward working both inside and beyond typical academic contexts."[35] Lastly, others such as Jeff Todd Titon see applied ethnomusicology as a distinctly "practical action in the world outside of archives and universities."[36]

The link between applied ethnomusicology and applied musicology is directly made in the skills that are attained in graduate work and preparation, as well as the job market for both disciplines. Conducting applied ethnomusicological or musicological work is not just about social activism outside of the classroom or library—although that is certainly a necessary and core value—but also opportunities for realizing change and impact beyond scholarship. As Klisala Harrison points out, in the current job market, nonacademic employers are increasingly interested in applied ethnomusicological and musicological work, and discussions with prospective employees are becoming increasingly relevant.[37]

Some universities have already responded to this increased demand through their academic programs. For example, Utrecht University has developed a master's program in applied musicology where students acquire skills to work within the "international musical industry." Utrecht lists possible careers as programmers or researchers at musical organizations, editors in written media, managers of cultural or educational institutions, programmers for festivals, and music supervisors at sound recording or film companies.[38] Many American graduate students in musicology and ethnomusicology are already cultivating strong skills in archival research, quantitative and qualitative analysis, writing, sound editing, and music production. While an explicit master's degree in applied musicology may be a helpful signal to potential employers, graduate students and their supervisors can also frame general PhD programs in musicology and ethnomusicology as supplying these practical skills for work in the nonacademic market.

Furthermore, "engaged musicology" can be another methodology that helps scholars rethink their relationship with the market outside of academia. In her recent book, *Black Opera: History, Power, Engagement,* Naomi outlines an analytical approach to music that can be broken into three rubrics.[39] These rubrics focus on how music is enmeshed in cultural signifiers, and they incorporate the vantage points of the diverse publics that are currently interpreting a work. This is especially true for the performing arts, where—unlike sculpture, painting, or novels—music (and theater and dance) is enacted by contemporary artists. While looking at the premiere of a work from the past can help us get a sense of its original historical context, performing these works now brings into play several issues about how the work resonates and is relevant today.

The first rubric for an engaged musicological approach looks at the text—the full musical work: what story is being told and how is it told? This narrative refers both to the "program" or semantic storytelling as well as to the form-style-historical context for a work without an explicit story (what has traditionally been called "absolute" music). Additionally, this first rubric considers how the text came to be and who the creators were—that is, the composer and collaborators (e.g., the poet, the director, the choreographer). How is representation articulated? If the creators are not representing their own identities and experiences, how are these depictions being informed? Bringing these two aspects together, the interaction between the creators of the work and the work itself is the beginning of understanding how meaning is created through the music.

The second rubric concerns the performance itself: Who is on stage? Who embodies and recreates the music? One question in opera gets to the heart of this theme: How does true-to-color casting matter for a specific role? What does it mean when a white singer puts on blackface makeup to sing the title role of Verdi's *Aida* or when a Korean singer takes the role of Mimi in Puccini's *La Bohème?* The third rubric involves the person interpreting the music. There is no single correct way to understand art; hence, the voice—of the discussant, the critic, teacher, audience member—is critical in shaping the meaning projected onto the music. Taken together, the three rubrics of engaged musicology can help scholars convey a rich and nuanced qualitative analysis that would also be insightful to hermeneutic or sociological work outside of academia.

In sum, an applied musicology (historical and ethnomusicological) explores the practice of how musicology can work in society, and an engaged musicology opens up the process of analysis to examine how music is assigned meaning and what those ramifications can do. Both approaches incorporate the goals of social justice to make the study of music and its sociocultural function more accessible and more equitable. Applied musicology and engaged musicology are thus complementary ways of thinking about research and scholarship, and they both emphasize the cultivation of tools and frameworks with relevance to employers of all kinds.

Thinking about the Future

It may be surprising that those with PhDs stick it out in the contingent labor market for so long in the hopes of obtaining the supposed holy grail of a tenure-track position, then to face the continued pressures of teaching multiple courses each semester, in addition to publishing one—or more—peer-reviewed books and articles before tenure. In fact, a recent study of five thousand humanities and social sciences PhDs by the Cornell Higher Education Research Institute found that those working in nonprofit jobs after graduating reported more satisfaction with their positions than their peers in tenure-track faculty positions.[40] The same finding holds true even for those PhDs who had initially intended to stay in academia. 93 percent of PhDs in nonprofit jobs said that they were "very satisfied" or "somewhat satisfied," compared to 88 percent in tenure-track or tenured positions. Additionally, 80 percent of PhDs in nonprofit jobs reported that they were satisfied with their compensation, compared to 61 percent in tenure-track jobs. Those who stayed in academia working in the gig economy were the least happy overall.

Another landmark study, conducted in 1999 by Maresi Nerad and Joseph Cerny for the Council of Graduate Schools, a nonprofit educational organization based in Washington, DC, discovered that job satisfaction among English PhDs employed in business, government, and nonprofit (BGN) sectors was higher in criteria of autonomy (92 percent vs. 90 percent), prestige of the organization (83 percent vs. 68 percent), work environment (83 percent vs. 73 percent), and career growth (78 percent vs. 67 percent), compared to only slightly lower satisfaction in "content of work" (87 percent BGN vs. 89 percent academia) and "flexibility in work" (82 percent BGN vs. 84 percent academia).[41] Theirs has been the most detailed examination of post-PhD career satisfaction to date, in this case, looking at English PhDs, eleven to fifteen years after their degree completion.[42] (Their analysis of job satisfaction criteria measures dimensions commonly associated with the privileges of academia.) Further research has shown that the skills and capacities developed in PhD programs (humanities and STEM) are transferable to many other professional contexts.[43] Narratives still persist, though, that nonacademic careers are consolation prizes for those who didn't make the cut.

Unfortunately, very few music departments are offering any sort of support or training for the many graduating PhDs who will not find a tenure-track position within six months of their degree. According to the 2012–13 Survey of Humanities Departments, musicology programs ranked dead last among humanities divisions in providing opportunities related to the job market outside of academia (best practices include presentations by employers, employees, or alumni, and internships in an employment context).[44] For example, 98 percent of art history departments offered internships as part of their graduate program, compared to only 13 percent in musicology; and 83 percent of English departments held occupationally oriented presentations (e.g., job fairs); in musicology, however, only 20 percent of departments did so. In terms of coursework or workshops focused on nonacademic employment, musicology came in second to last place (offered by 27 percent of music departments), ranked only above the history of science (14 percent of departments). We need to ask, why is musicology so far behind other humanities fields, and why is it not equipping our students for the workforce, in the broadest of terms?

Perhaps some of the reluctance to offer opportunities such as internships with local arts institutions, professional development training in hard skills like programming language literacy, or alumni visits from those working outside universities is related to a kind of academic brinksmanship when it comes to job placement. Senior tenured faculty supervising graduate students may fear that if too many of their PhDs leave academia, their department may attain a reputation of poor tenure-track placement; instead, they prefer other music departments to take on the "burden" of the nonacademic job market while they otherwise stay the course. Faculty have the power, though, to change the situation, just as students retain the agency to explore nonacademic careers. In the future, Michael, for example, hopes to integrate internships as a core component of his graduate seminars, including his seminar Philanthropy and Music. Certainly, internships need to be designed so that they provide valuable, real-world skills, rather than free labor to nonprofit organizations, but as it stands, we as faculty members can do much more to provide these types of experiences to our graduate students, and bureaucratic obstacles, interpersonal conflicts, or fears of loss of reputation should not be impediments.

Table 11.4. Humanities Disciplines That Offer Occupationally Oriented (Non-Academic Employment) Activities for Doctoral Students

Discipline	Occupationally oriented presentations by employers, employees, or alumni (%)	An internship in an employment setting (%)	Occupationally oriented coursework or workshops (%)
All departments	59	65	55
Art History	77	98	70
English	83	83	78
History	50	83	33
History of Science	29	29	14
Musicology	20	13	27

Final Thoughts

By way of conclusion, we can offer other resources in humanities disciplines that have been useful in advising graduate students.

The National Endowment for the Humanities explored in its Next Generation Humanities PhD ("Next Gen") grant program of 2016–17 the persistent obstacle that doctoral humanities programs "are too often designed to prepare students for only one career," that "students are told, often explicitly, that the only acceptable version of success is a tenure-track professorship at a high-intensive research university."[45] As the Next Gen program observed, the countervailing problem occurred when students were told that they "can do anything with their degree" but usually lacked the specific advice needed to pursue other options. Therefore, Next Gen supported capacity-building activities like creating databases of alumni contact information, developing partnerships with outside organizations, supporting internships, and exploring what other universities were doing to help their students.

Additionally, three service organizations especially active in this area have been the Modern Language Association (MLA), the American Historical Association (AHA), and the American Philosophical Association (APA). For example, the MLA's initiative Connected Academics helps prepare doctoral students for a variety of careers and offers various modules that faculty and graduate students can undertake together.[46] It covers aspects such as resource mapping, engaging alumni, and providing concrete suggestions and sample language for having conversations about career paths. It even offers advice for departments seeking to change their curriculum, including discussions with university deans and administrators. Both the AHA and the APA are active in cooperating with networks such as the Council for Graduate Schools and in publishing, as in the APA's *Beyond Academia: Professional Opportunities for Philosophers*, with a revised edition in 2016.[47]

Another catalyst for applying doctoral scholarship outside the tenure track has been the Mellon/ACLS Public Fellows program, begun in 2011. Recent PhDs in the humanities and social sciences are eligible for two-year positions at partnering government and nonprofit organizations. Fellows receive a stipend, health insurance, and professional mentoring. The program specifically "aims to expand the reach of doctoral education in the U.S. by demonstrating that the capacities developed in the advanced study of the humanities have wide application, both within and beyond the academy."[48] Fellows receive an annual stipend comparable to, if not slightly higher than, the salary of an assistant professor, individual health insurance, and professional mentoring. In 2017, for example, positions were held at the National Conference of State Legislatures as a legislative policy specialist, the Brooklyn Academy of Music as a program analyst, and the City of Seattle Office of Arts & Culture as an impact and assessment manager.

As a parting thought, and as scholars of color ourselves, we do want to emphasize that while the realities we have noted in this chapter affect all graduate students, we don't want to lose sight of the fact that graduate students of color and other graduate students from marginalized backgrounds are a particularly vulnerable population. Microaggressions, few faculty members of color who can act as role models, intersectional identities, structural biases, and discrimination—these experiences are all realities that negatively impact the success of our graduate students of color inside and outside of school.[49] Yes, affirmative action policies and increased funding opportunities for diverse hiring and admissions have changed the playing field, but the work heretofore has not been enough, and it is far from over.[50]

The academic pipeline is a minefield for graduate students of color, many of whom are first-generation students. Tenured faculty members of color are too few to advise the growing body of minority students—graduate *and* undergraduate—not to mention the fact that they often need to serve on "diversity committees" or provide indirect and uncompensated work (or "invisible labor," none of which counts for tenure) on top of their teaching and publishing.[51] While there is some evidence that colleges have been trying to increase their hiring of diverse faculty, the overall picture is still grim, and even when young scholars of color do get tenure-track jobs, they are not able to achieve tenure at a rate commensurate with their white peers, which is especially concerning given their high publishing record. Thus, we cannot bury our heads in the sand, some of us sitting from positions of economic security and some of us deciding to admit more students into our programs without preparing them for gainful employment after they finish. The problems will not miraculously fix themselves, so it is incumbent upon us to face these challenges with renewed vigor, perspective, and duty. The fate of US music studies will be deeply impacted by our actions.

Notes

The authors would like especially to acknowledge and thank Carol Oja and Charles Hiroshi Garrett, Matthew Leslie Santana, Ellie Hisama, Braxton Shelley, Tiffany Kuo, Lucille Mok, Jonathan Fanton, Robert Townsend, John Paul Christy, Maureen McCarthy, Susan Drange, and Adinawa Adjagbodjou.

1. The varied configuration of academic institutions, departments, and scholarly societies makes it difficult to arrive at a precise definition of musicology. Note that the studies of academia on which we draw face similar challenges.

2. The University of California at Berkeley, the University of Chicago, the University of Michigan, the University of Pennsylvania, and Columbia, Cornell, Harvard, Princeton, Stanford, and Yale attracted the largest number of winners of the Mellon Foundation's portable fellowships in the humanities. Ronald Ehrenberg, Harriet Zuckerman, Jeffrey Groen, and Sharon Brucker, *Educating Scholars: Doctoral Education in the Humanities* (Princeton, NJ: Princeton University Press, 2010), 1–2.

3. Ehrenberg et al., *Educating Scholars,* 1–2.

4. Ehrenberg et al., *Educating Scholars,* 10.

5. Ehrenberg et al., *Educating Scholars,* 16.

6. Ehrenberg et al., *Educating Scholars,* 2. Three music programs received GEI funding: Columbia, the University of Pennsylvania, and Yale. The "control group" was composed of Cornell, the University of Michigan, Princeton, Stanford, UCLA, and UCSD. According to the GES/GEI study, music programs fell under the category of having the smallest class sizes among the humanities.

7. Ehrenberg et al., *Educating Scholars,* 184.

8. Ehrenberg et al., *Educating Scholars,* 185. Furthermore, 38 percent of leavers received a master's degree from the department in which they were enrolled (177).

9. Ehrenberg et al., *Educating Scholars,* 188.

10. Robert B. Townsend, "New Study Highlights Prominence of Elite PhD Programs in History," *Perspectives on History,* October 1, 2005, https://www.historians.org/publications-and-directories/perspectives-on-history/october-2005/new-study-highlights-prominence-of-elite-phd-programs-in-history. Among the history faculty at the top 25 schools as designated by *U.S. News and World Report,* 58.9 percent had received their PhDs from top 10 programs; 74.9 percent had received their PhDs from top 20 programs, compared to 82 percent in economics and 74 percent in sociology. By comparison, top 10 programs conferred only 28 percent of PhDs in the discipline, and top 20 programs conferred only 44 percent.

11. Humanities Indicators is a project of the American Academy of Arts and Sciences with the National Endowment for the Humanities, the American Council of Learned Societies, and the National Humanities Alliance.

12. Humanities Indicators website, https://humanitiesindicators.org/content/indicatordoc.aspx?i=69, accessed November 16, 2020.

13. The other agencies include the National Institutes of Health, US Department of Education, National Endowment for the Humanities, US Department of Agriculture, and the National Aeronautics and Space Administration. NORC at the University of Chicago is an objective, nonpartisan research institution (and NORC is not an acronym). We are grateful to Ellie Hisama and Susan Drange for helping us to navigate through the NORC SED data to identify, as well as point specifically to, statistics pertaining to PhDs in musicology, ethnomusicology, and music theory.

14. Susan White, Raymond Chu, and Roman Czujko, "The 2012–13 Survey of Humanities Departments at Four-Year Institutions, HDS-2," Statistical Research Center, American Institute of Physics. Humanities Indicators and the American Academy of Arts and Sciences first administered the survey in 2008. The section on musicology noted that there was "a challenge in identifying departments and programs that award degrees in musicology" and that the results were based on data from "respondents who told us they offered a degree in musicology." In September 2018, the American Academy of Arts and Sciences received funding to undertake its third Humanities Departmental Survey (HDS-3) for 2017–18. The HDS-3 report is forthcoming as of the publication of this chapter.

15. The report focuses on PhDs awarded and does not include numbers for DMAs.

16. By comparison, there were 295 new hires in philosophy, 230 in religion, 630 in history, 10 in folklore, 900 in English language and literature, and 120 in art history. "Survey of Humanities Departments HDS-2," table MU14, "Faculty Tenure Decisions and New Hires," 171.

17. The data from 2013 to 2016 has aggregated Pacific Islanders into the American Indian category.

18. Data from NORC SED only includes US citizens and permanent residents and does not include noncitizen long-term visitors or undocumented immigrants.

19. Humanities Indicators, "Racial/Ethnic Distribution of Advanced Degrees in the Humanities."

20. The percentage of doctoral degrees awarded to women in the humanities has witnessed a strong growth, from 19.2 percent in 1966, to 36.2 percent in 1976, to 47.8 percent in 1986, to 51.1 percent in 1996 (the first year that more women obtained doctoral degrees in the humanities than men), 51.8 percent in 2006, and 53.8 percent in 2015. In the "Study of the Arts," women have received more PhDs than men, beginning with data from 1987 (55.2 percent) to the present (63.7 percent in 2015). While women have received more PhDs since 1987, however, as a percentage of faculty members within the field of musicology, they are only 39 percent (as of fall 2012), compared to 63 percent in English and 61 percent in history, but also 26 percent in philosophy and 31 percent in religion. "Survey of Humanities Departments HDS-2."

21. Ehrenberg et al., *Educating Scholars,* 105.

22. Ehrenberg et al., *Educating Scholars,* 197.

23. Ehrenberg et al., *Educating Scholars,* 203–4.

24. Ehrenberg et al., *Educating Scholars,* 203.

25. Ehrenberg et al., *Educating Scholars,* 209.

26. Ehrenberg et al., *Educating Scholars,* 210.

27. In our own field, see, for example, Ellie Hisama, "Colloquy: Race, Ethnicity, and the Profession," *Musicology Now,* December 1, 2016, https://musicologynow.org/colloquy-race-ethnicity-and-the-profession-part-4-of-4/, accessed April 9, 2021; Travis A. Jackson, "Rearticulating Ethnomusicology: Privilege, Ambivalence, and Twelve Years in SEM," *Ethnomusicology* 50, no. 2 (2006): 280–86; Tamara Levitz, "Decolonizing the Society for American

Music," *Society for American Music Bulletin,* September 2017; Alejandro L. Madrid, "Diversity, Tokenism, Non-canonical Musics, and the Crisis of the Humanities in U.S. Academia," *Journal of Music History Pedagogy* 7, no. 2 (2017): 124–30.

28. Allyson Hobbs, *A Chosen Exile: A History of Racial Passing in American Life* (Cambridge, MA: Harvard University Press, 2014).

29. Katie Rose Guest Pryal, "The Search for Stability as a Freelance Academic," Freelance Academic Series, September 14, 2017, https://chroniclevitae.com/news/1901-the-search-for-stability-as-a-freelance-academic, accessed November 16, 2020.

30. The panel also included Mark Davidson, Douglas Shadle, and Reba Wissner.

31. The survey results are accessible online at https://www.surveymonkey.com/results/SM-HJ9JXXTB8/, accessed November 16, 2020. The Forum for Early Career Professionals solicited voluntary and anonymous responses from the Society for American Music members.

32. See the recently published, *The Oxford Handbook of Applied Ethnomusicology,* ed. Svanibor Pettan and Jeff Todd Titon (Oxford: Oxford University Press, 2015).

33. The Society for Ethnomusicology, Applied Ethnomusicology Section, https://www.ethnomusicology.org/page/Groups_SectionsAE, accessed November 16, 2020.

34. Daniel Sheehy, "A Few Notions about Philosophy and Strategy in Applied Ethnomusicology," *Ethnomusicology* 36, no. 3 (1992): 323–24.

35. Klisala Harrison, "Epistemologies of Applied Ethnomusicology," *Ethnomusicology* 56, no. 3 (2012): 507.

36. Jeff Todd Titon, "Music, the Public Interest, and the Practice of Ethnomusicology," *Ethnomusicology* 36, no. 3 (1992): 315. Gage Averill is another important voice in this area. He believes that applied, public, or engaged ethnomusicology cannot be seen as an alternative career choice to academia but as an endeavor in which all ethnomusicologists should take part in "planning, advocacy, consulting, and other engaged roles, including acting as a social critic." Gage Averill, "Ethnomusicologists as Public Intellectuals: Engaged Ethnomusicology in the University," *Folklore Forum* 34, nos. 1–2 (2003): 49.

37. Harrison, "Epistemologies of Applied Ethnomusicology," 514.

38. Utrecht University, Applied Musicology, https://www.uu.nl/masters/en/applied-musicology, accessed November 16, 2020.

39. Naomi André, *Black Opera: History, Power, Engagement* (Urbana: University of Illinois Press, 2018).

40. Colleen Flaherty, "Where the Grass Is Greener," *Inside Higher Ed,* December 18, 2017; and Joyce B. Main, Sarah Prenovitz, and Ronald G. Ehrenberg, "In Pursuit of a Tenure-Track Faculty Position: Career Progression and Satisfaction of Humanities and Social Sciences Doctorates," *The Review of Higher Education* 42, no. 4 (Summer 2019): 1309–36.

41. Maresi Nerad and Joseph Cerny, "From Rumors to Facts: Career Outcomes of English Ph.D.s—Results from the Ph.D.'s-Ten Years Later Study," *Council of Graduate Schools Communicator* 32, no. 7 (1999): 1–12.

42. Overall, they looked at 814 PhDs from sixty-one US research universities.

The graduates were also predominantly white, 53 percent women, and on average thirty-five years of age at completion of their degree.

43. For example, see Maureen McCarthy, "Summary of Prior Work in Humanities PhD Professional Development," Council of Graduate Schools, September 2017; Thomas Bender, "Expanding the Domain of History," in *Envisioning the Future of Doctoral Education: Preparing Stewards of the Discipline,* ed. Chris M. Golde and George E. Walker (San Francisco: Jossey-Bass, 2006), 295–310; Maresi Nerad, "Confronting Common Assumptions: Designing Future-Oriented Graduate Education," in *Doctoral Education and the Faculty of the Future,* ed. Ronald G. Ehrenberg and Charlotte V. Kuh (Ithaca, NY: Cornell University Press, 2009), 80–92; from the STEM perspective, see H. Sauermann and M. Roach, "Science PhD Career Preferences: Levels, Changes, and Advisor Encouragement," *PLoS ONE* 7, no. 5 (2012), https://journals.plos.org/plosone/article/authors?id=10.1371/journal.pone.0036307

44. "Survey of Humanities Departments HDS-2," table 21, 30.

45. Maureen McCarthy, "Promising Practices in Humanities PhD Professional Development: Lessons Learned from the 2016–2017 Next Generation Humanities PhD Consortium," National Endowment for the Humanities, September 2017, https://cgsnet.org/ckfinder/userfiles/files/NEH_NextGen_PriorWork.pdf

46. For the online modules, see https://connect.mla.hcommons.org/doctoral-student-career-planning-faculty-toolkit/, accessed November 16, 2020.

47. The free pdf can be found at *Beyond Academia: Professional Opportunities for Philosophers,* https://cdn.ymaws.com/www.apaonline.org/resource/resmgr/docs/Beyond_Academia_2016.pdf, accessed November 16, 2020.

48. Mellon/ACLS Public Fellows Competition for Recent PhDs, https://www.acls.org/programs/publicfellowscomp/, accessed November 16, 2020.

49. For example, see David L. Burnsma, David G. Embrick, and Jean H. Shin, "Graduate Students of Color: Race, Racism, and Mentoring in the White Waters of Academia," *Sociology of Race and Ethnicity* 3, no. 1 (2017): 1–13; Julie R. Ancis, William E. Sedlacek, and Jonathan J. Moher, "Student Perceptions of Campus Cultural Climate by Race," *Journal of Counseling and Development* 78 (2000): 180–85; Sylvia Hurtado, "The Campus Racial Climate," *Journal of Higher Education* 63, no. 5 (1992): 539–69; Amy L. Reynolds, Jacob N. Sneva, and Gregory P. Beehler, "The Influence of Racism-Related Stress on the Academic Motivation of Black and Latino/a Students," *Journal of College Student Development* 51, no. 2 (2010): 135–49.

50. We are also reminded by Ellie Hisama that in the states of California, Michigan, and New Hampshire there are anti-affirmative action policies or laws, that is, Proposition 209 in California (1996), Proposal 2 in Michigan (2006), and House Bill 0623 in New Hampshire (2011). These policies are framed as nondiscriminatory, but have the effect of benefiting students from already privileged social and racial backgrounds.

51. For example, see Patricia A. Matthew, "What Is Faculty Diversity Worth to a University," *The Atlantic,* November 23, 2016; Mariam B. Lam, "Diversity Fatigue Is Real," *Chronicle of Higher Education,* September 23, 2018.

TWELVE | Collaborative Voices

Reimagining US Music Scholarship after AmeriGrove II

CHARLES HIROSHI GARRETT AND DANIEL GOLDMARK

Getting Started

GARRETT: Excitement and dread. It was summer 2004, and Laura Macy had just invited me to become the editor-in-chief of an updated version of the *New Grove Dictionary of American Music*, edited by H. Wiley Hitchcock and Stanley Sadie.[1] The opportunity to revisit this landmark publication, the first comprehensive reference work dedicated to the music of the United States, was compelling. I had consulted the dictionary for years, and I had studied with Wiley, whose memory I wanted to honor. But I also felt stumped and overwhelmed at the start of the process. What goes into a dictionary of American music? What should it look like? What gets included and what's left out? How does this work? I didn't know the answers, but I was sure that I would need plenty of help.

These questions resonated over the nine years it took for *The Grove Dictionary of American Music*, second edition, to reach publication.[2] Assembled during an age of great transformation in academic publishing, the dictionary—or as we shall refer to it in this essay, *AmeriGrove II*—appeared as a printed set and also as one of the many online resources maintained by Oxford University Press as part of *Grove Music Online* (www.oxfordmusiconline.com/grovemusic). Fueled by an explosion of scholarly activity over several decades, and expanded to twice the size of its four-volume predecessor, which appeared in 1986, *AmeriGrove II* includes more than eight thousand entries on significant people, places, objects, practices, genres, concepts, themes, and traditions. As the largest reference work devoted to music, musicians, and music-making in the United States, this encyclopedic dictionary is used by a wide readership of scholars, researchers, teachers, students, and interested readers. For some readers, it represents a trusted reference source; for others, it serves as a productive jumping-off point for further scholarly inquiry.

It was clear from the start that neither one individual nor even a small team could possibly complete such a complex and expansive project. Even the original, two-volume *Dictionary of Music and Musicians*, edited by George Grove (1879), sported fifty-six contributing writers, including Grove himself. Putting together *AmeriGrove II* required continuous teamwork and collaboration on a massive scale. The first step involved assembling an advisory board of specialists who offered planning advice and helped design the list of dictionary entries (or "headwords," in dictionary parlance).[3] They were joined by a large editorial team that was responsible for finalizing the list of entries, locating contributors, and editing each submission.[4] Rather than using a top-down model to dictate the contents of the dictionary, the advisers and editors of *AmeriGrove II* worked collectively, and this flexibility led to the dictionary growing from an initial projection of six volumes to its ultimate publication as an eight-volume set. The extensive technical and administrative demands of the project were also handled collaboratively by faculty at the University of Michigan, the project's institutional host, and by publishing staff at Oxford University Press.[5] Over time, the project came to involve more than sixteen hundred people, including editors, advisers, authors, experts in publishing, computing staff, copy editors, and fact-checkers. Dozens of meetings, hundreds of phone calls, and thousands of e-mails—without that level of collaboration, the project would have collapsed.

* * *

GOLDMARK: I had heard rumblings about the possibility of an *AmeriGrove* reboot, but did not really fathom the scope of what lay before us until the first "all hands on deck" gathering during a joint meeting of the Society for American Music and Music Library Association in 2006. I was humbled to be in a

> roomful of esteemed colleagues, many of whom had worked on the original dictionary and/or were founding members of the Society, and yet was also reassured by their presence, as I knew the formidable project ahead would involve some of the most talented people in the field. As a senior editor on the project, I managed entries relating to music and media (film, television, video games) as well as articles on music publishers since the late nineteenth century and record labels of the mid- to late twentieth century. The bulk of my work involved shepherding these entries, although I ended up writing a dozen short entries as well as revising and coauthoring several existing articles.

The senior editors shouldered most of the heavy lifting in the initial stages of the project, beginning by evaluating existing Grove articles and then proposing cuts, additions, and expansions.[6] Because we did not want significant musical figures or topics to slip through the cracks, editors were assigned subject areas that were designed deliberately to overlap into multiple domains, much like a Venn diagram. Peering through different lenses on musical life collectively generated an especially wide-ranging set of entries, even if it meant that separate editors sometimes proposed the same entries (e.g., separate editors for jazz, African American music, and popular music each nominated Ella Fitzgerald). Reconciling the intersection between proposed articles and editorial assignments became one of the earliest forms of collaboration: which editor ended up overseeing an article on "music video" (the person covering film music or the one responsible for popular music?) or "film musical" (film music or musical theater?) also influenced the choice of an author and the direction of the entry.

The process of generating a list of new headwords for each subject area, setting word counts for each article, and finding writers became the biggest task by far for senior editors. Sometimes many options existed for selecting writers, particularly for those areas well plumbed by scholars; who ended up writing which article often came down to availability. Identifying experts for newer topics proved much more challenging; entries related to orchestrators and record labels, for instance, led to an all-points bulletin among editors and contributors. The process of collaboration extended to communicating with individual contributors during the review process. Fortunately, once the commissions went out, an established style guide employed by *Grove Music Online* largely helped direct the writers as they began their work.

* * *

Voluminous reference works by necessity must be collaborative, simply because more people can offer more time, expertise, and collective experience than a single author. But the typical experience for nearly all authors who contributed to *AmeriGrove II* was not particularly collaborative.[7] After being contacted by an editor with details about an assignment—topic, description, word count, deadline—individual authors completed their work alone and received sole credit in the published dictionary. Each submission was reviewed and proofed as needed by the editorial staff, and numerous articles saw multiple revisions. Such publishing mechanics relied on communication between authors and editors and followed by-the-book procedure for reviewing solo-authored publishing. Looking back, it is difficult to imagine having adopted a different approach. Asking fifteen hundred authors to collaborate on cowritten entries would have been highly impractical, as many of those who wrote for the dictionary had neither time nor interest in teaming with coauthors. For that matter, the very idea of contracting cowritten entries runs contrary to the scholarly conventions that direct reference works. Above all, there was one thing that prevented us from pursuing a collaborative approach for producing dictionary entries: it did not even cross our minds at that time.

This oversight speaks to how deeply single-authored works are valued in the humanities, even though coauthored papers are the norm in the sciences (social and physical). By contrast, integrating collaborative elements within the administrative and editorial processes driving the dictionary project felt natural. This may have been related to the ways in which academia does encourage collaboration. Conferences and symposia, for example, are common settings for working with colleagues in and across the discipline, and academic societies offer various opportunities to work with peers. Serving on the governing boards of societies, coteaching courses, joining editorial boards, editing special journal issues, and coediting book collections are all accepted ways to work with colleagues.[8] Asking authors to contribute coauthored articles to *AmeriGrove II*, however, would have been seen as radically experimental at best and onerous at worst, both by contributors and by the editorial staff.

Our own perspectives on collaborative writing have shifted so dramatically over the past fifteen years that it is difficult to imagine not integrating coauthored contributions into a reference work produced today. We had both gone through the same graduate program (a few years apart) and had shared experiences and ideas, but had not teamed up on a publishing project until we coedited an anthology of essays with our colleague David Ake.[9] That book showed us just how much there was to gain from collaboration; we have since gravitated toward working together across academic settings, from publishing collaborative work to staging conferences to many other collective ventures. So we quickly jumped at the chance to participate in such a rare and extended undertaking as *AmeriGrove II*. Collaboration has continued to shape our thinking, led us to participate in the symposium that gave rise to this edited collection, and inspired us to work together on this essay. It is not that we invariably turn to collaboration to tackle every scholarly challenge but rather that we have come to appreciate this process for how it places us in dialogue and pushes us in unexpected yet fruitful directions.

Recognizing how much we have changed over the years prompted us to revisit our *AmeriGrove II* journey in this essay. We are not so interested in the question of "what if we could do it all over again"; rather, we wish to explore various strategies, some but not all involving collaboration, that point forward.[10] Together, we reflect here on the challenges and predicaments we faced during the construction of the dictionary, what that process tells us about the state of the field—where it has been and where it is going—and how our experience provides some guidance and inspiration for future scholarship.

The Question of "American Music"

"Amerigrove manifests what historians of American music have been moving toward for years: a full realization of how difficult it is to decide, musically speaking, what it means to be an American."[11] Richard Crawford's review of the original 1986 dictionary ended with this observation, which remains just as accurate decades later. Designing the updated dictionary involved addressing continually vexing questions: Who is "American"? What is "American"? What is "American music"? Rather than adopting a wider hemispheric definition of "America"—spanning the continents of North and South America—*AmeriGrove II* approached "American music" by placing the United States at its center and addressing musical life and cultures within the fifty states, the District of Columbia, and US territories. This editorial decision was shaped fundamentally by the nature of the commission: to update an established dictionary that had employed the same general approach to defining its subject. Retaining "American music" in the dictionary's title, rather than a more precise substitute such as "US music," similarly reflects an allegiance with the original work. How a dictionary might develop without close ties to an earlier model is a subject to which we will return.

Placing a nation at the center shaped the dictionary's overall design, the makeup and size of the editorial team, and subsequently the individual topics and central issues featured in the dictionary. At the same time, editors were acutely conscious of the ways in which a dictionary about "American music" could not simply offer a portrait of the United States in a vacuum, especially given our increasingly globalized world and the nation's sharply transforming demographics. While most members of the advisory and editorial boards possessed deep expertise in a specific period, area, genre, or tradition associated with music in the United States, several strategies were used to develop a broader chronological view and to foster transnational perspectives.

Following the editorial policy of the original dictionary, *AmeriGrove II* features extensive coverage of the history and music-making practices of native cultures whose occupation of these regions preceded European contact. Like its predecessor, the updated dictionary also includes numerous entries on foreign musicians who have shaped US musical life. The editorial board placed especially significant attention on musicians from Canada and Latin America who have been active in the United States, which resulted in a dictionary replete not only with US citizens and immigrants but also border-crossing figures such as Glenn Gould and Shakira. In an effort to further broaden perspectives, *AmeriGrove II* features more than a hundred newly commissioned topical entries—including "race and ethnicity," "intellectual property," and "sex, sexuality"—that range freely across genre, discipline, and period. These lengthy essays sought to intersect with and challenge the conventional elements of the dictionary's design. Furthermore, dictionary coverage in certain areas—including African American music, Asian American music, Hawaiian music, and Latinx music—saw extensive growth, and many related entries engaged closely with issues involving migration, diaspora, and cross-cultural activity. Finally, editors were encouraged to adopt a transnational philosophy in terms of framing individual articles. Foreign influences on musical activities in the United States and musical activities by US musicians in foreign countries were considered fundamental, not tangential, to the dictionary. The entry on hip-hop, for example, acknowledges its foundational relationship to Caribbean musical practices and its international spread over the last few decades.

Designing articles about musicians from outside the United States presented some challenges related to practical matters such as conserving dictionary space. Consequently, targeted entries on figures like Arnold Schoenberg and Igor Stravinsky place primary focus on the years after they emigrated to the United States. Similarly, the article on the Beatles addresses the inspiration they drew from US popular music, and their appearances and reception in the United States. Some figures who were far more active outside the United States were still included as a result of this editorial philosophy. A good example is the Viennese composer Erich Wolfgang Korngold (1897–1957). If he had stayed in Europe and only written operas and chamber music, he would have been an unlikely candidate for *AmeriGrove II.* But beginning in 1935 Korngold wrote the first of almost two dozen arrangements and original scores for films, including *The Adventures of Robin Hood* (1938), *The Sea Hawk* (1940), *Kings Row* (1942), and many others. He helped establish the sound of the film-scoring industry in Hollywood and influenced the careers of John Williams, Elmer Bernstein, Jerry Goldsmith, Howard Shore, and countless others. An entry on Korngold already existed in the standard *Grove* dictionary, yet comparatively little of the existing article dealt with his career as a film composer; the *AmeriGrove II* article places its primary focus on Korngold's life and influence as a Hollywood composer. Similar issues arose with other multinational composers, such as Ennio Morricone—whose sound not only influenced an entire generation regarding what we expect to hear in a western, but who also wrote music for many significant Hollywood productions (music from his "spaghetti" westerns also appears in recent films, such as *Kill Bill, Vol. 1*)—and Mario Castelnuovo-Tedesco, whose biography contains similarities to Korngold's. Editing entries about music publishers presented similar issues, as many foreign publishers—Peters, Ricordi, and so on—have conducted significant business in the Americas. Adapting these articles for publication in *AmeriGrove II* produced a narrow focus that makes them valuable for readers interested in their US activities. But it is fair to describe the overall balance of these articles as uneven, and readers unsatisfied by the US-centric lens would likely need to consult a different source to learn about the full picture. Compiling a dictionary will always result in some of these sorts of trade-offs, whether driven by practical constraints such as word count or guided by the conceptual philosophy informing the editorial policy.

Updating an existing dictionary is far different from designing one from scratch. As absorbing as our work became, the process led us to wonder about the future—that is, what different options, new configurations, and alternative possibilities exist for approaching a dictionary of "American music" today? The most fundamental issue, of course, involves acknowledging that "America" is not synonymous with the United States, even if that assumption often is made. Instead of a nation-based dictionary, we might take the lead from the Society for American Music, whose mission statement embraces "music of the Americas" as a broader, hemispheric definition that guides its journal, conference, and wider activities. Alternative frameworks for a dictionary of "American music" thus could place US music in a global context, as a node of the Black Atlantic, or as a key player in transatlantic or transpacific cultural exchange. Such approaches would highlight immigration, cross-cultural exchange, global politics, and other concepts that animate transnational studies; a model for work of this nature might be the *Garland Encyclopedia of World Music*, a series that places ethnomusicological concerns at its core. Repositioning the United States as one nation among many (and among differently configured groups of nations) would productively challenge notions of US exceptionalism. We'll come back to the notion of reframing *AmeriGrove II* presently.

What's *Grove*-Worthy?

GOLDMARK: Having come of age (so to speak) at a time when the *New Grove Dictionary of Music and Musicians* (1980) was still the main reference source for music students, I often found myself wondering (while poring over one of the *Grove*'s twenty volumes) why the topics that captured my interest had not been seen as significant enough to warrant an article in the dictionary. This was of course in the very earliest days of the internet, and long before many questions could be answered with a single online query. It wasn't until beginning work on *AmeriGrove II* that I discovered that the question of whether something did or did not receive attention in the *Grove* was a contested issue in itself, colloquially referred to by some as a topic's "*Grove*-worthiness." Given that the phenomenon we faced already had a nickname, we were not surprised to find that previous editors had grappled with the same problem; H. Wiley Hitchcock explained in the original *AmeriGrove* preface

> that "it is a critically organized repository of historically significant information, not a directory."[12]

As the dictionary evolved, editors needed to decide which topics mattered enough to merit a dictionary entry and which did not. No definitive "*Grove*-worthy" criteria coalesced: every time it appeared that an area was covered, an editor would end up making a strong case to commission a new article on an unforeseen topic. One area that saw significant growth was music for film, television, and other forms of visual media. The list of existing articles related to this topic in the original dictionary numbered all of fifty-eight entries, including broad surveys and profiles of composers best known for art music who had dabbled in composing for film. Almost every existing entry was updated or revised for *AmeriGrove II*, and close to one hundred new entries were added. Film composers who rose to prominence in recent decades or were overlooked by the original *AmeriGrove* were the first and most obvious additions, but changing perspectives on the notion of the "one composer, one score" approach (i.e., crediting work to one composer when a team of composers and other music professionals may have contributed) also led to commissioning brand-new entries about arrangers, orchestrators, and musical directors. Where to draw the line became a constant struggle for every editor; in the process we became acutely conscious of Glenda Goodman's observation that "dictionaries and encyclopedias are exercises in conferring legitimacy to some subjects and excluding others."[13]

As with all pursuits of knowledge, the harder we tried to cover bases, the more new ones would appear; a widening array of subjects only revealed more gaps in the dictionary's coverage. Since we did not, and could not, define a single standard for inclusion in the dictionary, we gravitated instead toward producing an updated "repository of historically significant information" that represented American musical life across the widest spectrum. The final product is distinctive for its diversity and breadth of coverage. This decidedly ecumenical approach was a luxury afforded by the willingness of Oxford University Press to expand the size of the dictionary beyond the original projections. What could have been an endless, ever-growing storehouse of material still had to be limited, leading some to question our final choice of topics and the length of individual entries. Debates about what to include became more spirited as we neared the present day. Taylor Swift and sound studies made the cut, but, regrettably in retrospect, Miley Cyrus and ludomusicology did not. The pace of change in musical life and the difficulty in predicting what would prove to have a lasting influence made such oversights inevitable. Sometimes articles were abandoned when it proved impossible to land appropriate authors; an entry on music and virtual reality, for instance, had to be shelved for a later time. In truth, the dictionary might have even more holes, had it not been for Jonas Westover, a nimble writer and jack-of-all-trades, who contributed more than three hundred articles to the dictionary on subjects ranging from charivari to the DJ Junior Vasquez to Lawrence Welk.

Space is at a premium for print publications, and strict word counts prove critical for authors, who tailor entries with a word limit in mind, and for readers, who often interpret the length of an entry as corresponding to its significance. Every editor who commissioned dictionary entries found assigning word counts challenging. Does Jenny Lind merit less or more space than John Coltrane or Jennifer Higdon? How many words should be allotted for the organ versus the synthesizer, the drum machine versus the saxophone? In the end, space in the dictionary was managed by assigning a collective word count to each subject area—an ongoing process that pushed editors through stages of negotiation, handwringing, adjustment, and acceptance—and empowering each editor to assign word counts for their set of entries. As much as these fixed limits sometimes troubled the editorial team, and as much as these choices miffed some reviewers of the dictionary, the word counts also served to keep the project on track. Had the updated dictionary been designed solely as an online resource, we would have had to debate whether to retain a strict word limit for the sake of practicality or to adopt a model that gave enthusiastic contributors the option to expand freely on their subjects of interest. While many writers worked perfectly well within the confines of their assignments, some struggled with keeping their ideas to the specified length. And why not? Asking any scholar to give a brief snapshot of a topic they know well inevitably presents a challenge. Some writers asked for more space; other entries had to be edited down. Occasionally, writers turned in fantastic articles that significantly exceeded the assigned word count. At such moments the dictionary process turned collaborative once again, as we entertained compelling arguments from authors, exchanged ideas about the best path forward, and found a solution satisfactory to all involved.

Assembling *AmeriGrove II*, and the Shape of Things to Come

Readers may anticipate when opening a volume of *AmeriGrove II* that it will deliver the latest word in musical scholarship. But putting together the dictionary made us keenly aware of the historicized nature of the whole endeavor. It took more than six years to assemble the dictionary, which meant that some individual articles had begun to age long before they appeared in print. Given the constant rush of musical life and the flurry of scholarly activity, the dictionary can only offer a snapshot of the perspectives and priorities held by this particular team of editors and authors at the start of the twenty-first century. We also recognize how powerfully the political and social climate in the United States shaped our editorial decisions. For instance, neither the original dictionary nor *AmeriGrove II*—which developed largely during the period when Barack Obama ascended to the presidency—contains an article devoted to music and immigration. Writing this essay during an era in which Donald Trump's administration enacted especially restrictive immigration policies, it is difficult to imagine a dictionary on any type of US artistic production that fails to more fully address issues involving citizenship and nation. We are equally interested in how ongoing initiatives might help *Grove Music Online* and other reference tools become more inclusive and equitable.

Accepting the dictionary as time-bounded was frustrating at first, but it did not make the final publication less valuable. We still use the dictionary, we advise our students to consult it, and we hope many others do so as well. But when we read it, we think of it as a historical document, not as a conclusive source or a living body of knowledge. Its time-dependent nature is not a problem: it's an important part of a dictionary's purpose. For this reason *Grove Music Online* archives all versions of Grove dictionary articles on its website: as a result, readers can see how different authors approached different subjects at different times. The fact that conventional dictionaries are fixed in time, and set in print, thus ends up being a distinctive strength, not a liability. At the same time, the monolithic nature of this approach to compiling information led the *Times Literary Supplement* to describe *AmeriGrove II* as "beautiful but a dinosaur."[14]

It is true that the eight-volume print version of the dictionary may be the last of its kind. What ushers *AmeriGrove II* into the twenty-first century is its dual-publication strategy of releasing a printed set and placing the dictionary online, which offers greater accessibility and allows for updates and expansions. Transitioning from a static print model to a dynamic online resource creates all sorts of possibilities for moving forward in new directions. In retrospect, we recognize our good fortune that the dictionary update was bounded by constraints related to the print edition. Having no limits in place for a solely online resource would have brought many new challenges, and perhaps the update would still be chugging along in earnest today. At the time, however, with practical limitations in place, we found ourselves wanting to incorporate more information, add more entries, consider new angles. It sometimes became frustrating to make editorial decisions based on the printed dictionary. This feeling became especially vivid when we looked to the sheer coverage offered by *Wikipedia*, with its global roster of volunteer authors seemingly able to address every topic under the sun: the site currently hosts around six million English-language articles, including thousands devoted to music. We admire the contributors to *Wikipedia* for maintaining and expanding an evolving archive, even if its quality and consistency may be uneven. The contrast between these two models highlights the tension between a publication produced by a limited pool of scholars in comparison to a crowd-sourced archive built by volunteers. An online scholarly dictionary may deliver top-notch quality but achieving *Wikipedia*'s breadth of coverage while providing continuous updates remains a challenge.[15]

"It is the responsibility of lexicographers to continue to push the boundaries of what dictionaries can do. It helps scholarship grow."[16] We take as a challenge Anna-Lise Santella's admonition about the possibilities for how reference works of the future might look: going forward, might it be possible to design a more sustainable balance of breadth, depth, and authority? Could some compromise—Grove with collective responsibility, or *Wikipedia* with scholarly oversight—be feasibly launched and maintained?

We are encouraged here by the *Stanford Encyclopedia of Philosophy* (https://plato.stanford.edu), a peer-reviewed, dynamic reference work directed by principal editor Edward N. Zalta, which as of March 2018 maintains nearly sixteen hundred entries freely accessible online. Developed over more than two decades, with support from Stanford University and numerous public funding agencies, the open-access encyclopedia is maintained by a large editorial board of more than 150 academics that manages contributions and updates from specialist authors. Whether a similar approach could scale successfully to a project as large as *AmeriGrove II* is difficult to envision, but the *SEP* demonstrates how scholars working together in a single discipline, given sufficient institutional support, can effectively produce and sustain what has become a foundational reference work in the field. We are similarly intrigued by *The American Yawp* (http://www.americanyawp.com/), one of the most innovative scholarly projects in recent years, which gathers over three hundred credentialed historians to produce an evolving open-source U.S. history textbook. This volunteer effort collaboratively maintains the textbook, supplemented by primary sources, and makes it available to teachers and students for no cost. *Yawp* also integrates Hypothes.is, an annotation tool that enables users to tailor the textbook for their own purposes. We see the *Yawp* approach as viable for producing, among other collaborative projects, an interdisciplinary, open-source textbook devoted to US music or music of the Americas. It is important to point out, however, that the *SEP* and *Yawp* models are far more aligned with *AmeriGrove II* than with *Wikipedia*: even if both projects rely on a large group of volunteers to produce an open-access reference work like *Wikipedia*, all of the participants are vetted scholars, and their contributions and updates are subject to thorough peer review.

The online platform now housing *AmeriGrove II* suggests a wide array of possibilities for expansion across various media so as to connect a web of scholarly sources. The online version currently incorporates text, citations, bibliographies, images, tables, figures, scores, and links to other Oxford/Grove articles and external databases; we imagine that future platforms could be extended to integrate digital archives of primary music sources, incorporate streaming audio/video, and establish links to outside reference works. Already we can imagine users browsing through an article on the music of Tin Pan Alley and having the ability to consult oral histories, view archival photos, page through published songs, listen to recorded excerpts, watch a video performance, scroll through a map of music publishers, or download key scholarly sources—all accessible through the same site. Technological advances that might connect online reference works to Spotify playlists today could bridge the gap between scholarly resources and music-intensive experiences offered by virtual reality platforms tomorrow. At what point will virtual assistants like Siri (Apple) and Alexa (Amazon) be able to consult scholarly reference sources when responding to queries from around the globe?

Consider the next step in discographical research. Websites like Both Sides Now (https://www.bsnpubs.com/) or the Encyclopedic Discography of Victor Recordings (https://adp.library.ucsb.edu/) have allowed most of us to get rid of—or at least put into long-term storage—the many discographical volumes for record companies that have been essential to so many areas of inquiry in musicology. Even more fortunate for future generations are the ongoing efforts to digitize thousands of recordings, which are being linked to the essential and yet resolutely silent data in these discographies. The Discography of American

Historical Recordings (DAHR) has begun the process of linking massive online discographies with digitized recordings, such as those from the UCSB Cylinder Audio Archive (http://cylinders.library.ucsb.edu/), so that users can not only find out information on when and where a song was recorded, but hear the actual recording (if one exists and has been linked to the session info). Perhaps the next step could involve a colossal store of *visual* media: if the DAHR linked the sheet music—be it the entire folio or even just a cover—from the Sheet Music Consortium website, sound, image, and discographical metadata might be united in a single location. Bringing all the known data and media for a song together in one location would allow for a vastly different understanding of how songs were produced, the manner in which they were marketed and promoted, and how the relationship between the visual (the sheet music) and aural (the recording) ultimately defined the popular life of a song.

Connecting such a web of online resources would certainly increase convenience and productivity for scholars. But as Doug Shadle observes, reference works like *AmeriGrove II* also could be expanded further to facilitate dialogue among readers, authors, and editors, to take greater advantage of an opportunity to engage with the public.[17] Thinking along these lines, it appears viable to design a set of scholarly tools that facilitate communication and initiate conversations between dictionary readers, perhaps by integrating the social media components of professional networking sites such as linkedin.com or academia.edu. Alternately, it might prove productive to draw on strategies employed by http://genius.com, a website that publishes song lyrics fleshed out by the incorporation of annotations from songwriters, recording artists, diehard fans, and pop music scholars. The flexibility of today's online annotation tools encourages various conversations. With the appropriate tweaks, dictionary users could gain the ability to add commentary, share extra information, or highlight points of contention within individual entries; individual readers would be able to decide whether to display or hide these annotations. The idea here would not be to detract from a dictionary's traditional function as a trusted reference source but rather to take advantage of the collective wisdom of a broad readership, to connect readers sharing similar interests, and to reposition the contents of the dictionary within a dynamic framework of discourse and debate.

As rewarding as it proved to update the original 1986 dictionary, we also wonder how it might have developed without constraints, without ties to an existing model. What are the possibilities for recentering, reimagining, reinventing? We are both drawn to the idea of building a dictionary designed with an interdisciplinary and multidisciplinary framework from the start. The *AmeriGrove II* editorial board and its list of contributors included participants from numerous disciplines, but musicologists were positioned at the core of the enterprise. More fully integrating experts in music theory, ethnomusicology, American studies, ethnic studies, Canadian music, Latin American studies, and other disciplines occupied with understanding music of the Americas would produce a new set of priorities, a broader range of authors, and an alternative configuration of disciplinary priorities and tensions. How might this approach reshape the approach of dictionary entries on cultural diplomacy, music and class, or Gustavo Dudamel?

An equally transformative approach could adopt a topic-based, theme-based, or event-based strategy. This would place concepts, practices, and events at the center of a reference work, assign editors to topics or themes (rather than to genres or periods), and then move outward to choose an appropriate set of entries on people, places, and genres to complement those themes. The online resource *International Encyclopedia of the First World War* (http://www.1914-1918-online.net) is an especially effective example of this strategy. Drawing on a worldwide network of researchers, the project complements conventional encyclopedia entries with a large set of transnational, comparative, multiperspectival contributions. Articles addressing the ways in which the United States intersected with World War I form one small aspect of a much larger tapestry that includes entries written from the perspectives of many other nations. We can similarly envision imaginative reference works revolving around key topics—music and identity, music and society, music and material culture, music and power, music and Indigeneity—that challenge conventional thinking about music in the Americas.

Expanding an existing scholarly resource by adding ancillary material and recasting the shape of such reference works in new thematic directions certainly represent significant transformations, but some of these transformations are hitched to an older, anchored model of conveying information. Far more flexible, dynamic, interactive models have revolutionized how we understand and represent such material with the emergence of the digital humanities in recent years. It is one thing to add extra components to an existing resource, but quite another to explore new relationships between multiple sources of information across different media using the digital tools of today. The variety of online experiences now being developed—by academics, museums, technical enthusiasts, and digital humanities collectives—recast our notions about music and musical practice and open up exciting vistas for exploring how music of the Americas may be understood in the years to come.

Michelle Urberg has characterized recent digital humanities developments in musicology as moving away from the compilation of data (source databases, image-based projects, sheet music repositories) toward "collaborative, cross-disciplinary projects that could not exist but in a digital form."[18] She points to projects such as Isabelle D'Este Archive (http://isabelladeste.web.unc.edu/) and Opening the Geesebook (http://geesebook.asu.edu/) as representing iterative, living archives. The D'Este project, for example, complements its primary sources with analytical tools and also affords scholars the opportunity to publish scholarship on D'Este as part of the site. Opening the Geesebook presents a multimedia palette—including text, image, and sound—that enables visitors to apprehend a medieval manuscript from multiple perspectives. We can understand these dynamic models as part of a larger paradigm shift of what it means to compile information. Many new archives do not serve as data repositories but instead present dynamic, interdisciplinary sites that "purposefully engage audiences outside of the field."[19] Along these lines, the New York Public Library for the Performing Arts maintains John Cage Unbound: A Living Archive (http://exhibitions.nypl.org/johncage/), which includes manuscripts, sketches, and ephemera alongside performance videos by professional and amateur musicians. Most significantly, the archive invites anyone who visits the site to film and upload their own performances of Cage's music, a curatorial policy that stimulates public engagement and continually refreshes the archive.

Recent advances in visualizing and manipulating data have also opened the door to fresh perspectives. Among the most exciting innovations in the realm of print media are a trio of atlases by Rebecca Solnit and her collaborators that rely on dozens of imaginative maps to illuminate the text,[20] and *Visualizing the Beatles,* which uses infographics—charts, graphs, timelines, maps, and splashy artwork—to present a highly visual and accessible history of the band.[21] Once we move online, musical visualizations become increasingly interactive. Southern Mosaic (https://adityajain15.github.io/lomax/), constructed by Aditya Jain, combines text, pictures, maps, journal entries, and recorded audio to imagine a journey taken by John and Ruby Lomax in 1939 to collect sound recordings. The Musicmap site (https://www.musicmap.info) enables users to learn about musical genres by navigating alphabetically or exploring visually, reading targeted entries, searching through dozens of genres and subgenres, examining charts of influence, and listening to individual recorded examples. Such developments usher in new possibilities for visualizing material gathered in *AmeriGrove II.* Its extensive data could make it possible, for instance, to develop an interactive map/timeline that allows users to select a place (e.g., Atlanta) and time (e.g., 1890) to obtain information on venues, institutions, and musicians who were active in that city at that moment.

Cultural geography and mapping have been gaining momentum for years, even before the easy availability of geographic information system (GIS) platforms for humanists. Ventures like the Musical Geography Project (https://musicalgeography.org/), led by Louis Epstein, have provided a creative outlet for the undergraduate music history classroom, enabling students not only to investigate a musical topic over time through archival research but also to show how we can understand data differently and fruitfully through the lens of spatial analysis. These interactive online platforms enable users to explore the transforming and shifting musical lives of cities, regions, or countries, as well as to show the interrelationships between musicians, events, and venues through their relative locations. These tools also hold special promise for modeling networks of exchange and communication for understanding music of the Americas through a transnational lens. Danielle Fosler-Lussier's companion website (http://musicdiplomacy.org/database.html) for her book *Music in America's Cold War Diplomacy* moves in this direction by mapping international musical and theatrical performances sponsored by the US Department of State. The extensive list of humanities GIS projects (http://anterotesis.com/wordpress/mapping-resources/dh-gis-projects/) maintained by John Levin shows that we're just scratching the surface of possibilities.

Musicians across the spectrum—Beyoncé, the Philadelphia Orchestra, Luke Bryan, Michael Bublé—have begun to explore virtual reality platforms to produce alternative, immersive, interactive experiences. For a speed metal band like Megadeth, this has meant creating a 360-degree environment where fans can experience the band playing their songs up close and from all angles. Singer-songwriter Imogen Heap has designed a virtual venue, modeled on her childhood home, that invites users with VR equipment to visit different rooms in the house, communicate with other virtual visitors, and enjoy a performance by a virtual 3D animated version of Heap in a specially designed space that bursts with special effects.[22] One of the most intriguing technologies of our moment, virtual reality thus appears poised to deliver the next big advances in entertainment, music, and video gaming. But a virtual reality encyclopedia? Is that something on the horizon?

In fact, that moment has already arrived. *Encyclopedia Britannica* currently produces targeted educational VR products for children, including "Virtual Reality: Dinosaurs." What the technology delivers is quite astounding. The package includes a book, virtual reality goggles, and an app for smartphones that enables kids to read about dinosaurs and interact with animated dinosaurs that roam around a 3D environment. Text and videos flesh out the educational experience. Altair VR, a company that operates virtual-reality education planetariums around the world, has been trying to take this a step further. In 2017, it launched an effort to create a virtual reality encyclopedia focused on the natural sciences. The project, which has not yet come to fruition, combines VR environments with a *Wikipedia* model, allowing different groups of contributors to design immersive experiences focused on chemistry, physics, astronomy, and related fields.

What might all of this mean for how we understand music? How about a dictionary that enables users to read about the history of the Los Angeles Philharmonic, listen to its recordings, and experience a performance by the LA Phil in 360-degree virtual reality (a VR experience that has been available since 2015)? We could learn about Duke Ellington while listening to recordings, paging through scores, viewing pictures, and reading about his early life while visiting the Cotton Club and other buildings from the 1920s and 1930s in the interactive world of Virtual Harlem (https://www.evl.uic.edu/cavern/harlem/). We could explore the musical history of New Orleans through a site that integrates historical elements, a virtual tour of the city (https://www.youvisit.com/tour/aaron.reissig/104451?id=162194), and VR performances by artists at Preservation Hall (http://live360video.com/vr-stream/live-music-now-live-in-vr/) and other storied venues.

Undoubtedly, the incorporation of immersive technologies will prompt debates surrounding the nature of a dictionary. Must text be at the center, with everything else just bells and whistles? Are we talking about an authoritative reference work here or an entertaining excursion? (Does it have to be either/or?) Rather than get bogged down about what these new technologies augur for the future of dictionaries or encyclopedias, it is surely more relevant to prioritize how best to reach new generations of students and scholars and interested readers of all sorts. Given our experience consulting reference works for decades, it is difficult for either of us to envision consulting a dictionary that does not feature a reliable textual component. Being able to read, print, or download a pdf with the information we need has become an ingrained part of our working lives—and that is something we would always hope would be available. But we also know, and are increasingly reminded at the start of each school year, just how differently our students navigate the world of information and media. The idea of reconfiguring a dictionary article—say, on Louis Armstrong—into an immersive virtual experience that is complemented by all sorts of media components and further enhanced by valuable text does not seem that far-fetched: visit this room to learn more about Armstrong's childhood; watch this early performance captured on film; click here to learn about his influences; read more about his time in Chicago; page through his discography. While it's unlikely the traditional, text-based version will disappear entirely, it's both exciting and stimulating how new ways of bringing that text to life continue to emerge.

The Promise of Collaboration

It is not coincidental that our thinking moves outward, across disciplines, media, and technologies. In part, these ideas respond to how dramatically the expectations held by media consumers continue to transform. We are not calling for an end to the dictionary as we know it; in fact, some of the projects we describe here remain highly dependent on the delivery of authoritative text. At the same time, we sense that today's media-drenched landscape encourages abundant opportunities for experimentation, and it is already past time to develop new resources that will prove useful for generations to come. Such projects, harnessing various forms of expertise, are nearly impossible to complete alone. Most call for collaborative partnerships that bring humanists together with musicians, scientists, librarians, technical experts, specialized programmers, and more. These transformations will push scholars to think differently, to engage with new ideas, to work in new ways. All of these developments will reshape how we understand the musics of the Americas.

But it doesn't end there. We have discussed the collective teamwork that energized the *AmeriGrove II* project, teamwork that has since shaped our thinking about the benefits of collaboration. Yet the dictionary in many respects was less collaborative than most of today's digital humanities initiatives. These projects rely on a collective approach from idea to implementation, and interdisciplinary groups often work together to craft the final text. A truly collaborative *AmeriGrove II* would have been coedited, and each of its subject areas would have been managed by editorial teams, rather than individuals. More significantly, as mentioned earlier, nearly every article was produced independently by a single author. Even in the case of most longer multiauthored topical essays (such as "opera" or "film music") individual authors took responsibility, and received publishing credit for, a section of the article rather than for the entire piece.

Our subsequent experiences with collaboration in general and with this essay in particular suggest that we missed a terrific opportunity. We will take that a step further. Embracing collaborative authorship, in our opinion, would profoundly reconfigure US music studies in many productive directions, enabling scholars to learn and grow together. While our purpose is not to provide a primer on collaborative writing, we wish to highlight that no aspect of this book or, for that matter, this very essay—the title, content, shape, structure, writing style, and tone—would exist in the way that it does if we had not collaborated. This piece itself only emerged while brainstorming about how we might contribute to the collection—Daniel suddenly proposed the idea and we ran with it together. It developed over time in conversation, sometimes by phone and more often through the process of writing and commenting on each other's ideas through an online writing platform, a technology that was not firmly in place when the dictionary update started and that we now take for granted. Collaborative writing certainly has its challenges, and it takes time to adjust to working together, but we really enjoy the process, appreciate how it sparks our shared imagination, and value how it pushes us forward together.

So, what might collaborative authorship have meant for *AmeriGrove II*? From a logistical standpoint, it would have been impossible to require collaborative submissions for every entry. There were times when it was challenging enough to enlist a single expert to write on a selected topic. And surely the idea would have met resistance—and rightly so—for anyone asked to hand in a submission of less than five hundred words. The longest essays, which ranged from five thousand to over fifty thousand words, are another matter. Like many contributions in this collection, topical entries in *AmeriGrove II* could have been designed to foreground interdisciplinarity. How might productive matches be made to bring together scholars from different fields? How would a trio of collaborators from American studies, musicology, and music theory tackle "popular music"? What could be gained in a joint entry on Bernard Herrmann by a film historian and a specialist in film music, or by inviting a historian of American politics to participate on an entry about "political music"? It is difficult to predict exactly how any of these articles would develop, for collaborative writing can produce measured synthesis, which is a common approach employed for dictionary entries, or it can advance competing narratives that acknowledge differences of opinion.

What we do know is that working together puts collaborators in conversation and presents the opportunity to examine things from new and unexpected perspectives. We want to read a dictionary with entries written by collaborators hailing from different disciplines. We would love to explore an online reference work in which every component is designed from the start by groups of scholars working in tandem with a team of experts in digital technology. When will we see an essay collection that brings together teams of music scholars residing in different nations? Is it time to start planning a multilingual dictionary of music of the Americas, featuring a diversity of voices in conversation? And will that collection have a print component at all, or will it exist entirely in a virtual configuration, one that can be expanded and updated as needed or desired?

Exactly how the next major encyclopedia of US music will take shape is impossible to predict. Although we anticipate those who lead the charge will have to grapple with many of the same questions and challenges we faced, new opportunities, options, and roadblocks will also almost certainly emerge. Of one thing we can be sure: they will need to work together in as many dimensions of the project as possible. Not only will teamwork make the task possible but it will also make the journey fulfilling.

Notes

The text of this essay was coauthored; vignettes offering individual reflections from each author are set off from the collective text.

1. H. Wiley Hitchcock and Stanley Sadie, eds., *The New Grove Dictionary of American Music*, 4 vols. (London: Macmillan, 1986).

2. Charles Hiroshi Garrett, ed., *The Grove Dictionary of American Music*, 2nd ed., 8 vols. (New York: Oxford University Press, 2013).

3. The advisory board members were Frances R. Aparicio, Lynne Aspnes, Harris M. Berger, José Antonio Bowen, Philip V. Bohlman, David Brackett, Dale Cockrell, James Deaville, Robert Fink, Kyle Gann, Mark Katz, Elise K. Kirk, Ellen Koskoff, Martin Miller Marks, Portia K. Maultsby, Judith McCulloh, David Nicholls, Carol J. Oja, Craig B. Parker, Katherine K. Preston, Thomas L. Riis, Deane L. Root, David Sanjek, Ann Sears, Magen Solomon, Amy Ku'uleialoha Stillman, James A. Strain, Timothy D. Taylor, Judith Tick, Sherrie Tucker, Graham Wade, Paul F. Wells, Deborah Wong, and Josephine Wright.

4. Members of the senior editorial board handled large subject areas or shared responsibility for separate subject areas. Serving in this role were E. Douglas Bomberger, Carolyn Bryant, Mark Clague, Kevin Fellezs, Daniel

Goldmark, Jere T. Humphreys, Tammy L. Kernodle, Beth E. Levy, Alejandro L. Madrid, Travis D. Stimeling, and Jacqueline Warwick. Contributing editors played a similar role for smaller, specialized subject areas. Editors included Elizabeth Aldrich, Bryan Burton, Raoul F. Camus, Esther R. Crookshank, David P. DeVenney, William A. Everett, Emily Daus Ferrigno, Thomas V. Fraschillo, Brian Harker, Loren Kajikawa, John Koegel, Paul R. Laird, Stephen A. Marini, Drew Massey, Michael Meckna, N. Lee Orr, Michael V. Pisani, Arian Sheets, Joanna R. Smolko, Stephanie N. Stallings, Judy S. Tsou, Paul F. Wells, Ron Wiecki, Stephen D. Winick. Sylvia R. Martin served as associate contributing editor for sacred music.

5. The project would not have gotten off the ground without the tireless efforts of Mark Clague and Jonathan Maybaum, two University of Michigan professors. As project director, design and development, Clague created an extensive project website that doubled as a shared database and a portal for communication for all dictionary participants. Maybaum, who developed this web-based platform, contributed advice, support, and specialized programming. Laura Macy, Tim Sachs, and Anna-Lise Santella served as hands-on Oxford/Grove editors over the course of the project.

6. Editors evaluated thousands of preexisting Grove articles from three sources: the original *AmeriGrove* (1986); the three-volume *New Grove Dictionary of Jazz,* 2nd ed., ed. Barry Kernfeld (New York: Oxford University Press, 2013); and the twenty-nine-volume *New Grove Dictionary of Music and Musicians,* ed. Stanley Sadie and John Tyrrell (London: Macmillan, 2002), the reference work at the heart of the Grove enterprise.

7. A small number of lengthy articles on broad subjects—such as "opera," "film music," and "popular music"—were commissioned to teams of authors and featured different levels of collaboration.

8. See chapter 10 of this volume for reflections on co-teaching by Loren Kajikawa and Daniel Martinez HoSang.

9. David Ake, Charles Hiroshi Garrett, and Daniel Goldmark, eds., *Jazz / Not Jazz: The Music and Its Boundaries* (Berkeley: University of California Press, 2012).

10. Anna-Lise Santella, the senior editor at *Grove Music Online* with whom we worked very closely on all aspects of producing *AmeriGrove II,* offers a valuable set of reflections about the role of reference works in the digital age. See Santella, "The Ideal Dictionary: Impossible Tasks, Frank Adjustments, and Lexicographical Innovations in the Creation of 'Grove Music Online,'" *Fontes Artis Musicae* 63, no. 3 (July–September 2016): 213–21.

11. Richard Crawford, "Amerigrove's Pedigree: On 'The New Grove Dictionary of American Music,'" *College Music Symposium* 27 (1987): 186.

12. Hitchcock, "Preface," to Hitchcock and Sadie, *New Grove Dictionary of American Music,* 1:ix.

13. Glenda Goodman, "AmeriGrove II: Perspectives and Assessments: Music before 1800," *Journal of the Society for American Music* 9, no. 4 (2015): 476.

14. Stephen Brown, "With the Beatles," *TLS* no. 5852 (May 27, 2015): 22.

15. Santella, "The Ideal Dictionary," 215–21.

16. Santella, "The Ideal Dictionary," 214.

17. Douglas Shadle, "AmeriGrove II: Perspectives and Assessments:

Nineteenth-Century Music," *Journal of the Society for American Music* 9, no. 4 (2015): 484.

18. Michelle Urberg, "Pasts and Futures of Digital Humanities in Musicology: Moving towards a 'Bigger Tent,'" *Music Reference Services Quarterly* 20, nos. 3–4 (2017): 137.

19. Urberg, "Pasts and Futures," 140.

20. Rebecca Solnit, *Infinite City: A San Francisco Atlas* (Berkeley: University of California Press, 2010); Rebecca Solnit and Rebecca Snedeker, *Unfathomable City: A New Orleans Atlas* (Berkeley: University of California Press, 2013); *Nonstop Metropolis: A New York City Atlas*, ed. Rebecca Solnit and Joshua Jelly-Schapiro (Berkeley: University of California Press, 2016).

21. John Pring and Rob Thomas, *Visualizing the Beatles: A Complete Graphic History of the World's Favorite Band* (New York: Dey Street Books, 2018).

22. Related technological advances have also led to full-blown concert tours in traditional venues featuring holograms of deceased artists, including Maria Callas, Roy Orbison, and Frank Zappa, as well as tours by 3D projections of virtual stars, including the Japanese virtual pop idol Hatsune Miku.

Contributors

Naomi André is Professor in the Department of Afroamerican and African Studies, Women's and Gender Studies, and the Residential College at the University of Michigan. Her book *Black Opera: History, Power, Engagement* (2018) won the Lowens Book Award from the Society for American Music and the Judy Tsou Critical Race Studies Award from the American Musicological Society. Her earlier books include *Voicing Gender: Castrati, Travesti, and the Second Woman in Early Nineteenth-Century Italian Opera* (2006) and *Blackness in Opera* (2012, coedited collection). She is the inaugural Scholar in Residence at the Seattle Opera and a founding member of the Black Opera Research Network (BORN).

Sarah Eyerly is Associate Professor of Musicology and Director of the Early Music Program at Florida State University. Her research interests include eighteenth-century music, sound studies, performance practice, and the geohumanities. Her recently published book and digital project, *Moravian Soundscapes* (Indiana, 2020; https://doi.org/10.33009/moraviansoundscapes_music_fsu), is a sonic history of eighteenth-century Moravian missions in eastern Pennsylvania. She has received fellowships and awards from the American Council of Learned Societies, the American Musicological Society, and the Society for American Music.

Charles Hiroshi Garrett is Professor of Musicology at the University of Michigan School of Music, Theatre & Dance. He is the author of *Struggling to Define a Nation: American Music and the Twentieth Century* (California, 2008), and he served as editor-in-chief for *The Grove Dictionary of American Music,* second edition (Oxford, 2013).

Cheryl Townsend Gilkes is the John D. and Catherine T. MacArthur Professor of African-American Studies and Sociology at Colby College (Waterville, Maine) and an ordained Baptist minister and assistant pastor for special projects at the Union Baptist Church (Cambridge, Massachusetts). She is the author of *If It Wasn't for the Women: Black Women's Experience and Womanist Culture in Church and Community*. Her published sermons have appeared in *African American Pulpit*, and in her spare time she is "Dr. Dr. Cheryl," the host of Colby College's gospel music radio show, *The Uncloudy Day*.

Daniel Goldmark is Professor of Music and Director of the Center for Popular Music Studies at Case Western Reserve University. He is the series editor of the Oxford Music/Media series, the author of *Tunes for 'Toons: Music and the Hollywood Cartoon* (California, 2005), and the editor of books on animation, film, and music.

Glenda Goodman is Assistant Professor of Music at the University of Pennsylvania. She works on the history of early American music. Her first book, *Cultivated by Hand: Amateur Musicians in the Early American Republic* (Oxford, 2020) is a material and social history of amateurism. She is currently working on a book about sacred music and colonial encounter in eighteenth-century New England. Her articles have appeared in several musicology and history journals. She is also working on a collaborative project, *American Contact: Intercultural Encounter and the History of the Book*, which will result in a volume and a digital humanities component.

Monica A. Hershberger is Assistant Professor of Music at the State University of New York at Geneseo and earned her PhD in historical musicology from Harvard University. She focuses primarily on the history of opera in the United States, including the depiction of sexual violence in opera. Her research has appeared in the *Journal of the American Musicological Society*, *Journal of Musicology*, *American National Biography*, and *Opera Journal*. She is currently working on a book about women in American opera during the 1950s.

Ellie M. Hisama is Dean of the Faculty of Music and Professor of Music at the University of Toronto. Her interests include the visual arts, dance, film, theater, collaborative works, and public engagement. Hisama is the author of *Gendering Musical Modernism: The Music of Ruth Crawford,*

Marion Bauer, and Miriam Gideon and has published essays on the work of Geri Allen, Joan Armatrading, The Cure, Julius Eastman, and Isaac Julien. She taught in the Department of Music at Columbia University from 2006 to 2021 and is Founding Director of "For the Daughters of Harlem: Working in Sound."

Daniel Martinez HoSang is Associate Professor of Ethnicity, Race & Migration and American Studies at Yale University. His research and teaching explore the contradictory labor of race within US political culture across a wide range of sites, including electoral politics, social movements, and cultural formations. He is coauthor (with Joseph Lowndes) of *Producers, Parasites, Patriots: Race and the New Right-Wing Politics of Precarity* and the author of *Racial Propositions: Ballot Initiatives and the Making of Postwar California.* He taught in the Departments of Ethnic Studies and Political Science at the University of Oregon from 2007 to 2017.

Composer-pianist **Vijay Iyer** has released over two dozen albums and has collaborated with Amiri Baraka, Wadada Leo Smith, Carrie Mae Weems, Teju Cole, Pamela Z, Henry Threadgill, Jennifer Koh, and numerous other artists across disciplines. He received a MacArthur Fellowship, a US Artists Fellowship, the Doris Duke Performing Artist Award, the Alpert Award in the Arts, and two German Echo Awards, and was voted Jazz Artist of the Year four times in the annual *DownBeat* International Critics' Poll. He is the Franklin D. and Florence Rosenblatt Professor of the Arts at Harvard University, with a joint appointment in the Department of Music and the Department of African and African American Studies.

Loren Kajikawa is Associate Professor of Music at George Washington University's Corcoran School of the Arts & Design. He specializes in twentieth- and twenty-first-century music of the United States, with special attention to hip-hop and the politics of race. His book *Sounding Race in Rap Songs* (California, 2015) explores the relationship between hip-hop beats and racial representation. From 2009 to 2018, Kajikawa served in the musicology and ethnomusicology program at the University of Oregon's School of Music and Dance, and was a participating member in the UO Department of Ethnic Studies.

Josh Kun is Chair in Cross-Cultural Communication and Professor of Communication in the USC Annenberg School for Communication and

Journalism. He is an author and editor of several books, most recently *The Autograph Book of Los Angeles: Improvements on the Page of the City* (2019), *Double Vision: The Photography of George Rodriguez* (2018), and *The Tide Was Always High: The Music of Latin America in Los Angeles* (2017). As a curator and artist, he has worked with SFMOMA, the California African American Museum, the Grammy Museum, the Getty Foundation and Getty Research Institute, Prospect New Orleans, and others. He coedits the book series Refiguring American Music for Duke University Press. He is the recipient of an American Book Award, a Berlin Prize, and a MacArthur Fellowship.

Panayotis League is Assistant Professor of Ethnomusicology at Florida State University, where he also serves as Director of the Center for Music of the Americas. He has published a number of articles on Greek and Brazilian music, dance, and oral poetry, and his monograph *Echoes of the Great Catastrophe: Re-sounding Anatolian Greekness* is forthcoming (Michigan). He is an active performer, composer, and recording artist in a number of Greek, Brazilian, Irish, and American idioms, and enjoys the distinction of being both an accordionist and a bagpiper.

Alejandro L. Madrid is Chair and Professor at Cornell University's Department of Music as well as Teaching Faculty in the Latina/o Studies Program. He is an author and editor of several books, including *Tania León's Stride: A Polyrhythmic Life* (forthcoming, 2021); *Experimentalisms in Practice: Music Perspectives from Latin America* (2018; coedited with Ana Alonso-Minutti and Eduardo Herrera); *In Search of Julián Carrillo and Sonido 13* (2015); and *Music in Mexico* (2013). Madrid is the recipient of the Dent Medal from the Royal Musical Association and the Premio de Musicología Casa de las Américas, among many other national and international awards. He edits the book series Currents in Latin American and Iberian Music for Oxford University Press and coedits the journal *Twentieth-Century Music*.

Misako Ohta is Associate Professor in the Graduate School of Human Development and Environment, Division of Human Expression at Kobe University in Japan. Born in Tokyo, she studied musicology at Tokyo University of the Arts (BA) and German literature at Gakushuin University (MA). Her PhD in music history (University of Vienna) examined artistic intention and its public impact on Kurt Weill's musical theater in the 1920s and 1930s. She teaches Western music history within its cultural contexts and transnational perspectives and has been a music critic for the regional edition (Kansai area) of the *Yomiuri shinbun* since 2003. She is completing a critical biography of Kurt Weill in Japanese.

Carol J. Oja is William Powell Mason Professor of Music and Professor of American Studies at Harvard. Her *Bernstein Meets Broadway: Collaborative Art in a Time of War* won the Music in American Culture Award from the American Musicological Society, and her *Making Music Modern: New York in the 1920s* won the Lowens Book Award from the Society for American Music. She is a member of the American Academy of Arts and Sciences. Her current book in progress is tentatively titled: *Civil Rights in the Concert Hall: Marian Anderson and the Struggle Against Racial Segregation in Classical Music.*

Samuel Parler is Assistant Professor of Music History at Baylor University. His research focuses on issues of race, class, and genre formation in US popular music. His work has appeared in the *Journal of the American Musicological Society* and the *Journal of the Society for American Music.* He is currently writing a monograph on race and respectability politics in country music media prior to 1950.

Kay Kaufman Shelemay is the G. Gordon Watts Professor of Music and Professor of African and African American Studies at Harvard University. Shelemay's most recent books include *Pain and Its Transformations: The Interface of Biology and Culture* (2007, coedited with Sarah Coakley); *Creating the Ethiopian Diaspora* (2011, coedited with Steven Kaplan); *Soundscapes: Exploring Music in a Changing World* (3rd ed., 2015); and *Sing and Sing On: Sentinel Musicians of the Ethiopian American Diaspora* (in press for 2021). Shelemay has published numerous other monographs, articles, editions, and recordings. A past president of the Society for Ethnomusicology, Shelemay is a fellow of the American Academy of Arts and Sciences, the American Academy for Jewish Research, the Ethiopian Academy of Sciences, and the American Philosophical Society.

Braxton D. Shelley is Assistant Professor of Music in the Harvard Faculty of Arts and Sciences and the Stanley A. Marks and William H. Marks Assistant Professor at the Radcliffe Institute. Shelley specializes in African American popular music with research and critical interests that extend into media studies, sound studies, phenomenology, homiletics, and theology. His recent article, "Analyzing Gospel," in the *Journal of the American Musicological Society*, and his forthcoming book, *Healing for the Soul: Richard Smallwood, the Vamp, and the Gospel Imagination,* construct a theory of the black gospel tradition.

Sarah Suhadolnik is Lecturer in Musicology at the University of Iowa, where she teaches courses in American music, jazz, pop, and Western art music. Her research centers around overlapping ideas of music and place—particularly those that highlight the ways in which public perceptions of dynamic musical landmarks, such as New Orleans, are shaped by their popular musical representation. She has served as a member of the editorial staff for both the Music of the United States of America series and the University of Michigan Gershwin Initiative.

Michael Sy Uy is the Allston Burr Resident Dean of Dunster House, Assistant Dean of Harvard College, and Lecturer in the Music Department. His published work appears in *American Music, Journal of the Society for American Music, Journal of Musicology,* and *Music and Arts in Action.* His main areas of scholarly research focus on patronage, philanthropy, arts education, cultural policy, expertise, and connoisseurship. His book *Ask the Experts: How Ford, Rockefeller, and the NEA Changed American Music* (2020) explores the grantmaking of these three institutions after the Second World War. He is the recipient of several teaching awards, including the Mindich Program in Engaged Scholarship's Curricular Innovation Award, the Derek Bok Center Excellence in Teaching Award, and the Distinguished Faculty Award by the Harvard Foundation.

Lucie Vágnerová is a New York–based music scholar, who earned her PhD in historical musicology from Columbia University. Vágnerová's work engages with issues of gender, race, and labor in electronic music, digital media, and higher education. She has taught graduate and undergraduate courses on music, gender, and digital culture at Columbia University, Montclair State University, and New York University; she also leads classes in the Adult Learning program of the Brooklyn Public Library. In 2018, she directed the second installment of the public outreach initiative "For the Daughters of Harlem: Working in Sound."

Rachel Wheeler is Associate Professor of Religious Studies at Indiana University-Purdue University Indianapolis (IUPUI). Her book *To Live upon Hope: Mohicans and Missionaries in the Eighteenth-Century Northeast* (Cornell, 2008) was a finalist for the American Academy of Religion's prize for best first book in religious studies. She has received funding for her work from the National Endowment for the Humanities, the Fulbright Foundation, and the American Council of Learned Societies.

Index